The *International Herald Tribune*

James Gordon Bennett, Jr., as *Vanity Fair* saw him, shortly after completing cable communications across the Atlantic and contemplating a Paris edition of his *New York Herald*.

THE

Herald INTERNATIONAL Tribune

THE FIRST HUNDRED YEARS

CHARLES L. ROBERTSON

New York
COLUMBIA UNIVERSITY PRESS
1987

Grateful acknowledgment is made for permission to reprint selections from the following:

News Is What We Make It by Kenneth Stewart. Copyright 1943 by Kenneth Norman Stewart. Copyright © renewed 1971 by Kenneth Norman Stewart. Reprinted by permission of Houghton Mifflin Company.

Paris Was Yesterday: 1925–1939 by Janet Flanner. Copyright 1925–1939 (inclusive), © 1972 by *The New Yorker* Magazine, Inc. Copyright 1934, 1935, 1940, copyright renewed © 1962, 1963, 1968 by Janet Flanner. Reprinted by permission of Viking Penguin Inc.

Paris Herald: The Incredible Newspaper by Al Laney. Copyright 1947 by Al Laney, renewed 1975 by Al Laney. A Hawthorn book. Reprinted by permission of E. P. Dutton, a division of NAL Penguin Inc.

Library of Congress Cataloging-in-Publication Data

Robertson, Charles L.
   The International herald tribune.

   Bibliography: p.
   Includes index.
   1. International herald tribune. I. Title.
PN5189.P3I587   1987   070   87-6355
ISBN 0-231-065652-0

Book designed by Laiying Chong.

Columbia University Press
New York   Guildford, Surrey
Copyright © 1987 Charles Robertson
ALL RIGHTS RESERVED

For
Denise, Christina, *and* Claudio

Contents

Preface

THE EUROPEAN EDITION of the *New York Herald Tribune* was the first newspaper I ever looked at regularly, back before World War II, when I was a small boy in Belgium. I read it again—somewhat less regularly—when I went back to Europe in the American army at the end of the war, and again when I spent a Fulbright year at the University of Strasbourg in 1950. Since then, whenever I have spent time in Europe, the paper has been to me what it has been to countless other Americans abroad—a constant and valued companion. I have taken for granted its presence wherever I may be, and grumbled when the one or two copies disappeared from the kiosk in some remote Alpine town before I had a chance to get to them. When stewardesses pass out the newspapers on the plane to or from Europe, the *Herald Tribune* is the one I ask for.

I suppose that explains why, when I was grading a student's paper at Smith College a few years ago and ran across a reference to the *International Herald Tribune*, I wondered idly whether anyone had ever written a history of the paper. That bit of idle speculation led to an intense seven-year affair with the newspaper, an affair that took up most of my spare time and whose result is this book. It is therefore happenstance that it appears just as the newspaper is celebrating its 100th anniversary and its new global image, but I am pleased at the coincidence.

Innumerable people working for the paper or who once worked on it helped me out. I am particularly grateful to Lee Huebner,

Richard Morgan, and Walter Wells, who read parts of the manuscript and gave me their comments, as well as to Roland Pinson and Micheline Personnaz, who were among the many people at the newspaper's offices in Paris who became my friends and gave me open access to the often disorganized files from the past and the more regular ones of recent years. There, and in the New York Public Library and the Library of Congress, I read through thousands of issues of the paper and masses of correspondence and reports. Publishers, editors and columnists, accountants, market analysts, advertising salesmen, and mailroom distributors all gave freely their time and their often conflicting accounts of the past, and I owe them all a debt of gratitude. I have listed their names in the bibliographical note at the back of this book. I should also like to thank the Kaltenborn Foundation for a grant that paid for my first trip to Paris to see if the project was at all possible.

Newspaper people are, by and large, a fascinating lot, and the story I pieced together involved a remarkable group of people. But the story of a newspaper is also the story of a business within a changing social and political setting, of that business's links to a rapidly changing and often challenging technology. The modern newspaper was a phenomenon of the growth of nineteenth-century mass society, and newspapers have come and gone as mass society itself has altered over time, cities have been transformed, and developments in communications and transportation technologies have accelerated. Most recently, facsimile transmission has allowed a single newspaper to be printed in multiple locations, while word processing, photocomposition, and offset printing have made whole categories of skills obsolete, and worker resistance to change has been widespread and in some cases disastrous. Newspapers that were once the personal creations of strong men, bearing their imprint on almost every page, have become corporate entities run by boards and committees and subject to complex legislative regulation.

The history of the hundred-year-old *International Herald Tribune* mirrors all these changes as well as others: begun by one man,

James Gordon Bennett, Jr., for a new Europe-wide cosmopolitan class that he exemplified in his own life-style, the paper weathered the collapse of the world it was created for during a single week in 1914; it then had to secure new audiences at each turn of international events of the next half century, to face a stream of competitors, and to survive the collapse of its parent newspaper in New York. Its very nature changed with each change in its setting, and it grew only by fits and starts. But in recent years that growth has been steady. The paper now calls itself the world's first global newspaper, it is printed in more than half a dozen locations scattered through Europe, Asia, and the United States, and it is distributed in more than 160 countries. Its history is a remarkable success story.

All this I have tried to tell. And while I owe thanks to so many whose names appear in the text and in the bibliographical note, the story and interpretation are my own; so are the errors. Art Buchwald, one of the first people to encourage me to write this book, once said that the *Herald Tribune* was the only newspaper he had ever loved. I hope that he—and some of the countless readers of what is one of the best and most respected newspapers in the world—will enjoy reading its story as much as I enjoyed putting it together.

PART I
THE BENNETT ERA

CHAPTER 1

James Gordon Bennett, Jr.

ON A CHILL, gray October morning in 1887, horse-drawn carriages began to make their way across Paris from a cramped printing shop in the rue Coq-Heron to distribute packages of a new, four-page newspaper to kiosks and hotels in the more elegant sections of the city. The awakening *haut monde* of the most cosmopolitan center in Europe found the European Edition of the *New York Herald* waiting for them on their breakfast tables. There was no explanatory word or opening editorial and no mention of the name of the publisher or editor in the paper, whose masthead bore the legend Whole No. 18,670, and whose price was listed as ten centimes in Paris, fifteen centimes elsewhere. Three days later, though, when a letter appeared expressing delight at the appearance of the new paper but adding that the reader had missed the usual article of greeting and explanation of purpose, the publisher, James Gordon Bennett, Jr., whose name was to appear in the newspaper only upon his death some thirty years later, took the occasion to reply: "You are mistaken in one respect, this is not a new newspaper. The *Herald* is over a half a century old. The fact that we have chosen to publish a European edition is a detail. We do not, moreover, believe in buncombe articles about 'long felt needs' and telling what one intends to do, and what not to do. A good newspaper speaks for itself."

The reply was disingenuous. Bennett was, indeed, the publisher and owner of the *New York Herald,* founded in 1835 by his father. But what Bennett had launched in Paris was, in fact, a wholly new venture so well suited to time, place, and social conditions that it would rapidly carve out for itself a unique position among European newspapers. What no one could foresee was that its successive owners and publishers would be able to build on the foundations that Bennett had laid, and that what began as an intensely personal four-page paper would outlast all but two of the newspapers then being published in Paris, and, through an almost miraculous process of adaptation, survive and surmount the terrible and extraordinary changes of the next hundred years.

The Paris *Herald,* as people came to call it, was an almost instantaneous success, soon to be read by the right people in all the capitals and worldly resorts of Europe, and for this Bennett must take the credit. "Success" is a relative term, however. Albert S. Crockett, who worked for Bennett with great devotion for a dozen years, estimates that during Bennett's time, up to World War I, no more than 12,000 copies a day were ever sold in the winter, and perhaps 20,000 in the summer. In the final years of the Great War, when American doughboys streamed across the ocean into France, circulation rose rapidly to a peak of some 350,000 a day. It would soon sink back to the prewar figure when they left.

The European Edition of the *New York Herald* was obviously a paper of limited circulation. Its continued existence was the result of Bennett's willingness to sink a good part of his personal fortune into it, year after year, even when a London counterpart, begun two years after the Paris Edition, failed within eighteen months, and even when his New York newspapers began a fatal decline in the face of competition from publishers Joseph Pulitzer and William Randolph Hearst. The Paris *Herald* was put together by a small staff of miserably paid men and subject to the increasingly erratic whims of the aging Bennett. Yet by the time the world for which it was designed came crashing down before the guns of August, it had become a by-word throughout Europe and probably one of the best-known papers in the world, and would go on to establish an even greater reputation during the war years.

The story of the *International Herald Tribune* must start with one man—James Gordon Bennett, Jr.

The younger Bennett was born into wealth created by the success of his father's *New York Herald.* The elder James Gordon Bennett had done in New York what the younger was to do on a smaller scale in Paris forty years later: see the new elements in an evolving situation and seize the time. In 1835, when, at the age of forty, the elder Bennett founded the *Herald* with $500 and a plank laid over two barrels in a basement office, the United States was beginning a period of rapid economic growth. Increased public schooling and spreading literacy, more rapid forms of communication and the beginnings of mass production, recent reforms that had spread the franchise, all forced the prevailing ruling circles to appeal to a more widespread electorate. Bennett appealed to the same people by scandalizing and printing scandal about the upper classes, referring to legs and arms rather than "extremities," campaigning against "upper class hypocrisy," and earning the undying hatred of the society of his time.

Bennett produced graphic, illustrated descriptions of disasters such as fires and floods. He employed special correspondents: by the end of the Civil War, he had sixty-three correspondents in the field. But he also initiated the printing of detailed financial news and daily Wall Street reports, daily weather reports, and detailed shipping news—and sent boats out to meet incoming ships so as to get the news before anyone else. He wrote editorials about anything, without fear of reprisal. In fact, his was really the first modern mass-circulation newspaper keyed to the rise of industrial-ization and modern commerce; when, in 1840, the other New York publishers mounted a joint attack upon the man they counted as a blackguard, trying to organize an advertising boycott and carrying on a vendetta in their editorial columns, he could point out that the *Herald* had a circulation far greater than the rest put together. James Parton, in *Famous Americans of Recent Times,* published in 1867, wrote that "his paper is generally read and its proprietor universally disapproved." Opponents might call him an "obscene vagabond," "loathsome and leprous slanderer and libeller," "in-famous blasphemer and profligate adventurer," and "venomous reptile" but he and his paper seemed to thrive under the attacks, and when Henry J. Raymond, founder and editor of the *New York Times,* thrashed him in the streets, Bennett could not wait to get back to the office to write a front-page account of the incident!

His marriage in 1840 to a lovely, recent Irish immigrant of "respectable family" did nothing to stem the torrent of abuse poured upon him. When James Gordon Bennett, Jr., was born on May 10, 1841, the *Sun* suggested that the elder Bennett was not the father. (Bennett sued and won.) Subsequently Mrs. Bennett was to stand by in helpless horror while her husband was beaten by a gang headed by John Graham, a candidate for district attorney whom the *Herald* had helped to defeat. Unable to stand the atmosphere in which her husband worked, she removed herself and young James and his sister Jeanette to Paris, where she could rear her children in a more civilized atmosphere. The elder Bennett stayed on in New York to improve the *Herald*'s news coverage, outdo his rivals, increase his circulation, prestige, and advertising, and make himself—and then his son—one of the richest men in the United States.

Thus it was that James Gordon Bennett, Jr., received his education from French tutors, went to the Collège de France, and was taken care of by governesses and a mother who spoiled him. Mrs. Bennett returned to the United States from time to time, and young James accompanied her as he grew older. At least one witness told Bennett's biographer Don Seitz of seeing the sixteen-year-old boy thoroughly drunk at a party. "Isolation abroad," wrote Seitz, "combined with plenty of money, made him dissolute when young."

But his father doted on him and began to prepare the rakehell son to take over the *Herald* at some indefinite date. In the meantime young Bennett, tall, handsome, and with a certain cosmopolitan charm, an unmatchable arrogance, and a penchant for women, drink, and outdoor sports, became a member of New York's fast set and quickly made both a name for himself and a circle of boon companions. He became a member of the Union Club, the Jockey

Club, and the youngest member ever to be admitted to the New York Yacht Club, of which he was subsequently elected Commodore. His ever-indulgent father bought him the 70-ton sloop *Rebecca* and then the 160-ton *Henrietta,* which young Bennett volunteered to the Union cause during the war. He and the *Henrietta* served with no perceptible distinction for a year in the Revenue Cutter Service, cruising off the coast of the Carolinas, and when the *Henrietta* was decommissioned, he resigned his lieutenancy and went back to his desultory service on the *Herald* and to his wealthy companions and their pastimes.

"Coaching"—driving a coach pulled by four horses—was a favorite sport, but Bennett carried it to extremes, racing at breakneck speeds, yelling as he went, and—at night—stripping off his clothes and riding stark naked through the countryside. In one coaching accident he spilled a young woman who, luckily, was only shaken up. She was the daughter of his friend Leonard Jerome, her name was Jennie, and she would later be the mother of Winston Churchill. He also got into brawls at his favorite restaurant, Delmonico's. One night, drunk as he too often was and dressed in evening clothes for dinner at Delmonico's, he tried to direct firemen who were fighting a raging conflagration, shoving them around until they turned the fire hose on him. He was taken home by his friends, and the next day, on reaching the *Herald* he asked his friend Flynn, "What did I do last night?" "Made a big fool of yourself," came the answer, with a frank account of the proceedings. Bennett ordered a rubber overcoat for every man in the fire department. "I was never so wet in my life!"

With the August Belmonts, Jr. and Sr., Bennett helped found the Belmont Park racetrack—where he once won a footrace and a $6,000 purse against walking champion John Whipple after a thirteen-mile walk from downtown. He later introduced polo to the United States, bringing equipment, a team, and instructors over from England, and founded the Westchester Polo Club. After a scandal at the Newport Casino, he had one of the outstanding architects of the area, Stanford White, design and build a new casino across from his own luxurious Newport mansion, complete with private club and tennis courts, where the national tennis championships were held until 1914, when they were moved to Forest Hills. (The casino is still there, though the mansion has been replaced by a parking lot.) In 1875 he was a founding member of the Coaching Club of New York, along with the Belmonts, Pierre Lorillard, Leonard Jerome, James Roosevelt (father of FDR), Alfred G. and William K. Vanderbilt, and William C. and Harry Payne Whitney.

Bennett's erratic behavior when drunk—and the fact that only a couple of drinks could produce it—would have mattered little were it not for what happened on New Year's Day, 1877. The previous year, to everyone's surprise, the perennial bachelor, whose amatory bouts involved actresses, singers, and dancers, had become engaged to the young, beautiful, and wealthy Caroline May. The family was congratulated on her having landed one of the richest eligible young men in New York, and her trousseau was brought over from Paris. But on that cold and snowy January 1 of 1877, having imbibed at several other parties, and downed more punch at the reception at his fiancée's house, Bennett proceeded to un-button himself and urinate into the roaring fire in the fireplace. (Some accounts have it that it was into the grand piano; for several reasons, including the physical difficulties involved, the former version seems more plausible.) In any event, Bennett, who in his sodden state seems not to have realized what all the fuss was about, was escorted from the room by scandalized fellow guests amid confusion and recrimination. He sent no apology and received a note declaring the engagement at an end. Two days later he ven-tured forth to dine at the Union Club; emerging after his meal, he was met on the steps outside by Caroline May's brother Frederick, who thrashed him with a horsewhip as club members looked on from the window. At first Bennett failed to defend himself, but then he grappled with May and the two fell into the snow, flailing away at each other until separated by two of Bennett's fellows. Two days later Bennett challenged May to an illegal duel. May, at the required signal, turned and fired into the air. Bennett missed, though accounts differ as to whether it was on purpose or not. The two were formally reconciled, but New York society was not, and Bennett found the door to mixed gatherings barred. Enraged, since he had treated the world of fashion with dignity and respect in the pages of the *Herald* where his father had previously poked scurrilous fun at it, he determined to leave. Within the year he had reestablished himself in Paris, the scene of his upbringing. There, he figured, society would accept with indulgence the occasionally erratic behavior of a wealthy and imperious American.

And it did. One of his old friends, Lawrence Jerome, joined him for the first of the forty years of Bennett's self-exile. Together they continued the mad coaching as of old, and the story goes that Bennett drove wildly up the Champs Elysées stark naked. Certainly it is true that in the summer of 1892, roaring drunk, driving at a mad pace toward the porte cochere of his apartment on the avenue, he disregarded the warning cry of a policeman and was swept off the box as his head collided with the archway. Only the skills of a surgeon saved him after he crashed to the cobblestones below, where he lay with a fractured skull, bleeding from the mouth, nose, and ears. (But before he was operated on he calmly dictated to his secretary for an hour, putting his affairs in order. The story got around: *that* was the grand manner!)

He and Jerome would ride the Paris-Bordeaux express and play jokes on the other passengers, with Bennett pretending to be a betrayed lover pursuing Jerome in the role of the betrayer, or one attempting suicide at great length while the other tried to dissuade him before the horrified passengers. One night Jerome was hastily summoned to Bennett's deathbed in a private hospital, to find him swathed in bandages, surrounded by a suspicious number of rather voluptuous nurses. When he bent over Bennett in sorrow, Bennett reared up before the surprised Jerome and yelled out to the nurses to bring in the medicine. And as they brought in the champagne Jerome learned that the "hospital" was one of the better Paris bordellos, which Bennett had hired for the occasion.

In time, in addition to the apartment at 120, avenue des Champs
Elysées, Bennett acquired a house on the avenue d'Iéna, a beautiful
villa on hunting grounds near Versailles, a shooting lodge in Scotland kept ready for the grouse season, and a sumptuous Mediterranean villa beneath towering cliffs at Beaulieu-sur-Mer, on the
Riviera, which he made his winter headquarters. These were in
addition to the two residences always kept ready for him in New
York and his mansion in Newport. He kept his palatial, seventy-
five-meter-long steam yacht, the *Namouna*, in the Mediterranean,
but supplemented it with a smaller one, the *Serena*, which could
thread the French river and canal system and serve him in the
summers in the North.

In 1901 he sold the *Namouna* to buy the even more luxurious
Lysistrata, which rivaled any other yacht in the world. She was
frequently redecorated inside, carried a crew of 100, and was
equipped with a turkish bath and a padded, fan-cooled stall for
two Alderney cows to supply him and his distinguished and royal
guests with fresh milk. The yacht was named, said the Commodore,
for a Greek lady who was known to be very fast, and the escapades
aboard, amorous and otherwise, assumed legendary quality. In the
winter Bennett would take her for four-and five-month cruises,
stopping at Mediterranean and Adriatic ports where he received
royal treatment, and where the resident American consuls would
come aboard to pay their respects. On occasion he took her through
the Suez Canal to make a tour of south Asian and Far East ports,
or across the Atlantic to Jamaica and Bermuda, stopping at Mar-
tinique and the Canary and Balearic islands. On a cruise down the
east coast of Africa he visited the Emperor Menelik II of Ethiopia,
who presented him with a monkey which Bennett then lodged in
an elaborate cage in his garden at Beaulieu, where he kept his flocks
of Pekinese dogs. His old friend Jenny Jerome, now Lady Randolph
Churchill, joined him on board with her young son Winston. The
Lysistrata ended her days in the service of the Russian Red Cross,
to which he sold her during the Great War, but she still exists in a
beautiful miniature at the Musée de la Marine, in the Trocadero,

The palatial *Lysistrata* moored before the Doge's palace in Venice for one of Bennett's imperial visits.

only 300 yards from where Bennett's body lies in an unmarked mausoleum in the Cemetery of Passy.

Bennett's escapades on the Riviera made him almost as famous and notorious as his vast wealth. His often cruel and capricious pranks—walking through a restaurant and pulling off the table-cloths, sending the table settings crashing to the floor, walking rapidly along a quay, pushing fishermen into the water, invading a market and scattering the produce on the ground—were redeemed by the princely compensation he would award to his victims. He could also be kind and generous to strangers and generous to the community in which he lived. For his own amusement he established a series of seasonal coach services between Nice, Cannes, and Beaulieu to entertain and serve the other millionaires, grand dukes and duchesses, princes, and assorted royalty with whom he mixed.

Bennett's arbitrary and arrogant social behavior was matched by his behavior toward his employees on his newspapers, whom he hired, fired, promoted, and demoted with a seemingly equal capriciousness. After a period in Europe he took to calling people to come and see him from wherever they might be. He might then receive them graciously or send them curtly home without a word. One familiar story is that Bennett once cabled William Reick, his trusted city editor and chief link to the New York newspaper, to send a particular man from the New York office to work for him in Paris. Reick cabled back that the man was "indispensable" in New York. Bennett then supposedly asked him for a list of the indispensable men on the New York paper, and when Reick supplied it, cabled back, "Fire them all. I want no indispensable men working for me." Some of his men rose suddenly in favor, were richly rewarded, and then as suddenly demoted, fired, or given reason to quit; the able Reick was one of these who, humiliated, went over to the *New York Times,* where he helped it to overcome the *Herald*'s lead in foreign reportage.

At the time of Bennett's death E. D. Dewitt, publisher of *Editor and Publisher* and previously general manager of the *Herald,* wrote an affectionate tribute to his former boss, praising the man and his "long distance vision." The European Edition, he wrote, was "probably read by more rulers, potentates, and men of high officialdom than any newspaper published." But he also recounted the story of how Bennett received an anonymous telegram to the effect that he, Dewitt, had grown fat and lazy, and immediately cabled Dewitt to come and see him in Paris. The athletic Dewitt appeared, the Commodore looked him over and, satisfied, ordered him back to New York!

Yet there is the other side to these stories. Another of Bennett's trusted men, R. D. Blumenfeld, acknowledging Bennett's capriciousness, and recounting how Bennett sent him off someplace just after he had signed a lease for an apartment—which Bennett knew about—also tells that when Bennett decided to move the *New York Herald* uptown to 34th Street to a new two-story building designed by Stanford White, to put Pulitzer's new sixteen-story skyscraper to shame ("We'll show them that we need not let offices to pay for our building!"), he argued with the Commodore, summing up the problems that the move would cause. Bennett listened, but dismissed the arguments and told Blumenfeld to go back to London, and draw up papers that would make him and Reick one-third shareholders in the *Herald*. Then he said, "And, by the way, reduce your salary by ten pounds a week for having tried to tell me my business." But Blumenfeld notes, "I only paid attention to his money whims when on similar occasions he asked me to raise my salary." There were, in other words, ways of getting around Bennett's arbitrary ways.

Whatever it was, it was an adventure working for the Commodore, and many stayed as long as they could stand it. He seemed to have a certain contempt for journalists—he once brought one to the Riviera, had the young man accompany him alone on a mysterious trip to the interior, and then, when his eye alighted on a suitable Alderney cow, which he bought, ordered the reporter to bring the cow back to the city of Villefranche on foot and put it aboard the *Lysistrata*. The contempt did not extend to those who did the mechanical work. A mechanical genius named Frank Cohick was brought over in 1898 when the Commodore imported the first Linotypes to be used for typesetting on the European continent. Previously—and for some time to come on other European newspapers—all type had to be set tediously by hand. Cohick was to supervise only the installation and initial operation of the machines, but he ended up staying for thirty-five years, frequently telling the Commodore where to get off. (At one point, on one of those drunken evenings when Bennett descended on the *Herald* offices and indulged in his whims, he fired the whole editorial staff and bellowed down the stairs to the composing room to Cohick that he was now editor-in-chief, charged with hiring a whole new staff. No one paid any attention and the whole incident was forgotten.)

One of Bennett's men, Thomas G. Alvord, tried to explain the Commodore's behavior this way:

> The seemingly erratic, unjust, contemptible conduct now and then shown the most deserving members of the staff was designed to put to the severest test the loyalty of the individual whose seeming fealty, expecting a reward, had been proven a dozen times. Came he through demotion, reduction of pay, undeserved suspension, designed humiliation, and still remained, steadfast in his devotion to the *Herald* and its master, taking his dose without complaint or the seeking of a place on some other paper, then Mr. Bennett believed he might be trusted in great temptation and relied on in all emergencies. In no other way, in his opinion, could a thoroughly reliable corps of newspaper employees be built up and maintained.

Indeed, says Seitz, in his biography of Bennett, "Some who were discharged or demoted were never themselves again. They missed their shirts of hair and the excitement of accomplishment which was always plentiful in the *Herald* office. Thus, for all their contemptuous mistreatment, men were attracted to the *Herald*. There was something compelling about the tigerish proprietor with his fickleness and brutality. Women are said to be fascinated by such characters. Certainly, newspapermen were."

This, then, was the man who took over formal control of the *New York Herald* from his father in 1868, went into exile and continued to run the paper from Paris in 1877, and founded—or began—the European Edition of the *New York Herald* in 1887.

Before he did any of these, though, one event in his eventful life appears to have worked something of a transformation in the young man-about-town. An evening of brandy and cigars and talk at the Union Club in the fall of 1866 led to a $90,000 bet that Bennett's *Henrietta* could beat two other yachts, the *Vesta* and the *Fleetwing*, in an unprecedented transatlantic yacht race. The race took place that winter, in freezing and dangerous conditions. Bennett was the only one to skipper his own boat, and he nosed out the other two vessels—to find himself lionized in England and toasted by society in America. Before, he had been bored. Now, by all accounts, he threw himself into the daytime activities at the office. In 1867 he started a second paper, the *Evening Telegram*. In 1868, in the face of his son's change, the elder Bennett handed the *Herald* over to him.

Historians rate the next fourteen years—particularly the decade after 1872, when old Bennett died—as the golden decade of the *New York Herald*. The paper was supreme in New York and now respectable, the younger Bennett rejuvenated the staff, and his lavish use of funds to secure news and scoops paid off. His reporters were encouraged to use the transatlantic cable freely; the *Herald*'s prestige soared as it began a more thorough coverage of the world news that now began to be important to the rapidly industrializing United States. In England the *Herald* became a power when it consistently beat the British with dispatches from colonial wars and made them available to London newspapers. The *Herald*'s important weather reports were better than anyone else's, and the Commodore initiated the first "real estate" section in any newspaper, giving it a lead in real estate advertising which it never lost.

It was in this era, too, that Bennett began to make the news as well as cover it: in 1869 he sent Henry M. Stanley to find the aged Livingstone in the heart of Africa when everyone in England was speculating about the older man but no one was doing much about finding or helping him. Stanley's account of the interview has often been repeated. After his initial surprise at Bennett's demand the prospective explorer asked, "Have you considered seriously the great expense you are likely to incur on account of this little journey?"

"What will it cost?" Bennett asked, abruptly.

"Burton and Speke's journey to Central Africa cost between £3,000 and £5,000, and I fear it cannot be done under £2,500."

"Well, I will tell you what you will do. Draw a thousand pounds now, and when you have gone through that, draw another thousand, and when that is spent, draw another thousand, and when you have finished that, draw another thousand, and so on; but *find Livingstone.*"

Stanley, of course, did find him, and other Bennett-financed expeditions followed.

Upon his self-exile to Paris, Bennett retained tight control of the New York newspaper by cable. It was then that he discovered the costs of the Western Union cable monopoly, control of which had been seized by that prince of financial buccaneers, Jay Gould. For some time Bennett brooded over the extortionate rates: he had already decided to establish a new cable company and had opened a public subscription for one million pounds when John W. Mackay, who had made his fortune in silver at the famous Comstock Lode, approached him. Could they work together? The result was a rare combination for the time; the two men plunged into the fray together, drawing heavily on their resources, first to establish the Mackay-Bennett Company, to equip a special steamer named the *Mackay-Bennett* to lay a new transatlantic cable, and then to fight off Gould's price-cutting counterattacks. In addition to price-cutting, Gould used his pyramided control of American companies to try to stop distribution of Mackay-Bennett cables within America once they had crossed the Atlantic. But the man was overextended. He complained, "There's no beating John Mackay. If he needs another million or two he goes to his silver mine and digs it up." In the meantime the *Herald* benefited from the competitive rates, increasing its foreign coverage. Gould eventually had to give in and accept a stable and much lower rate structure for transatlantic cables. For years thereafter the European Edition of the *Herald* carried on its editorial page the circular logo of the Mackay-Bennett Company.

There were two immediate effects of the bitter struggle. Bennett's resources, already strained by his style of living in Europe, were further depleted by the battle, and he cut back on expenditures for the New York paper, at the same time that Joseph Pulitzer bought the *World* from Gould himself and entered the New York fray. Most historians of the press mark this as the beginning of the long, gradual decline of the *New York Herald,* a decline interrupted only by the *Herald*'s preeminent reporting of the Spanish-American War. The second consequence was that Bennett began his Paris Edition.

People have speculated on what prompted Bennett to start the Paris Edition in 1887. The new, cheaper cable rates were an essential prerequisite, making the whole enterprise possible. It became useful to have Paris as a central gathering spot for news from all over Europe, Africa, and the Near East, from which it could then be transmitted to New York. It was this, Bennett later explained, that justified the "appalling loss" he sustained in the first months of publication.

Other technical developments played an equally essential but more underlying role. Steamship and railroad transportation underwent an astonishingly rapid development after 1850. Competition between shipping lines like Cunard, White Star, and Inman provided both speed—the Inman Line's *City of Berlin* made the westbound crossing in seven days, eighteen hours, in 1874—and a new standard of comfort: vast and spacious accommodations, private staterooms with individual toilets and bathrooms, comfortable dining lounges with good food and wine, electric refrigeration, electric lights, elevators—in short, virtually all the amenities of modern travel for those who could afford first class.

Meanwhile, on land, railroads had made equally amazing progress. In 1876 the Compagnie Internationale des Wagons-Lits was formed, and soon all-Pullman *trains-de-luxe* with the typical European configuration of individual compartments and a side aisle were crisscrossing the Continent. Dining cars became standard when coach-to-coach communication was made possible by the development of vestibules. By the time Bennett began the Paris *Herald,* the famous Train Bleu had already been in operation for four years, picking up English travelers in Calais, speeding to Paris where coaches from Berlin and St. Petersburg were attached to it,

and then making its overnight run to the Riviera, stopping in
Marseilles, Cannes, Antibes, and Nice.

Industrialization created a wealthy bourgeoisie that mingled
freely with the older aristocracy, and now rapid and comfortable
transportation in conjunction with communication by cable was
to produce a truly cosmopolitan class. Wealthy people could move
back and forth across the Atlantic and throughout Europe with an
ease denied their parents, all the while keeping in touch with home
and business or with one another. A traveler could move from
Baden-Baden where he had taken the waters, to Deauville-Trouville
to be by the sea, then to Paris and then on to the Riviera or Venice—
all without a passport or a visa. A man could deal in Munich street-
railway bonds one day and Cleveland municipals the next, with
never a thought for exchange-rate regulations: all currencies were
based on gold and freely exchangeable. It was the era that Henry
James was to write about in his first group of international novels;
he had settled in London the year before Bennett established himself
in Paris. Daisy Miller's mother would surely have read the European Edition of the *Herald* for world news, to keep abreast of what
was going on in the United States, to find out what her friends—
or those she would have liked to have as friends—were doing and
where they were doing it, to keep an eye on her market holdings,
to know what the weather was going to be like at their next stop,
and to know how to get there. The cosmopolitan setting was there,
in the midst of a period of industrial and commercial prosperity:
France had recovered from the disaster of the Franco-Prussian War
of 1870; trade and colonization flourished and news from overseas
gained in importance; thanks to recent technical developments,
wood pulp for newsprint cost one-tenth what it had cost a decade
earlier. And once more, as seems inevitable when one deals with
James Gordon Bennett, Jr., there is a story to it: an owl prompted
him to start the paper.

The owl was always a fetish with Bennett. Owls of a hundred
descriptions ornamented his study, and an owl always distinguished his stationery. When he built the *New York Herald* build-

ing uptown in 1894, modeled on the Palazzo del Consiglio in Verona, he installed great bronze owls all around the roof perimeter, glowering down at the New York streets with eyes that lit up at night. (One of these still decorates the office of the publisher of the *International Herald Tribune* in Neuilly.) There are, again, varying stories of how he came to adopt the owl as his symbol. C. Inman Barnard, his private secretary, maintained that his father recommended the owl to him when the younger Bennett failed to stay at the paper until it went to press: "Young man, your future career depends upon night work on the *Herald,* and eternal vigilance. Otherwise, after my death, the *Herald* will belong to someone else. Bear in mind that as long as you live the owl—the bird of Minerva—should be your fetish, and not the eagle nor anything else." Another story, however, has it that the younger Bennett once went to sleep on watch on the *Henrietta* during his Civil War patrolling, and when an owl hooted, awakening him and saving him from running ashore on a sandy reef, he proceeded to adopt it as an omen of luck. Whatever the truth, the owl, perched on a crescent moon and surrounded by the motto "La nuit porte Conseil," was to figure prominently on the editorial page of the Paris *Herald* until after Bennett's death. And so the story goes that one night in 1887, fresh from the success of his Mackay-Bennett enterprise, toying with the idea of a European Edition to serve the new cosmopolitans, the Commodore stood on the balcony of his Paris apartment and heard an owl hoot. He took it as an omen and made his move.

There were already two English language newspapers in Paris at the time: the venerable but decrepit *Galignani's Messenger,* founded in 1814 and famous primarily for having been the first newspaper in Paris to report Napoleon's defeat at Waterloo. Bennett tried to buy it, but a clause in Galignani's will blocked the effort. (The Commodore was subsequently to refer to it as "our venerable scissors and gum-pot contemporary" in *Herald* columns, and the *Messenger* died off in 1906 when the *London Daily Mail* established a Continental Edition. Its memory is enshrined in Galignani's Bookshop in the rue de Rivoli.) The other newspaper had begun publication in 1874—the *Morning News*, printed in both an English and French Edition, the brainchild of William Alonzo Hopkins of Brattleboro, Vermont. Hopkins was willing to sell Bennett the English Edition, but continued to publish the French half as *Le Matin*, a newspaper that later became a power in Paris. With this purchase, the Commodore had a base from which to operate.

On September 3, 1887, a French language dummy version of the *New York Herald*, European Edition, appeared, in order to mark possession of the title. Within weeks Bennett had assembled an English language staff—primarily English—and was ready to go. Beforehand he invited them to his home for lunch and there delivered himself of the following famous speech: "I want you fellows to remember that I am the only reader of this paper. I am the only one to be pleased. If I want it to be turned upside down, it must be turned upside down. I consider a dead dog in the rue du Louvre more interesting than a devastating flood in China. I want one feature article a day. If I say the feature is to be Black Beetles, Black Beetles it's going to be."

CHAPTER 2

"The Most Serious
of Frivolous Newspapers"

THE FIRST ISSUE of the Paris Edition of the *New York Herald* set a pattern that would be more or less maintained for all the years that Bennett ran his paper.

The front page of the paper carried four main headings: "New York Letters," "Wall Street," "Capel Court," and "At Friedrichsruh." The first two ("By Commercial Cable to the *Herald*") carried what was then a vast amount of cabled information from across the Atlantic. There were stories on the Knights of Labor convention and on coming political campaigns. The Wall Street letter carried a half-column listing of the previous day's stock and bond prices, followed by a listing of the French bourse. It also had a series of financial stories: "Successful Bear Attack on St. Paul Stock" and "Jay Gould's Latest Coup." "Capel Court" ("By the *Herald*'s Special Wire") carried news of the London financial markets and a half-column listing of British securities. The fourth column, with a wide variety of news stories cabled from all over the world, expanded in the next few weeks as the financial sections were moved back to page 3. And as the new paper found its way, the front page blossomed into an unusually good roundup for its time, even though much of it was in summary form, cabled from New York or from London, where it drew heavily from the news printed in London papers.

Much of what it printed might seem frivolous today, yet in the context of the times was not. The revolution begun in 1789 spread all across Europe, but in 1887 liberal institutions hardly reigned supreme. Old dynasties and aristocracies had made uneasy compromises and still retained power in most places; court news was still of real importance. And despite Bennett's speech to his editors, a dead dog in the rue du Louvre received short shrift in comparison with a famine in China. Within a few days the *Herald*'s front page was full of detailed reports of one of the periodic scandals that marked French bourgeois society of the time and rocked the precarious Third Republic to the point that they nearly toppled it; in this case, the sale of government decorations. The first picture to appear in the new paper ornamented the front page of the October 14 issue: it was of General Boulanger, who had been arrested for having made statements linking the Minister of War to the traffic in decorations.

Hard news occupied a large part of the paper, but page 2 chronicled the doings of society in all the main cities of Europe. "Mr. William K. Vanderbilt will return from London to the Bristol on Wednesday." "Mr. James G. Blaine and family arrived at the Hotel Vendome Sunday from Geneva." At the same time that Bennett began to print the *Herald* on the rue Coq-Heron, he also opened a business office in the heart of Paris, at 49, avenue de l'Opéra, where, besides advertising offices, a register permitted visitors to Paris to inscribe their names and see them appear a day later in the *Herald*. The practice began within a week of first publication, and continued on and off until World War II. From the start the *Herald* printed letters from its readers, with frequent editorial rejoinders. Both in its columns and in the offices at the avenue de l'Opéra the *Herald* quickly became a place that Americans in Europe could use as a link to other Americans and to home, and where they could find help and advice in how to cope in a foreign and sometimes hostile environment. When American students came to attend the opening of a new Sorbonne building the *Herald* served as a clearinghouse for information. A year after it began publication the French government issued a confusing decree stringently regulating the domicile of foreigners in France, and the *Herald* devoted much of its front page for several weeks to clarification, responses to letters, and reports of administration of the decree. (It also revealed that the census of 1886 found about 1 million foreigners among 38 million Frenchmen and women; 100,000 were British, but only 10,000 American.)

By adding reviews of the English and French press, English court news and English gossip, the "Talk of Paris" news and gossip column, French language stories on Paris, and a "Sporting Gossip" section to its sports news on page 3, the *Herald* also began to attract the attention of English and Continental readers. Their names, too, appeared in the new *Herald*. Despite Bennett's own pronouncements and the comments of later chroniclers, alongside the jumble of names, the paper performed useful services, produced a wide mixture of news both important and exciting, and soon was able to attract genuine advertising to fill its back page, much of which, in the first number, had been filled with dummy advertising or ads from the New York paper. From the beginning, Bennett's staff knew how to attract advertising: early on the paper ran one story that said Brentano's was about to open a bookstore in Paris, then a second one to the effect that when members of the Anglo-American community had queried *Herald* staff members as to the truth of the matter, they were "politely informed that everything is true which appears in the *Herald*." Within the year Brentano's ran a regular full-column ad on the back page!

Bennett did everything possible in the way of promotion, and some of his devices reveal why people thought of him as a genius in his field. A few weeks after the *Herald* began publication a notice appeared on page 3: "English governesses living in any English, Russian, French, Spanish, or Italian families and sending to us the proper credentials of their position will be sent a free copy of the *New York Herald* (European Edition) for one year." Who knows how many nannies actually took advantage of the offer? If they did, members of the well-to-do families within which they worked could hardly fail to see the new paper. We may assume that at least a few families took advantage of the offer to get the newspaper free for themselves. But even if few subscriptions resulted, people were bound to talk about the novel offer.

Within two weeks after the first number a special edition was prepared for an incoming steamship, *La Bretagne,* with a summary of the week's news. It was sent out to the ship by steam tug so that passengers received it well before docking at Le Havre, and, the *Herald* reported, "News spread like wildfire through the ship as all asked for a copy." Passengers, while catching up on the news that had been denied them during their week's crossing, also noticed the newspaper that provided it. Success of the stunt prompted the Commodore to make it a regular practice for the arrival of every major transatlantic vessel. Within a few years a note to advertisers alerted them to the fact that copies of the *Herald* were delivered to incoming steamships not just at Le Havre, but also Boulogne, Southampton, Liverpool, and other ports.

A "Traveller's Guide" column soon appeared that listed trains between Paris and London and Paris and Nice. A column of shipping news announced arrivals and departures, and Bennett went to the expense of using cables from New York, enabling the paper to print the names of those who would be arriving on incoming steamers. Within a month, it started publishing a regular listing of *Herald* agencies where the European Edition could be bought; not just in France, but also in England, Belgium, Germany, Italy, Sweden, and Switzerland.

The *Herald* always went in heavily for self-advertisement, carrying out in a rather curious way Bennett's early dictum that the paper spoke for itself. A week into publication one story explained what was meant by the phrase "By *Herald* Special Wire" attached to the stories from England. The *Herald* was the only Paris paper to have its own private, direct cable connection to London. The negotiations for an international line had been arduous and expensive, the *Herald* told its readers, and informed them that all nighttime dispatches had to be sent by a British government operator, with one copy going to the government; none could be shared with other newspapers. The *Herald* would always explain its *modus operandi* at great length, and heavily publicize its technical or journalistic innovations.

Bennett's social and political views began to make themselves known from the beginning. Economic expansion might be the general mark of the times, but so was the growth of anarchism and other forms of protest or revolt. The paper was full of accounts of anarchist activity, of sedition, rioting, and possible revolt. Three weeks after the start of the European Edition Bennett printed a three-column letter from Prince Peter Kropotkin, the anarchist theorist, which was mainly a plea on behalf of the Chicago anarchists on trial in connection with the Haymarket riots. Bennett prefaced the letter with a comment that the *Herald* had never favored revolution. "For anarchy and anarchists it has no respect whatever. But the *Herald* loves fair play and believes in presenting both sides of a question." Besides, the piece was certainly another attention getter.

The pervasive anti-Semitism of European upper classes and of the French right found reflection in the *Herald,* but Bennett's reaction, on the whole, does him credit. A letter of July 9, 1889, reproved the *Herald* for a piece about an English adventurer who was referred to by another gentleman as "an ass, a cad, an adventurer, and a Jew." "By that statement, one must come to the conclusion that you consider it to be a disgrace to be a Jew," the letter went on. "With such anti-Semitic statement you ought to transfer your paper to Berlin or Vienna. There such a statement could be relished, but I doubt if such is the case in Paris." The *Herald* replied that it had printed a letter verbatim, containing the statement attributed to a certain person. "It had nothing to do with the *Herald,* which never allows itself to be used as the mouthpiece of class or sect." Within months the paper had printed an interview with the Marquis de Morés, a depressing figure who was mounting a new campaign against the Jews because they controlled the Third Republic. But editorially it attacked his views and warned him: "He who sows the wind will reap the whirlwind. Let the Jews alone."

The *Herald* covered the Dreyfus trial thoroughly, devoting three pages and a series of courtroom sketches to the verdict. The subsequent trial of Emile Zola received equally intensive coverage, and in both cases the *Herald* was clearly on the side of the defendants. But it was also clear that the *Herald* was in a delicate position as an American in Paris.

When Bennett launched the Paris Edition he may not have realized just how delicate this position would be. He seems to have had that peculiar American conviction that news reporting could be "objective," that "factual" reporting and "letting the facts speak for themselves" did not reflect a point of view. Sometimes the attitude was disingenuous. In 1896 and 1900 the *Herald* inveighed against the American presidential candidacy of William Jennings Bryan, whose free-silver campaign threatened prosperity and whose platform, the *Herald* declared, was put together by a coalition of "Anarchists, Socialists, Populists and silver lunatics." It advised a vote for McKinley. But later, in 1904, when it called Theodore Roosevelt "dictatorial," "imperialist," and "ruthless," the paper asked rhetorically whether it was taking a position. No, it was merely laying out the situation for its readers, who could draw their own conclusions! When it came to reporting French political events and news, however, the situation was more complicated—in part because every election in France continued to be a virtual referendum on whether France should even be a republic or not.

In 1889 General Boulanger, backed by a coalition of anti-Republican forces, had hit upon the technique of getting himself elected to Parliament from a number of different constituencies, and while the *Herald* did not overtly champion his cause, it gave extensive coverage to his appearances among cheering crowds. In early 1889 he was campaigning in Paris for election from the Department of the Seine, and the *Herald* reported on him at length. "The people of Paris worship the hero of the moment. . . . Everybody asks . . . 'will he be elected?' The Boulangists are in high glee." Then, within days, its editorials took a different turn and began to warn against the Boulangist campaign: "Boulangism is a weapon, an expedient to break down the Republic. . . . It represents every element of Bonapartism but the genius of Napoleon." Boulanger won that particular election, but the *Herald* continued to inveigh against him: by July it could refer to him as "an adventurer" who practiced "despicable demagoguery"

Accused at that point in a letter to the editor of having taken government money, Bennett defended himself vigorously: the *Herald,* an editorial declared, supports the institutions that be. "It attends to its own business and therefore does not meddle with that of others." It denied equally vigorously reports that Mackay money had gone to support the general, and later thanked French papers for reporting the denial. The *Herald*'s stance, it said, was like the Monroe Doctrine: "Leave us alone and we will leave you alone! . . . The *Herald* holds itself aloof from French politics." But the editorial went on to comment that in the recent local elections in which Boulanger had lost heavily, "France proved on Sunday her sound common sense!"

Bennett's noninterventionist stand when it came to French politics may have been somewhat peculiar in execution, but he later shed some light on the *Herald*'s stance on the Boulanger affair. The occasion was a protest strike by French workers against some action taken by the Paris prefect of police in which the editorial staff of the *Herald* planned to take part. Bennett, it is reported, assembled the staff and told them that he had once been inveigled by a noble French lady into giving General Boulanger the full support of the *Herald,* believing that it was in the best interests of France. He was, he recounted, then called in by the Minister of the Interior, who addressed him coldly:

"Mr. Bennett," he said, "I understand that you have a fondness for France and that you enjoy making your home in Paris. We, too, enjoy having you with us and respect and admire you for the part you play in our capital city by publishing there a European edition of your great American newspaper. But, however great your paper is, we cannot overlook the fact, of which we are now compelled to remind you, that you are publishing here a foreign newspaper to which we have granted the fullest degree of hospitality.

"Now, Mr. Bennett, you have chosen to take sides with an element which is attempting to undermine and even overthrow our system of government, and that, we cannot, under any conditions, countenance. We have troubles enough of our own. We must therefore ask you to refrain from giving aid to those who are opposing us, or this Government shall find itself compelled to ask you to leave this country and take your paper along with you."

Bennett went on to tell his workers that he saw the justice of the point, ordered the staff at the time never again to take sides in French politics, and warned them now that their planned strike—not directed at the paper, but at French government action—would result in his sending their names to the Ministry of the Interior for the same medicine he had received.

In fact, Bennett had stretched the truth to prevent the strike. He had reported the Boulanger campaign generously, but never gave the general editorial support, and always continued to publish pungent comment on French politics. In later years he was to feature a daily column in French by a well-known playwright, Pierre Veber, reporting the doings of the National Assembly in a fashion so wickedly witty that it drew bitter protest and the threat of prosecution of the writer . There is no evidence that Bennett paid any attention. His aloofness from French politics, in other words, was never very complete.

The Commodore was an expatriate, banished by New York society. "I love America, but I hate most Americans," he once told Alfred Jaurett, his longtime advertising manager. He also loved the country he had chosen to live in and the city of Paris itself; he refused to live in America, yet he did not change his nationality. He once said to an editor: "My foreign policy is simply this: if a nation is friendly to America, I wish the *Herald* to be friendly to that nation, but if a nation shows an unfriendly policy, I wish the paper to adopt an unfriendly tone. This may not be patriotism, but it is the course I wish the *Herald* to follow." And for all the years that he ran the *Herald* he did much to encourage Franco-American friendship, especially during the Spanish-American War, when feeling in Europe ran high against the United States.

Bennett was accused of being merely another jingo during the war. He was not. When the U.S. battleship *Maine* was blown up during a visit to the harbor of Havana, Bennett counseled America to keep cool. The Senate's ardor, his paper declared, was embarrassing to presidential diplomacy; if the House could block the passage of the belligerent declaration passed by the Senate, diplomacy might yet succeed in averting war. When the Spanish Minister Dupuy de Lômes' unflattering description of McKinley as "weak and a popularity hunter" was made public in the rival *New York Journal,* Bennett advised smoothing over the affair: "Delay makes for peace." By early April, when a diplomatic solution seemed in sight, the *Herald* ran half a page of letters from its readers and breathed an editorial sigh of relief. Nevertheless (in line with Bennett's perennial fascination with technical detail in general and naval affairs in particular), it published articles on "How Submarine Mines Are Fired," a pictorial glossary of an American battleship, and pictures of "The Holland Submarine Torpedo Boat Undergoing Trial."

Once war was declared, the *Herald* went fully about its business of reporting the war, and its pages became full of portraits of American and Spanish military leaders, maps, photos of naval vessels. It was, in fact, the *New York Herald*'s reporting of the war that regained the paper all its earlier influence, and carried it to its apogee and a circulation of over 500,000. Bennett threw himself into the effort, sparing no expense but also avoiding the sensationalism that marked his New York rivals. *Herald* dispatch boats, shared with the *London Times* and the *St. Louis Globe-Democrat,* shuttled back and forth between the fleet off Havana and the coast of Florida, carrying news and pictures. Richard Harding Davis, already famous, increased his reputation as the chief *Herald* correspondent. A *Herald* journalist stood on the bridge when Admiral Dewey steamed into the harbor of Havana to destroy the Spanish fleet, and on June 8 the front page of the Paris *Herald* carried a heroic portrait of the Philippine patriot Aguinaldo, with an account of his guerrilla campaign against the Spanish forces.

Yet Bennett was also concerned with the anti-American feeling that ran high in France. He printed an article based on interviews with French laborers—trade unionists and Socialist deputies—to show that they were favorable to the United States. But the paper also received and published a mass of letters recounting insults and slurs directed by Frenchmen against Americans in public places; one letter asked the *Herald* why it did not stop its campaign in favor of the French. Bennett replied in a biting editorial: he would stop publishing some of these "puerile complaints . . . a feeling of *amour propre* prevents their publication." Americans should not be so sensitive; French newspaper opinion was now wholeheartedly pro-American, the United States was winning every battle, why then complain of an occasional slight? And in short order the *Herald* published a long article assuring its readers that the Grands Magasins—the Magasin du Louvre, the Bon Marché, the Maison de Blanc, the Belle Jardinière, the Samaritaine, the Trois Quartiers, the Magasin de l'Opéra—had pledged to show only courtesy to American shoppers.

Somehow or other, the whole discussion of French anti-American opinion on the subject of U.S. imperialism has a familiar ring!

But the *Herald* was equally concerned that American policy be just, so that it would earn foreign approval. "The war," the paper said sternly on May 31, "has been largely brought about by the jingoes and by the shrieking of the yellow press." It was to be hoped that McKinley would give in no further. The *Herald* raised a significant question after the victory at Manila: "Has Admiral Dewey Caught a White Elephant for the U. S.? Accidents Create National Policies." It argued—on June 1, before the American forces landed—that the psychological moment for peace had arrived and was rapidly passing. Delay would prolong the war, and the United States should avoid further fights and be generous. Canvasing the possibilities that existed with regard to the Philippines, the paper argued that they could not be returned to Spain, nor sold to Britain—a move that would embroil the European powers—nor simply be left alone to be fought over. The only solution was an American protectorate that would allow full self-government, and, if it would serve to end the war quickly, a joint protectorate with Spain. To the *Herald*'s dismay the war did go on; the paper warned that Aguinaldo had begun to play a dangerous game by turning to the Germans for support. "Peace," it declared, "Gives Way to Imperialism." A change of opinion was evident in the United States. And then, with perhaps a touch of pride, "Europe is assisting at a great spectacle: the genesis of a nation. The United States will now be a factor in world politics."

The *Herald* had never been pro-McKinley. It had opposed William Jennings Bryan in 1896 and opposed him again in 1900, not only for what it felt would be disastrous domestic policies that would destroy prosperity, but also because Bryan's free-silver, easy-money campaign would destroy American credit abroad. It was against McKinley's "ruinous" protectionism, but free silver was more dangerous. In 1900 Bennett declared: "McKinleyism has already produced a plentiful crop of trouble: war with Spain, discontent in Cuba and Puerto Rico, an apparently endless conflict in the Philippines, and now military interference in a China-European affair [the relief of Peking during the Boxer Rebellion] . . . a record of bungling during four years of Imperio-McKinleyism . . . justifying the nation in a longing for a return to the old liberal policy of non-intermeddling in other people's difficulties."

The whole episode of the Boxer Rebellion, the murder of European ministers, the siege of Peking, and gathering momentum for a Western relief expedition filled the front pages of the *Herald* in 1900 and led Bennett to an even stronger statement of his views of American foreign policy. There could be no suggestion that the President should join other Western powers in sending an expeditionary force. "The very existence of the Republic hinges upon the rigid confinement of the President's powers within the limits laid down by the Constitution." Any armed intervention would be "a flagrant breach of the Constitution which emphatically forbids the President to make war on a foreign people or to send troops abroad without the formal sanction of Congress." Americans might deplore the loss of life and the outrages perpetrated by the Boxers, but "Europe is to blame for sowing the whirlwind in China by trying to carve it up; the quarrel is Europe's; let Europe fight it out. Few will deny that the Chinese have been harried until a rising was inevitable."

Besides, the editorial went on, "if there is one people on earth that has no right to meddle in China's internal affairs, it is the American," for in America Chinese have been "attacked, set upon, beaten, harassed by petty, iniquitous annoyances enacted by Congress. . . . driven out of the country. China has not sent an armed expedition to enforce the right of her subjects to the justice due to all human beings, civilized or uncivilized. . . . To use Prince Bismarck's phrase, the Administration's clear duty is to be the 'honest broker' in matter—nothing more." And once the powers—including the United States—had relieved Peking, the *Herald* consistently supported use of the Hague Tribunal to settle matters, and withdrawal of the American contingent.

During the presidential campaign of 1904, the paper declared, "The *Herald* neither 'supports' Judge Parker, nor 'opposes' Mr. Roosevelt . . . it endeavors to put before the people, frankly, fully and impartially, the facts . . . *the people will have to decide*," but it was fully ready to help them decide.

Three years of Mr.Roosevelt as President have cleared away all illusions as to his ideals. His conduct in the "floating" of the Panama Republic, his ruthless disregard of public sentiment in the South, his dictatorial assumption of authority in every department of the public service have sufficed to show the people that his ideal of government is Imperialism, that he regards brute force as the equivalent of right and his will as the equivalent of legality. . . . The issue before the people is: Imperialism or Democracy? Which is to rule in the U.S.? The people will have to decide.

In 1908, when Bryan ran against Taft, the *Herald* declared that Bryan had mellowed. He was still a demagogue, but after all the country had survived eight years of demagoguery—i.e., Roosevelt!

Bennett had long had the rather petulant habit of forbidding criticism of certain people in his papers' columns or of publishing and publicizing the names of others. Reick once asked a friend on the New York *World* whether they had any list of "sacred cows" to be treated with discretion. When he was told no, Reick replied that *he* had a full stable. "How in hell can I be expected to carry the names of all the members of the Union Club in mind?" The forbidden list changed with the times; William Randolph Hearst and Theodore Roosevelt were both to feature on it, along with the Kaiser, though it was never as strictly observed as legend would have it.

During the 1912 presidential campaign all the animosity Bennett had long felt for Roosevelt came to a head when the latter bolted the Republican party to campaign as a Progressive under the Bull Moose banner, even though, in fact, the *Herald* supported Wilson. For a brief time one could read about "the Third Term candidate who has split the Republican Party wide open," or how "the Bull Moose is gaining almost all his support from the Republican Party." "Bad Times for the Bull Moose," read an editorial in September after a previous one headed "The Third Termer's Senile Socialism." But Roosevelt's name could actually be found in the text of cable dispatches. Bennett relented during the Great War when Roosevelt took a belligerent stance similar to that of Bennett's and in contrast to what Bennett considered Wilson's wishy-washy attitude. His change of heart about Roosevelt culminated in 1915 when the *Lusitania* was sunk: all through the page-long report of the sinking a phrase in italics punctuated the paragraphs: "What is President Wilson going to do? What a pity Mr. Roosevelt is not President!"

Briefly, in 1908, Bennett's anti-imperialist stance took a back seat. He took a trip to the Far East, visiting Java, the Philippines,

China, and Japan. Sensing that the Anglo-Japanese naval treaty of 1902 had given the Japanese too much free rein and that they might become aggressive, he conceived of the idea of a Chinese-American alliance, and began to campaign for it at length in the *Herald*. As Albert Crockett recounts it, Bennett recruited a bright young Chinese reporter named Li Sum Ling, brought him to Europe through the Suez Canal, and was planning to send him on to New York. At every stop *Herald* reporters were instructed to interview him at length about the proposed alliance, and the interviews were reprinted in the *Herald*. French newspapers were induced to print synopses of the interviews and these were then cabled to the *Herald* in New York to display the degree of French interest and support. During the campaign the Paris *Herald* declared, "It is the manifest destiny of America to enter into a reciprocal agreement with China; to keep the Philippines, and to play a predominant part in the development of Asia. *Westward the Star of our Empire Takes its way* and shall take its way, *peacefully* or otherwise." The alliance proposal, of course, never got off the ground.

Much has been made of Bennett's dislike of the Kaiser, and many have attributed it to some real or fancied slight. One story has it that at one point Bennett was not invited aboard the Kaiser's yacht during the German royal regatta at Kiel, and as an intimate of royalty, enraged at the snub , he sailed off, forever after hostile to the German Emperor. The *Herald* itself, however, reveals that while he may have had strong personal feelings, they were tied to political analysis. As early as 1889, a year after William's accession to the throne, an editorial noted with concern the young Kaiser's expressed determination to start a new contest with Britain by building a new high seas fleet for Germany. At the start of 1892 the *Herald* aimed a remarkable editorial in his direction, demanding that he recall Bismarck, whom he had dismissed in 1890:

Sire!
People ask whether you wish to become the Prince of Peace or

whether you are content to remain merely a soldier-King of Prussia.
. . . Your policy may force you to struggle against the Russians and
against the French . . . may also precipitate war between the Slavic
race and the Germanic race and between the Germanic race and the
French race and even between the French race and the English
race. . . .

Or on the other hand, peace! If [the latter] . . . then place beside
you the man who, having already become great in war, can now
only wish for peace!

Do this and nations will worship you . . . [otherwise] you will go
down in history as the Little German Emperor of the end of the
century . . . people will curse you.

A week later, under the heading "An Imperial Busybody," the
paper noted that three years after William's accession to the throne
he had "managed to offend the susceptibilities of almost every class
of his subjects." By 1901 the Commodore was convinced that the
Kaiser was incorrigible. He sent one of his correspondents, Sidney
Whitman, to Germany to write a series of articles about Germany's
aspirations to world domination. "I have picked out Whitman,"
he wrote to a friend in England, "because he is familiar, from
personal contact, with Bismarck's policy, which was imperialistic
for Continental purposes: but this young man now on the throne
has gone beyond that. His idea is to conquer the world and make
us all his vassals. I don't like it and I am going to stop him."

The Kaiser, according to legend, learned that he had unintentionally snubbed Bennett, and he tried to make amends by sending
him a personal invitation to attend an important function in Potsdam. Bennett did the unthinkable: he refused to even acknowledge
an invitation from the All-Highest, and the Kaiser, hurt, apparently
brought up the matter with every American thereafter. Whether
the reason was personal animosity, a generally Francophile attitude, a distrust of German militarism, or reasoned political analysis, Bennett would have none of the Kaiser and, once the war
broke out, savaged him mercilessly in the columns of the *Herald*.

Across these early years the Paris *Herald* carried a very substantial serving of news reports from all over the world. They were quite frequently borrowed by French newspapers—and the *Herald* was not loath to point this out. Even the poor old *Galignani's Messenger* did some borrowing which the *Herald,* though condemning the practice, excused on the basis that imitation was the sincerest form of flattery. Colonial wars, the Balkan wars, developments in the military balance of power, political changes, financial and economic developments, all received wide coverage. From the outset the paper featured a frequent roundup of the French press, lengthy excerpts and summaries of stories in American newspapers, and in the 1890s, by special arrangement with the *London Times,* it printed a front-page column, "What the *Times* Says Today."

Bennett continued to try to make news, as he had done earlier with the Stanley expeditions, but now in the field of international politics, as he tried to drum up opposition to what he conceived of as the Kaiser's belligerency, and support for his American-Chinese alliance. Political reporting was interspersed with more sensational items: murders, trials, or reports of duels. Four of six columns could be devoted to a duel between the Count of Turin, nephew of the Italian King, and Prince Henri d'Orléans, whom the count accused of insulting the honor of the Italian army. The coronation of Czar Nicholas and Czarina Alexandra drove all else off the front page, as elaborate descriptions of the pageantry and of those attending vied with illustrations and articles on the political significance of Nicholas' ascension to the throne. The tragic death of Crown Prince Rudolf of Hapsburg at the hunting lodge of Mayerling filled the front pages in early 1887; the mystery of whether it was apoplexy, accident, or assassination, the grief of the old Emperor, the political ramifications, and the account of the obsequies took up much space. Reports of this kind might jostle for space on the front page with journalistic firsts like an interview with Count Herbert Bismarck, the German Foreign Minister, son of the Chancellor, or Signor Crispi, the Italian Prime Minister.

Newspapers had begun to play a role in diplomacy that they would never relinquish, and the *Herald* was a part of the development. Two-thirds of the front page might be devoted to Jack the Ripper, complete with maps of the Whitechapel area indicating where the victims had been attacked. And extensive reports of the last Indian wars in the western United States (a correspondent was with the cavalry, and reported on "How Sitting Bull Fell") might share the front pages with reports of the Christmas and New Year's festivities in New York and Paris, and of the unusual freezing over of the Seine, with bonfires and dancing on the ice after the police failed to keep the crowds off. A column of worldwide political reports might be headed "How the World Wags Politically," while another, on Franco-Italian-papal politics with the subhead "A Curious Chapter in the Diplomatic History of Europe," was headed "Si Non E Vero—" The siege of the legations in Peking might share the front pages with a tragic fire on the Hoboken docks, Mrs. Chetwynd's divorce, the first day at Henley, and the successful trial of a new German zeppelin. The fact is simply that the *Herald* was rarely dull!

Some Americans in Europe objected to the coverage of European social events and to the growing number of articles in French: "The *Herald* is supposed to be English-written . . . it is a shame not to give a little American news instead of all the departures, arrivals, etc. of the lords and ladies of England," wrote one. Said another, "Your paper may cost you a lot, but if you printed more American news instead of elaborate accounts of what the Spanish nobility is doing in private life . . . eliminate the details as to the decorations, etc., of the many English social functions . . . in short cut out what to Americans, who are desirous of reading an American paper, would call trash and spend a few dollars on cablegrams of what is going on in America, your paper would not then be a financial failure." Signed, "An American."

Bennett must have been provoked. A day later the editorial page noted that that day's paper contained 3,953 words from the United States "and 'An American' wants more!" A week later it took space to tell readers it contained 4,354 words cabled from overseas. "Can 'An American' want more?" After several more of these editorials, another letter writer calculated that the number of cabled words the *Herald* boasted about totaled only 13 percent of what the *Herald* printed and, signing his letter "Daily Reader," appended a P.S., "who expects to get his editorial scolding now, too." But the *Herald* called the whole thing off.

It is certain that Bennett's personal views very much influenced the news coverage. The Commodore was a wealthy man of his times; he enjoyed to the utmost the status quo; he foresaw continued improvement in society, largely as a result of technical progress—which fascinated him and which he recorded in great detail in the *Herald*. He hoped for an amelioration in the condition of the working classes, and he himself contributed large sums to charity and for relief during times of financial crisis or famine. He insisted editorially that the charges made against the Belgian administration of the Congo be thoroughly investigated, and improvements be made. But he was never a crusader for social reform. He accepted the class system of his time, and geared his paper to a particular one of those classes. He opposed all use of violence to bring about change, and condemned revolutionaries or anarchists of all stripes. His views on socialism are on record: in 1908, complaining about the vagaries of the French telephone system— "Nothing could be worse, except, of course, the French telegraph"—and the problems it caused for the paper, he went on to observe: "And to think that there are people who advocate the State ownership of railways and other public necessities when they have before their eyes the French telegraph, the French telephone, the French cigarette and the French match! It is charitable to conclude that such people are merely crazy."

Perhaps two French journalists, Louis Vauxcelles and Paul Pottier, describing the *Herald* in 1904, came closest to the mark. They claimed that the *Herald* skimmed off the cream of the cable dispatches that poured in from all over the world before relaying the body of them to New York. "The political information is precise, up-to-date, sometimes sensational, with no padding, no ideological considerations." They referred to the daring displayed by the Commodore in starting the newspaper when he did; the technical developments that made it possible were new and largely untried. The *Herald* may have been "a sportsman's caprice," and "Bennett's favorite sport," but it was also "the most plagiarized newspaper in Paris" and "the most serious of frivolous newspapers."

CHAPTER 3

The Most Frivolous of Serious Newspapers,

or

"Decidedly Rosy Prospects for the Coming Grouse Season"

JAMES GORDON BENNETT could feed his cosmopolitan class hard news. But the news had to be interspersed with more than scandal, trials, and disasters. The paper also had to chronicle the doings of the new class, entertain it, and serve its members in a variety of ways, and the success of the Paris *Herald* rested on how Bennett did this.

It took a few months for the Commodore to really get going and discover what he could cram into his four-page format, what with most of the last page given over to advertising. On page 2 "Paris, People and Places" soon came to be followed by social news of London, Berlin, and other cities. A "London Court Circular" gave readers essential information about London society; a condensation of "London Press Notes" added to it. The "Talk of Paris" soon took two columns; "Births, Marriages and Deaths" were registered for the entire Continent. "Yacht Movements" was obviously a popular column; by 1892 the *Herald* could note that it had contracted with Lloyds of London to receive news of all yacht sightings and landings. Yachtsmen would always be able to keep in touch with one another, and more sedentary mortals could keep up with their gallivanting friends, family, and employers—through the *Herald,* of course. Sports concentrated on such high-life affairs as horse racing and polo. The "World of Sports" might give an account of the races at Caen (with a word about the special deluxe train from Paris in the morning, complete with report of the table d'hôte in the dining car). "Sporting Life" would give predictions for Croydon. For fifty years, starting with "Coq-Heron Selects," the *Herald* would give its own favorites at Paris races to its readers. (When John Hay Whitney—a descendant of some of Bennett's close New York friends—bought controlling interest in the Paris *Herald Tribune* in 1958, one of his early inquiries was whether the Paris paper could carry more American horse-racing news.)

It was on page 2 that the *Herald* informed its American visitors of what amusements were available in Paris and London, the location and opening hours of "Places of Interest" like the Arc de Triomphe, the Louvre, or Les Halles. Within a few years of the start of publication the paper could include a list of *Herald* reading rooms in other cities: Nice, Berlin, Dresden, Leipzig, Lugano, Mainz, Munich, and Stuttgart; it bore a few brief paragraphs in French under the title "Coups de Lorgnette"—soon to be expanded into whole pages in French. "Her Majesty's Navy" and "U.S. Navy" told the whereabouts of both countries' capital ships and the names of commanding officers, while a listing of boat trains came to occupy more and more space.

The register at 49, avenue de l'Opéra began to yield a long list of names: in September 1889, Bennett opened up a reading room there, grandly called a *salle de dépêches et de lecture,* with American, English, and French newspapers and periodicals available. According to the *Herald,* 200 Americans had registered there every day for the previous six months. Not only did their names duly appear in the Paris paper; they were cabled back to New York and then sent to be published in the visitor's hometown newspaper. In later years Bennett would expand the services provided at the avenue de l'Opéra offices. Hotels could send mail there addressed to Americans who had left without a forwarding address and the

The *Herald* Registry and reading room on the Avenue de l'Opera, about 1900, with the MacKay-Bennett Commercial Cable offices next door.

paper would advertise them in an unclaimed letter column. "In nine times out of ten," it boasted, "the addressees are heard from"; in one day eighty letters were forwarded.

But it was in the *Herald*'s first year that Bennett came up with an idea that led, ultimately, to one of the most characteristic features of the paper up until World War I: he invited "bright and gossipy" correspondence of 800 to 1,000 words from the leading watering places giving accounts of daily life, of the latest arrivals, anything of public or social interest. He would pay fifty francs a letter and more if it was very good. Letters must be exact in their facts, not mere "puffs," and they must avoid anything libelous or malicious.

On August 11, 1888, the whole front page and much of page 2 were made up of the first of the fall's crop of letters, among which were "Trouville Temptations," "Sunshine from Etretat," "The Delights at Aix," and "At Wagner's Shrine." In later weeks readers could enjoy "Engadine Breezes," "Grindelwald Climbing," "Exquisite Evian," and "Queenly Brighton." (It was a regular correspondent, however, who came up with "Shooting in the Schwarzbach: Emperor William Enjoys Two Days' Bad Sport," thereby providing both social reporting and a dig at the Kaiser.)

With his competition for amateur correspondents Bennett accomplished several objects in one stroke. He brought the attention of those attending the fashionable resorts to the newspaper, to the fact that it would chronicle the resorts' doings, and created a bond with their hotels and restaurants, thereby assuring the *Herald* of a circulation in each of the resorts. And since the clientele was a mobile one, it would take its newly acquired taste for the *Herald* with it. Within a couple of years the page 3 listing of towns and hotels where the *Herald* could be obtained had lengthened to include virtually all of Europe. Special notices would occasionally appear: "The Paris Edition of the *New York Herald* may be purchased at Trouville during the Race Week of the Concièrges of the Hotel des Roches Noires and of the Hotel de Paris."

The amateur correspondents continued to appear in later years: "Merry Montreux," "Bits from Baden" and "An Adamless Eden: Woeful Dearth of Gentlemen at Aix-les-Bains." The device must have been immensely popular: each summer until the turn of the century would see a new crop. The instructions given to amateur correspondents were quite specific: pieces must be "newsy and social"; "guidebook descriptions" of scenery, trees, sunsets, and so on would not be published. "Letters should mention the arrivals, departures, and movements of well-known Americans, English, French, Russians, Germans, Austrians—in a word, of all persons of note, of whatever nationality, at frequented watering places such as Trouville, Dieppe, Vichy . . . Spa, Homburg, Ems, Carlsbad, Marienbad . . . Lucerne, Zermatt, Lausanne." And, as the paper expanded and included more and more pictures, the contest was extended to photographs of "views and scenes of social or sporting interest." In 1896 the paper reported receiving over 300 such letters.

In later years the *Herald* dropped the contest aspect and used regular correspondents in the very large number of fashionable resorts on which it reported. Albert Crockett, vacationing at Aix-les-Bains on the Commodore's orders in 1902, learned that any *Herald* correspondent would be extended extraordinary "courtesy" by the managers of fashionable hotels, although Bennett disapproved of the practice. At the Ritz, in Paris, Crockett had already been assured that the luxurious suite he was given was the smallest room vacant and that he would be charged what the cheapest room cost. Dinner, at M. Ritz's orders, was not to be billed at all. In Aix Crockett decided to look up the local correspondent, who proved to be an Italian "cavalière" with an American wife who did the actual writing. When they dined or lunched it was always with a lot of people whose names figured in the Aix correspondence. In the winter the couple "corresponded" from a resort in the south of France. At the Commodore's request Crockett traveled on to Baden-Baden and Marienbad to check out the two correspondents in each place and give them a little coaching. Baden-Baden authorities had complained that despite a large ad they had taken out in the *Herald* the newspaper did not seem to be using the material they had furnished to one of the correspondents, and Bennett was concerned that there might have been an illicit commission involved.

Once the paper had expanded to six or eight pages in the early 1900s, two whole inside pages might be filled on a Sunday with resort news with the titles running across the top of the pages: "Society, Hunting, Kennel, Theatrical, and Racing News from All Parts of the World." On other occasions it might be "Society, Grouse Shooting, Yachting, Tennis, and Racing News." or "Society, Automobile, Balloon, Football, and Racing News." The two French journalists, Vauxcelles and Pottier, wrote, "There is no waltz that takes place in the depths of the Engadine in a villa of St.

Moritz at 1800 meters' altitude of which the *Herald* does not give the first names of the dancers."

But if the wealthy, cosmopolitan clientele of the *Herald* moved from resort to resort, engaging in every sport, buying luxury luggage and expensive clothing and staying in the chic hotels, eating at the best restaurants—all advertised in the *Herald*—it also spent much time in the major cities. By the turn of the century, the Paris columns, for example, covered festivities in the Bois, the salons, the concerts, sales at the Hotel Drouaut, "Chez les Antiquaires," diplomatic functions, the Cercle des Patineurs, etc., and Vauxcelles and Pottier remarked that "the untiring *labeur de fête* is analyzed minutely."

Bennett was a bit of a nut about a number of things, and the weather was one of these. He had scores of centigrade thermometers hanging on trees at his Versailles estate and one on a wall of every room in his houses and offices; he always carried a pocket thermometer that he consulted at regular intervals and he conceived it to be one of his several missions in life to convert the English-speaking world to centigrade. There was, however, some reason to all this. The Commodore was interested in the weather as only a yachtsman or other seafarer might be; also, the growth of commerce had made regular weather reports a virtual necessity and he understood this. When, using the Atlantic cable, Bennett was able to give warning in Europe that storms were approaching across the Atlantic from America, he outflanked every newspaper in Europe. There were, thus, "*Herald* Warnings" of "*Herald* Storms," and rather smug accounts of the damage done as prophesied.

In fact, the Paris Edition began at the start with rather brief notes about the weather in Paris. As the paper began to print more illustrations, the weather reports featured charming young ladies standing under a tree or an umbrella, drawing up their skirts to avoid a puddle; or a young man holding a tennis racket and holding out his hand while looking up at the sky. In the *Herald*'s manner, the weather would not be described merely as "mostly cloudy" but rather as "damp and cheerless." Bennett's concern about centigrade was evidenced by a picture of a double thermometer, with side-by-side Fahrenheit and centigrade scales. But as the paper began to receive Europe-wide distribution it became obvious that weather in all the major cities had to be included, and the column grew accordingly. Then, Christmas Eve in 1899, came one of the most famous of all letters to the editor—second only to Virginia's letter about Santa Claus.

> To the Editor of the *Herald:*
>
> I am anxious to find out the way to figure the temperature from Centigrade to Fahrenheit and vice-versa. In other words, I want to know, whenever I see the temperature designated on a Centigrade thermometer, how to find out what it would be on Fahrenheit's thermometer.
>
> OLD PHILADELPHIA LADY
>
> Paris, Dec. 24, 1899

None of the people who responded to the old lady's query could have known that her letter would appear every day in the *Herald* for the next nineteen years, even when the Great War cut the paper down to a thin single sheet. No one is quite sure how she got there—whether her second appearance was a printer's error that the Commodore, once twitted about, decided in his fashion to keep on, or whether it was his decision to reprint the letter from the start as part of a campaign to convert everyone to centigrade. He later told C. Inman Barnard (who thought Bennett himself had composed the letter) that that was why he went on printing it. But to others he said that he would reprint it as long as it kept on provoking people to write annoyed, amused, or curious letters—and it did, by the hundreds. Some were from innocents who had just started to read the newspaper and endeavored to give an honest answer. But most were either filled with abuse or mildly amused. Some threatened to cancel their subscriptions unless the old lady disappeared, and carried out their threat. "Your silly tactics have driven many a reader to the *Daily Mail,*" wrote one Englishman.

One man's duty at the office was to edit the "Old Philadelphia Lady" letters, and his task became somewhat more varied after he was instructed also to see to the regular reprinting of a cartoon from *Leslie's Weekly* magazine that had amused the Commodore: "What are you doing now, Patrick?" asks the young girl pictured on a house porch as Patrick holds a string from the porch floor up to the base of the thermometer on the wall. "Sure, your mother told me to see how high the thermometer was." Patrick's frequent reappearances brought more indignant letters, and the pleased Commodore worked out a schedule of days on which he should appear.

The Old Philadelphia Lady was, incidentally, resurrected on December 22, 1944, when the Paris Edition exultantly reappeared after the end of four years of the German occupation of Paris. Geoffrey Parsons, Jr., the new editor, reprinted her with a ringing afterword: "The Mailbag is Now Declared Open!" And on special occasions she still occasionally turns up.

Barnard records that Bennett once told him, "Bear in mind that the weather is more urgent than politics, social events, theaters, sports or anything else," and in its full bloom the weather column reflected the Commodore's view. On a typical day in the early 1900s it would be adorned with a sketch of a lovely young woman paddling a crescent moon through the clouds. Patrick measuring his thermometer might follow. Then would come a long list of resorts: "Aix-les-Bains—Hotel Regina, noon, 22°C. Splendid Hotel Excelsior (on the terrace), noon, 21°C. Fine." And so on down the list, through Baden-Baden, Barcelona, and Beaulieu to Zermatt. Selected hotels at each resort would wire the weather to the *Herald.* "The readers of a foreign newspaper on the continent appreciate weather news perhaps more than any other kind of information," it declared, and if a hotel clerk was too optimistic, the *Herald* immediately received corrections from its readers.

The resort weather would be followed by Paris weather, always to the accompaniment of a sketch of the Tour St. Jacques and in full paragraph form: "No reasonable person could object to the brand of weather which was served to Parisians yesterday." A paragraph on weather in the United States would be followed by one on the English Channel and three on the British Isles, along with special notes on Dover and Folkestone. (The channel was always of concern to those peripatetic cosmopolitans, and both the Hamburg-American Line and Nord Deutsch-Lloyd advertised that their seven-day crossings to New York from Cherbourg avoided the channel.) For years a noted French astronomer, Camille Flammarion, with whom Bennett became friendly, wrote a regular column on atmospheric phenomena.

If the weather was one of the Commodore's hobbies, it was a welcome one. His mobile clientele did, indeed, want to know what it was going to be like at the next stop. And while he conducted some purely personal campaigns in the paper, such as those for antivivisection and against tarring roads—a practice which, he said, gave the landscape a funereal effect, was unhealthy, and was promoted only by antidust faddists—most were shrewdly related to important current developments. In the mid-1890s the paper began to be filled with cycling stories, as a virtual mania seized the urban population. "Cycling Notes," to the extent of several illustrated columns, concerned themselves with technical developments, questions of safety, and organized trips. Readers wrote in with tips on "pleasant parcours," and the *Herald* inveighed against the dangers of "scorching" and "over-gearing" which could put a strain on the heart, had undoubtedly already killed some men, and from which the prominent cyclist M. Huret was suffering. It recorded "An Accident to the Prince of Wales: His Royal Highness While Out Cycling Falls from His Machine."

In a jocular vein the paper editorialized that the bicycle had done much for the emancipation of women. "They can now face the world in bloomers, divided skirts, and other forms of this dress after which their souls hankered." The cycle had freed humanity from that instrument of torture the piano, and "the endless strumming that formerly drove people with delicate nerves to the verge of distraction." Best of all it was displacing the uncomfortable and inartistic stovepipe top hat, as men were forced to switch to the soft felt hat, the casquette, and the straw hat. The *Herald* reprinted a cartoon from *Collier's Weekly* of a little girl asking her grandmother, "Grandma, when I am an angel, will I have wings?" "I hope so, dear, why do you ask?" "Cause I think I'd rather have a bicycle!" There were poems, articles about cycling schools, and on one day when a half page was devoted to "Cycling Scenes at Suresnes" and several more columns to other varied cycling topics, the *Herald* editorialized that the bicycle was "the most potent agent of true democracy since the French Revolution!" Why? Because for the first time in history the lowliest could move from place to place as easily as the grand seigneur.

By the late nineties the automobile began to rival the bicycle as the object of attention, and the attention to dangers of "scorching" was now turned upon the rapidly developing problem of the automobilist—and more especially the chauffeur and "chauffeuse." In 1898 automobiles were limited to twelve kilometers per hour in the city and twenty in the country—but what policeman could catch those that exceeded the limits? The *Herald* forecast that the automobile would drive out the railroads just as the railroad had put an end to mail coaches. "Walking will be a lost art." The first Salon de l'Auto took place that year under the sponsorship of the Automobile Club de France, and the *Herald* gave it two-thirds of a page, with illustrations. It reported the suggestion that each automobile be given a unique number that could be affixed to the outside for purposes of identification. Despite adoption of this device, the paper reported a few years later that the police were sporadic and inefficient in stopping what it now called "speeders," and it put forth the idea that a private membership League Against Speeding might be effective in taking down numbers and reporting them. By 1912—does this have a familiar ring?—it was invoking "the ever increasingly difficult problem of regulating the dangerously congested street traffic of Paris, particularly on the Avenue des Champs Elysées. . . . the chief fault lies with the Paris drivers themselves, who show a disregard of established regulations which the police seem powerless to cope with."

Bennett's readers, of course, were among the first to take up the automobile, both for urban use and for touring. In the early 1900s the *Herald* began to provide the sort of personalized service that the *Guide Michelin* would never be able to provide in later years. Under the rubric "En Automobile" the paper registered the arrival of automobile parties in hotels all over Europe. Not only were names given, but also the make and horsepower of the car in which the party arrived, thus giving people an idea of which makes were the most popular and what power people were seeking out. Like all such columns it was handsomely illustrated with a photograph of one of the hotels mentioned, framed in elaborate flower and scrollwork. The *Herald* paid for the telegrams from hotels announcing the arrivals, and was not loath to advertise the fact. At first, it said, hotel owners were unwilling to believe that the *Herald* would pay and that they would get the resulting free publicity. After mentioning the cost, the paper took the occasion to rub in a point: "And to think that there are people who imagine a foreign newspaper on the continent is a profitable undertaking! Such ignorance is pathetic!" At another point it reported that at Biarritz the automobile craze had caused flagging attendance at casinos and a decline in bathing.

It was an exciting time of technical and scientific innovation, and only a handful of romantics had really questioned the benefits of the new technology. Bennett was an avid promoter of all that was new—automobile racing, aeronautics, motorboating, radio; the construction of the Metro was proceeding apace in Paris, and the Commodore became a habitual user. To encourage technical progress he established a series of international prizes: in 1900 the Coupe Internationale de l'Automobile became the first international automobile road race, to be run on a circuitous route between Paris and Lyon. A French driver, Fernand Charron, won, driving a twenty-four-horsepower Panhard, even though he collided with a Saint Bernard dog at sixty miles an hour. The Automobile Club de France subsequently took over patronage of the event, and it became the French Grand Prix. The races were, of course, reported at length and in detail in the *Herald*, though the cup, which became generally known as the Gordon Bennett Cup, was never referred to as such in the paper. During the running of the Grand Prix, bulletins would be posted in the windows for the excited crowds that gathered outside the *Herald* office on the avenue de l'Opéra.

In 1906 the Commodore came up with another and even more eye-catching award, the Coupe Internationale des Aeronautes, for balloon racing. Success was immediate and enthusiasm widespread. The balloonists in the first Bennett Cup balloon race were to leave from the Tuileries, in the heart of Paris:

> By three o'clock in the afternoon the place de la Concorde, the quais, the lower part of the Champs-Elysées and the Tuileries Gardens were black with spectators. Traffic was at a standstill. . . . A walk round the enclosure before the start was very entertaining. It was a study in itself to mark the various types of aeronaut present—the stolid German, the sprightly Frenchman, the indifferent Spaniard and the cool Englishman.

Sixteen aeronauts sailed off to the west, including Santos-Dumont, "the hero of the 'heavier than air theory.' " An American, Frank Lahm, won. The races, interrupted by the war, continued until 1934—and were resumed in California in 1979, under the aegis of the *International Herald Tribune*! Although the newspaper's accounts of the races had to compete with such minor matters as the Balkan wars, they always occupied a large part of the front pages, with photos of contestants and the starting point and maps of previous results.

In 1907 Bennett gave a cup for motorboat races, and in 1909 he established the Coupe Internationale de l'Aviation. The first airplane cup race attracted 100,000 spectators to Reims, including the cream of international society. Frenchman Louis Bleriot set a world speed record, and later emerged unhurt from a crash; the lone American, Glenn Curtiss, bested him twice and won the first Gordon Bennett Airplane Cup. And the *Herald* had an extraordinary field day.

All these events and accounts of other technical developments in the field of transportation and communication were grist for the Commodore's mill; he had them reported in detail, fully illustrated. A young reporter assigned to cover Wilbur Wright's flights at Le Mans in 1908 became the first journalist to actually fly when Wilbur invited him along. Bennett also assigned a reporter to cover the work of an Italian named Marconi. The reporter's enthusiasm led Bennett to provide financial backing for the Italian, and to commission him to provide wireless coverage of the 1899 America's Cup yacht races. Subsequently, during World War I, Bennett established his own wireless station at Wellfleet to keep in touch with ships at sea and helped finance Lee De Forest in his attempts to improve radio transmission.

Some of the Commodore's fads and fancies, however, seemed purely personal, although at times they helped to promote the newspaper's reputation or circulation. All through these years of improving transportation the Commodore continued to promote his old sport of coaching. Edwin Howlett, an English coaching expert, came to Bennett to ask permission to run a public coach from the *Herald* offices to Versailles. Bennett's enthusiasm was aroused, and on May 2, 1889, a regular coach service began during the summer months, running from the avenue de l'Opéra out to Versailles. The "well-appointed Coach, the Magnet" left at 10:45 A.M. and returned at six in the evening. Liveried coachmen blowing silver trumpets announced the departure and arrival, and soon there was a regular audience along the avenue for the event. It was so popular that the next year coaches with names like the Comet, Rocket, and Meteor ran to Saint Germain and Maisons Laffitte, Poissy, and Rambouillet as well as to Versailles, and the *Herald* began to publish a regular column of "Coaching Notes." The coaches from Rambouillet would return laden with game during the shooting season, much to the delight of spectators. Later, coach

A Bennett coach and its liveried drivers preparing to leave from the Avenue de l'Opera offices for the suburbs of Suresnes and Ville d'Avray.

services were established in resorts like Cannes, Trouville, and Cabourg. The regular "whips" or drivers became popular figures; the Commodore himself was known to frequently take the reins.

Bennett liked to eat well, although his favorite dish appears to have been mutton chops. When in Paris he usually lunched at the Tour d'Argent. And when he ran across a place he really liked, it usually made for a story in the *Herald*; a few such stories and the place was made. There are, as usual, conflicting versions about some of the restaurant stories. The most popular one is that once, when he went to a favorite place in Monte Carlo with a terrace overlooking the sea, he was refused a table outside because these had been reserved for drinking, with food being served inside. In a rage, he arranged to buy the restaurant that afternoon, presented it to his favorite waiter, an Italian-born Egyptian named Ciro, and told him to get the tables back outside. Renamed Ciro's, it then became one of the great restaurants on the Riviera. Other Ciro's restaurants sprang up in other towns, and as Richard O'Connor says, "Like the Ritz among hotel names, the Egyptian waiter's name, glorified by a Bennett whim, has been made synonymous with fashionble catering."

But Albert Crockett, who frequently ate at Ciro's, says that Ciro ran a small pastry shop until Bennett chanced to taste one of his confections one day, advised him to branch out and make himself fashionable, and then gave him a story in the *Herald* to encourage him. With the free publicity and by personally giving parties in Ciro's new establishment, the Commodore made the man and the place. And each year a *Herald* correspondent was told to go and eat at Ciro's at the *Herald*'s expense and write a story on the "prospects for the season." This account is a little less romantic but gives an indication of what the Commodore and the *Herald* might do for a man.

There are conflicting stories, too, about another episode in the *Herald*'s Bennett era. In the spring of 1904 the *Herald* came out printed in blue ink. A few days later the color changed to green and then red and purple and finally, after a couple of weeks, back to black. What, people asked, had happened? In one version, Bennett, who always insisted on the best white *papier de luxe* and the best ink, became dissatisfied with the quality of ink he was receiving from his usual supplier, and took this method to show him that he had better shape up. Another—for which Crockett is again the witness—is that although experts considered the newspaper to be an excellent piece of presswork, some friends of Bennett's told him that the black on glazed white dazzled their eyes, and the rainbow hues were merely the puzzlement-provoking result of Bennett's desire to experiment!

In those days of fewer specialized periodicals the *Herald* tried to cover everything. New works and performances of well-known masters would be reported on the front page: reviews of the first performance of Gilbert and Sullivan's *Yeoman of the Guard* on October 4, 1888, the first Tchaikovsky *Sleeping Beauty*, Glinka's *Life for the Czar* and an Irving performance of *Macbeth* were all full-column items, to be found between international events or developments in American politics. People have written that the Commodore was more concerned about printing *who* went to the opera than what happened there; one obituary went so far as to say that "there were no critics on the European Edition of the *New York Herald*." The charge is untrue. David Belasco praised Bennett as the "first newspaper proprietor to give the theater its rightful place in news columns," and when Bennett began to print Sunday supplements two years after the start of the European Edition, alternate numbers carried full-page articles about different French theater companies. Reviews of art exhibits and stories about new, young American artists were frequent. The *Herald,* in 1888, estimated that of the 7,000 Americans resident in France at the time, 1,000 were artists, of whom 500 lived in Paris. As the paper expanded, it began to issue art supplements as a fairly regular Sunday feature; by the early 1900s these were elaborately illustrated rotogravure sections, focusing on antiques, on a particular painter, or on a recent salon. The tone, in general, was conservative, but the *Herald* reported controversy.

The supplements were mainly in French, with a well-known and prolific French playwright, Pierre Veber, providing some of the comment, and the prominent Henri de Rochefort the rest. Veber, who wrote over 100 plays, also did theater criticism, and Eric Hawkins, an Englishman hired in 1915 who stayed for forty-five years, recounts in his memoirs the story of how the playwright subsequently moved on to other things. Veber had been challenged to a duel, with attendant publicity. Bennett was happy to report duels in his newspaper, but was furious at having a member of his staff mixed up in them. He called in his theater and art critic to tell him he had disgraced the paper, but Veber, expressing regrets, explained that since the duel was a matter of honor, publicity would have been worse had he refused to fight. Bennett considered the matter for a moment, then suddenly proposed that Veber write a daily column of French politics. Veber protested: "I don't know anything about politics. I write plays." And according to Hawkins, the Commodore replied, "Good. That ought to make you a damn fine political writer. There's comedy in politics. Bring it out." And Veber went on to great success! On another occasion C. Inman Barnard, returning from Egypt, was ordered to write 2,000 words on the current salon within the next three days despite *his* protestation that he knew little about art. The Commodore wanted to keep him on his toes.

In the history of modern French literature the *Herald* has some significance for having published, serially, books and articles by some of the leading authors of the time: Paul Bourget, the conservative Catholic novelist, Marcel Prevost, whose novels dealt primarily with modern woman, the political satirist, Anatole France, Pierre Loti, the French naval officer turned novelist, and the Italian poet and novelist Gabriele d'Annunzio. The *Herald* ran short story contests and published the winners. Edouard Herriot, later to become Prime Minister and the grand old man of the Radical Socialist party, was hired to do French literary criticism, and the *Herald* gave him liberal space. Anatole France recorded that he was well paid but Herriot admitted that he was not, though what he got, when still a young man, was "manna from heaven."

Unfortunately, the editors also felt it a part of their mission to lighten the paper with humor, and some of the early cartoons reprinted from *Life* or the "Jokes and Jingles from the Jocose Journals" are better left buried. The "News in Cartoons" half-page section that began to appear in the 1890s has a certain historical interest, and at least one of the regular columns was actually funny: an early version of what someone much later called "fractured French," it was headed "Our Own Special Translator" and under the category "Games," for example, contained such items as "Are the stakes high?" translated as "Les biftecks, sont ils d'une mauvaise odeur?" But it should be noted that the column was not original. It came from the English magazine *Punch*.

When it came to the status of women, Bennett was no more ready to rock the boat than he was on other matters. Large parts of the *Herald* were devoted to matters traditionally of interest to women as they were—the sections on fashions, society doings, the arts, and the lengthy weekly "What the Doctors Say," chronicling new developments in medicine. On occasion, of course, the issue was raised when suffragettes forced it to public attention, but Bennett had no taste for the violence with which they advanced their views at the turn of the century. But when the issue arose of whether lady barristers should be allowed to practice in Belgium and France, an editorial answer pointed to the success of female lawyers in the United States, surely proof enough for anyone. On the other hand, in 1904 a long article asked, "Is Woman To Be Trusted at the Automobile Steering Wheel?" and the answer, based on interviews with both men and women, was that they could certainly tour with any high-powered machine as safely as men could, but would never become expert at such high speeds as fifty miles an hour. At least the *Herald* avoided the simple clichés about women drivers!

What none of this conveys is the extraordinary charm that the paper developed over the years. It began in a rather cramped and straightforward style, although from the start headlines gave promise of things to come: "America by Cable" might have as a subhead "Little To Talk About Except Politics and the Weather," and two years after the start of publication headings that had been simply "America," "France," or "the Continent" began to become more descriptive: "Clouds of Calumny" (on a French libel suit) or "Primroses in Order" (on a fine Good Friday in England). "Wall Street," we are told, "After a Day of Inordinate Dullness, Has a Lifeless Close." The engravings that began to appear more and more frequently, particularly those illustrating fashions, were delightful; those illustrating articles on naval developments, for example, would be collector's items today. When, in 1890, the *Herald* began to print photographs, it started a tradition of printing them framed in a variety of ways, which held good until World War I. In a straightforward article illustrated by a single photo the frame might be simply several straight lines. But in a feature with several photos one might find them mounted at angles, overlapping, en-

closed by elaborate scrolls, flowers, or leafy "art deco" back-
grounds, with delicate engravings of appropriate subjects set off
against the more literal photographs. After the turn of the century
virtually all the feature columns had their illustrated heads; even
the column of stock and bond listings bore a golden calf at the top!

The supplements became more numerous and more sumptuous
as the years wore on, and give testimony to a graciousness that
could be found in the midst of the life that the *Herald* chronicled
at the turn of the century. Rumblings of discontent with the established order of things constantly made themselves felt; socialist
political parties gathered political momentum, trade unions struck,
anarchists created for themselves their bomb-throwing image, and
the hungry rioted for food. Overseas the European empires felt
only occasional tremors, though the Boxer Rebellion and the Japanese successes against czarist Russia foreshadowed things to
come. But through it all the *Herald,* serene in Bennett's faith in
progress, pictured beauty in the life that was. In the mid-nineties
the Christmas supplements would have stories, songs, and poems
illustrated in full color, and full-page colored engravings—"Too
Late for Christmas Dinner, 1794 and 1894" with a horse and
carriage stuck in the snow in one and a train in the other, or, with
a reproduction of a Venetian painting, a story in French, "Le
Parabole de l'Homme Riche et du Pauvre Lazare," by Gabriele
d'Annunzio. A full page of color illustrated "Love Me, Love My
Dog," with women hanging decorations as their dog looked on.
The cover of the 1896 Christmas supplement bore an elegant lady,
resplendent in a cream-colored satin and flower-embroidered lace
gown raising a champagne coupe: "A Merry Christmas!" while
inside the Queen of the Mistletoe drove a sleigh pulled by cherubs.
Another bore a cutout dollhouse of Bennett's new Herald Square
building, complete with the owls along the parapet. And all were
printed on paper that is still, eighty or ninety years later, a dazzling
white.

We can learn something of the life of those cosmopolitans from
the advertisements that sometimes filled several pages and became
more elaborate as the years wore on. Many of them were for

products or services still available: when the *Herald*'s readers traveled, they used Louis Vuitton luggage and made their arrangements through Thomas Cook; they took photographs with their Kodaks, stayed at hotels like the Meurice on the rue de Rivoli, bought their art from the Knoedler galleries or from Duveen, and went to the Moulin Rouge, the Folies Bergère, or the Olympia music hall to be entertained. They shopped at the Grands Magasins like the Printemps, the Samaritaine, or the Bon Marché, though they also went to Tiffany's. If they drank familiar brands of champagne, they also used Vichy water and Perrier. They brushed up on languages at the Berlitz School, improved their complexions with Cuticura soap, bought comfortable Walkover shoes, and used Houbigant perfumes. And as a full travel page would indicate, the hardier souls, rather than merely staying in the Grand Hotel in Venice or the Badrutz Palace in St. Moritz, might take an automobile tour through Morocco or Algiers, staying in first-class French hotels. "Americans in Paris" were told in one ad that they "will find genuine ice cream soda, candies and cakes at Fuller's, 4 rue Daunou"—just across the street from where a more famous establishment would appear in 1924, at number 5—Harry's New York Bar.

At one point in 1912 a faithful reader wrote in to say that the *Herald* had gone overboard in its opposition to Theodore Roosevelt, and as a nonpartisan paper it should—as it usually did—give facts from all points of view. The letter gives some inkling of what the *Herald* had come to mean to Americans in Europe:

> Remember that the *Herald* is more than a mere newspaper for us Americans in Europe. It is a national emblem and oracle. It is the most patriotic and American thing in Europe, not excepting the Diplomatic Corps. We cuss the *Herald* and find fault with it. But we all of us buy it, couldn't do without it. Even the Old Philadelphia Lady makes most of us feel cozy. . . .
>
> But the very position of the *Herald* should make it more than usually careful in giving all the news from a truly impartial standpoint. . . . Eat'em alive in your editorial columns once in a while, and print the sassiest things you can find in the American press, but give us some of the other side too.

CHAPTER 4

The *Herald* as an Organization

ENNETT'S *Herald* establishment was always spread around Paris. The advertising business offices and reading room in the heart of Paris on the avenue de l'Opera served to advertise the newspaper, with their large and visible "New York Herald" sign. The Commodore had two apartments on the avenue des Champs Elysées, with his own personal office in one and a sort of daytime editorial room in the other, where mail to the *Herald* was sorted out and letters judged of particular importance to Bennett were sent over to him. The rest were sent to the editorial offices, first on the rue Coq-Heron, and then, in 1890, after a brief interval at the rue Montmartre, to a new building at 38, rue du Louvre, overlooking the belly of Paris—Les Halles. Here the Commodore had leased the basement and the first two floors and installed his own presses, and here the paper stayed until December 1930, when it moved west to the rue de Berri, off the Champs Elysées and near the Etoile.

The different establishments were conducted separately, and unless ordered otherwise by Bennett, an employee at one was not supposed to appear at any of the others. Bennett apparently felt the arrangement protected him from intrigue. The offices were eventually connected by the precarious French telephone system, but messages generally travelled from one to the other in the hands of a small corps of grooms dressed in olive-green livery, with each uniform bearing a small golden owl. In any event, given Bennett's nature, the true center of affairs was always where he was, whether at his office in Paris, shooting in Austria or Scotland, at the villa in Beaulieu, or cruising the south seas on the *Lysistrata*. At the office at 120, avenue des Champs Elyées he eventually installed the former skipper of the *Lysistrata*, a Captain Hutt, who had been invalided ashore, but who lent a fine presence to the office where most visitors called, and who also edited the "Mailbag" column.

Albert Crockett, called by Bennett from New York in 1901 and told to spend two weeks at the rue du Louvre before going over to London as a correspondent, has given us some sense of what the newsroom was like. Going in at the normal hour, five o'clock in the afternoon, he was introduced, he says, to "such a varied collection of sub-editors and copy-readers as could be equaled in few offices. Some of them were men of considerable education who had seen better days, and were now working for a miserable pittance; for very few men hired in Paris by the *Herald* were paid more than twenty-five dollars a week . . ." Some were Americans left behind after the tide of the Paris Exposition of 1900 receded. And some were, as Laney put it in his memoirs of years on the paper, "the usual lushes and derelicts of the type which seemed to cling to the Paris *Herald* all the years of its life."*

People in 1901 worked until five in the morning, when the paper finally went to press, and Crockett describes what he calls "an atmosphere of anemic gloom . . . of men who were oppressed by fate or circumstances, but had not the strength to rebel." The staff was usually heavily English, because, as Bennett once explained, British employees were easily obtainable, the channel not being so wide as the Atlantic. Besides, he admired their writing style. And according to Eric Hawkins the staff also felt that it was because they didn't have far to travel once they were fired. There was generally an "editor-in-charge," but to avoid letting a man go stale in the position Bennett had the habit of appointing one man or another to the position every few weeks, until World War I imposed a manpower shortage.

*Al Laney, *Paris Herald: The Incredible Newspaper* (New York: Appleton-Century, 1947), p. 37.

Drinking was always a problem, and given the small staff there was often reason to wonder how the newspaper could get out. Bennett was ready, however, to fire anyone for alcoholic indiscretion, despite his own proclivities. One story ended happily, though. The staff always bribed Bennett's butler to notify them when he left his apartment so that they could prepare for one of his descents on the newsroom. One night they had piled their empty beer bottles in front of the young sports editor, Billy Bishop—chosen for that position, typically enough, because he had once demonstrated some knowledge about Pekinese dogs in front of the Commodore—and Bennett walked in unheralded. The warning system had somehow broken down. Were the bottles Bishop's? he demanded. Bishop, unwilling to implicate his fellows, admitted that they were. Whereupon the Commodore raised his salary by fifty francs. "He needs it to pay his beer bills."

On another occasion a somewhat raffish employee, George Cooper, arriving at the office with a bit of a brandy glow, found the Commodore poking around the office sourly. Disregarding the danger signals, Cooper slapped him on the back cordially and shouted: "Come along Bennett, I'm going to show you Paris!" To everyone's amazement the Commodore cheered up and the pair went off arm in arm—and Cooper's salary was doubled.

Other evenings would not end so happily. Sometimes the Commodore dictated editorials that the staff conveniently lost; on others he would storm in angry about something he had read in the paper. It was of these occasions that people lived in fear.

Bennett had indefatigable energy and slept little; he was one of those men who could get along on four or five hours a night. Despite his other activities, when he was in Paris he arose before five o'clock in the morning, and began by reading cable dispatches that had arrived from New York during the night, reports from his New York paper, and then every line of the Paris paper, a copy of which was sent to him marked up in red and blue pencil, indicating who had written what and who was responsible for what part, along with a half-dozen reports that gave him a list of the staff on and off duty and their working hours, the number of editorial columns filled, and the press times for each edition. When he was in Beaulieu or on his yacht he would keep in constant and expensive communication by cable. Alfred Jaurett, his business and advertising manager and one of his few long-term employees, related that when Bennett was in a good mood aboard the *Lysistrata* he would go through the mail carefully with a secretary at hand, the deck would be covered with papers and a stream of his blue memoranda would issue forth; on other occasions, if the weather was foul or the Commodore awoke with a hangover, he would kick the mail sacks from the *Herald* into the Mediterranean and steam into port to a favorite restaurant. The result, Jaurett claimed, was a considerable volume of lost mail and advertising! (Other paid ads disappeared because the Commodore, at night, liked to go down and visit Cohick in the composing room, where he would look over the classifieds and order that this one or that one be removed. Cohick, amused, would tell him it was already paid for, but Bennett would snap back, "I won't have it in my newspaper!" and out it would come.)

Bennett's habit of working from his yacht lost him at least one good man, the brilliant Samuel Chamberlain, son of one of the ablest of *Herald* journalists. Chamberlain, a bon vivant in his own right who got along famously with the Commodore, had been acting as Bennett's secretary for years and helped found the Paris Edition. Soon after, cruising on the *Namouna* with the Commodore at the helm, the yacht's sailing master pointed out that the *Namouna* was set on a collision course with a unit of the United States Navy. Doggedly determined that the Navy vessel should shift course, Bennett refused to change his own, despite Chamberlain's expostulation about what the collision would mean. Only at the last moment, as guests and Chamberlain protested together, did Bennett make the necessary move to avoid the collision. But he was furious with Chamberlain for interfering, and the story has it that only his guests' intervention prevented him from marooning his secretary on a small island. Chamberlain then left him to help make *Le Matin* one of France's leading journals.

When R. D. Blumenfeld came to Paris in 1890 to get orders about closing down the London Edition that Bennett had started eighteen months earlier, he wrote in his diary "He is a strange, fascinating, enigmatical figure. If he had not been born rich and had to earn his living, he would have been the world's greatest journalist. But he has been hopelessly spoiled for many years, and is now just like an Eastern potentate. His word is law." The same image came to Albert Crockett, who entitled his memoir of his years with the Commodore *When James Gordon Bennett was Caliph of Bagdad*. To others, commenting on Bennett's working methods, the imate was of a Captain of a ship, whose command had to be absolute—in principle. Bennett himself conceived of a newspaper this way. The command was his and no one else's. Therefore, generally speaking, the responsibility was his and the credit was his. Reporters never received a byline. Only feature writers like Veber or Flammarion or writers like Anatole France had their names at the end of their columns, and most of Veber's editorials were unsigned. And Bennett would be angered when a reporter's work received special credit or notice from anyone other than himself. As Seitz put it, "There could be but one known man in the shop—Bennett."

The problem, of course, was that command could be absolute in principle but not in practice, and ways and times developed to avoid the all-too-often eccentric orders that issued from wherever Bennett might be. It was the resulting uncertainty that drove men away, although a handful stayed and played an important role in maintaining the paper: Alfred Jaurett, the advertising and business manager, who later on, in the twenties, is credited by Al Laney with having maintained the *Herald*'s lead over its rivals; Percy Mitchell, long his secretary and chief assistant, who played an increasing role in directing the paper in the Commodore's last years; the indefatigable Cohick on the production end; and Veber on the French language pages.

There are innumerable stories that the Commodore chose his employees on the basis of whether his dogs appeared to like them when they first appeared, or whether he approved of their appearance. It is true that he once fired music critic Charles Henry Meltzer because the latter refused to have his long hair cut. (The critic sued and won). A new prospective employee named Creelman was to be interviewed aboard the *Lysistrata* but was not allowed aboard because he refused to shave off his beard to meet the Commodore's injunction that all men aboard the ship had to be clean shaven. Bennett did see him later in Paris, liked him, and took him on, beard and all. And the story goes (with variations) that John Burke, who later became editor-in-charge during the first two years of the war, passed the dog test by dousing himself in anisette, which he had been told dogs loved. The variations have him tucking pieces of liver into his cuffs and his hat!

But again, whatever the stories, most people also agree that Bennett had an extraordinary capacity for picking out good people who would be top-flight journalists. Subsequent arbitrary treatment drove some away, but there were many, French and American alike, who wrote later of his generosity and encouragement; John Russell Young, who ended his career as Librarian of Congress, wrote that Bennett paid him three times as much as he was paid at the rival *Tribune*. From Paris, where Bennett used him as a roving reporter, Young wrote to his brother, "I was quite astonished with his appreciation of my merit and the princely way in which he went beyond my desires, my deserts, or my expectations" and, much later, that Bennett had an "unerring instinct for news; instant appreciation of the important features in dispatches arriving late at night; a kind of devination of events to come and changes in public sentiment amounting to genius."

In Bennett's waning years, on one of his rare visits to the United States, news of the *Titanic* disaster reached New York. It was Monday, April 15, 1912. There was little way of getting more of the story, but Bennett was up to the task. When a bulletin came in giving the names of ships going to the rescue, Bennett called for the passenger list of one of them, the *Carpathia,* which had sailed from New York only a few days before. He spotted the name of

May Birkhead, about whom the *Herald* had printed a story a year earlier. She was one of a new breed of tourists: she had made the money for her European trip by making and selling shirtwaists in her hometown in Missouri. He immediately cabled her on the *Carpathia:* "Wireless all operator can take on Titanic." She had never written a word for a newspaper before, but she interviewed survivors, had sketches made, and wired what she could, and when the *Carpathia* returned to New York, she came to the *Herald* with her notes and sketches. As a result the *Herald*'s coverage was both the most complete and most graphic. When Birkhead finally made it to Paris Bennett called her into his office on the Champs Elysées and offered her the job of social correspondent. She proved to be the best society editor the *Herald* ever had, and many credited her with appreciably increasing the paper's circulation. During the war she became an accredited war correspondent, and her friendship with General Pershing, the commander of the American Expeditionary Force, led to many newsbreaks. She stayed with the *Herald* until 1926.

When Bennett first took over the *New York Herald* in the 1860s he abolished his father's old list of taboos. As the years wore on, however, and his crotchets manifested themselves in so many ways, one was an increasing list of stylistic dos and don'ts. Eric Hawkins writes that when he joined the *Herald* in 1915 one man, Gaston Archambault, was famous for knowing by heart the purported 483 don'ts, rules, and orders laid down by the Commodore, many of which were pasted up on the long wall of the editorial room, opposite the windows that looked down over the markets of Les Halles. The French Linotype operators, too, were familiar with them, and would usually catch something missed at the copydesk. Thus, a liner never "sailed." It "steamed," "departed," or "left." A theatrical performance could never be called a "show." A diplomat was a "diplomatist," and the word "minister" could only be applied to a diplomatist—and so on. Many of these rules applied English rather than American usage, and it was not until the 1920's that the *Herald* became Americanized.

Albert Crockett once cabled an interview to Paris from London about British naval experts' views on the lessons of the Russo-Japanese war. He received a telegram back: "In interview this morning you spoke about armor-plating back of smoke-stack. Avoid this Americanism in English news in future. Use word funnel instead." But Crockett took it upon himself to have one of the English experts point out to Bennett that "smoke-stack" was just as good an English word as "funnel," and the result was that during the rest of that season Crockett found it impossible to please the Commodore. Bennett did not like being shown up as wrong.

There are two ways to look at the expansion of the Paris *Herald* in the years between its birth in 1887 and the start of World War I. One is that in spite of the aging Commodore's whims and often expensive eccentricities, the *Herald* was a success, growing and developing into a paper with much more solid news as well as those features so dear to the hearts of the Commodore's cosmopolitan clientele. Or one can look at the *Herald* itself and its growth as a costly whim, and one that helped hasten the decline of Bennett's two New York newspapers.

For the decline of the *New York Herald* is easy to document. It began in the early eighties when Bennett, in Paris, cut back on its expenditures just when Joseph Pulitzer bought the *New York World* from Jay Gould and began an aggressive expansion program, and when the Commodore began to display that arrogance in the use of his power that would cost him dearly in personnel. The decline was arrested during the Spanish-American War and during the years that Reick served as Bennett's alter ego in New York. But in 1906, after Bennett battled and helped defeat another rival newspaper publisher, William Randolph Hearst, in the latter's attempt to be elected Governor of New York, Hearst's manager, S. S. Carvalho, took legal action against Bennett that cost the *New York Herald* heavily. Its classified ads had been one of the most important sources of revenue, but the popular "Personals" column that covered the whole front page on a Sunday became a venue for advertising for houses of prostitution after Charles Parkhurst's campaign to close down open prostitution in New York City. Despite the vigilance of proofreaders, obscene ads in the form of ingenious anagrams crept in, along with open invitations to pleasures. The *Herald* and Bennett were indicted and convicted. The fines amounted to only $31,000 but the "Personals" column was discontinued and the battle hurt the *Herald* badly. Bennett swore he would never return to the United States, but he did come back, marched into the courtroom, heard the sentence, contemptuously plunked down 31 thousand-dollar bills out of his pocket, and sailed back to Paris. The *Herald* soon sank from first place in Sunday circulation to third, and never recovered. By the time the Great War began, circulation of the *Herald* in New York had slipped to 60,000 from its turn of the century 500,000, and even during the war it never really revived.

It is hard to determine what the financial situation of the Paris *Herald* actually was, partly because there are only isolated bits of evidence to piece together, partly because it is hard to disentangle Bennett's own finances from those of the paper, and partly because the Commodore insisted on spending large sums to make the paper be what he wanted it to be, even if this never increased the circulation beyond 25,000. Only the best paper and best ink would do. Linotypes were brought in in 1898—and the event was the occasion, as usual, for widespread promotion; French newspaper publishers were invited to inspect the machines, so that stories about them would appear throughout the French press, and the *Herald* itself published a long and detailed explanation of the marvels of the six new machines. In 1907 new American presses and stereotype equipment were bought. And in the meantime the paper was continuously expanded. Two years after it started, supplements began to appear; by the turn of the century it ran to six or eight pages on weekdays and eight to ten on Sundays. Four- and six-page art and fashion supplements were now a regular feature, and the slick-paper Christmas and Easter supplements also made their appearance. Color began to be used in supplements in the early 1890s and in 1897 there appeared a full-page colored ad for the Hamburg-

America Line. (Eighty-two years later the *International Herald Tribune* reintroduced color for advertising!) In 1903, with a twenty-four page Christmas supplement—mostly in French—the December 20 issue totaled forty-eight pages.

As early as 1893 the Commodore began to publish a second edition that contained summaries of the English press for the same day, and were available in the center of Paris by 9:30 A.M. Election day always called for special editions continuing until results were definitive. In 1904 the *Herald* introduced the Sunday colored comic section to the Continent, and the startlingly surrealistic "Little Nemo" made his appearance. That same year Bennett initiated automobile delivery to Trouville during the summer season. He did it, of course, with a flair and publicity that drew everyone's attention to the event. The vehicle used was a big, red, eighty-horsepower Mercedes racer; leaving the ruc du Louvre at 3:45 A.M., it roared through the tiny towns along the highway to reach Trouville, 130 miles from Paris, by 6:30 A.M. As a result, the *Herald* was on every breakfast table in every fashionable hotel.

Until August 20, 1908, the *Herald* was delivered to railroad stations and Paris vendors by three horse-drawn vans and seven cyclists. On that day, with the usual promotional fanfare—"The Auto Revolutionizes *Herald* Delivery"—two gray-painted vans with "New York Herald" in red on their sides (and bicycles strapped to their roofs just in case) left the rue du Louvre at 4:00 A.M. to leave bundles of paper at the Gare du Nord, the Gare de l'Est, the Gare de Lyon, the Gare d'Orsay, and, perhaps, most important, the Gare St. Lazare, which served Trouville, Le Havre, and Cherbourg. There were mishaps at first—one truck headed down a street that ended in steps and one driver found the Gare d'Orsay all closed up and had to scale several barriers to deliver the bundle. But the van delivery added up to a considerable saving in time, and delivery reports were made by 9:00 A.M., an impossibility in the past.

All of this cost money. So did the establishment of the *Herald*'s own photo-engraving shop in 1908, which advertised that it could do contract work for other illustrated papers and magazines. So did the cabled reports for the "En Automobile" rubric, and the cabled or telephoned weather reports from hotels all over Europe, and the full-page stock reports on Mondays. Nothing was too good for the Paris *Herald*. These devices all brought in advertising. In the early 1900s there might be three and a half pages in a ten-page paper, including a full page of classified ads. Department stores like the Galeries Lafayette took out full-page illustrated advertisements. But was it enough?

In 1889 Bennett told Baron Alphonse de Rothschild that the paper had already begun to make money; to friends a decade later, however, he said that the paper had cost him between two and two and a half million dollars. In an editorial in 1908, the Commodore commented on plans to establish another English-language Continental newspaper, backed by several wealthy Americans.

> This latter detail shows the horse-sense of the paper's publisher. . . . Wealthy backing is about the only thing that can keep an Anglo-Saxon journal alive on the Continent. A Continental newspaper . . . is not a profitable affair. *C'est magnifique, peut-ĕtre, mais ce n'est pas "business."* A *newspaper* on the Continent means running expenses of close on two million francs a year. It has cost the *Herald*, for example, about thirty-six million francs in twenty years to establish the European Edition . . .

Which translates into over seven million dollars by 1908.

Too, Bennett had wasted money on another venture earlier in the game. Initial success of the Paris Edition led him to establish an English Edition that first appeared on February 2, 1889. The Commodore aimed high. He had leased a five-story building on Fleet Street and installed his own rotary presses. He promised that the new paper, modeled on the Paris Edition, would be "on lines essentially cosmopolitan." Three hundred thousand English residents were directly interested in the United States through ties of marriage, relationship, or business, and an enormous class of rich American tourists visited England regularly. As a new departure for English newspapers, it would appear seven days a week, an innovation which raised an outcry that probably delighted Bennett. He was attacked for publishing on Sunday by, among others, Cardinal Manning, the Archbishop of Canterbury, the bishops of London, Manchester, and Bedford, and the Duke of Argyll. The *Pall Mall Gazette* blasted the *Herald* for an opening wedge that would lead to the seven-day work week, and the *Globe* published "The *Herald*'s Chorus—with apologies to Gilbert and Sullivan"

> The screw may twist and the rack may turn
> And Prigs may scream and bishops burn
> O'er London town and its golden hoard
> I keep my sabbath watch and ward—

Other English papers mocked the *Gazette* for its attack, noting that Monday papers were all put together on Sunday anyway, though the *Gazette* had called Sunday "the rest day for our profession."

Initial publicity was great, and a flood of ads made an eight-page paper necessary. But the paper contained too much American news, the American audience failed to materialize, and the British stuck to their own papers. In September of 1890 the Commodore had had enough. He called over R. D. Blumenfeld, then editor of his *New York Evening Telegram,* and instructed him "to conduct the funeral, so to speak . . . I've lost £1,000 a week now for over a year on that silly London edition . . . I hate the very name of London now." And Blumenfeld had to dispose of the machinery and property at considerable loss, as well as pay off the staff. Bennett was estimated to have drawn thirty to forty million dollars for his own personal use from the profits of the *New York Herald* and the *Evening Telegram* during his lifetime, and he spent them largely on his own lavish living. But many millions must have flowed into the two European Editions.

At the time of Bennett's death Henry S. Brown, who handled the Commodore's affairs in New York, wrote that the paper had finally

begun making a profit by the time of the outbreak of the Great
War, and "would have returned the proprietor all the outlay he
had made through the long years that it had been eating up money."
The war, of course, ensured that it could not. For months, the
paper was reduced to a single or double sheet, there was no advertising, and the whole market beyond the Rhine was abruptly cut
off. As the war wore on, however, some degree of a strange normality was reestablished and advertising reappeared. Then the
United States finally came in, and as American doughboys swarmed
into France sales shot up. Percy Mitchell came to the Commodore
shortly before his final illness to tell him that the Paris paper had
begun to accumulate funds.

"Impossible!" declared the Commodore, and dismissed him.
Mitchell came back again and persisted, showing Bennett the figures. "What shall I do with the money?" he asked. "Why—er—
just leave it in the bank!" The Commodore was evidently not used
to a profit.

Those were golden years for many people, those years before
August 1914. Technical and political progress and increasing
wealth seemed to go hand in hand. International trade and finance
knit nations together. Armies and navies increased in size, but in
1911 Norman Angell proved that war could not pay, in *The Great
Illusion*. Aristocratic diplomats, mingling with the European rulers
who all seemed to be related to Queen Victoria, knew that their
task was to preserve peace unless the vital interests of their countries
were threatened. People with money still traveled without passports
and visas, visited and worked where they wanted to. The rumblings
of discontent were there, but the House of Lords' power was curbed
in England in 1911, the Duma and the Stolypin reforms took care
of matters in Russia, Bismarck had introduced the welfare state to
Prussia, and in France, where Catholics had been told by the Pope
to accept the Republic, that Third Republic survived all the scandals
and the assaults that the reactionaries had mounted upon it. As

Turkey, the first of the great empires, crumbled, and the Balkan wars erupted, the other powers resolved matters. China might be in upheaval and the powers might have to intervene, but even there an archaic dynasty had to give way to republicanism based on European thought. In India or Africa tribal warfare and border troubles would be smoothed over by small European armies and local levies and the soothing activities of diplomats—or "diplomatists," as the *Herald* was forced to call them.

For the *Herald* chronicled it all under James Gordon Bennett's direct control. A glorious newspaper told of a glorious time, in the way that Bennett wanted it to. No marketing or promotion or advertising department, no board of directors or publisher's weekly conference, affected what went into the paper. Like some other papers of the time—but unlike any today—the *Herald* bore in full the imprint of Bennett's direction. It was his, and he did what he wanted to with it. Bennett knew what his cosmopolitan public wanted and he loved to provide it. He was a snob who might inveigh against snobbery, but he was a member of that society whose doings he so elaborately chronicled, and which, as some have said, he helped make conscious of itself. The *Herald* was, after all, a main means of communication between members of that cosmopolitan world. Two hundred copies of it a day were even dispatched to the Czar's court in Russia. And Bennett was not about to alienate people of influence and fashion anywhere in Europe. While sometimes cynical and derisive about individuals in European society, he was a part of it. Even his dislike of the Kaiser did not mean that in July 1914, for example, the *Herald* would not chronicle the excitement of the great international naval review at Kiel. It recorded the enthusiastic cheers that British sailors gave the Kaiser as his yacht sailed by the great line of British capital ships— "their cheers rang out stronger and sturdier than the rest."

But the *Herald* was far more than an entertaining society paper. If it did not influence politics directly before 1914, it influenced society and the social structure of the day through its elaborate reporting of change—both political and technological—and through its encouragement of the latter. On the occasion of Bennett's death a Paris paper, *L'Information,* insisted upon the immense influence the *Herald* had had on French journalism: its concise, worldwide news reports were adopted by French papers and replaced the casual "causeries" that had characterized them until then; its headlines that told the story were also copied (and many of its stories were copied, too). Unlike much of the press in France and England that was directly subsidized by a political interest—in England the textile interests supported newspapers that promoted free trade, while iron and steel subsidized the imperialist press—the *Herald* was "independent" in that it represented only the views of its owner. But, to the admiration of the editors of *L'Information,* Bennett allowed other views to be aired in the admirable "Mailbag" column and, by printing matter that did not fit into his scheme of things, in effect separated editorial opinion from reporting. There were, as the two French journalists Vauxcelles and Pottier declared in some amazement, no paid public relations handouts in the paper.

French newspapers copied many of the "features" that Bennett introduced, as well as many of his technical innovations. The Linotypes which French publishers at first felt were too expensive were soon adopted by all newspapers; so were half-tone photographic illustrations, with their sense of immediacy, in the place of engravings; rotogravure sections caught on although the colored Sunday comics section never did.

What the *Herald* could not do, and what no one in retrospect could expect it to do, was analyze what lay behind that sunny, golden time: how archaic autocracies had managed to come to terms with bureaucracies and the upper-middle-class bourgeoisie produced by the industrial revolution to produce a new and precarious stability based upon an enduring hierarchy—and a corruption of the spirit. Behind the glitter and extraordinary wealth of the cosmopolitan fusing of these ruling elements there existed a peasantry still living in feudal misery and urban poverty unimaginable in the Europe of today. Real wages rose throughout the nineteenth century, though the rise was punctuated by crises and bad times and the famines that drove millions to seek an uncertain new life in the New World. The fantastically luxurious and expensive living and the revels the *Herald* described in detail coexisted with the conditions that produced revolutionaries and reformers of every stripe. Anarchists and extremists condemned both the conditions and the reformers who hoped to ameliorate those conditions.

Bennett and the *Herald* believed in progress and improvement, but the *Herald* was a newspaper of its times and like its owner a part of the hierarchy of those times. Implicitly, it shared in the peculiar view that the upper classes could give pleasure to the lower classes through their displays of wealth and luxury. It shared, too, in the tonic of scientific discovery, and technical progress—even if it remained wary of new music, new art, and experiments in literature.

Bennett lived those times in his own wild way, and more recent biographies and sketches have concentrated on his bizarre behavior and his squandering of a fortune. But he was an extraordinary promoter when it came to the Paris *Herald,* and his personal iden-tification with the *Herald* meant that, in effect, his style of living and his passionate interest to the point of eccentricity in such matters as the weather and the centigrade thermometer, and his substantial expenditures on the promotion of aviation and auto-mobile races or on technical developments in communications, all scrved to promote the newspaper. If Henry S. Brown was correct, by 1914 the Paris *Herald* was beginning to make money. Moreover, Bennett himself had changed in his old age. For several years he had been calmer; on his doctor's advice he had had to abandon the long cruises on the *Lysistrata.* The main influence upon him, how-ever, appears to have been that of a woman whom he married on September 10, 1914 in the American Cathedral Church of the Holy Trinity in Paris. He was seventy-three at the time, but he had known her for years. She was the former Maud Potter, long married to Baron de Reuter. Her marriage to the Baron was an unhappy one, but she did not want a divorce. The baron's death in 1909 left her

Bennett at Villa Namouna, in Beaulieu-sur-Mer, with Pekingese, guests, and Maude de Reuter, the future Mrs. Bennett, on the left. (Collection Andre Cane)

free to marry Bennet, and after a decent five-year interval, she did. In the meantime she seems to have had a settling effect upon the aging Commodore.

The other event, of course, that radically altered the lives of Bennett and the *Herald*—and of so many million others—took place in far-off Sarajevo on Sunday, June 28, 1914, where the Serbian nationalist Gavrilo Princip succeeded in assassinating Archduke Francis Ferdinand of Austria-Hungary, heir to the throne of the dual monarchy, and his morganatic wife, Sophie, Duchess of Hohenberg.

CHAPTER 5

The End of an Era

T HE SUMMER OF 1914 was one of the loveliest and most brilliant ever throughout Europe. The *Herald,* on June 23, reported on the tide of tourists pouring in from the United States, calling it "An American Army of Invasion," and interviewed the famous, listing those who had advance reservations at the Ritz. There was a three-column head on the Jack Johnson–Frank Moran heavyweight fight about to take place in Paris, and another headline told about the "Americans Prominent Among Brilliant Throng Who Witness Race for the Prix des Drags at Auteuil." The front page on June 26 offered a vivid description of the reception given the Kaiser's yacht *Hohenzollern* as it entered the harbor at Kiel where the international fleet was anchored, accompanied by a photograph of the Kaiser "in a happy mood" as he watched the yacht races, following his informal visit to Admiral Sir George Warrender on the 27,000-ton British flagship *George V,* anchored just astern the German flagship, *Friedrich der Grosse.*

The prospects for the grouse season appeared to be good, the London-Paris aeroplane race drew excited attention, ads displayed the virtues of Baden-Baden, Wiesbaden, the Hotel Adlon in Berlin, and the new Englischer Hof in Frankfurt-am-Main. The *Herald,* in an editorial, declared that the reason the Atlantic was now being crossed by such splendid British liners as the *Mauretania* and the *Acquitania* was the spur that had been given by German competition—which might now even lead to improvement in the P. & O. liners that steamed out to the Pacific.

On Sunday, June 28, a headline announced Jack Johnson's easy win on points. The paper carried a sixteen-page art supplement in French and the four-page colored comics section. Among the usual columns there were the special Sunday features: "What the Doctors Say," "Books," and a relatively new one, a map next to the columns of shipping news, showing the position of all transatlantic liners on that day. Veber's and Flammarion's features were to be found on the French pages, American visitors were informed of the three classes of Paris taxi fares, the "En Automobile" rubric was in full summertime swing, while in a serious vein the *Herald* proceeded with its revelations of Big Business' role in the Mexican revolution.

On Monday a banner headline announced the assassination of the Archduke and his duchess at Sarajevo. The *Herald* took two pages to give the story, with details of the earlier, failed attempt that same day and the mischance that led the chauffeur to stop the car right where Princip was standing, making the archduke an easy target. It pondered the strange fate that had pursued the Hapsburg dynasty in recent years—and published a brief note to the effect that the Kaiser had stopped the yacht races at Kiel to return to Berlin.

History books have recorded that few people foresaw any grave consequences as a result of the assassination. Edmond Taylor, in *The Fall of the Dynasties,* gathers together the records of some reactions. Lenin, who had written to Gorky a year earlier, "War between Austria and Russia would be very useful to the cause of the revolution in Europe, but it is hard to believe that Francis Joseph and Nicholas will give us this pleasure," did not change his mind when he learned of the assassination. Britain's King George V wrote in his diary: "Terrible shock for the dear old Emperor." "There is nothing to cause anxiety," wrote the military commentator of *Figaro,* while the Kaiser is said to have remarked, "I cannot imagine the old gentleman in Schoenbrunn will go to war, and certainly not if it is a war over Archduke Francis Ferdinand." And the poor old gentleman in Schoenbrunn, upon learning the news of his nephew's death, sat first in stunned silence and then declared that divine retribution had struck down his heir to punish the dynastic sin of having made a morganatic marriage. "A higher power has restored the order which I unfortunately was unable to uphold."

The *Herald* was somewhat more prophetic. The day after the assassination it commented on the revelation that there seemed to have been a widespread conspiracy, and declared that while "all humanity must sympathize with the aged Emperor Francis Joseph . . . the tragic event . . . is fraught with fateful consequences for the Austro-Hungarian Empire, and may mark an epoch-making date in European history." But for the next three weeks, though it recorded the Austrian nobility's protest at the lack of honors shown the slain archduke, the *Herald* had little to say about Balkan tension. "The Exodus to Europe Attains New Record," it declared on July 2. The regatta opened at Henley, England, under glorious skies while London baked in unaccustomed heat. When German driver Lautenschlager won the French Grand Prix again in a Mercedes, with two other Germans coming in second and third, the crowd, whose sympathies were naturally with a French driver, nevertheless gave the Germans a rousing ovation. On July 17 101 new American arrivals signed the register at the avenue de l'Opera; 104 others were reported as arriving at Paris hotels. The number of visitors at the French spa Evian-les-Bains was greater than ever, and the season there promised to be as good as at all the German watering places, whose ads filled the back pages of the *Herald*.

Two days later, on the nineteenth, a single column on the front page reported some Austro-Serbian tension, but observed that it had relaxed since the Emperor and Count Berchtold, the Austro-Hungarian Prime Minister, opposed coercive action. Alarmist dispatches turned out to be fakes, and the *Herald* noted editorially that "perfect tranquillity reigned in Belgrade," the Serbian capital, where the main concern in the streets was with "pretty girls in dainty white frocks and smart-looking officers, presumably ogling the aforesaid pretty girls." A day later the *Herald* correspondent learned from the Serbian Premier that his country desired nothing but friendly relations with Austria-Hungary and anticipated no intervention.

With matters well in hand the *Herald* could afford to give a three-column head to the departure of the *Shamrock IV* to sail in the America's Cup race, and then to devote the next few days' front pages to the sensational trial of Mme. Caillaux, wife of the former Finance Minister, for the murder of Gaston Calmette, editor of *Figaro,* who had been carrying on a campaign to get Caillaux to resign and had planned to publish incriminating love letters written to her by M. Caillaux—before the latter's divorce from his first wife.

Suddenly, although few yet realized it, the bottom fell out of the world the *Herald* served so well. On July 25 the Caillaux trial had to be relegated to the bottom half of the front page; the top was taken up with a story under a banner headline: "The Brutal Tenor of Austro-Hungarian Note to Serbia Makes Its Acceptance Impossible." Other heads followed: "Official Italy Fears Possibility of War . . . Germany Angered at Austria's Act." Germany, the *Herald* declared, had undoubtedly supported Austria in the affair, but had no idea that "such a fiercely inelastic ultimatum would be the result." In Russia it was announced that France and Russia must take the initiative for concerted negotiations between Austria-Hungary and Serbia to prevent the outbreak of a new Balkan war; the French press was reported as severely condemning the tenor of the Austrian note, and editorially the *Herald* suggested recourse to the Permanent Court of International Arbitration at The Hague.

A day later the *Herald*'s first editorial referred to its shipping chart, showing the position of sixty-seven transatlantic liners. It seemed to be taking comfort and refuge in this proof that the world was still going on as before, that cosmopolitanism would win out. A second, more melancholy editorial expressed hope that the impending hostilities could be localized—for now, indeed, the front page bore witness to the fact that the incredible had happened. Serbia's virtually complete acquiescence had been deemed insufficient by Austria, and war fever was reported to be rampant in Berlin.

On Tuesday, July 28, with the Caillaux case still occupying the bottom half of the front page, the top half bore another banner head: Europe Asks Anxiously: Is It Peace or War? Italy Is Hopeful That Peace Will Prevail; Britain Invites Powers To Confer, Hoping To Localize Conflict." On Wednesday Mme. Caillaux's acquittal was removed to the second page; page one was filled with Austria-Hungary's declaration of war, and Germany's refusal to join the British-proposed conference. The next day's front page related news of mobilizations and of President Poincaré's return from St. Petersburg to cheering Parisian crowds. Inside, the paper still reported forlornly on the *Herald* Cup for the pony races at Maisons Laffitte, the King George stakes at Goodwood, the tipping question, and society news from Lucerne and Aix-lex-Bains. But it also reported that war fever had cast a pall over Carlsbad and that the great ocean liners that had so recently been bringing in the flood of Americans were now jammed with returnees whose one subject of conversation was war.

August 1 was a Sunday. The *Herald* still put out a Sunday paper, with a twelve-page fashion supplement and the colored comics. Inside it still bore a correspondent's story to the effect that the Bavarian resort of Joachminsthal was coming to rival Carlsbad, Marienbad, and Franzenbad. But it also reported that Americans in Austria and Germany were besieging consulates, while shipping offices everywhere were jammed. A panic had developed within twenty-four hours, and the *Herald* published Ambassador Myron T. Herrick's appeal to Americans to keep calm.

The fashion supplement was to be the last the paper would publish for a decade, and the comics would disappear a week later. On August 2 the *Herald* reported the inconceivable: the Germany of William II had declared war upon the Russia of William's cousin

Czar Nicholas, whom he had always addressed as "Dear Nicky";
France had ordered general mobilization; Belgium declared its neu-
trality and expressed the hope that all the powers would respect it.
On August 4 the *Herald* reported the German declaration of war
upon France; on August 5, that England had entered the war when
Germany rejected its ultimatum on respecting Belgian neutrality.
The last war in which men of all nations would march off cheerfully
singing had begun.

Only in that one last week that began on July 25, when the
Austro-Hungarian note to Serbia broke into the news of the Caillaux trial like a bombshell, could any reader of the *Herald* feel a
chill of fear; what was true of the *Herald* was true of other papers,
too: none had foreseen the coming of a general war. After all, there
on the front page was the Kaiser, cheered by British sailors, in a
happy mood after visiting the British flagship; there was German
racing-car driver Lautenschlager, cheered by the French crowds
when he won the Grand Prix; there was also the news of Carlsbad,
Marienbad, and Franzenbad, the opening of the Englischer Hof in
Frankfurt, the regatta at Henley, the inaugural voyage of the great
new German transatlantic liner *Vaterland,* presumably destined to
bring back more of that flood of Americans upon its return trip. In
one week that whole world disappeared. And most of the old Paris
Herald disappeared with it.

On August 4, virtually bereft of ads, it appeared as a four-page
paper, and began to assume the role it would play for the next few
months, but which it could define only a month later, when it
explained that because of lack of advertising revenue it was losing
35,000 francs a week, and therefore had to raise its price to 25
centimes a day—or else suspend publication.

> It may be journalism, but it is not business!
> We believe that it would be inadvisable to suspend publication.
> There are in Paris several thousands of American citizens who for
> various reasons are remaining here during the war. . . . The *Herald,*
> as a medium of communication between Americans believes that it
> ought also to remain.

It is a neutral organ, it represents a neutral nation of one hundred millions; and as such may be able to render a public service on the Continent in the present trying times.

When general mobilization was declared on August 1, all of Paris life changed. Shops closed down, most public transportation ceased to run, and people fled the city. At night the streets were dark and deserted. Foreigners had to register, and for those who wanted to stay the necessary *permis de séjour* involved a lengthy involvement in what was already a notorious French bureaucracy—now disrupted because the young men in it had been called up. It was believed that 40,000 Americans were in Europe, 7,500 of them in Paris, and 1,500 of these were stranded with inadequate funds. On August 3, in the rue Scribe where all the major shipping lines had their offices, everything was closed down.

From the start Ambassador Herrick moved vigorously to help, receiving the support of the wealthy and prominent Americans residing in Paris. An American Ambulance was organized in Neuilly, using the Lycée Pasteur and the resources of the nearby American Hospital; the ambassador created an American Relief Committee to coordinate the efforts being made to help out Americans;* Dr. Watson of the American Cathedral Church of the Holy Trinity opened the church's doors to let stranded Americans sleep there. And the *Herald*'s pages, with their war communiqués and maps and narrow columns of compressed world news, were full of information of these activities as well as long lists of Americans who had registered at the *Herald* offices. It served, quite simply, as the major means of communication among the thousands of stranded and resident Americans and between them and the authorities. It published the ambassador's instructions and French orders; it published lists of Parisian pensions that had called in to

---

*Percy Mitchell, the Commodore's longtime secretary and aide, unfortunately left us no record of his service to Bennett, but wrote an account of the American Clearing House, as the Relief Committee came to be called.

tell the paper that they had space. It told people where to go, what to do, and how to get in touch with each other. In short, it was a vital part of the official and unofficial efforts to cope with the emergency.

And it did all this when a large part of its own market simply disappeared overnight, which happened to no other newspaper— for no other newspaper depended as much upon international circulation—and when its own staff was sorely depleted. Most of the French workers downstairs had been called up, and many of the English staff left for England. But the seventy-four-year-old Bennett was roused to take a hand in putting out the paper as he had never done before. He told the wives of married employees that they would receive full salaries as long as their husbands were in uniform. He came to the office every day, took off his jacket and worked in either the editorial room or composing room; on foot or using what little public transportation was available he served as his own Paris reporter, going to see Herrick personally to get the latest—and frequently inside—news. Protective of Americans, he attacked the French authorities editorially for allowing only telephone conversations and telegrams in French, when so many Americans could not use the language.

The news those days was mainly of heavy German losses, as German armies attacked such virtually impregnable fortresses in Belgium as Liège, of French advances into Alsace-Lorraine, of massive Russian troop movements. The *Herald* complained that French regulations were so limiting that, in fact, "the War Correspondent's occupation is gone." It had to rely on the optimistic official communiqués, which it printed in full, on maps and photos, and what comment it could provide on these. On August 18 the paper told of how German soldiers feared bayonet charges, and reported that they were "worn out, hungry, and disillusioned by the energetic resistance of the Belgians." When calling for Japan to enter the war on the side of the Allies in the Far East, to neutralize the German shipping which had threatened to become preponderant in the area, it now added the phrase "but for this war which

Emperor William provoked." This was the first time Bennett blamed the Kaiser, but it would soon become a major theme. On August 26, after more reports of German discouragement and defeat, the *Herald* declared that Allied armies were now in an excellent position to take advantage of the Germans' exhaustion.

But official optimism could not conceal the evidence of the influx of refugees and British and French wounded. The terse communiqués began to document a relentless advance of the German right wing; the French had allowed too much of their strength to be diverted to the attack upon Alsace. On August 30 the first German airplane to drop bombs on Paris also dropped a German banner and a letter addressed to the Paris populace advising surrender, and the bombing became a daily afternoon event. On August 31 General Gallièni, the new military governor of Paris, ordered all newspapers to confine themselves to two-column heads to avoid spreading panic. Three days later the French government moved to Bordeaux in order to be able to continue conducting its business and organize the fight for victory.

The *Herald,* of course, carried the news on its front page. The official explanation appeared in full below the horrifying headline; the government must be able to continue to conduct its business. The Germans were virtually at the gates of Paris, fighting in Senlis and Compiègne, only thirty or forty miles to the north. Gunfire could be heard from within the city! Bennett called his staff together and told them, "Those of you who wish to quit may do so. This place will be under the protection of the Stars and Stripes and I will defy those Prussians to disregard it. If they come and you stay, I will do what I can to ensure your safety. In any event, the paper comes out."

On September 5 the *Herald* was reduced to a single sheet, in English on the front, French on the back. Hawkins recalled that when he arrived that day at the Gare St. Lazare, on one of the few trains still running, the *Herald* was the only paper available. "Germans Spreading to the East of Paris," read its headline. But it assured Parisians that the Germans could never invest Paris; the circle of forts around the city would prevent it, and it announced that Ambassador Herrick and the *Herald* would both stay. It was no bravado. Henry S. Brown then headed the London bureau and he recalled urging the Commodore to leave. But Bennett had reassured him. He had followed closely the progress of the German troops on a map in the office, and knew they were falling into a trap. "You are entirely wrong to be bothering your heads about us here in Paris. The Germans are coming and coming fast, but the French and English are getting ready for them faster." Bennett, said Brown, foresaw the Battle of the Marne with prophetic vision.

Bennett's decision to stay in Paris when most other publishers moved to Bordeaux gave him a permanent place in French history; Ambassador Myron T. Herrick's decision to stay, along with the Spanish, Swiss, Swedish, and Norwegian representatives, had the same effect. Said *Le Matin,*

> Of all the diplomats accredited to France, it was Mr. Herrick who took the gallant initiative to remain in Paris, and Parisians deeply appreciate this. . . . Mr. Herrick said that he regarded Paris not only as the capital of France but as that "Metropolis of the World" spoken of by Marcus Aurelius . . . it is at one and the same time to Paris, in its period of trial, and to the fatherland of the human race, that Mr. Herrick wishes to give the pledge of his affection,

and it then went on to refer to the "Sister Republic across the sea."

Herrick told his biographer, "James Gordon Bennett was a delight. He dropped in to see me frequently, and his explosions at least I could enjoy more than the enemy's bombs." At one point Bennett came to tell him that thirty of his men had departed for London without notice; he didn't see how he could continue to put out the paper. Herrick urged him to keep trying as long as possible. The *Herald* was indispensable as a bulletin of general information for Americans. Its disappearance would add to apprehension. To Bennett's credit, he never missed a single one of those dark days. Copies of the *Herald* and large-type bulletins were posted in the rue du Louvre and the avenue de l'Opéra, and the crowds that gathered to read them there were so large that the police had to come and control them on several occasions. (Two months later, after the battle for Paris was over, the police politely requested that the bulletins be discontinued since the crowds obstructed traffic.)

All this has given rise to the oft-repeated story that the *Herald* was the only newspaper to remain in Paris during the Battle of the Marne and the only source Parisians had for news. Ambassador Herrick himself contributed to the myth when he said, on his departure later in the year, "They were exciting days in Paris, of course. It was great to have the European Edition of the *Herald* published throughout this terrible period. Its daily and uninterrupted publication even when all others had ceased, was one of the great sustaining influences of the trying days in Paris." Many papers did move to Bordeaux, but several stayed in Paris, including *Le Matin* and *Le Figaro,* and on September 11 a new, small English language newspaper appeared, the Paris *Daily Post,* although it was not destined to last. Distribution was sporadic, since Gallièni had requisitioned everything with wheels to rush reinforcements to the front on the Marne.

But certainly the *Herald* never missed a day, and it became one of the chief sources of information for English, Americans, and French alike. As a result, it achieved a new status. So did the Commodore, who appeared now not so much as a wealthy eccentric but as a gallant and heroic old fighter. A new bond developed between him and the French, exemplified by the fact that each night for the duration of the war a group of union printers, when they had finished in their own shops, made their way over to help put out the *Herald.* In those few days of the Battle of the Marne, by the moral support it gave to Parisians and to France, the paper became a Paris institution in a way it never had been before.

The "entrenched camp of Paris" was ready for a siege; the Bois de Boulogne looked like a cattle ranch, and Bennett's Versailles hunting grounds served as a troop bivouac. But on September 10 the *Herald* could report that the line was holding; the next day, that the enemy was in retreat; and by the fifteenth it resumed publication of a four-page paper, reducing its price again to fifteen centimes on weekdays. The German attack on Paris had failed.

But just as no one in July foresaw the complete collapse of that golden world of 1914, no one now foresaw the horrible stalemate of trench warfare that would last for another long four years.

In the meantime Bennett had taken time out to get married. On the day that the German retreat became a certainty, September 10, he and the Baroness de Reuter were married, first in the Town Hall of the ninth arrondissement, then in the American Cathedral Church of the Holy Trinity, where Dr. Watson had confirmed the old bachelor the day before in the Episcopal faith. The wedding party was a small one, but overworked Ambassador Herrick abandoned his post long enough to act as a witness for Bennett, along with a well-known French scientist, Albert Robin. There was, of course, no mention of the event in the *Herald*.

Bennett's attitude toward U.S. involvement in the Allied war effort evolved gradually. At the outset the *Herald* was concerned with only two things: reporting the war news and being a part of the organization that Herrick created to help the thousands of stranded Americans caught in Europe. Bennett soon blamed the Kaiser for the war. In late September when Ambassador Herrick narrowly escaped being hit by a German bomb dropped on Paris, the *Herald* reported it with the comment that "it brings home the iniquity of German warfare" to Americans. (The bomb killed two people and shattered a young girl's leg.) The paper printed letters arguing that America might be neutral, but Americans could not be impartial, and by October it gave reasons why the Dutch, the Danish, the Italians, and the Romanians should *not* remain neutral: the German bombardment of Antwerp and Reims, violation of Belgian neutrality, the bombing of Paris, the burning of Louvain. On the occasion of the first wartime Christmas, "A Festival of Hope," it listed the anti-Christian acts of the enemy, who had "destroyed cathedrals, churches, convents, shrines, hospitals, and beautiful buildings of many towns of Belgium and northern France." Christmas was a "solemn festival," because "Germany has forced upon Europe a mad war that makes the message of the great Christian festival—'Peace on Earth, Good Will Toward Men'—a mockery." And it reported a new German "outrage"— bombardment of British coastal towns.

The *Herald,* then, gave moral support to the Allied cause, which had all its sympathies. But on October 7, editorially, it found the U.S. attitude admirable. America's "first duty," it declared, "should be strict neutrality . . . second, humanitarianism. . . . Its third, minding its own business, is being attended to." Some people, it went on, have tried to shout "peace." The moment is inopportune "because, no matter how horrible, this war must go on until broad principles of security and civilization are re-established." In other words "peace efforts" now might allow Germany to emerge un-scathed, might give it an opportunity to back out of a losing situation without having taken the consequences of its actions. The *Herald* supported the Allies in their determination to press on to real victory, yet approved the American policy of neutrality. It printed an English letter thanking it for its support of the Allied cause and, in mid-November, a Ridgeway Knight cartoon from the New York Edition showing Columbia comforting French Liberty: "Brave France! you have my grateful and sisterly sympathy."

But the attitude of the paper began to sharpen with the passage of time. In December another Ridgeway Knight cartoon appeared from the New York paper; under the title "American Awakening," Columbia sat pondering a map with the caption "It would have been my turn next." In January, when zeppelins raided British towns, the editorial not only raged against the act and "the usual toll of life: women, children, non-combatants . . . worst, the evident intent of the Germans to assassinate the King and Queen of England," but went on to declare, "This is only one of the numerous reasons why Americans cannot be neutral at heart in this struggle. . . . Let the mastermind that made this war triumph in Europe and there will not long be peace and security in America." The Allies' fight had evidently become the American fight, too. But the Commodore was not yet ready to call for American entry into the war, although he printed letters deploring the shame of America standing by or of Americans protesting at British interference with commerce. A front-page cartoon from *Life* showed the Kaiser riding in a Roman chariot, whipping the defeated nations that dragged it, including a John Bull saying to Uncle Sam, "If you'd helped us, Sam, we wouldn't be here now." Material support, at least, should be given.

During the course of the year 1915 the paper began to be filled with stories of German plots and German propaganda in the United States, and the dubious loyalties of German-Americans and particularly the German-American press. German submarine warfare came quickly to be qualified as the worst form of "piracy." The sinking of the *Lusitania* on May 17, with the loss of 1,198 lives, including 124 Americans, cemented this point of view.

Eric Hawkins has given us a picture of that night at the *Herald*. Bennett was desperate for more manpower, and he called John Burke, his editor-in-charge, to tell him to find someone, anyone, right away. Burke had a yellowing application letter from Hawkins, who'd been scraping a living in Paris acting as a correspondent for two English papers. Burke sent a deskman out to find him, and Hawkins spent his first night on the *Herald* sorting out a continuous flow of dispatches listing the *Lusitania*'s survivors and casualties.

The headline read "The *Lusitania* Sunk off Irish Coast by German Pirates." The accompanying story called the sinking "piracy on a vaster scale than any old-time pirate ever practiced," and in an accompanying box the next day, alongside further stories of the sinking, the paper quoted Theodore Roosevelt (about whose last political defeat it had exulted only eight months earlier): "It is inconceivable that we should refrain from action. We owe it to humanity."

On May 10, with stories of German—and German-American—celebrations of the sinking, the *Herald* went all out. Small black boxes punctuated the front page, bearing the legend "In Memoriam of the Men, Women, and Children Lost on the *Lusitania.*" A cartoon depicting the Kaiser—as always—cloaked and in a spiked helmet had him facing an Uncle Sam standing behind a flag draped over the bodies of children, with Uncle Sam's arms spread as he says, "Here are the 'facts.' "

President Wilson came through, however, to the satisfaction of the *Herald.* On June 15 it approved the stiff terms of his note to the Kaiser: "The Germans must abandon piracy. Now peace or war with the United States is up to Germany." And it exulted that Secretary of State William Jennings Bryan had resigned in protest against the firmness of the note. "The whole country is aligned against Bryan."

The war dragged on and the *Herald* continued its chronicle of the carnage on the western front, in East Europe, on the high seas, and in the Turkish Straits. It applauded Italy's overdue entry on the side of the Allies, who more and more incarnated virtue against the Central Powers' evil. Its inside pages were filled with news of increasing private American aid to France and features on the various organizations: the Field Service of the American Ambulance at Neuilly, the American Red Cross, the Depew Ambulance, the Edith Wharton War Charities, the American Clearing House with its warehouse at 79, rue Pierre Charon, donated by the Comtesse de Talleyrand, née Gould. And the paper carried on a constant war with the French and English censors, begun back in August of 1914 when it was not allowed to print news of the arrival of the British Commander Sir John French, when all the French newspapers were full of the story. Observing that it was frequently forced to leave blank a space that other newspapers filled, it quoted Clemenceau approvingly: "Nous sommes en pleine incohérence." In fact, witnesses to Bennett's explosive telephone battles with the censors and his attempts to circumvent prohibitions feel that any other paper would probably have faced suspension.

On that night early in the war when so many men left that Bennett told Herrick he didn't think he could continue, he turned out a single sheet with long blank spaces. According to the ambassador,

Bennett said that he'd spent the night in the office getting out the paper: "I think now I can continue to issue it with the aid of the censor, for see these long blanks in the place of articles and news which I am not able to get or print!" The practice hardly endeared him to the authorities, who felt it reflected upon them. As the war continued the Commodore came to the office less and less, communicating mainly through Percy Mitchell, who would bring over the editorial orders. He left the censorship battles to Eric Hawkins, who translated the communiqués and was told by Burke, "You must be diplomatic. Try and beat the guy as much as you can without getting him mad." On occasions that the censor did something really outrageous, the Commodore himself might still intervene. When told by the censors not to publish the names of officers arriving at hotels, he wrote back stiffly, saying that other papers continued to publish them. He would comply, of course, but considered the censor to be taking an "unfriendly attitude."

By the beginning of 1916, exasperated by Wilson's attempts at evenhandedness, Bennett was ready to take an even stronger stand on the issue of American policy. Wilson temporized too much. The issues were clear. When the British P. & O. liner *Persia* was sunk in the Mediterranean with a high loss of life, including that of an American consul, the Commodore exploded:

> Americans have seen murder of wives and children—
> And the American Government has done nothing!
> They have seen American factories blown up, railways sabotaged,
> ships in port destroyed—
> And the American Government has done nothing!
> They have seen their Government flouted by the same foe—
> And the American Government has done nothing!
> They have seen the same foe violate every principle of humanity,
> repudiate every pledge, commit the most infamous crimes
> against civilization.
> And the American Government has done nothing!
> . . . It has merely written. "No wonder" said an American yesterday,
> "that Henry James has changed his nationality. He can now
> declare it without a blush of shame."

The *Herald,* later in the month, wrote of Wilson's "supine attitude." "We are drifting toward the abyss," it said. "Good Lord
Deliver Us!" By midyear it was inveighing against the ineffectual
intervention in a Mexico being incited by Germany, an enterprise
which turned attention away from the real enemy. There could be
little surprise, once the conventions were over and Charles Evans
Hughes, the Republican nominee, had repudiated the support of
"hyphenated Americans," that the paper should declare its support
for him.

In the summer of 1916 Bennett made his last trip back to the
United States, to sound out opinion about the war and influence it
if he could, and to try to revive the flagging fortunes of his New
York papers. A photograph of him at the time shows a deeply lined
face, angry eyes, and the look of an obstinate bulldog. He could
do little about the papers, for the money needed was simply not
available. It must have hurt to see the state of his New York
enterprise about which he had boasted at the turn of the century,
"Nothing can hurt the *Herald.*" It is said that during the visit he
even proposed to Adolph Ochs a merger of the *Times* and the
Herald, and that Ochs turned him down. But he returned to France,
his wife, and the Paris Edition, pausing only to send Burke back to
see if he could do anything to revive the flagging New York paper.

The election of 1916 was a cliffhanger. Wilson won on the slogan
"He kept us out of war." Knowing that the longer the war lasted
the more danger there was that the United States would be drawn
in, the President attempted a mediating role in late December 1916,
asking all the belligerents to declare their war aims, which, he went
on, had never really been stated.

Bennett exploded again. To rank the aggressors and defenders
in the same way when their aims were well known was unconscion-
able. The *Herald* ran a daily editorial: "Germany's Defeat Essential," "Playing with Fire," "An Untimely Note," "War Aims Well
Defined." Their tenor was simple: Wilson was now playing
Germany's game; Germany would welcome peace now since her
plans had been thwarted and the war not won. "She is moving

heaven and earth to induce some neutral busybody to save her from the punishment which she has merited and will receive." Letters poured in from the Committee of 500, formed to attack the President's proposal. On Christmas Eve Dr. Watson preached a peace sermon at the American Cathedral Church which set matters right. "Wrongs must be righted before true, just and Righteous Peace can be established." And, with little consideration of what its earlier stand had been, the *Herald* went on to attack Wilson for not having helped to prevent the present war by telling Germany that the United States would fight if Belgium were attacked. The President had tolerated the crucifixion of this people unprotestingly.

On January 24 Wilson was attacked again for his "Peace Without Victory" speech to the Senate. His view was incompatible with reality, and utopian in tone. Allied reaction was correct: there could only be peace *with* victory. One week later Germany resumed unrestricted submarine warfare. Bennett champed at the bit: "It Is Up to You, Mr. Wilson," a head proclaimed, while on the back page Veber declared in French that "Mr. Wilson must awaken from his pacifist dream." Three days later when news of the U.S. rupture of diplomatic relations came over the wire, the *Herald* reported that its offices "seethed with excitement" while "Americans in Paris Rejoiced."

The rejoicing was premature. Both President and Congress were slow to act, hoping that war might still be avoided. In early March the English leaked the notorious telegram from German Foreign Secretary Zimmermann offering Mexico the return of Arizona, Texas, and New Mexico if Mexico would enter the war on the German side in the event of American entry on the Allied side. Even this calculated leak failed to rush the administration. Mid-March brought startling events, although censorship limited news sources and wishful thinking served to confuse them. Coincident with reports of internal collapse in Germany came the utterly unforseen news presented in a banner headline on March 17: "The Tsar Of Russia Abdicates." Citing a statement of Bonar Law to the English Parliament, the *Herald* interpreted the event as a revolt by the Duma, the army, and the people against pro-German influence around Nicholas and his court. Bennett's editorial called it "A Good Augury for the Allies," and three days later, in the face of these events, cried, "Dare To Act, Mr. Wilson! Do It Now!" On March 24 in utter exasperation the paper asked, "What is the matter with Mr. Wilson? Is he in a hypnotic trance of self-admiration?" There was silence for a few days, broken only by a white, completely censored, editorial. But finally, on Wednesday, April 4 (a bit prematurely, since it took two days for the Senate and House to debate and vote and the President to sign the proclamation), the *Herald* could display the banner that Bennett had so longed to use: "America Is At War With Germany." The whole front page was given over to Wilson's war message and to reports of a national "transport of joy."

The next few days saw war news largely displaced by news from America. Opponents of the war were castigated by the *Herald,* although it expressed sympathy for the lone woman in the House who had voted against the declaration—Jeannette Rankin (who would do so again twenty-four years later, tears streaming down her cheeks, when another President would ask again for a Declaration of War). Two months later Bennett could exult across six columns again: "Paris Wildly Welcomes General Pershing And First American Fighting Unit In Historic Demonstration." Pictures showed the general disembarking at Boulogne and being cheered by immense crowds in the place de la Concorde as he waved from the balcony of the Hotel Crillon. The iron-jawed, ramrod-straight general and his 100 men symbolized the outpouring of American manpower and might that would, at this crucial moment, turn the tide and crush the hated Boche after those three long years of grinding trench warfare. To Bennett it must have seemed almost a personal triumph. But the headline itself was slightly misleading, representing something in the way of wishful thinking; Pershing's 100-man advance party was hardly a "first fighting unit."

Moreover, American fighting men were slower in coming and

getting into action than the impatient Bennett and the Allies had hoped; Pershing recorded in his diary on July 28, "Had luncheon with James Gordon Bennett and found him more aggressive than ever." The publisher was unhappy with the general's decision not to allow small American units to be integrated with those of the other Allies pending the arrival of a sufficient number of American soldiers to constitute an independent army.

The Paris that Pershing came to had changed in many ways since those days of the Battle of the Marne when the whole city appeared to be closed down. The French had sustained unbelievable losses in the trenches; the wounded were omnipresent, and every family seemed to be in mourning for someone. But life went on, and a society and economy that was geared up to support a war effort in a way unimaginable in the past was also able to sustain a semblance of normality. Social life revolved around officers on leave, but it was frequently gay. Resorts had reopened, even if they served mainly as rest areas for men back from the front. Shops had re-opened, too, although in 1917 meat rationing was instituted for the first time. And while transportation was mobilized in service of the war effort, it also served the civilian life necessary to contin-ued conduct of the war.

All of this was reflected in the columns of the *Herald,* particularly after July 1917, when the real American influx began. Advertising, which had disappeared in August 1914, reappeared in sufficient quantity so that in June 1917 the *Herald* complained it simply didn't have enough space for it all and would have to institute a waiting list for some types, since paper restrictions kept the paper from being enlarged. In fact, earlier in the year, it had been forced to reduce itself to a single sheet on Mondays (though it joked that the size of the *Journal Officiel* of parliamentary debates made it hard to see how a paper shortage could really exist).

Advertising revenue more than doubled between 1915 and 1917. Theaters, Swiss resorts, banks, and bookstores all increased their ads. Today's up-to-date drinkers would certainly have noticed an eye-catching ad prompted by the American army's arrival:

Standard Bearers of America!
You have come to the home of Perrier
The champagne of Table Waters
Drink it Today!

The *Herald* had taken once more to printing the weather at resorts, although the list was a sadly restricted one. Arrivals at hotels and on the Riviera were now to be found alongside Red Cross and YMCA news. Society notes alternated with the long lists of the wounded.

The American entry into the war, however, changed the nature of the paper once more. Ever enterprising, the Commodore created a weekly Sunday summary of news events, soon to be issued as a single page sold separately for ten centimes, with YMCA news on the back. On regular days sports news and YMCA and Red Cross activities began to take up more and more space; on occasion the whole back page would be devoted to features and news for American troops. The paper printed columns of letters from soldiers asking the whereabouts of friends in France. The *Herald* had found a whole new audience, one that expanded at a fantastic rate. Bennett was not about to fail to adapt to it. At the start of the century there may have been Gordon Bennett cups for aeronauts; in 1917 there were *Herald* cups for army and navy and YMCA baseball teams. The *Herald* had run contests for stories from readers twenty years earlier; it now ran literary contests for authors and poets of the American Expeditionary Force. But it worried, too, about these raw American recruits. "Americans!" one head ran, "Steel Your Hearts Against the Enemy and Realize His Iniquity. . . . Uncle Sam's fighters seem almost too good natured for the work before them."

If the *Herald* responded to a whole new audience, so did other newspapers. Far-off, in the Midwest of the United States—the heartland of America, as many would have it—another brilliant newspaper publisher who would later develop almost as curious a reputation as James Gordon Bennett, Colonel Robert R. Mc-Cormick of the *Chicago Tribune,* began to worry that American troops were going to get their news and information from a newspaper that not only was an Eastern, New York one, but perhaps even worse, had been based in and subject to the corruption of Europe for years. The carefully timed result was the appearance of the European Edition of the *Chicago Tribune* on July 4, 1917.

It was the first real challenge to the European Edition on its home ground in a long time. But the ground, after all, had shifted, and McCormick, at least, must have felt he could make a go of it. The new paper nevertheless had a hard time in its first months, losing money consistently despite the influx of troops. In March of 1918, according to Jaurett, *Tribune* employees were told it was going to fold, but the decision was then reversed. McCormick, he said, was vexed that after creating a newspaper for the soldiers, an official paper with the same goals had then come into being—the weekly *Stars and Stripes,* launched in February 1918. As it turned out, there was room for both the *Herald* and the *Tribune,* both of which expanded so much in 1918 that the *Herald,* with a circulation that reached an utterly unprecedented 350,000, had to be printed in five different plants scattered around Paris, with all the attendant problems of distribution.

The landing of the Yanks and the heavily censored news of troubles in the French ranks led the *Herald* to make known and spell out what the enhanced Allies' war aims must be. Pacifists and philosophers should stop babbling; discussions of postwar organizations could wait; the first order of business was "On to Berlin! . . . crush Prussia . . . thoroughly humiliate her, force her to disgorge her plunder and pay the penalty of her crimes, and leave her not even the shadow of a possibility of again becoming a danger to the peace of the world." This was what three years of war had done to Bennett—but also to those around him, who continued to take this point of view after his death. Too, it colored the attitude of the paper toward another series of events: the Russian Revolution.

The toppling of the Czar had elicited nothing but cheers at first; it would lead to a strengthening of the eastern front just as America's entry would lead to a strengthening of the western front. The knockout blow to the enemy could hardly be far behind. In June and July of 1917 the news was still good, although German armies seemed to have taken the initiative here or there. The New York newspaper had sent special correspondent Herman Bernstein to Russia. Bernstein's dispatches radiated the same confidence manifested by Elihu Root's official U.S. mission to the Russian government. The coalition government was increasing its authority, the Russians applauded Wilson's ideals, the cause of freedom was practically won, and the Belgian Socialist Emile Vandervelde, interviewed by Bernstein, called Kerensky, the Minister of War, "the idol of the masses and the nightmare of the Leninists."

For there was one fly in the ointment, and the *Herald* was quick to point him out: Lenin, the man whom the Germans had transported from Switzerland to Russia. The Germans would not have made the move if they were not going to benefit from it. Lenin, therefore, must be head of a pro-German faction. Bernstein went further, however: on July 23 he revealed that Lenin was a German agent-provocateur, acting on behalf of a vast German plot to take Russia out of the war. Lenin and his colleagues were not merely playing the German game, they were actually German agents. It was this that explained why Kerensky had had to seize the reins of government from Prince Lvov on July 22, following pro-German riots and disturbances in Petrograd. Frontline military reverses in late July were therefore easily explained—"Traitors Bring Fresh Reverses to Russians."

News from Russia was crowded off the front page for the next three months, but in late October, taking note of an improvement of the situation in Russia that meant "traitors such as Lenin, visionaries such as Gorky, and narrow-minded doctrinaires such as Trotsky" were excluded from government, the *Herald* then recorded its horror at the statement of peace aims brought from Russia to the inter-Allied conference in Paris. Skobolev, the Russian delegate, called for a plebiscite in Alsace-Lorraine, an *international* indemnity to Belgium, neutralization of the Panama and Suez canals, no economic blockade of Germany, and a plebiscite in the

"Italian" areas held by Austria. Pierre Veber attacked the statement violently on the back page, while the page 2 editorial called it a proposal for a German peace, a move to back down before the Germans just when the Russians should have indicated a continued resolution to fight, so that Germany could not continue to mount its massive attack against the Italians or to strengthen the western front.

The month of November brought one fresh blow after another: "Petrograd in Throes of Fresh Crisis" the *Herald* reported on November 8. On November 9 a four-column head read: "Kerensky Deposed by Maximalists; Soviet Acclaims Traitor Lenin; How Trotsky Prepared Coup." On November 11 and 12 it reported that Kerensky had marched upon Petrograd with 200,000 loyal troops and routed the Leninites. A week later wishful thinking disappeared as the paper confirmed that the Leninites held power in Moscow and in the capital; two days later, that they had called for an armistice on all fronts; and in another two days, that Trotsky had decided to publish the texts of Russia's secret treaties as a "hostile demonstration toward the Allies."

The paramount consideration was what the events would mean for the Allied war effort. Now that Lenin was ready to take Russia out of the war, it was even more obvious than before that he was a German agent. In December the *Herald* published dispatches that took a different tack—one analysis to the effect that whatever the Russian government, the Russian people now desperately craved peace, and another to the effect that Trotsky and Lenin were genuine Russians and not German agents. But an editorial headed "Back to Chaos" declared that Bolshevism in Russia was "perfectly clear. Partly it is the product of secret German funds. Lenin and Trotsky, the paid agents of Prussianism, have earned their pay by disarming Russia." For the rest, Bolshevism was "socialism carried to an extreme limit," while Trotsky was described as "a primeval savage, seizing what he wanted and holding what he could." On May 4, at the time of the signing of the peace of Brest Litovsk between Germany and Russia, Trotsky was depicted in a cartoon receiving thirty pieces of silver from the Kaiser as he handed over captive Russia on a stake, gazing longingly at a dove. In the meantime, reports of the Czar's death received scant notice. History had passed him by, just as it had passed by Francis-Joseph, whose death in 1916 hardly seemed to matter. The dynasties were falling, but other matters preoccupied the *Herald*.

The peace of Brest Litovsk enabled the Germans to move forty divisions from the Eastern front to the western front. Blockaded from the sea, worn out economically, the Central Powers' last chance lay in knocking out the Allies before the full weight of American manpower could reach Europe and be thrown into the fight. In March 80,000 American troops reached Europe and in April, over 100,000. They were still in need of training and could not be put into the front lines, where in March a tremendous German assault began against the British sectors, designed to split the British and French forces and drive the British back against the channel ports. The German offensives would be checked and renewed; in May they came within forty miles of Paris, which the Germans had been shelling with an extraordinary long-range gun known as Big Bertha, from some seventy-five miles away. In late July the Germans launched their final offensive. It was rapidly checked by the Allied forces which were now, finally, under the control of a single Allied commander-in-chief, Foch. The joint Allied counteroffensive, drawing heavily for the first time on the million Americans in France, would end only in the final defeat of Germany and the armistice of November 11.

James Gordon Bennett was not alive to see it. On May 15 a black-bordered issue of the *Herald* announced his death at Villa Namouna, in Beaulieu-sur-Mer, with a banner headline. It was the first time his name had appeared in the paper.

He had been ill the previous November, and never fully regained his strength. Mrs. Bennett took him to spend the winter in Beaulieu, where he kept his usual constant contact with the paper. The Bennetts had lived quietly since their marriage—a returning *Herald* reporter told James L. Ford, who recorded it in *Forty Odd Years in the Literary Shop,* that "the old, drunken, money-spending Jim Bennett is dead. In his place has come a Scotch miser." It was perhaps an exaggeration. The two entertained quietly but frequently at home, both in Paris and Beaulieu. (Visitors left a record of only one quarrel. Bennett refused absolutely to publish pro-German dispatches in New York when the Germans intimated that they would liberate Mrs. Bennett's interned son if he did. The young man was later released in an exchange of civilian internees and recuperated with the Bennetts on the Riviera.)

This time, though, the couple did no entertaining. Mitchell saw to it that word of Bennett's illness didn't get out to even the local papers, so that few suspected anything was wrong. In December, as he sat in a wheelchair, a deputation presented him with a copy of a motion of recognition for his services to France voted by the Departmental Assembly and General Council. An attack of bronchopneumonia late in the winter weakened his robust constitution; though fatally stricken on May 10, his seventy-seventh birthday, he remained mentally alert, writing in his own hand to C. Inman Barnard, his former private secretary, two days before his death, ". . . I hope we may both live long and prosper, as old Rip Van Winkle used to say, and that our galvanized constitutions will pull us through to a far future. Ever yours, B." It was not to be. Early in the morning of the fifteenth, he died, with only Mrs. Bennett present.

There was a memorial service in Beaulieu, for which it seemed that the whole town turned out. Then a special car attached to the Nice-Paris express bore his body to Paris, where he was buried in the Cemetery of Passy, near the Trocadero, after brief services in the Trinity Church. His tomb was built according to instructions: a gray granite mausoleum, with a single owl carved in stone over the entrance, under a Maltese cross. There is no name on the tomb. But in the rear wall a small stained-glass window provides some further measure of identification: unlike those with Virgin and child in other nearby tombs, it pictures a yacht.

Tributes poured in to the *Herald* in Paris; memorial services in

New York and remembrances in newspapers and magazines gave evidence of the influence, fame, reputation, and notoriety he had gathered. In France the tributes were enormously affectionate. All else might be forgotten: this was the man who had stood by France in her darkest hour, thrown his influence and what was left of his fortune into keeping alive French hopes for American support and aid, used his New York papers to champion the Allied cause despite pro-German boycotts.

But all else would *not* be forgotten: his paper had influenced French journalism, encouraged the arts, promoted scientific development, and warned against the Kaiser's ambitions, and Bennett, modestly, had refused all honors and decorations across the years. There were no others like him. French astronomer Camille Flammarion, recalling his years of service to Bennett, whose name he could now mention in the paper, wrote that he had agreed to do his regular column for the *Herald* when he discovered Bennett was extraordinarily well read in astronomy and had even read Flammarion's own book, *Lumière,* some twenty years earlier. He had dedicated another book, *Stella,* to the Commodore, to whom he now paid homage, calling him "a man of extraordinary imagination, intellect, physical capacity, and a free and independent spirit." And the indefatigable Pierre Veber, after a long recital in *Figaro* of the great things Bennett had done, and an attack upon the French authorities' lack of reciprocity in refusing him his one modest wartime request, that he be allowed to wire his bureau in English, went on to say, "During the torment of 1914 one American's friendship was effective—our children should not forget it." A few months later, at the time of the armistice, when a victory parade led by the mayor of Beaulieu passed by the Villa Namouna, the mayor stopped, turned to the crowd, and called out, "Vive la France, vive l'Amérique, vive Gordon Bennett!"

In the United States there were the expected fulsome tributes. *Editor and Publisher* called him a "towering figure in journalism" and published eulogies and tributes from all over "to the man, his magnificent courage, his initiative . . . his public service, uncompromising patriotism, his capacity for doing big things in a big way." There were, of course, the more measured—even sour—notes; James B. Townsend, one of his former employees, called him "too much the faddist to be a great newspaperman . . . too changeable, mercurial, actuated by suspicion."

It was not yet the end of the Bennett era. This would come only two years later, when the paper changed hands and a new director came on the scene. Under Bennett's will the papers were to be run by trustees, and in Paris Bennett's trusted Percy Mitchell would continue to exercise overall control. In the week following his death the front page continued to print tributes to Bennett, from Georges Clemenceau, now Prime Minister and War Minister, from President Poincaré, General Pershing, Ambassador Sharp, Bennett's old bête noire Theodore Roosevelt, the American Club and the Chamber of Commerce in Paris—the list was almost endless. And a five-column headline announced his burial in the Passy Cemetery on May 24. All of this for a man who had never allowed his name to appear in the paper during his lifetime. And the day after Bennett's burial the censors forbade the printing of weather reports for the first time. There was a reason: German air raids had increased in intensity as the renewed German offensives approached Paris. Bennett, one feels, would have accepted the explanation, but certainly regretfully. To outward appearances, nevertheless, the paper looked the same while Mitchell guided it through the period of transition. He even kept the Old Philadelphia Lady for seven months, until December.

The paper continued to be full of news of the German offensives; large blank spots announced the continued assiduous attentions of the censors. On July 4, with Wilson's announcement that over a million fresh American troops had reached France, Paris helped the Americans to a tremendous celebration. On July 5 the city inaugurated the avenue du President Wilson in the sixteenth arrondissement. Two weeks later the Allies would finally go on the offensive. In the meantime the *Herald* was involved in battles the

Commodore would have fought with zest. Hachette, their French distributor, dissatisfied with its share of a *Herald* price increase, had decided to boycott the *Herald.* The *Petit Parisien* came to its rescue, sharing its own distribution service. But Hachette had a state-granted monopoly of railway station kiosks and refused to allow the *Herald* to be sold in them. The issue became one of freedom of the press, necessitating parliamentary intervention. Parliament also intervened on another occasion when three deputies objected to Veber's characterizations in his column. They accused the *Herald* of participation in a campaign of defamation and requested that Veber be banned from the Chamber. In both cases the French press raised a hue and cry in support of the *Herald,* and the issue was dropped.

And in mid-1918 Bennett's old foe, the censors, decided that advertisements other than classifieds might possibly be used for the transfer of coded messages. They therefore forbade shipment of newspapers to both neutral and Allied countries unless all the advertisements were obliterated. Mitchell then found out that several weeks' worth of papers destined for England and the United States had been held up, and that while the *Herald* was being implored to save on paper and transport, it was being allowed to print and ship papers that were then stopped and stored—and was being notified that they would now be sold as newsprint to defray storage costs! Monsieur le Bureaucrat, wrote the *Herald,* was now saying "L'Etat C'Est Moi!" How Bennett would have raged!

Of primary interest, however, is the attitude the paper took to the confusion of events the headlines recorded as the war drew to a close: revolts in Germany, the abdication of the Kaiser and of the Emperor Karl of Austria-Hungary, proposals from all sides as to what armistice and peace terms should be, Vienna's demands for an immediate separate peace, announcement of Turkey's capitulation, and discussions of whether and how long the economic blockades of the exhausted and hungry Central Powers should continue. In all these matters the *Herald*'s editorials continued to take the uncompromising line Bennett had earlier adopted. The full flavor of what four long years of war had produced can only come from the language the *Herald* itself used.

It refused to be hoodwinked by German "democrats or revolutionists . . . who at heart are all pan-Germanists." Military victory, it declared, must result in the complete crushing of Germany. Under the heading "The Debt Shall Be Paid" it spelled the point out further:

> Germany, to escape the punishment of her crimes, is pretending to reform her governmental system. . . . The system is the product of the nation; it faithfully reflects the nature of the most abject savages that ever disgraced the human race, arrogant and merciless in victory, grovelling and treacherous in defeat. . . .
>
> Those who try to distinguish between the people and their masters fill one with contempt for the naiveté . . . or duplicity of those making the efforts. . . .
>
> . . . The people's share in this most ghastly enterprise of brigandage in the history of the world is enormous and the penalty must be paid by the people. . . .
>
> Nothing was said [in criticism] so long as the fortune of war seemed to be favoring the criminal nation; no one, from prince to peasant, condemned the nameless horrors committed in France and Belgium, the ruining of entire provinces, the razing of towns, the driving forth of hapless citizens, the torture and maltreatment of women and girls, the deliberate destruction of hospitals and murder of wounded, the creating of awful deserts where once were fertile fields and orchards.
>
> For all this hideous work of bestial ferocity the German nation has a direct and crushing responsibility, and whether the new Germany be imperial or democratic, the crimes will have to be atoned for and a full reparation made by the people.

On November 10, on a single sheet, the paper announced "Abdication of the Kaiser: Revolution in Germany," and went on to call the fallen ruler "an object of horror and disgust . . ." "For two centuries," it declared, "the Hohenzollerns have outraged every principle of Right." The next day the *Herald* could proclaim, "The

War Is Won!" For a day joy rather than hate pervaded the pages of the paper as it described how, at the sound of the thousands of bells and cannon, "people listened to the wonderful music a few seconds in ecstasy" and then poured madly into the streets to join their countrymen in singing the "Marseillaise," dancing, decorating everything with bunting, kissing and hugging Allied soldiers.

The celebration lasted. The *Herald* recorded the joy in Metz and Strasbourg as Allied armies entered with Marshal Pétain at their head. Simultaneously in Paris the statue of Strasbourg in the place de la Concorde was shorn of the veil it had worn since the Germans had annexed Alsace in 1870. But the peace could not wait, and the *Herald* resumed its campaign. German efforts to soften the impact demonstrated the hollowness of the political revolution: "The one object of the enemy now is to obtain peace without paying for it."

President Wilson's problems with the peace were foreshadowed in reports from the United States of the midterm elections, which would guarantee him opposition, and of the attacks upon him and the idea of the League of Nations in the Congress upon the eve of his departure. The *Herald*'s attitude toward Germany further foreshadowed what the President would find in France. Nevertheless, the President's arrival called forth one banner headline and page of photographs after another: "Paris Meets the President and Takes Him to Her Heart," "Two Million Londoners Give Wilson Reception of His Life." And on December 25, as the paper reported that Wilson celebrated Christmas with American troops, its Christmas editorial could give a resounding "Merry Christmas—a greeting exchanged for the first time in four years with a joyous heart," and it went on to say, "If the many portents and signs are not misleading, mankind may strike out into the future without misgivings."

In the meantime, the censors had allowed the resumption of weather reports, the Old Philadelphia Lady disappeared in December, on Friday the thirteenth, and Cunard was able to publish the first announcement of a sailing date since the censors had forbidden them early in the war. There were over two million American soldiers in Europe, the French opened up French colleges to doughboys awaiting redeployment, and the circulation of the *Herald* rose in the next month to 350,000.

How slow the change from wartime conditions to peace must have seemed! Some restrictions could immediately be lifted; others persisted. The *Stars and Stripes,* having reached a peak circulation of over 500,000 copies in February, was phased out in mid-June. (The *Herald,* reporting on this, mentioned the name of one of the *Stars and Stripes'* three managing editors, a private named Harold Ross—later the fabled editor of *The New Yorker* magazine.) The *Herald* itself kept to its wartime format: world and U.S. news on the front page, a brief column of "Personal Intelligence" on page 2, where letters and editorials were featured, a half page still devoted to troops and army activities, a half page in French, and the last page, sports and finance, shared with advertisements. Among the ads were an increasing number for resorts and hotels in France and Switzerland. Articles extolled French spas as far superior to the popular old prewar Boche spas. The State Department chilled expectations by announcing that no American tourists could come to France until 1920, though it would sanction limited business travel. But the opening of the Pershing Stadium for inter-Allied games during the peace negotiations enlivened the atmosphere a little.

In the meantime, as best it could, the *Herald* chronicled the making of the peace. When the text of the Versailles Treaty was published, the *Herald* found that the treaty had "glaring defects." Among these was the fact that "the peace terms are severe, but not too severe, indeed not severe enough." Pierre Veber was even more emphatic: the treaty was extremely disadvantageous for France, crushed first under the burden of war and now of peace. Nevertheless, the *Herald,* with the headline "World Peace Pact Signed," recommended ratification. (Later, in different conditions and with a different editor, it would reverse its stand, condemning the harshness of the Versailles peace and approving the idea of revision.) When the ratification battle began in the Senate it defended the

Senators' right to take plenty of time and to make the revisions they thought necessary. But when the Senate rejected the treaty on November 19, 1919, the *Herald* was not around to comment. A wave of strikes swept over France, and this time the *Herald* was not immune. It failed to appear for three weeks.*

The cosmopolitan world served by the *Herald,* and to which it may be said to have even given a consciousness of itself, collapsed in a single week in 1914. That world had grown out of changes that took place before the turn of the century, grafted onto an older society. After August 1914 the technology remained, but the society disappeared. The *Herald* survived because it became a different newspaper. Bennett used it first to serve the thousands of Americans stranded in Europe by the outbreak of the war. Then, when other Americans stayed on to help France in an hour of need, Bennett and the *Herald* changed again. The Commodore had lived in France for thirty-seven years when the war broke out; the devastation of the north and the decimation of a generation of Frenchmen told upon him as it did upon the French. The paper came to serve not only the Americans who served the Allied cause, but the Allied cause itself, and Bennett made it his business after 1915 to help bring American military support to that cause—something he did not do at the outset. The coming of the American army and all the services that revolved around it worked another change in the paper. It grew enormously as it provided the army with a link to home and information on what was going on both in the theater of war and off duty. The question, of course, became: what happens when the doughboys go home, and that old cosmopolitan world is merely a heap of ashes—and there is no James Gordon Bennett to chart a new course?

In the meantime those left in charge after Bennett's death con-ducted a campaign completely in line with that taken by Clemen-

---

*A fact which shatters another myth promulgated by Eric Hawkins, who wrote that the paper never missed an issue before World War II.

ceau. If England had suffered ten times the casualties the Americans had, France had suffered almost twenty times as many, and the north of France had been devastated into the bargain. The fault was Germany's to begin with, and the consequences were Germany's to pay. What had to be done to establish peace was clear. What would happen to the *Herald* was perhaps less so.

PART II
THE INTERWAR YEARS

CHAPTER 6
Back to Normalcy

ON FRIDAY, January 9, 1920, a headline in the *Herald* announced, "American Army Fades Away as Dream in Sunny France." A day later it reported the final departure of the 330 officers and men of General Connor's staff from the Gare du Nord at ten-thirty in the evening. A few French officers, a handful of Frenchwomen, and one *Herald* reporter were there to say good-bye. Official farewells had already been said at the embassy and government offices. It was, the reporter wrote, a melancholy ending to an enterprise that had brought to Europe some 2 million men— and an enormous public for the *Herald*.

One week later a front-page box announced the purchase of Bennett's properties by Frank Munsey from the executors of the Bennett estate. Ten days after that another box announced the merger of Munsey's New York *Sun* and the *New York Herald*. And Laurence Hills, Munsey's reporter at the Paris Peace Conference, was named director of the Paris Edition, a post he would maintain until May 1940 when the Germans, this time, marched into Paris.

Behind all this lay some fairly complicated maneuvering and the parlous condition of Bennett's New York newspapers. Bennett's will had left it up to the trustees to decide what to do with the newspapers. It provided for substantial annuities totaling $142,000 a year for several of his longtime associates, and for one favorite

project: a retirement home for deserving and indigent newspapermen, to be established in memory of his father.*

The problem the trustees faced was that there was not enough
money to carry out Bennett's will. The home was incorporated,
but by the time the annuities and taxes were paid there was no
money for it, and yet requests from old employees kept coming in
for help. Either the trustees would wait until deaths liberated the
money to be paid out in annuities—which might be a long time—
or they would sell the papers. In the meantime they discovered the
million dollars Bennett had stowed in the bank in Paris during the
palmy days of the American Expeditionary Force, and they tried
to get their hands on it for use in New York; Jaurett and Mitchell
were able to block them in court.

Frank Munsey then entered the picture. He was a sort of Yankee
trader from Maine, who had made a fortune from a chain of
groceries and then of magazines, and had then launched on a
peculiar career of buying, selling, combining, and killing off newspapers, making more money on each occasion, and earning a reputation as a sort of cannibal of the newspaper business. He offered
$4 million for the three Bennett properties, and the trustees ac-
cepted. He merged the *New York Herald* with his own morning
Sun and later combined the *Evening Telegram* with another purchase, the *Evening Mail.*†

Munsey's purchase provided the money to maintain the Bennett
home. But in Paris it created havoc. What would Munsey do with

*There had long been a rumor that Bennett was going to leave the papers to his employees.
The rumor was traced back to a *Figaro* interview of a decade earlier, featuring a fairly
liberal interpretation of what the Commodore had said. One biographer called it a last sour
joke on his employees. It's a dubious interpretation.
†Four years later he would sell the two *Heralds* to the Reids, publishers of the *Tribune,*
thereby creating the *New York Herald Tribune,* and to the Scripps-Howard chain the
Evening Telegram along with his *Evening Sun,* previously merged with another purchase,
the *New York Globe and Commercial Advertiser.* The Scripps-Howard people combined
the *Sun* and *Telegram* with yet another paper, the *World,* to create the *World-Telegram
and Sun.* The story finished only in 1966, when the *World Telegram and Sun* merged with
the Hearst *Journal-American* and the Whitney-owned *Herald Tribune,* to create the *World-
Journal-Tribune*—which died only a few months later.

a property whose circulation had sunk from 350,000 in 1919 to perhaps 10,000 one year later, once he had gotten his hands on the million dollars it had previously earned? Everyone knew that he was a great admirer of Bennett, and that the purchase of the *New York Herald* was something of the culmination of an ambition. But everyone also expected him to kill off the Paris Edition. He had been heard to say that the paper never could do anything but lose money, and probably was not worth it.

What he did, however, was to install his own man, Laurence Hills, as director, instruct him to keep expenses down, and then leave him and the paper pretty much to their own devices. Munsey took an annual trip to Europe, but—in complete contrast to James Gordon Bennett—there is no record of his ever interfering in the paper's affairs.

This meant that three men were primarily responsible for making a go of things during the four years of Munsey's absentee ownership and in a period of straitened postwar circumstances. One was Alfred Jaurett, Bennett's old advertising and business manager, a man completely conversant with the Paris newspaper and business world, who looked like an old boulevardier. He knew that most of the potential advertisers were not the kind of people who actually read the paper, so he made it a point to meet and know anyone for whom it might be a useful medium. In those days the *Herald* staff prepared most of the advertisements themselves, and Jaurett, spurred on by a percentage agreement he had negotiated earlier with Bennett, personally secured the advertising of luxury shops that would never use the French newspapers, both by suggesting the format and by emphasizing the kind of readership the *Herald* had. He foresaw the increased flow of Americans in the mid-twenties and managed to snare 75 percent of the English language advertising done in Paris; the *Chicago Tribune,* the *Daily Mail,* and another short-lived twenties competitor, the *Paris Times,* never came close, and house ads in the *Herald* always cheerfully pointed it out. There were always critics ready to emphasize that the *Herald* of those years attracted heavy resort advertising through its special pages of puffery. But whatever else one may say about them, they helped make the newspaper pay—and a newspaper has to live.

On the managerial and editorial side Laurence Hills, Munsey's man, and Gaston Archambault, a Bennett holdover returned from four years of military service, battled out the shape of the paper. Hills wanted to Americanize the *Herald:* the personnel, the spelling, and the makeup and typography. Archambault, a handsome, pipe-smoking, English-speaking Frenchman with a handlebar mustache, not only resisted the changes fiercely, but also had the personality to do it. He was invaluable—he knew how to perform the one essential job on the newspaper, that of taking the skeletonized dispatches that came over the wires from New York and London and padding them out to full-length stories. But he was an authoritarian who bullied those around him.

What probably made it possible for Archambault and Hills to work together was that in those four years Munsey kept Hills busy as chief Paris correspondent for both the *New York Sun* and the *Herald,* as well as director of the Paris paper. Hills' experience was as a reporter and Washington bureau chief for the *Sun.* As chief correspondent in charge of reporting on the peace conference for the *Sun* he covered Woodrow Wilson's trips to England, Italy, and Belgium. Once Munsey bought the *Herald* and named him director, in his capacity as correspondent he nevertheless went off to Geneva to report on the opening and the first four Assemblies of the League of Nations, and traveled to Italy to interview Mussolini after his Fascists seized power in 1922, with the result that Archambault was left to mind the shop a good part of the time.

Nevertheless, after a few years the dissatisfied Archambault persuaded an American named Courtlandt Bishop, of Lenox, Massachusetts, to finance a new afternoon newspaper in 1924 called the *Paris Times,* of which Archambault became editor. The *Times* was put out by a minuscule staff and, though readable, never achieved a wide circulation. Bishop used it as a tax break; when the Depression hit he didn't need one anymore and it folded. But Hills seems to have resented its existence and had an undue fear that Archambault would beat him out on some news story. Much later, when Archambault was writing interpretive stories for the *New York Times* from the front in World War II, Hills was to write of him, "I had many rows with him when he was under my command. But he was unusually interesting and well-prepared."

In 1924, when Ogden and Helen Rogers Reid purchased the *Herald* from Munsey, they gave Hills the title of editor and general manager. He presided over both the expansion of the paper in the last half of the twenties and its sad contraction in the thirties. The consensus among newsmen of those years was that he was temperamentally unsuited for the job—irascible and unstable. Yet his own letters to the Reids frequently praised the enterprise and courage of *Herald Tribune* correspondents and the Paris *Herald* staff.

Certainly the *Herald,* in those immediate postwar years, was a rather sorry paper. In 1920 its four pages appeared on cheaper, more acid newsprint; Munsey's injunction to Hills about expenses was obviously being followed, but one may imagine what the Commodore's reaction would have been. The Bennett era had really come to an end. Much of the sports reporting disappeared when the American army did, and the full French page with Pierre Veber's editorial contribution reappeared. The front page chronicled the postwar difficulties: the flu epidemic, the great wave of strikes, the difficulties of postwar settlements in the Middle East, the Mediterranean, and the Balkans, the continued bickering over possible Senate ratification of a modified Versailles Treaty—even as the other Allies began to put the treaty terms into effect. It recorded the developing sourness between the former Allies. In 1920, following Munsey's lead, it stood foursquare for Harding. His triumphant inauguration in March 1921 had to share the front page with the expiration of the Allied ultimatum to Germany on reparations and the Allies' subsequent advance into the Rhineland. But the *Herald* had the time and the space to comment on the profundity of the new American President's thought.

In 1919 hotels and resorts returned to advertise in slender numbers and restricted space. "Chamonix," the *Herald* reported, "Presents Many and Varied Attractions," as winter sports resumed; tourists in large numbers were also seeking sunshine at Biarritz. Wagner's music was applauded with demonstrations at the Salle Gaveau, although the same issue that recorded this also printed a letter deploring the pro-Boche trend in both music and politics. The *Herald* continued to mock modernist movements, and its "Personal Intelligence" columns remained short. The great Central European hinterland was no more. Still, even without it, the paper was able to boast in a house ad, "The *New York Herald* Has a Larger Sale in Europe Than Any Other American Newspaper."

What the paper also began to testify to was that the Great War had left behind a more permanent if less affluent American community. The American Chamber of Commerce advertised the creation of its center for American businessmen; a reception was held for YMCA women remaining in France to help in reconstruction; American ex-servicemen staying on in France formed American Legion Post No. 1 amid great enthusiasm. By mid-1920 the column "News of Americans Day by Day" began to increase inexorably; the French page shrank; Pierre Veber's chronicle of the proceedings of the Chamber of Deputies and his accompanying political analysis disappeared without a word, ending a long relationship. And on March 14, 1921, the "Sporting Gossip" column appeared on the back page with a new name appended to it—"Sparrow" Robertson. The column itself was not particularly noteworthy. It was the usual sort of thing: a paragraph on a potential Dempsey-Carpentier heavyweight fight, and another on a man who trained horses that ran at both Maisons Lafitte and St. Cloud. But it was a harbinger of things to come—of what the *Herald* would be in the twenties and thirties, and "Sparrow" will reappear in this account.

In the next three years, although the paper showed no great distinction and sadly lacked the personal eccentricity that marked it under Bennett, it slowly expanded in advertising lineage, in size, and in circulation. Hills' Americanization of the *Herald* began to take hold. The reputation Paris gained during World War I attracted a new flow of American tourists and expatriates. Prosperity came to America—but so did Prohibition. What better to do with new money than to find relief, in France, from thirst? And as Americans got thirstier, the *Herald*'s sales increased.

On July 17, 1923, the *Herald* headlined the inaugural voyage of the *Leviathan,* flagship of the United States Lines. She was the reconditioned *Vaterland,* whose maiden voyage in that fateful month of August 1914—nine years earlier—ended ignominiously in internment in New York Harbor. Now she would run into trouble in attracting passengers by trying to comply with Prohibition's prohibitions, while the French Line published the news that for each man, woman, and child traveling to the United States their ships would stock ten bottles of red and white wine, three of champagne, and half a liter of mixed liquors. This, it was calculated, would be enough to take them to and from the three-mile limit!

In fact, one of the chief editorial concerns of the *Herald* in the early 1920s was over the transatlantic friction created by the American attempts to enforce Prohibition upon liners that docked in the United States; the paper stood very strongly for some sort of reasonable compromise. And this—apart from expressions of distaste for communism—was one of the strongest editorial positions it took. It would agree that the United States had an interest in European affairs, but say little about how it should be expressed; in a bold editorial marking the anniversary of Adam Smith's birth (though placing it a century late) the paper advocated a reading of *The Wealth of Nations* for all who wanted wisdom in the field of political economy. Fascism in Italy it described as originally a movement of war veterans clubbed together to further their interests but now a recognized political movement directed against the spread of Bolshevism as a result of the "frankly revolutionary" policy of the Socialist government of Italy. When Mussolini's march on Rome brought him to power it called the Fascists "a national force bent on restoring Italy to her rightful place among the European powers"; the Fascist cause might be justified, if not the means. If Italy escaped upheaval it would be "because the Fascists realize the responsibility of power."

If the editorials had none of the old bite that they had when the Commodore dictated their content, it was also true that the Americans in Paris who were reading the paper were not the same people as those from before the war. Former servicemen returned to settle down to middle-class existence. Business and professional people mixed with writers, artists, students, movie stars, and sports figures, some on the Right Bank and some on the Left. Refurbished liners now offered tourist or cabin class instead of steerage, and the myth soon spread, assiduously promoted by the lines themselves, that it was more fun to go tourist than first class. But when Sinclair Lewis' Sam Dodsworth crossed on the fictitious *S.S. Ultima* he—like other American businessmen—went in the style to which his social superiors before the war were accustomed. The social superiors were still there. But with Central Europe no longer what it had been, they were fewer in number, had a smaller stage, and shared it with all the new elements. In 1924, when the *Herald*'s circulation reached 12,000 Jaurett looked at the shipping lists and forecast that in a few years it would reach 50,000.

Some of the old touches reappeared in the *Herald*. Noting that there were only 300 permanent American residents in Rome compared with the 3,000 there had been before the war, the *Herald* nevertheless reopened a bureau there with reading, reception, and restrooms, a name and movement registry, hometown newspapers, and information for transients. It was five minutes from the embassy and in the heart of the tourist quarter. Within a couple of years the *Herald* listed registries in Nice, London, Brussels, Vienna, Florence, and Genoa in addition to those in Paris, Berlin, and Rome. In March of 1922 the first fashion supplement appeared, comparable in layout and on as smooth, white stock as in prewar times. In 1923 occasional art supplements reappeared, with stories on present tendencies, new painters, and exhibits, but always with a strong admixture of what was at the *antiquaires*—usually in French—and what Old Masters were to be found. In one supplement it noted happily, "Younger American Artists in Paris Calmly Conservative: only rare exceptions show savage appetite for cubism or other radical schools. Fondness for classical composition, however, does not destroy inventive genius." The 1923 Auto Salon was also an occasion for several extra pages. Stories featured names like Peugeot and Fiat, but also, from America, Studebaker and Packard, and for real buffs, Hispano-Suiza, Panhard-Levasseur, and Delaunay-Belleville.

In a very real sense these art and autosupplements tell something important about the *Herald* of those years: its pages show little concern with either the modernist movements in art, literature, and music that began to flower in France before the war, or with the effect the war then had on artistic and literary sensibility. Cubism, Dada, the music of the Six or Stravinsky, Ezra Pound, e. e. cummings, even the springtime ballet season with its galas and costumes and decor by Braque, Chirico, Juan Gris, Marie Laurencin, Fernand Léger, Picasso, Rouault, and others, all receive short shrift. Harding and normalcy set the tone more than the impulses of despair, absurdity, or renewal and revolution. The *Herald* was resolutely Right Bank American.

Five years after the end of the war the *Herald,* though still not a moneymaker, had the look of a prosperous newspaper. It was normally six pages on weekdays, eight on Sundays, and would soon get even thicker. It also had the appearance of a typical American product. The front pages mixed news of world events, politics, scandal, and murder. The unexpected death of President Harding occasioned a black-bordered issue: "The Whole World Mourns President Harding," it said. "The French Press Calls Harding a Great Friend." Munsey happened to be on one of his periodic visits to Paris, and he supplied the editorial himself. He wrote that Harding "was not one of the greatest Presidents America has had, but in sincerity and honesty of purpose and faithfulness to the duties of his great office, he was one of the best. There has been none better." Later, and somewhat regretfully, the paper reported Coolidge's firmness on the war debts, an issue that perpetually clouded Franco-American relations. Approached by American bankers on cancellation as a step to reestablishment of normal exchange rates and consequent regaining of normal foreign markets, the new President had said he was "unalterably opposed to any cancellation."

The paper reported at the same time the rallying of 75,000 Klansmen in Dallas, Texas, and troubles in Germany, where separatism in the Rhineland and putschism in Munich vied for attention. In the "plus ça change" category it recorded the fall of the Belgian cabinet over the long-standing language dispute; a little later it reported that H. L. Doherty, the financial wizard of petroleum who had put together Cities Service Company, predicted the end of U.S. oil before 1936. It also recorded events in Russia: Trotsky's defeat and exile were the occasion for headlines. But so were monkey glands: the Thirty-Fifth French Surgical Conference refused to hear Dr. Serg Voronoff talk about the results of implanting them in men. And the Florida East Coast Railway's filling operations for its route to Key West occasioned a flurry of headlines about its possible diversion of the Gulf Stream and a resultant threat to the European climate.

The inside pages reveal even more of what had happened to the *Herald*'s world and to the *Herald* itself. Cosmopolitan Europe had fractured irrevocably, even though in those years recovery gave rise to some semblance of the return of old times. It was an illusion; the war meant that recovery would be on a nationalist basis that would only be strengthened by time. One of the earliest letters written by poet Ezra Pound, who would become an indefatigable letter writer to the *Herald* in years to come, railed against "the passport idiocy." In prewar times, after all, cosmopolitan Europe had required no passports or visas; they had been introduced as a wartime control measure. "What possible form of protest," he wrote, "could penetrate the mind of an American Senator or any other official?" The answer, of course, was that none would. The national state had begun to strengthen its peacetime hold on its citizens, and passports and visas were merely a manifestation of this. Others joined in the campaign—Representative Sol Bloom showed up in Paris to try to arrange for a reciprocal abolition of visas—but they would get nowhere.

Although the *Herald* soon began to carry columns of social events in Italy and Germany and advertisements for their revived resorts, the emphasis was never again the same. The *Herald* was clearly published in Paris, in France. It might be read by American residents elsewhere and by American tourists traveling throughout the Continent, but the concentration was on events and developments in Paris and France as it had never been before. News of "Americans Day by Day" accompanied notes on the Paris stage, where to dine, "Today's Calendar of Events," what to see in Paris, what the art galleries were showing, a directory for visitors, a long double-column listing of hotels, restaurants, and pensions, and—in place of the Old Philadelphia Lady—instructions on how to change from centigrade to Fahrenheit. The columns in French took much less room and would shrink further as Hills made the paper become more and more the organ for Americans in Paris.

In these years the "Mailbag" gave more of its space to tourist complaints than in the past—a reflection of the fact that a different, less experienced, class of people now traveled. There were still train times and, for the first time in 1924, an air schedule between Paris and London: travelers could leave the Crillon Hotel on the place de la Concorde at 9:15 A.M. and reach the Hotel Victoria in London at 1:30 in the afternoon. Lists of transatlantic liner arrivals began to lengthen, and more and more of a new brand of people called "celebrities" appeared on them—stars of stage and screen, and sports figures.

May Birkhead, whom Bennett had recruited at the time of the *Titanic* disaster and who had done so much for the social columns of the *Herald* subsequently, now began to spice them with fashion notes and increase the paper's fashion coverage. Soon, when the season of new showings began, the *Herald* would list American buyers in town as well as at the openings. The practice begun then continued into the 1960s. The Sunday paper, while not yet publishing a regular rotogravure section, frequently contained a whole page of photos and tips devoted to a single resort such as Vichy. As if to emphasize the new nature of the newspaper, the *Herald* began, in 1924, to publish a yearly *American Guide to Paris*, containing police and passport regulations, sightseeing information, guides to hotels, shopping, theaters and amusements, and so on. By 1923 it returned to the early habit of publishing elaborate spring and Christmas magazine-style supplements of forty or fifty pages.

While the Paris paper under Hills, Archambault, and Jaurett returned to a semblance of its prewar prosperity in a somewhat different guise, back home the parent paper was in trouble. Munsey poured three-quarters of a million dollars into it in 1923 in an effort to stem a decline in circulation and advertising, but nothing happened. Adolf Ochs' *Times* and Pulitzer's *World* were brilliantly successful rivals, while the *Herald* seemed to share a fixed audience with the smaller *Tribune*, a newspaper that could boast a glorious past under Horace Greeley and Whitelaw Reid and appealed to the same people the *Herald* did.

To Munsey the situation was absolutely clear: there were too many morning New York newspapers, and the *Herald* and *Tribune* would have to combine. A paper that used the best features of each would be a new power in New York. And Ogden Reid, the *Tribune*'s owner and editor, agreed. But Munsey wanted to buy the *Tribune* to merge it with the *Herald,* and Ogden Reid had it the other way around. It seems that Mrs. Elizabeth Reid broke the stalemate. She was Ogden Reid's mother, and the *Tribune* was a monument to her late husband Whitelaw, who had not only owned and edited the *Tribune* but had also been a diplomat of note. She herself was a power in shaping the *Tribune* (as her daughter-in-law Helen Rogers Reid would be in the future.) In the face of Munsey's every effort, she remained immovable, and following his own logic, Munsey agreed to sell the *Herald* to the Reids. There followed hard haggling over price and details; James Gordon Bennett's will made it mandatory that the name *Herald* be retained, although the Reids didn't like it. Munsey wanted to hold on to the Paris *Herald*, but the Reids insisted it be a part of the deal. In March the agreement was consummated, and in May Ogden and his mother sailed on the *Aquitania* to take over the Paris paper.

And so on May 20, 1924, another announcement appeared on the front page in Paris:

> The *New York Herald* appears today as the European Edition of the *New York Herald Tribune*. Laurence Hills will continue as Editor. . . . Plans are being developed for the enlargement of the *New York Herald*. Americans visiting Europe now have the opportunity of obtaining the views of the *New York Herald Tribune* the same day they are published in New York.
>
>   Ogden Reid, President

In New York Frank Munsey was $5 million richer, and hundreds of men on the *Herald* were out of work. In Paris, on the other hand, men rejoiced. Living under the shadow of Munsey had never been comfortable; knowledge of the *Herald*'s parlous state in New York produced nothing but uneasiness among men who were afraid he might shut down everything despite the progress the newspaper had made in Europe. The Reids' announcement promised expansion just at the moment that Jaurett was sure the conditions were right. And Helen Reid, now director of advertising of the *New York Herald Tribune*, wrote to her mother-in-law that the Paris *Herald* was a "real treasure . . . more of an asset than we had any idea of," because of the number of advertisers who wanted to reach the new tide of Americans.

The timing couldn't have been better.

Ogden and Helen Rogers Reid aboard the *Aquitania*, off to inspect their new Paris acquisition. (Bettman Archive)

CHAPTER **7**

Golden Years

$\mathbb{I}$N 1923 the *Herald* publicized a fund drive by the American Hospital in Neuilly to finance a new expansion made necessary by the growth of the American colony in Paris and the increased flow of tourists. It was symptomatic; just about every American institution in Paris began to expand or reorganize at the same time. The congregation of the little American Church on the rue de Berri decided that it had outgrown its quarters there and purchased a site on the Seine opposite the Grand Palais, where it built the much larger structure it still occupies. A couple of years later American Legion Post No. 1 began a fund to buy a large, handsome mansion at 49, rue Pierre Charron, off the Champs Elysées (where it is still lodged), and again the *Herald* publicized the drive.

The American Library, having originated simply as an organization to distribute books to rest camps and hospitals of the American Expeditionary Forces, blossomed by the mid-twenties into the most comprehensive grouping of American books on the Continent. It acquired a permanent home and became a membership library, as well as the English language branch of the Bibliothèque Nationale, making loans to lycées all over France.* Membership in other clubs and organizations zoomed. To cap it all off, the American embassy made plans to move to a new home near the place de la Concorde.

*When Sylvia Beach, over on the Left Bank, published the first edition of James Joyce's *Ulysses* in 1922, an angry Gertrude Stein came by her bookstore, writers' center, and lending library called Shakespeare and Company to tell Sylvia that she and Alice B. Toklas were transferring their membership to the Right Bank American Library. They would have nothing to do with Joyce's filth.

The rush was on. Americans came in droves and frequently stayed as long as they possibly could, and American institutions in Paris planned their expansion accordingly. On the Left Bank, artists and writers migrated to St. Germain and Montparnasse, flocking to the Deux Magots, the Dome, the Select, the Closerie des Lilas, and later, the new Rotonde and Coupole. Some were poseurs who spent most of their time in cafés; others worked hard but made little mark; still others gave a solidity to the legend of the Left Bank—Ezra Pound, Gertrude Stein, Dos Passos, Hemingway, Miller, Fitzgerald, MacLeish, and so many others. Small publishing houses rose and fell, and so did little magazines. The American expatriates felt the need to leave the Babbitry of America, the repressive mores and laws that kept them from publishing their own work—or from washing down their food with good wine. Besides, the revolution in art and literature was taking place in Paris—not the Paris of tourist sights and sounds, but the Paris of real people.

On the Right Bank the middle-class Americans formed a wholly different but equally ubiquitous society. They haunted Harry's New York Bar (American tourists were told to "Just Tell the Driver Sank Roo Doe-Noo," in what was probably the longest-running *Herald* ad ever), acquired in 1924 by Scotsman Harry McElhone, and equipped with a long bar and dark woodwork shipped over from New York. It was conveniently around the corner from the Opéra, the Café de la Paix, American Express, and the rue Scribe, where all the transatlantic lines had their offices; celebrities, tourists, and journalists used it as a sort of clubhouse. Henry's Bar, nearby on the rue Volnay, was a more sedate gathering place for the older generation of the American business colony; sportsmen drank at Dickson's Silver Ring, whose owner, Jeff Dickson, enjoyed success as a promoter of sporting events at the Palais des Sports and the Salle Wagram. Between the Opéra and the Madeleine, Luigi's, an Italian-American bar-restaurant, had an upstairs cabaret and eventually a gambling club called the Franco-American Association. For years the *Herald* carried the same ad for Luigi's, featuring cartoonist Briggs' comfortable characters, familiar from his comic strip "Mr. and Mrs.." Over in the Champs Elysées area the rue Pierre Charron emerged as another entertainment center for Americans. Johnny's was an ornate place down one flight of stairs, opposite what would become the American Legion Building, with its own bar.

For nightlife all of Montmartre lay before the Right Bank American and it, too, was well stocked with American-run night clubs and bars, all recorded by the diminutive and indefatigable Sparrow Robertson, "Sporting Gossip" columnist for the *Herald* of those years, as he made his rounds. Sparrow seems to have spent virtually all his time going from one "thirst emporium" to the other, pausing only long enough to come into the office to peck out his column on a battered portable typewriter or to go to an occasional event at the Palais des Sports, where he shared front row seats in the press box with Eric Hawkins of the *Herald*, Jules Frantz, managing editor of the Paris Edition of the *Chicago Tribune*, and the *Trib*'s sportswriter, Herol Egan.

And the Right Bank colony had its own newspaper, the *Herald*. Hills might be afraid of inroads from the *Tribune* or the *Times*, but the solid Americans bought and read the *Herald*. For them it chronicled the doings of the American Club, to which it gave perhaps more space than to any other subject. It reported in detail the art shows, concerts, and parties at the socially distinguished American Women's Club, with its own handsome building in Passy. Readers were constantly advised of events at the American Church, the American Cathedral Church on the avenue George V, the Christian Science and Methodist churches. The American Chamber of Commerce, the Rotary Club, American Legion Post No. One, the Washington-Lafayette Club, the American University Women's Club on the rue de Chevreuse, and innumerable other clubs and schools called in about their dinners, wiener roasts, luncheons, and picnics, all of which were reported in "Paris Clubland"; the American undertakers called in death notices; the boat trains, large hotels, and the embassy constituted a regular beat for several *Her-*

ald reporters and provided a stream of copy, not only in the form of lists of transients, but in hundreds of interviews that filled the *Herald*'s pages. The 20,000 or so resident Americans were augmented by a continuous flow of tourists, celebrities, clothes buyers, and transient high society, and the *Herald*, as its enlarged crew of reporters covered their beats, merged their accounts of these transients with those of the resident community.

Circulation rose from 12,000 in 1924 to 39,000 in 1929; advertising went from 800,000 lines in 1922 to 2½ million in 1929. The house ads trumpeted this frequently: "The New York *Herald* has a larger sale among Americans than any other American newspaper—and a larger sale among Europeans." Another ad, referring directly to its competitors, said, "An Important Fact—the New York *Herald* is sold on its own merit and is not given away or distributed in hotels as a common handbill." In October 1929 the paper boasted of having printed seventeen times as many classified ads as any competitor; during the 1928 Salon de l'Auto, it printed 86 percent more ads than two years before, far more than any other American paper. "Si vous voulez atteindre les Américains en Europe faites de la publicité dans le *New York Herald*." And almost as if to rub it in, the paper noted that its sales on the Riviera were "Five Times Greater Than the Sale of All the Other American Papers on the Continent Combined."* Ogden Reid, on a visit in early 1927, wrote home to his mother that "the Paris *Herald* has had an extraordinary good year. Laurence Hills is entitled to great credit . . . costs have gone up enormously but he has succeeded in raising his rates proportionately. I wish we could do the same in New York," where, unfortunately, the *Herald Tribune* did not have the advantage in prestige that the Paris Edition had, so that the *New York Times* could even then get more lineage at higher rates.

The *Herald* began to make a profit in the last months of 1924, following the sale to the Reids, and it continued to do so all through

---

*Even though it was, for a while, the late, great James Thurber who put out the Riviera Edition of the *Chicago Tribune* virtually singlehanded.

the 1920s despite an expansion in size and in staff and increases in the staff's remuneration. (The *Chicago Tribune*, on the other hand, sent over an accountant named J. H. Hummell at about the time the *Herald* changed hands and began its expansion. He earned the nickname "Give 'em half Jack" after trimming many salaries by half and inviting staffers to quit who didn't like it. In its own way the *Tribune* was then also able to make a slim profit in the fat years, paying salaries of fifteen dollars a week –half what was paid on the *Herald*.) In mid-1924 the *Herald*, incorporating a number of the New York *Herald Tribune*'s syndicated features, moved to a regular eight-page format. Within a few years it regularly had twelve to sixteen pages, with a second section on Sundays and, as of June 1928, a four-page rotogravure section incorporating, for the first time, two pages in color. Introduction of the rotogravure section, the *Herald* noted, came within days of thirty years after Bennett introduced the first Linotype machines.

What it did not note was that those same Linotype machines were still in use, along with the decrepit American press and stereotype equipment bought in 1907. As the paper grew even larger— hitting a total of thirty pages on special occasions and putting out an American Legion special edition of fifty-six pages to greet returning Legionnaires in 1927—it became clear that the dilapidated building and the antiquated equipment needed replacement. And so Hills and the Reids decided that like all the other prosperous American institutions in Paris, the *Herald* must make a move. The times were good and getting better; the franc was stabilized and back on gold; Coolidge would be succeeded by Hoover; there were more and more Americans in Paris with more and more money. Since the American Church had moved off the Rue de Berri a new building could be put up there. Paris was moving west, the *Herald* should be in the heart of things. For three million francs, it told its readers, it had acquired the site; for seven million more a splendid new building would be ready by mid-1930.

Built with a floor plan in the shape of an H, it would have a courtyard front and back so that despite a narrow lot most offices

The composing room in the Rue du Louvre, shortly before the move to the Rue de Berri.

would have outside windows. Nine stories tall, it would have space for all the *Herald* offices, with a brand-new Walter Scott press in the basement, and a gravity feed system so that from the editorial rooms above copy would go by tube to the composing room one floor down and from there to the presses below. Myth has it that the designers forgot to include a staircase, which explains why the two elevators were so tiny—space had to be taken from the elevator shafts for stairs. But certainly the gleaming, white-faced building was a contrast with the grimy old rue du Louvre building, and a fitting symbol for the *Herald*'s prosperity. Offices for rent on the top floors would have a fine view over all of Paris. There was plenty of room besides for the *Herald* offices that had previously been located on the avenue de l'Opéra: administration, circulation, accounting, publicity, and visitor's bureau. As a result it could sublet most of the Opéra space to the Italian Tourist Bureau and retain only a small visitor's bureau. The ground floor of the new building had a spacious reading room in twenties modern style, with a table for bound volumes of the paper in the middle.

But a lot happened to the newspaper besides sheer expansion between the time of the Reids' purchase in 1924 and the move to the new building in December 1930. The Reid purchase brought a first and immediate change: the inclusion of features from the former *New York Tribune* now appearing at home in the combined *Herald Tribune*. Some of the columns came and went; one can regret the rather rapid departure of the poems of Samuel Hoffenstein ("My heart leapt up / when I beheld / the face of my friend Katzenfeld"). Others became permanent fixtures, and so did some of the cartoons. No one who read the interwar European Edition can forget the gentle Briggs and Webster panels—"Mr. and Mrs.," "Life's Darkest Moment," "Bridge," "The Thrill That Comes Once in a Lifetime," "How To Torture Your Wife" (or Husband.) Hills increased financial coverage substantially. Most important, perhaps, was increased cable news transmission from New York.

Journalists who worked on the *Chicago Tribune* and the *Herald* testify that the most valuable characteristic a deskman could have in the 1920s was the ability to take a twenty-word cable and make two columns out of it. William Shirer, on the *Tribune*, calls getting out the paper then "primarily a work of the imagination." A young fellow with thick glasses named Jim Thurber was the best one at it, Shirer recalls, particularly in taking a cable that said, for example, "Coolidge to Legionnaires Omaha opposed militarism urged tolerance American life," and writing a column and a half of what Coolidge had said. It came to the point, according to Shirer, that Thurber simply made up whole Coolidge speeches out of Coolidge clichés when the President hadn't even spoken at all. Most of the deskmen seemed to find this daily exercise rather exhilarating. Stories were padded out with information from a battered encyclopedia, from memory, and from invention.

The front page was often made up without the stories to fill the various columns, and Don Donaldson, in charge of front-page makeup, would see to it that obscure items would be blown up to fill them. On one occasion, near Christmas, when there was little news, Donaldson still had nothing for the lead story that demanded a three-column head. One of the men came up with a three-line item in the French news service Agence Havas "flimsy" mentioning a typhoon that seemed to be centered near the Island of Yap, a tiny spot in the Pacific over which the United States and Japan had come into conflict prior to the Washington Naval Conference of 1922. Within minutes one rewrite man had written a dramatic and excited half-column story to fit the head "Tidal Wave Sweeps Yap; Thousands Feared Lost," and a "shirttail" of another half column filled people in on background about the island. The next day the *Tribune*, commenting on the *Herald* story, pointed out that there had been little if any damage to the islet, since the storm, not too strong to begin with, had hardly touched Yap. But no one seemed to mind.

On another occasion, with half the first page more or less blank below the "fold," seven men were told to write stories of at least two paragraphs each on whatever they wanted. The results were interesting—the reappearance of a bandit believed long dead in Nevada, the discovery of a new monster in the deserts of New Mexico—and no one ever seems to have known that they were made up. Occasionally, of course, there was a real gaffe, but a correction and an apology could take care of it.

Part of the fun was that men on the rival papers kept tabs on each other. The *Herald* once published an agency photograph purporting to show current bread riots in Moscow. At the *Tribune* the late Waverley Root, then assistant to the managing editor, recognized it as an illustration of the 1917 attack on the Winter Palace, and editor Jules Frantz simply ran it the next day, identifying it correctly. "For weeks thereafter," wrote Root, "Eric Hawkins, my opposite number on the *Herald*, never ran into me without shaking his head dolefully and groaning, 'not cricket, old boy, not cricket!' "

Stretching the skeletonized cables out into full-length stories would always be a desirable art and a sheer necessity in the interwar period. In 1926, however, Roland Kilbon, the New York correspondent since Bennett's days, was given an extended leave to visit the Paris Edition. Kilbon was the man who routinely sent the few hundred words of condensation from the New York paper that formed the backbone of serious *Herald* coverage, and who occasionally had to reply to cabled inquiries from Paris. Now he sat on the receiving end as his replacement cabled from New York. As a result, once he returned to New York he saw to it that the Paris paper received far better service than before and paid more attention to the deskmen's requests than to the harried demands of Laurence Hills. It was probably a symptom of the second change for the better: both in New York and Paris the paper was being taken more seriously. The shadow of Munsey no longer hung over it, staff began to stay longer and to be better paid, and in general morale improved—and with it, the paper itself.

The *Herald* never took a strong editorial stand in the interwar years, except on the matter of dog droppings on Paris sidewalks. Wrote one newsroom staffer, "It [the *Herald*] is as easily predictable as Mr. Coolidge . . . it stands on every fence that was ever erected." And Hills had a hard time deciding whether the *Herald* was a small-town newspaper for the 20,000 resident Americans or whether it should be something more cosmopolitan for the vast number of tourists. In either event it would be resolutely for Americans in Europe. But it began to attract good men who tried to make it a better paper.

One was Al Laney. For eight years he worked as city editor and night editor and then moved back to the *New York Herald Tribune*. He was and had been essentially a sportswriter, specializing in golf and tennis. Like so many others, he was shipped off to Europe with the American Expeditionary Force in 1917, and—like many others with hardly a cent left in their pockets—he landed a job on the *Herald*. But unlike others he stayed. The memory of him is of a

Director Laurence Hills makes his first trans-Atlantic telephone call with Eric Hawkins looking over his shoulder from behind him and *New York Herald Tribune* correspondent Leland Stowe on the other phone.

soft-spoken, competent man, a careful stylist who helped others with their prose.* He, in turn, learned from another cultured and dignified man, Willis Steell, a successful Broadway playwright marking time as a copyreader and then Sunday feature editor on the *Herald* so that his daughter could study for an operatic career. Laney himself writes that change for the better began when a young man named Ralph Barnes showed up at the rue du Louvre in the autumn of 1925. On sheer nerve he managed to wangle a job when many more experienced had failed. Enormously energetic, enormously concerned with the state of the world, he learned fast. But

---

*In 1978 the Metropolitan Golf Association awarded Laney its Distinguished Service Award for his sensitive reporting for the New York paper before its death—and his retirement—in 1966.

more, he seems to have inspired his colleagues at the paper at just the time that several were joining battle with Hills over whether certain matters should see print. One man, John Elliott, had already left, having given it up as a bad job.* But Barnes stuck it out, just as the increased wire copy from New York and the possibilities of taking on more staff changed the whole complexion of the news- room. A regular staff of reporters assigned daily by a city editor began to take shape as a group separate from the copyreaders and rewrite men working at night.

Barnes worked hard, for example, to get news of the momentous events taking place in China into the paper. Ned Calmer, later a CBS correspondent and author of four novels, gives a fictionalized picture of the young Barnes in *All the Summer Days*. He has him telling the city room about a speech in the House of Commons, finding "ambition in Italy, fear in Russia, resentment in Germany, suspicion in France, danger in Poland, confusion in the Balkans, mistrust in the United States, and war in China." "Keep the story down," he is told by the night editor. "It's too pessimistic!" And when he announces the important retreat of the northern armies in China he is told, "We have no room for any Chinese stuff tonight. Dave, give him that cable on the U.S. heat wave—fifty-nine dead did you say?" "Do you know how many are dying in China every hour?" Calmer's Barnes-figure asks. He is greeted with laughter, and a reference to the last resort copy being handed in: "Prince of Wales wore soft cuffs with his tuxedo when he went gambling at Touquet. And Spence (Barnes) thinks China has a revolution!"

There is no question that Barnes was fighting against heavy odds. In a thoughtful account of his own life in journalism published in 1943, another former *Herald* deskman, Kenneth Stewart, has a brief chapter on his stint on the *Herald*.

> Newspapermen dropped in uninvited and unannounced, working for a while on the *Herald*, the Chicago *Tribune*, or the little *Times*,

---

*He would go on to become one of the best of the New York paper's growing staff of foreign correspondents, and would come back to Paris in the mid-thirties, as chief of its foreign service.

corresponded for papers back home, played a while on Montparnasse or Montmartre, moved, returned to the States, vanished. . . .

On a normal evening at the *Herald* the nightside would straggle in at about eight o'clock, well wined and dined, to take over from the day staff, which had leisurely collected the tourist registrations at the Right Bank hotels, recorded the comings and goings from the Riviera, interviewed arrivals on boat trains, listened to the talks on international amity at the Anglo-American and Franco-American luncheons. Richard, the French copyboy with the old man's face, would grin at us as we came in and mutter something about "les américains fous."

After a few preliminaries, we would drift out again to the corner bistro for coffee or a liqueur, come back to de-skeletonize the cables which Roland Kilbon had filed from New York, translate a few odds and ends of politics and crime from the Paris papers. Sometime during the evening a minor crisis would have to be solved in the composing room. Few of the printers read or spoke English and they often ran into trouble following the copy.*

There are dozens of stories about the "franglais" used in communicating between the composing and press room people and the editorial staff upstairs, and everyone tells them with nostalgic amusement. Barnes figures in many of them. As he followed the China story, Laney writes, he would come blundering downstairs shouting to makeup men to hold the page until the last minute, so that he could insert the latest information. The printers took to calling him affectionately "Insert Barnes," pronounced "An-sair Bar-nez." But he made everyone around conscious of the importance of events in China, just as he would do later on a larger scale when he became one of the *New York Herald Tribune*'s foreign correspondents in Italy, Spain, and Nazi Germany; and he finally lost his life in a British bomber over Yugoslavia.

In 1926 international news made big headlines: Allied troops evacuated the zone around Cologne; Germany renewed the Rapallo Treaty with Russia and entered the League of Nations; England and France settled the schedule of repayment of their war debts to

*Kenneth Stewart, *News is What We Make It*, pp. 62-63.

the United States, and the French franc hit an all-time low—attracting more American visitors. Hirohito became Emperor of Japan, and Chiang Kai-shek emerged to prominence in China. The *Herald* recorded all these events, but to the journalists on the paper these were mere rewrites from cable sources. The big stories were about the channel swimmers, which reporters actually covered. It was when Gertrude Ederle finally made her first successful crossing that Ralph Barnes' resourcefulness became evident, when he beat out the other reporters on the job. And the heavyweight championship Dempsey-Tunney fight, Laney remembers, was the occasion for a real change in the atmosphere of the editorial room.

For the first time since the war it was decided to put out an extra, and careful preparations were made. Interest in the fight was high and people were prepared to stay up all night to get the results; the fight in Philadelphia would take place at 3:00 A.M., Paris time. Kilbon, back in the States, would file twenty-five words each round, the cyclists would rush over to the paper with the wire from the telegraph office, a rewrite man would construct the story, and within forty-five minutes or so the extra could be ready, since everyone confidently expected Dempsey to knock Tunney out in two or three rounds. The first edition was put out with much of the preliminary fight story and everyone got ready for the extra. What happened, however, was that the place became a madhouse. Harry McElhone, of Harry's New York Bar, had sent over a case of brandy which Sparrow Robertson distributed to all and sundry. Hundreds of Americans and Frenchmen eager for the news congregated hilariously in the editorial room—including French reporters eager to get the results for their own papers. By the time the fight was over, with the stunning news of Tunney's victory, everyone decided the hell with the short lead Kilbon was sending over, this called for a banner headline.

Hills had given strict orders against any banners, concerned that some of the new staff wanted to play with the makeup a bit. It was an inflexible rule. But the extra was an enormous success and sold out immediately, and no word of censure came down from on high.

"The immediate result of this incident," writes Laney, "was a new feeling of freedom among the staff . . . they had got away with something and they might get away with something more. It got to be more fun working in the rue du Louvre." And, he goes on, it was Harry McElhone, a Scot who seldom gave anything away, who should be credited with an assist on this play. Without his brandy it would never have happened.

The year 1927 was a big one for the *Herald*. The Locarno treaties appeared to have stabilized the European situation two years earlier, and the start of 1927 brought the final withdrawal of occupation troops from Germany. Successful inter-Allied debt and reparation negotiations led to the stabilization of the French franc. In America and Europe men and women prepared to cross the Atlantic in droves. Several thousand Rotarians passed through Paris in June on their way to a Rotary convention in Belgium; on one single August day seven transatlantic vessels docked in Le Havre to pour 5,000 passengers onto fifteen boat trains, while the paper recorded that eleven more ships cleared New York Harbor for Europe on that same day. Seventy thousand American Legionnaires prepared to embark for a September 10 anniversary celebration of the landing of American troops in France during the Great War. A handful of others, however, were ready to fly the Atlantic, to compete for the prize offered by hotel owner Raymond Orteig for the first nonstop New York to Paris flight.

Yet it was a bad moment in Franco-American relations. Ambassador Herrick had been returned to France by the Harding administration, and if any diplomat could be said to have been loved it was Herrick, France's great friend in her darkest hour. In his diary, however, he recorded the contributions to increasing tensions: the Coolidge stand on war debts, the prolonged agony of appeals in the Sacco-Vanzetti case—widely covered in the French press—the bad behavior of so many of the new flood of American tourists, who drank too much and too rowdily, but who complained in turn of unpleasant incidents directed against the unwary and innocent in their midst.

The *Herald* avoided reporting these tensions, while giving space and headlines to gestures like the Rockefeller gift of $1 million to help reconstruct the Reims cathedral and Fontainebleau and Versailles. Most important of all, it could turn its attention to the attempt at the first nonstop transatlantic flight between Paris and New York. There was a long list of contestants; far down on the list was a crazy American named Lindbergh who planned to make the thirty-odd- hour trip alone, in a single-motored Ryan monoplane, and on whom Lloyds of London refused to even give odds.

In mid-April the favorite, Richard Byrd, was delayed when his trimotored Fokker made a crash landing. Ten days later Noel Davis was killed in the crash of his *American Legion*. On May 8 two French wartime pilots, Charles Nungesser and François Coli, took off from Le Bourget in their Levasseur flying boat. The *Herald* scooped the French newspapers, having its stories ready beforehand, needing only a line or two to fill in at the last moment, and taking chances the French papers were unwilling or unable to do. The *Herald* carried a banner headline the next day: "All New York To Greet French Fliers at Battery." Excited French crowds gathered in the Paris street and began wild and elaborate celebrations; expectations were roused to fever pitch when rumors flew that the fliers had been spotted off Newfoundland. The *Herald*'s bulletin boards on the avenue de l'Opéra were jammed by masses of people waiting for the final news to flash, and Paris newspapers poured out into the street to report the safe landing in New York Harbor— while the *Herald*, receiving no confirmation, reported nothing.

As the hours went by, disappointment and disillusion were succeeded by anger at the paper's silence. The *Herald* offices had to be given special police protection, and the Paris police begged Eric Hawkins to at least put up a notice to the effect that *Herald* cables had been delayed. At the offices of *Le Matin*, where great American and French flags were intertwined, the mob forced the paper to take down the American flags. Soon it became apparent that Nungesser and Coli were lost. French newspapers printed unfounded rumors in the next few days to the effect that the American Weather

Service had either refused to cooperate by furnishing the Frenchmen with their reports or, worse yet, had actually falsified them. Under the circumstances, Herrick warned Washington that no new flights should be undertaken. Given the ugly mood and the mystery surrounding Nungesser and Coli's failure, such a flight could well be "misunderstood and misinterpreted."

It was in this setting that news flashed across the Atlantic of Lindbergh's takeoff on the morning of May 20. Pandemonium ensued among the journalists as they tried to cover his landing in the midst of a crowd of hundreds of thousands at Le Bourget. The rest is history. Barnes was the first journalist to interview the young pilot after Herrick had given him refuge from the crowds in the American embassy. The paper was full of what seemed to be the biggest story since the armistice; other events paled beside this one—even Bill Tilden's defeat of René Lacoste in the French tennis championships, in progress when news of Lindbergh's takeoff was first announced. Lindbergh's success dispelled almost as if by magic all the sourness. His modest demeanor, his ready and apt responses to the flowery welcomes and congratulations, and the very fact of his being there produced a general feeling of celebration that no one who was there could forget. A single man, without fanfare, had done it, and the French fell for him.

Myron T. Herrick shepherded him through what followed. The French President and the Prime Minister both wanted to see him. He was invited to the National Assembly and the Senate, which he addressed with the perfect self-possession that seems to have marked all his appearances. A medal was struck in his honor and presented to him at the Hotel de Ville where, in conclusion, he said:

> I hope my flight is but the precursor of a regular commercial air service uniting your country and mine as they never have been united before. That is my hope today as I believe Bleriot hoped his flight across the English Channel in 1909 would be the forerunner of the commercial aviation of today; and I believe that if those gallant Frenchmen, Nungesser and Coli, had landed in New York instead of me here in Paris, that would also be their desire.

THE NEW YORK HERALD

EUROPEAN EDITION OF THE NEW YORK HERALD TRIBUNE

PARIS, SUNDAY, MAY 22, 1927.

LINDBERGH ARRIVES ON RECORD-BREAKING FLIGHT

The *Herald*'s biggest interwar scoop.

I have one regret, and that is that New York was not able to accord to these brave Frenchmen the same reception that Paris has accorded to me.

No wonder that all Paris feted him! And he was given the same kind of reception everywhere he went. There were, wrote Herrick, forty million people in France, not to speak of the rest of Europe, to whom Lindbergh was of more importance at that moment than Kings, Presidents, or politics. In twenty-four hours a "period of petulant nagging and quarreling between the French and ourselves" was completely dissipated. "No earthly power could have created the outburst of enthusiasm which began with his arrival and never abated one jot or tittle during his entire stay."

The mood persisted. Western Europe seemed to have gone mad over fliers in general, and fliers wanted to prove that Lindbergh's accomplishment was no simple fluke. At the time of the Nungesser and Coli misfortune several authorities had declared that the art and science of aviation was insufficiently advanced to permit regular Atlantic crossings; the surviving aviators of the crew that assembled to compete for the Orteig prize were out to show the critics they were wrong.

On June 29, five weeks after the Lindbergh flight, Richard Byrd and his crew finally set out in their carefully prepared Fokker. They arrived over Paris to find all of Western Europe blanketed in rain and fog. Their compass went awry, radio connections failed, and after several hours of circling blind they headed back in the general direction of the coast where the pilot was able to bring the plane down to a landing in the surf off a village called Ver-sur-Mer. In the meantime, on the ground, newsmen kept an all-night vigil, the *Herald* having finally gone to press with a headline that said only "Byrd Vanishes in Storm Somewhere Near Paris." Calculations demonstrated that the plane must surely have run out of gas and crashed when word came in of the fliers' safety in Normandy, and reporters were rushed to the scene by a plane held in readiness at Le Bourget, despite the field's official closing to all flights. Again the *Herald* scooped the opposition with extensive reports, and this despite the fact that both Lindbergh and Byrd had been signed up to exclusive stories by the *New York Times*.* (The latter paper threatened legal proceedings and lodged a complaint in Paris duly reported back in New York. Hawkins remembered the reply he received from the New York office: "Let the heathen rave!")

Only the execution of the anarchists Sacco and Vanzetti in Massachusetts for murder and robbery marred the good relations cre-

---

*Waverley Root is the source for the story that the *Herald* had done its normal preliminary job of preparing a front page with the usual background stories, leaving only space at the beginning for a lead reporting the details of the arrival when it occurred. The rewrite man, however, had chosen to fill in the space temporarily with a fictitious story of the arrival and an interview, to be replaced with the real story later. When Byrd's arrival was delayed the page was mistakenly clamped to the press and printed. It was caught, of course, but not until hundreds of copies had gone out to newsstands. Everyone at the *Herald* was sent out to buy up copies, but the *English Daily Mail* and the *Tribune* both managed to find a copy to print and comment on the next day, just for the fun of harassing the *Herald*.

ated by Lindbergh's and Byrd's success. On August 24 headlines read, "Paris Police Fight Angry Mobs Attempting To Reach Embassy: Sacco and Vanzetti Die Bravely." The story reported a night of rioting, looting, and bloodshed; another acknowledged that the French press, by and large, deplored the execution, and a third reported protests elsewhere. The *Herald*'s own editorial approved the execution as one that "relieved the world of a pretext for lawless agitation which should never have existed." Yet the uproar was short-lived, a generally cheerful mood seems to have remained, and the *Herald* could turn its attention to happier matters—the American conventions in Europe—revealing the lengths to which Hills and the new-style *Herald* were willing to go. In early June a horde of Rotarians descended upon Ostend, where the *Herald* established a headquarters with a special correspondent assigned to cover the convention. For the week that it lasted the *Herald* published accounts of the meetings, a daily program of events, a Memo Book of general notes ("Rotary Spokes"), a daily column on life in Belgium, and a series of articles and pictures. One article noted that war debts, race issues, and American tariff barriers were taboo questions; another reported, "Rotarian Hits Mencken and Lewis," terming them "destructive critics." Throughout, the stories emphasized the service functions of what had become one of the largest international organizations.

This was a mere prelude to the big event in September: the tenth-anniversary Legion convention. Two men were told in the spring to prepare a special ad-filled fifty-six page supplement to greet the Legionnaires on their arrival. For two weeks before the convention began the *Herald* filled pages with stories of accounts of their arrival, their visits to the vast battlefield cemeteries, their gifts to French families who had befriended them, preparations, plans, and schedules. There were, in fact, only 20,000 coming; from the space and time devoted to the event a reader might have gathered that half a million were about to arrive. September 19, the day of their parade down the Champs Elysées, was declared a French national holiday; the Opéra-Comique arranged three gala programs; President Poincaré and Ambassador Herrick prepared to open the convention proceedings, and a whole building on the cours de la Reine was given over to the Legion as headquarters. Legion stamps were put on sale by the French post office, department stores were decorated with flags and bunting, Citroen donated six taxis for official Legion use, and the *Herald* published a picture of the last Taxi of the Marne still in use. By the start of the convention it began to issue a three- or four- page supplement every day, with full-scale reporting of all events.

The high point was the march down the Champs Elysées: "All Paris Crowds Streets To Watch the Great Parade." It was a friendly crowd. Americans in Paris had lived in some dread of the approaching event; American Legion conventions back home were not noted for propriety, and everyone was still touchy about possible French anti-Americanism. Police Commissioner Chiappe—always a friend to Americans—had instructed the Paris police to be more lenient with these particular foreigners, and all nightclubs had been ordered to close at midnight. But though some cut up drunkenly, filled with the unaccustomed wine and liquor, on the whole the Legionnaires were well behaved, and there was much that was deeply touching in their return.

One sad event that September 19, fifty-odd years ago, went almost unnoticed in the coverage of the Legion parade: the funeral of Isadora Duncan, who had participated vividly in the Sacco and Vanzetti protests, and who had died only a few days earlier on the Riviera when her long red scarf caught in the spokes of an automobile wheel and broke her neck as the driver started the car. Her funeral cortege, on the same day as the Legion parade, led by her brother Raymond in his usual Greek tunic, moved all the way on foot, in the drizzle, from Auteuil along the Seine, avoiding the Champs Elysées district, and finally crossed the rue de Rivoli to get to the place de la Bastille, from which it would go to the Père Lachaise Cemetery. At the rue de Rivoli it was momentarily halted by French soldiers guarding the approaches to the place de la Concorde against Sacco and Vanzetti sympathizers who had threatened to disrupt the Legion parade. Then it was allowed to pass. The *Herald* relegated its account of the funeral to the back pages. The headline read, "Few Attend Isadora Duncan's Rites as Compatriots Parade." No reporter had been sent to the Père Lachaise, where, in fact, some 5,000 people attended what was a moving ceremony. The *Tribune* and the *Times* did no better.

In 1928 the newspaper entered what was probably the most prosperous period it ever had except for the brief time of sales to doughboys in 1918–19, and certainly a "richer" one than any time in the future until the 1970s. There were more than thirty people on the editorial payroll; Whit Burnett, who ran the day desk, and Martha Foley, a copyreader whom he married, demanded more money of Hills, and the whole staff's economic situation improved. Hills added United Press service to the Associated Press and Agence Havas news services the paper already received. With this, the skeletonized cables from New York and London, and a staff of half a dozen local men, the paper's rewrite men could put together a creditable newspaper, and they frequently did. The *Herald,* like the *Tribune,* could draw from a floating pool of very good newsmen, attracted to Paris by all that brought so many Americans in the twenties. Newsmen who worked on the post–World War II paper always say that the *Herald* was a very bad paper in the interwar period, and that they made it a much better one in the 1940s. It's a pardonable exaggeration; journalists who worked for it and afterward wrote about it tended to write more about the workings than the product.

Whit Burnett and Martha Foley's caustic piece about the *Herald* in Mencken's *American Mercury* for January 1931 included much gossip. They wrote that an Englishman who had graduated from proofreading to become managing editor—i.e., Eric Hawkins—had once changed "so's your old man" to "and so is your father" in Arthur Moss' "Around the Town" column. Moss himself was still angry about it thirty-five years later! But Hawkins, smarting over the general tone of the article in his *Memoirs,* published thirty years afterward, says the change was made as a joke by Don

Donaldson, chief of the copydesk. Unhappily, he says, this and other stories were picked up and repeated in the weekly news magazines. Burnett and Foley, to underline their contention that the paper was too much a mouthpiece for the Embassy, recount the time that the phone rang one night; it was Ambassador Herrick, who told the journalist who had picked it up that there were two moons in the sky, and said to him amiably that if he hadn't noticed it he should go to the window to look, and make sure that something appeared about it in the paper the next morning. This, they said, was probably the single occasion that the paper did *not* print what an official U.S. spokesman had asked them to. Laney repeats the story in somewhat different form in his book on the *Herald*. But Hawkins insists that at the time there was a regular crank call from some drunk in Montparnasse who would begin each conversation with "This is the American ambassador speaking," and would then go on to tell whoever had answered some absurd and presumably funny story. Hawkins himself had been the recipient of two such calls.

In fact, the *Herald* gave wide and quite ample coverage to most of the news of the day in its first two or three pages. Typically it might have a story or two devoted to the Kellogg-Briand Pact (of which it took a skeptical view), stories on the continued fraud trials resulting from the Harding administration's difficulties, and a report of William Z. Foster's fifteen-minute acceptance speech over NBC's station WEAF as Communist party presidential candidate. It noted that Miss M. V. Burr, deputy attorney general of Pennsylvania, had become the first woman to be admitted to practice before the United States Supreme Court, and it told of the wounding of Leon Trotsky in exile in Alma-Ata, Kazakhstan. The paper recorded that the president of the American Chemistry Society defended chemical warfare as a most powerful defensive weapon that was also a most efficient way of saving lives, since it gave affected combatants a far better chance of survival than other weapons. And it reported that the Boy Scouts of America had been asked to give up their campaign to get women to stop smoking. "The Viennese," it wrote on another occasion, "Cheer Strauss and Jeritza at Spectacular Premier of Opera"—Richard Strauss conducting his own *Egyptian Helen*. While the rotogravure section ran heavily to photographs of arriving celebrities and pictures of places such as the Ritz Hotel garden at teatime—"Where Fashionable People Meet"—it also showed Gorky addressing a welcome crowd in Moscow and a picture of Soviet athletes.

The headlines were often still devoted to aerial spectaculars. On June 19, 1928, the *Herald* welcomed "Lady Lindy"—Amelia Earhart, the first woman to cross the Atlantic by airplane, in a Fokker named *Friendship* piloted by Wilmer Stoltz. Pacific and polar flights, and the first flight of a woman from Capetown to Cairo, were all grist, although nothing was ever again to equal the Lindbergh event. In October of 1928 the "Graf Zeppelin's" first transatlantic flight merited several days' front-page headlines.

Of somewhat more interest is the testimony of the paper's pages to the reintegration of Central Europe into European society. The new Versailles-created entity of Czechoslovakia features not only in news dispatches, but in the travel pages and their advertisements; some of the old Austro-Hungarian resorts familiar from Bennett's days reappear: Carlsbad, Marienbad, and Franzenbad. A section on Hungary acquainted *Herald* readers with the *Herald* bureau in Budapest, where files of the paper were available and visitors were welcome. There were sections on Germany with ads for Bad Ems, Bad Nauheim, Wiesbaden, and Baden-Baden. Columns reported on racing in Mannheim, and theater in Dresden, and there were advertisements for Bad Gastein—"the world's most radioactive thermal baths[!]" * When the International Advertising Association held its four-day convention in Berlin in August 1929, the *Herald* devoted a special color rotogravure section to the meeting, published a daily special edition in Berlin, and followed up with the arrival of the regular edition later in the day by plane. It advised

---

*One dispatch in mid-June 1928 told readers that a small town nearby had supplied Munich with a fine vaudeville troop. The town's name was Dachau.

the delegates that the $500 million market of Americans in Europe constituted the forty-ninth American state for advertisers who could, of course, reach it through the *Herald*.

If these were golden years for the newspaper, they were golden years for the Third Republic too. A large measure of reconstruction had taken place; production, in general, was well above prewar; Poincaré had stabilized the franc. Frenchmen will look back and tell you that these were probably the best years of the Republic. Memories of the war years were still strong, but at least some of the bitterness had faded. One *Herald* story is rather revealing about how this manifested itself in nearby Belgium. In Louvain the library of the burned-out university was being rebuilt, largely with American contributions. The architect, Whitney Warren, and Belgian Cardinal Lemercier wanted the balustrade over the entrance to bear an inscription: "Destroyed by German Fury—Rebuilt by American Generosity." The rector of the university, Monseigneur Ladeuze, reflecting the change in feeling, opposed it. Warren and Lemercier won—and perhaps felt vindicated a few years later. On a happier note the paper could report that the French Film Control Law had been changed, with the four-to-one import ratio suspended to permit the import of 200 films, but that in Peking, on the other hand, the censors forbade kissing on-screen.

Laurence Hills had seen to greatly expanded securities tables and increased financial news. The paper printed a number of columns originating in the United States, but it could afford to contract for a large number of columns from stringers in Europe, and many of these made delightful reading. George Slocombe, who would reappear after World War II, published a series of "French Sketches." In "Roads and Inns," for example, he noted that each road out of Paris led to an inn at the end of a ride: the Hotel de la Poste, for example, usually came at the equivalent of a day's postal coach ride. The various Hotels de France, on the other hand, marked the broadening outlines of French royal control over the centuries. The Hotel du Commerce often replaced a name that had previously honored King or nobility until the time of the Revolution. But nowhere, he noted, were there inn signs honoring Marat, Danton, or Robespierre.

A. C. Fox wrote "Little Stories of Everyday Paris" and "Stories Picked Up in Paris Streets." Whit Burnett, though day editor, contributed pieces like the one on "Married Artists Who Work in Sympathy." There were occasional columns like Helen Mulvaney's "Soak in the Rue Mouffetard Language." The paper had two regular art and music critics, George Bal and Louis Schneider, neither of whom has left any discernible mark in the history books.

There was considerable movement back and forth of personnel between the three Paris American newspapers. Elliott Paul was fired from the *Tribune* in the late 1920s because he led too many young staff members into all-night drinking bouts; he then worked for the *Herald* on and off. For a while he ran the "Mailbag," bringing it to a certain artistic height: he often wrote his own letters, as well as answers, all designed to provide controversy and stimulate a flow of genuine contributions. But he was also given fairly free rein to simply contribute columns on subjects that interested him. Some of them foreshadowed sections of *The Last Time I Saw Paris,* with its loving account of the rue de la Huchette.

For a time Paul did the art gallery column. One fanciful piece told about how all the statues on the outer walls of the Louvre had suddenly come to life, stepped down from their niches, and danced along the Seine. The aunt of rewrite man Larry Dame was so enchanted that she sent Dame a note with a check—variously estimated at either two or four thousand francs—telling him to "take dear Elliott to a good restaurant and regale him." Upon reading this note Paul marched into Laurence Hills' office and said, "Sir, I fire myself." Hills is said to have looked at him in some amazement, whereupon Paul explained that only a few months earlier Hills had laid down the rule that any journalist who got drunk *on the job* would be fired. He had been working since morning, was now going out to get drunk—and therefore he was firing himself. The clear distinction had to be made that since Dame was a night man and was going to get drunk *before* coming to work, nothing would happen to him. (It was, incidentally, almost the last time Paul came to the *Herald*. He returned several years later, having lived through revolution on the island of Ibiza and written *The Life and Death of a Spanish Town,* and walked into the office, over to the clothes rack, and asked, "Where's my hat, goddamnit? I left it right here!" The new people who made up most of the staff stared at him in some amazement, and he strode back out, for the last time.)

Arthur Moss, who with Florence Gilliam edited *Gargoyle,* a little magazine of the early 1920s, and later *Boulevardier,* wrote a regular column for Archambault's *Times,* "Over the River," as well as contributing a regular one for the *Herald,* "Around the Town," which rather tended to poke fun at Left Bank doings. The *Herald* gave considerable space to book reviews. But here a digression is necessary.

People acquainted with Paris and the *Herald Tribune* generally tend to associate the *Herald* with much of the Parisian literary and artistic ferment of the 1920s. But Colonel McCormick's *Chicago Tribune,* European Edition, and even the tiny *Times* were far more involved. Hills himself never seems to have recognized that anything of much importance was going on over on the Left Bank, and Hawkins' memoirs would certainly have marked him as the complete philistine in Left Bank eyes. In fact, the *Herald*'s early coverage is rather delightfully innocent, drawing as it does on the paper's usual style of reporting. In 1924, in an unsigned column called "Latin Quarter Notes," it apprised readers that

> Ezra Pound, the American poet, is back in the Quarter after a visit of several months in Rapallo. . . . He will shortly present Georges Antheil in another concert.
> Miss Djuna Barnes, author of "My Book". . . has returned to the Quarter from Cannes.
> Ernest Hemingway is assuming the editorial duties of the *Transatlantic Review* in the absence of Mr. Ford Madox Ford who is now in America.

In spite of later attempts to match the *Tribune's* liveliness about the arts, a 1931 "In the Latin Quarter" still comes up with items like: "Back in Paris, for the winter, Miss Gertrude Stein, the prominent modern writer, is seen frequently walking in the Luxembourg Gardens not far from her home."

Few of the big names of those years ever worked for or contributed to the *Herald*—Hemingway, Pound, Stein, Eliot, or Fitzgerald, for example. Henry Miller contributed a few columns at one point or another, though no one can be sure how many, since they would have appeared under a regular contributor's name. On the other hand, he worked as a stock table proofreader for the *Tribune* (and gives a rather vivid description of the job and its effect upon him in *Tropic of Cancer*) and contributed a large number of columns. Despite the *Tribune's* general rule of printing mainly its own staff's pieces, it did buy pieces from Joyce and Ford Madox Ford—at eight to ten dollars apiece. William Shirer, whose major Paris stint was for the *Tribune* rather than for the *Herald,* records that when he first came to the *Tribune* in 1925, the deskmen included Elliott Paul, and Eugene Jolas, James Thurber, and Virgil Geddes, who published poetry under the imprint of the Black Manikkin Press and wrote plays. Paul, Jolas, and Robert Sage were working on the *Tribune* when they began to edit the influential *transition*, aided by Jolas' wife Maria. (Robert Sage would later edit and translate Stendahl's diaries and end his years on the *Herald,* to which he went in 1934 and to which he returned as travel editor after World War II.) *Transition* was virtually an outgrowth of the *Tribune's* Sunday magazine and art supplement, and published or discussed virtually all Left Bank writers. The *Tribune* attracted and even published dozens of the Left Bank crowd, was read by them, and actually influenced the artistic and literary scene in a way the *Herald* never did.

In part responsibility must go to a man whom many current readers of the *International Herald Tribune* would know—the late Waverley Lewis Root, author of, among other books, *The Foods of France* and *The Foods of Italy,* and in the 1960s and 1970s a regular contributor of a learned and sometimes recondite column on food. (Mr. Root once went to the trouble to deny the rumor that his real name was "Alimentary Canal.") Root actually began his career on the Paris *Chicago Tribune* in the mid 1920s as its literary editor while simultaneously serving as a Paris correspondent for Danish and Swedish newspapers and later as the *Tribune*'s night editor. Root, while critical, was closely attuned to what was happening on the Left Bank. He was willing to print contrasting reviews as well as to write reviews himself, with the result that the *Tribune* might print Root's critique of Robert McAlmon's *The Indefinite Huntress and Other Stories,* published in Caresse Crosby's Continental Edition Series, and then McAlmon's rejoinder, a reply by Root, and finally a defense of McAlmon by Kay Boyle. No exchange of this sort would be found in the *Herald.*

Root found most of Gertrude Stein's work to be ephemeral; he reviewed her *Lucy Church Amiably* with a parody of her style, though he later heaped praise on *The Autobiography of Alice B. Toklas.* In other words, the *Tribune* did not indulge the expatriates; one of its regular critics, Alex Small, was well known for the scorn he poured out on those in whom he detected pose rather than accomplishment. But it all puts into relief what everyone at the time knew: the *Tribune* was a livelier and more intellectual paper than the *Herald,* even if it could not cover either international or Paris events in the detail required to make it sell to the Right Bank and to the tourists.

There was some interchange of personnel; many of the *Herald* journalists took to living on the Left Bank, and mingled freely with its personalities. Al Laney, and perhaps others, are supposed to have helped to type parts of Joyce's *Ulysses* for Sylvia Beach, although she does not mention it in her autobiographical *Shakespeare and Company.* Some went on to become well-known writers in later years. But in the main, legend rubbed off on the *Herald* because of the later confusion of names, because the *Herald* did provide some of the context, and partly because some of the *Chicago Tribune* people put in a briefer stint on the *Herald*—Shirer, Elliott Paul, Jolas, Harold Stearns.

Perhaps because newsmen are an irreverent lot, perhaps because the *Chicago Tribune* had as managers people like David Darrah and then Jules Frantz instead of a Laurence Hills, the *Tribune* seems to have inspired much more affection in those who worked for it and in some ways, more admiration by those who knew the circumstances in which it was put out. Burnett and Foley write that it was "brilliant one day and a gross mistake the next," while they call the *Herald* "spiritless." Frantz himself, as a way of contrasting the two papers, recalled the occasion that Hills told Root in agitation, "Do you know what those madmen at the *Tribune* have done now? They've used the word 'bordello' in a headline!" And he remembers the time that his sportswriter Herol Egan came back from Spain to write about bullfighting. If the fight was a good one, Egan wrote, the matador may be awarded one ear; if unusually good, two ears. But if it was superb he gets both ears "and a piece of tail." Frantz let it go through; Hills or Hawkins, he was sure, never would have. Instead of being the voice of the real, midwestern America in Europe, as Colonel McCormick had intended it to be, the Paris *Chicago Tribune* became, as Shirer puts it, the irreverent "organ of the expatriates of the Left Bank, mostly written and entirely read by the bohemians of Montparnasse."

How could it continue? Frantz's answer was simple: no one in Chicago much bothered reading it. He was sent "A" and "B" editorials, with orders to print A and choose among B. He frequently ignored both, and no one complained. Certainly the Colonel, had he read it regularly, would have fired everyone on it. Only when he received a direct objection did he act. The Colonel ordered that the writer of a favorable interview with Roger Baldwin of the American Civil Liberties Union be fired when the column was called to his attention. Waverley Root was the author, but luckily the column was unsigned and the Colonel was informed by return cable that the offending staffer was already gone. Shirer had to be fired when, during his absence, his assistant filed a mistaken report about film actress Anna Mae Wong, who threatened to sue.

Deskman Spencer Bull went to the *Herald* as a result of a kind of silly joke common to all newsrooms. Deskmen on both papers were forever inserting fake bits in their stories to see whether the copyreaders or proofreaders would catch them before they got into print. Bull took a handout about the Prince of Wales' opening of an orphanage and added an imaginative bit about one of the children talking back to him, whereupon the prince took his cane and bashed the little fellow over the head. The copyreaders read only the first, routine part of the story, and the rest got through, with the result that there was hell to pay with the British government. McCormick ordered Bull fired, and Hills, obsessed with the idea that the *Tribune* was livelier, took him to lunch, where Bull poured out his ideas about what was wrong with the *Herald*. Hills hired him, but he didn't last. Colonel McCormick himself was responsible for hiring May Birkhead for the *Tribune* in 1926, after she left the *Herald*. He had hopes that her prestige might bring more of the important and affluent Right Bank readership to the *Tribune*. She stayed until the paper closed down in 1934, but apparently to little effect.

In fact, there was a friendly, amusing, and—many felt—healthy rivalry between the two papers. Newsmen tried to scoop each other, editors tried to outguess how the others would play important news, each tried to outpoint the other. When the Colonel ordered that there be an eight-column banner on each number of the *Tribune,* the staff was sorely taxed. Either it had to find worthy news stories, or it had to be even more imaginative than usual in blowing up minor ones. The result was—on occasion—rather hilarious. A minor item about locusts in America grew to the dimensions of an enormous plague under a banner head; Hills, greatly disturbed that the *Herald* had missed the story, cabled the Paris Herald correspondent in New York, Everett Walker, asking him how come they'd let the *Tribune* scoop them.

Despite all the efforts of the staff and the liveliness of the *Tribune,* the *Herald* attracted the advertising that allowed it to put out a bigger paper, pay more to a bigger staff, and thereby provide the coverage that more people wanted. Janet Flanner could refer to it as "the dear old *Herald*" in one of her *New Yorker* columns. It was an institution, and neither the *Tribune* nor the *Times* could shake it. Its readers could follow "Doctor Cadman's Daily Counsel," check out events in "Today's Calendar," amuse themselves with what happened "Thirty Years" and "Ten Years Ago" in the *Herald,* survey the "Art Scene" and "Art Sales" with Georges Bal, "Music and Musicians" with Louis Schneider, check out "Life in Berlin" and its "Art Galleries" and "Czechoslovak Economic and Resort News." They could do the crossword puzzle, try out the problems in the bridge column, and—as the food feature suggested—pass on its American recipes to their French cooks.

A column told them what to see in Paris shops; "In the Latin Quarter" continued to tell them sedately about the not-so-sedate denizens of the Left Bank; thanks to Hills they got two full pages of "Financial Reports" and the "Continental Bourses"; Willis Steell reviewed books; elaborate fashion supplements told them what to wear. There were a half page of shipping news, a half page "Directory of Hotels, Restaurants and Pensions," three columns of "Paris Amusements," and a full page of sports was capped off with Grantland Rice's American sports column—and the inimitable Sparrow Robertson's "Sporting Gossip," now sporting a picture of Sparrow himself, wearing his trademark battered fedora. A house ad told readers, "Keep Up with American Athletes by Reading Sparrow Robertson's Sporting Column Daily in the New York *Herald,*" and thousands upon thousands of readers did.

Robertson was by all odds the most widely known and perhaps the most colorful figure of the *Herald* of those interwar years. Even today one or two French employees of the paper remember him, and mention of Sparrow Robertson will light up a face and bring forth the phrase "ca, c'était un personnage!" The tiny, wizened man must have been well into his sixties when he showed up at the end of the war and asked Hills for a job on the strength of having occasionally contributed sports items to the *Sun* back in New York. Neither his age nor the fact that he had come over during the war for the YMCA were things to be mentioned in his presence. It was only when his column began to move from sports strictly speaking to gossip about sporting figures that he hit his stride; when he began to retail his own adventures as he moved from one Paris hangout to another, each populated with his "Old Pals" whose names and activities would appear in the next day's piece, his popularity mounted. No one could accurately reproduce his twisted syntax; Hawkins received innumerable letters attacking Sparrow's daily appearance. But far more typical was Eugene O'Neill's declaration, from a village outside of Tours where he was living and writing at the time, that he had to go into town each morning to get the *Herald* since he could not start the day without Sparrow's column: "Why, he's the greatest writer in the world!"

Everyone testified that Sparrow hardly ever slept and hardly ever paid for a drink. His presence was welcome in all the "thirst emporiums" he visited—and where he frequently ordered drinks for his Old Pals—simply because he was the best publicity they could get. He was frequently accompanied by a crowd of hangers-on (who would drop off one by one as the night progressed—few could ever stay the course with the little man), and crowds of visiting tourists would come to the places simply to see or meet him. His disregard for all else but sports, sporting figures, and thirst emporiums is perhaps best illustrated by the time he traveled to Marseilles to witness a fight in the company of his Old Pal Jules Frantz of the *Tribune*. The fight ended in a riot sparked by the actions of an American judge who happened to be linked to one of the fighter's managers. Frantz reported the whole affair, and it was spread across the front page of the Paris *Chicago Tribune*. When he joined the Sparrow in a bar Frantz asked him if he'd sent a good story. "I sent them a blow-by-blow rundown," the Sparrow replied. "Nothing else?" "Get away with that stuff! I came here to cover a fight, not a riot!"

Sparrow Robertson at his most usual place of business, Harry's New York
Bar, with Harry McElhone on the right.

He was really in his element in the late twenties, when Old Pals
by the thousands came pouring across the Atlantic seeking relief
from the Great Thirst. Sparrow himself traveled occasionally to
report on sporting events outside of Paris, and at one point even
went to the United States. In his column he wrote:

> From time to time I will shoot something over from America to
> my column and when I return I will give the general lowdown on
> how I found things over home. My visit home will be a short one
> and, during it, I will often think of the dear Old Pals I have in Paris
> and throughout Europe. . . .
> . . . In New York all was not well.
> I visited the soft-drink places on Broadway now frequented by
> the city's sporting characters and I spoke with many of same. I was
> brought into contact with what is now being passed off in New
> York as genuine Three-Star.

The old town still has a hold on me, though. I went to see my Old Pals and was sad to see what has happened to them. It is their diet. You should see the food and drink they put away. I would like to be able to provide a rest cure at Henry's in Paris for all of them. Back in Harry's I'll have to tell the boys that New York's not what it used to be, although I still have a great deal of regard for same.

The *Herald,* like its parent paper, supported Hoover vigorously during the 1928 election, finding in Al Smith a man who was "not of national stature," and foreseeing disaster with "Tammany in the White House." Election night afforded Hills the opportunity for elaborate coverage: special editions issued periodically from the rue de Berri throughout the early morning hours, and open houses at numerous hotels and cafés received returns by courier from the *Herald.* The largest groups were at the paper itself and at Harry's New York Bar. The complicated election night operation went smoothly, and the final edition, remarkably complete, bore a banner about Hoover's history-making, smashing victory, earning him 444 electoral votes to Smith's 87—even though, as the *Herald* acknowledged the next day, Smith got more votes than any candidate in history with the exception of Hoover. That day the paper congratulated itself on the front page: "We submit that in Europe such a complete service on a vital election in the United States under the onerous condition of a difference in time ranging from five to eight hours is without a parallel." Of further interest is the fact recorded by Al Laney and Ken Stewart that only one of the newsmen on the *Herald* had even bothered to vote. The election held little interest for them.

The *Herald* continued on its sedate course in 1929, happily celebrating the inauguration of the new American President in March, but mourning the death of Ambassador Myron T. Herrick on March 31—friend of France, friend of the *Herald,* friend of James Gordon Bennet, Jr. Few warning voices were raised about the economic or financial situation in the United States; the *Herald* recorded that some Frenchmen had demonstrated against the new Hawley-Smoot tariff, which 1,000 American economists petitioned

Hoover not to sign. But no one understood what its consequences might be; most forecast continued good times, and with all that money Americans continued to sail across the Atlantic in increasing numbers. The surviving prewar *Mauretania* and *Aquitania* of the Cunard Line and the *France* of the French Line were still favorites. They were joined in the mid-twenties by the *Paris,* and then the all-time favorite, the *Ile-de-France.* In mid-1929 the first of the modern superliners marked German reentry into the field: the *Bremen,* soon to be joined by her sister ship, the *Europa;* both figured largely in the *Herald*'s rotogravure section. That summer the *Bremen* crossed the Atlantic in four days, seventeen hours, forty-two minutes, capturing the blue Riband from the *Mauretania,* which had held it longer than any other ship.*

All of the ships were packed with Americans, and the *Herald*'s ship advertising columns fattened the paper. Travel and resort led the rest of the ads, but luxury goods—perfumes, clothes, jewelry, gloves, furs—followed closely. Tourists who ate breakfast or light lunch at Louis Sherry's on the Rond Point des Champs Elysées might decide to travel through Europe a new way, on a Motorways Pullman Tours bus, equipped with tables, a buffet, separate armchairs, and a toilet, with the driver properly separated out front, limousine-style.

1929 was the year that Sparrow Robertson instituted what became known as the "Death Watch": keeping visiting firemen up all night drinking in various "thirst emporiums" until the time came to drag them to the Gare St. Lazare and pitch them into their compartment on the boat train. It was also the year that Wall Street ended it all. But it took a long time for people to realize what had happened, and in a sense, for the *Herald,* the end of the era came in December 1930, when it moved, somewhat prematurely, into a brand new building at 21, rue de Berri, rather than in October 1929.

---

*Mussolini's Italian Lines got into the game a little too late. The beautiful *Rex*'s maiden voyage was only in 1932, and her sister ship, the *Conte de Savoia,* came even later. But when the *Rex* sailed, Eric Hawkins sailed on her, by invitation of the Italian government.

For one thing, 1930 continued to be a pretty good year for the *Herald,* although the little *Times* folded on December 1, 1929, a month or so after Black Thursday. The effects of the crash were not yet universally felt, the American colony was not yet decimated, and tourists still came to France in sufficient numbers to bring in the advertising the *Herald* lived on. The rotogravure section shrank slightly, but the *Herald* continued to publish its annual *American Guide to Paris* (138 pages and a map in 1930), and sold tickets to Paris theaters at the Information Bureau on the avenue de l'Opéra. Advertisements enticed the buyers to come hear Maurice Chevalier, see Mistinguett's famous legs, or cheer for the beautiful Josephine Baker, who had made such a splash in Paris five years ago dancing with nothing but a string of bananas around her waist, and who was now the established reigning star of the Folies Bergère in an all new and nude review, "Paris Qui Remue." Special travel sections called people to Greece or Hungary. Germany was big: "US Middies and Sailors Conclude Visit to Berlin," or Nuremberg, Wiesbaden, Dresden, or Aachen. Information about resorts, hotels, travel, and shopping could still be supplied by the *New York Herald* Information Office at 11, Unter den Linden, in Berlin. A house ad flaunted the new system of aerial delivery. Planes flew the early edition from Le Bourget to London, Vienna, Munich, Berlin, Amsterdam, The Hague, Rotterdam, Cologne, Le Touquet, and Strasbourg, ensuring rapid delivery to nearby towns.

Henry Ford, leaving New York for Bremen in the summer of 1930, told the *Herald,* "The United States is just beginning to recover from a severe illness." The paper added new features: Will Rogers' brief daily column, cabled directly to the paper, and a column of almost stupefying banality contributed by Calvin Coolidge. A *Herald* editorial urged all Americans who wanted to be informed to read the former President's daily contribution, "a product of deep thought and wide knowledge." A typical column musing on how the automobile, radio, and movies had molded Americans into one nation pointed out that "they are outstanding examples of how commercial activity ministers to the spiritual welfare of the people. Diligence in business has carried us to a higher mental and moral plane." When Coolidge ended his column a year later, the *Herald* congratulated him for giving his fellow citizens "a daily fund of calm, level-headed advice" in the face of a complicated world. And Helen Reid wrote to Hills that the columns had caused "a great deal of comment and contributed substantially to circulation."

On September 5, 1930, "Topics of Wall Street" noted that for the first seven months of the year American automobile production was down a staggering 66.2 percent.

Kenneth Stewart, a copyreader for the Paris *Herald* in 1928 and 1929, recorded his experiences and reflections about the *Herald* in *News Is What We Make It,* and they are more thoughtful than those of most other participants.

> Most likely, if you had asked any newsman coming back from Europe at the end of 1929 what he had seen and heard in Paris, he might have mentioned a few recent political events, but more likely, he would talk about the fine food at the Restaurant Lapérouse or La Reine Pédauque, about the soft glow of sunrise on the Seine, about Bill Tilden or the races at Auteuil, about the saucy songs of Bricktop on the Rue Pigalle, about the paintings in the Louvre . . . the Folies Bergère . . . the Hemingway imitators at the Dingo and the *transition* crowd at the Dome—the list is endless and fruitless. . . .
>
> Our sins were sins of omission, and not so great as those of our superiors. Editorially, the papers we worked for never said anything that might annoy the power-seekers of Europe and frequently said things that gave them aid and comfort. . . .
>
> Our crime, if crime it was, was indifference, nonchalance, and escape from responsibility. . . . We let the play choke off our concern as citizens.

The new building on the rue de Berri was not yet ready in December when the move was made there from the rue du Louvre in time for Laurence Hills to take his annual American trip to report to the Reids. As a result, the gravity system for feeding copy to the composing room below blew hot air upward; electricity was inadequate for the linotype machines; the brand-new presses printed only a gray blur the first night, spurring a frantic race back to the rue du Louvre plant, happily still intact after an all-night drunken party. It took a week to establish that inferior watery ink and not the press was at fault, and the paper was finally able to issue from the home it would have until March 1978.

Only a few months before the *Herald*'s move to the new building, the Fondation des Etats-Unis had opened its doors at the Cité Universitaire as a residence for American students; three months later the American Country Club was inaugurated outside of Paris, at Ozoir-la-Ferrière. In April 1931 the American Legion Building on the rue Pierre Charron was finally completed, though not to be dedicated until October 2. All of these, like the new *Herald* building, were planned in the opulent years, with the expectation that every day in every way, things would get better and better. This was certainly true for the *Herald,* whose profits since 1924 had been sunk into first enlarging the paper, and now into the building at 21, rue de Berri. The timing for all of these buildings could hardly have been worse.

CHAPTER **8**

The Unhappy Thirties

ON NEW YEAR'S DAY 1931 the *Herald* announced that
1931 would inevitably be far better than 1930. Will Rogers
wrote that God had just imposed a little necessary humility on
Americans who thought they had it licked. And so for a while the
paper looked much as it had in the lush years. In October Walter
Lippmann's thoughtful columns began to appear.* The 1931 edition of the *Pocket Guide to Paris* came out as scheduled in early
summer; Fourth of July activities and ceremonies took up a lot of
room, and the *Herald* reported that American Chief of Staff Douglas MacArthur visited with the French Minister of War, a man
whose name would one day become a household word—André
Maginot. On an entirely different level, the *Herald* pictured Charlie
Chaplin visiting with Gandhi in London, and then waving from
the Hotel Crillon balcony to crowds that cheered him like a king.
The Automobile Salon pages featured a large number of American
cars whose names are now enshrined in the history books: Packard,
Studebaker, Reo, Pierce-Arrow, Hupmobile, Auburn, Cord, Franklin, and Willys/Knight. Some of them were reported to feature free-

---

*When the Pulitzers' *World* folded in New York, Lippmann was much in demand. He had
firm offers from, among others, Adolf Ochs to head the *New York Times* Washington
bureau, and a more tempting one, which he took, to do a regular column of political
comment for the *Herald Tribune*. Elizabeth Reid worried about bringing such a well-known
Democrat and former writer for the *New Republic* onto the Republican *Herald Tribune*,
but Helen Reid persuaded her that he was a great catch, and indeed he was: his columns,
while stimulating opposition, also provoked a constant flow of letters in praise both of
Lippmann and of the *Herald Tribune* for printing someone with whom it often differed
editorially.

wheeling for economy, but it didn't do much good—the Depression doomed most of them.

The *Herald* managed to rent out some of the offices in the new building; the *New York Herald Tribune*'s Paris bureau moved in, of course, and so did the Scripps-Howard chain's European bureau. But the paper had trouble filling the building in the first year; it continued to advertise available space on the upper floors (though in 1933, full, it brought in less rent than half full in 1931). Perhaps Jaurett could have done better; he had retired a relatively wealthy man. His successor, Hubert Roemer, who had been at the paper since 1925, acted as both advertising manager and assistant to Hills while Mlle. Renée Brazier, Hills' confidante and secretary, became business manager, a post which she retained until shortly after the *Herald* resumed publication in 1944, after a wartime hiatus. People remember her as a harsh taskmaster—a "holy terror," said one—who kept watch on whether people were working hard enough, and who reported everything to Hills. But the worsening financial condition of the paper might have made anybody seem harsh. Its circulation began to drop; from 39,000 in 1929 it decreased to roughly a third of that within four years. It began to lose money and would continue to all through the thirties. Taxes, mortgage charges, and upkeep on the new building were not met by rental income, and even so, the *Herald* had to reduce its rents drastically to keep the space filled. In October of 1931, as advertising started to decline, the paper began to appear on only eight pages during the week, and features diminished accordingly. On the day of Roosevelt's inauguration in 1933, after consultation with Ogden Reid in New York, Hills also announced discontinuation of the Sunday rotogravure pages (for a saving of $300 a week). There was little job printing to do, so that the large composing room, stereotype, and printing staff were underused, making for heavy overhead costs.

In 1931 Hills had to begin payment on the mortgage and indebtedness incurred in connection with the new building. The result was that an overall loss of $35,000 that year grew to over $64,000

21, Rue de Berri, for fifty years the Paris *Herald*'s home.

in 1932. Hills, taking his own cut, reduced salaries drastically in 1932, and when a second cut was made in New York, Hills worried that a further 10 percent cut in Paris would bring pay down "too low almost for existence." It would be difficult to keep any competent staff at all. Many in the business departments made the equivalent of $15 a week, and New York should realize, he said, "how much overhead and salaries have been held down here even in good times, which naturally accounted in those years for our good profits."

Despite all the economy moves, losses continued to mount, and Hills continued to consider other drastic economies: cutting the size of the paper while raising its price, printing on thinner, cheaper paper, and diminishing margins. He balked, though, when Ogden Reid suggested standardizing it at six pages, instead of maintaining it at eight with an occasional reduction to six. Worst of all, perhaps, was cutting allowable returns from distributors. As he wrote to New York, the policy of distributing 40 to 50 percent more papers than were sold and paid for dated back to James Gordon Bennett, Jr., "who felt that the best promotion of the paper was a very complete newstand coverage of all the places in all the countries in Europe likely to be visited by American or English tourists or advertisers." It was too expensive now, Hills admitted, and he had cut back. He was still printing 21,000 copies a day, but net paid circulation had sunk to less than 10,000 in 1934. He asked the French government for a delay in tax payments, sounded out the French news agency Agence Havas and the *Petit Parisien* on a possible takeover of the *Herald,* and even suggested trying to sell the building, of which everyone had been so proud, and converting the Paris Edition to a smaller, tabloid-size paper.

None of this happened, but the record does show that by the end of 1936 the New York paper had transferred over $265,000 to Paris to keep the Paris Edition going—and would advance a similar sum over the next five years. The journalists may not have been continuously conscious of the details of the situation, as Hills and the office staff were, but they certainly knew about it when periodic reductions in staff and salaries took place: as the local American colony declined, so did local news, and Hills let three local reporters go.

On several occasions in those years of Depression and labor upheaval the paper could not be printed or distributed, and the new assertiveness of labor with government support troubled both New York and Paris. Hills was surprised to learn in a letter from Reid's executive assistant that both Walter Lippmann and Dorothy Thompson were members of the Newspaper Guild. The rest of the letter gives some flavor of the bitterness engendered by New Deal legislation:

> All the Jews in our employ are active in the movement with one or two exceptions . . . we are called upon to meet with a little Jew named Kaufman . . . Under the Wagner Act employees may select anyone they please to negotiate with us . . . there is no reason why they could not select a Negro from Harlem, a Jew from the Bronx and a Chinese from Mott Street. We would be obliged to meet with such a committee and negotiate with it . . . Mayor LaGuardia in New York is a red and is also in sympathy with most any labor union activity.

Hills sympathized. Negotiations in New York were bound to affect those in Paris, where editorial personnel had tried to institute collective bargaining in pursuit of a fixed wage scale and one or two other guild demands. He intended to raise salaries somewhat in 1937, but only on an individual basis. As for the effect of Popular Front laws, "I am constantly having to explain our actions and policies to delegates who are not much more than office boys. In the mechanical departments it is even worse."

The bad times and the move to the new building brought the departure of many good men. Warwick Tompkins wrote to *Time* magazine in 1939: "We left, almost all of us, when the *Herald* quit the drafty but colorful old rooms overlooking Les Halles and moved into splendor and near bankruptcy near the Etoile . . . but I think our records in our chosen fields indicate that the *Herald* was staffed, at one time, anyway, by an able, imaginative and productive crew."

Al Laney, who stayed on as night editor until 1935, remarked that a certain increased drunken irresponsibility made it more difficult to get the paper out. The links with the Bennett past were disappearing, too. In October an obituary appeared for Wilfred D. Bishop, who had spent most of his forty years with the paper picking horses. He was the young man whose salary, many years previously, was so unexpectedly raised by the Commodore when the latter came upon him with everyone else's beer bottles in front of him.

The financial troubles of the early thirties, of course, did not spare the *Herald*'s main remaining competitor, the Paris *Chicago Tribune,* and Jack Hummel, its business manager, approached Hills on several occasions about possibly combining the two papers. In early 1932 Colonel McCormick himself raised the possibility in New York, declaring that without a merger both papers might have to fold. However, Ogden Reid's executive assistant, Wilbur Forrest, confirmed Hills' own view. He told McCormick's representative not to worry: "The *Herald,*" he said, "was deeply rooted in Europe and would remain so after its competitors had faded out." The only solution, therefore, was a sale of the *Chicago Tribune* to the *Herald* at a reasonable price. When rumors cropped up again in Paris in 1933 that New York might be arranging a merger, Forrest wired back, "Purest bunk!"

Yet in early 1933 when Hills calculated that the *Tribune* must be selling fewer than 3,000 copies a day, Jules Frantz began to make some significant improvements in the *Tribune:* he came out with much better-looking body type—a move that worried Hills, who had always considered the *Herald*'s type a great advantage— added increased cabled material, braced up the financial pages, increased resort correspondents, and in general seemed to be spending more on editorial material. "I am afraid it may mean more serious competition," the surprised Hills wrote, convinced as he was that the *Tribune* lost heavily every day, carrying—by his own figures—60 percent less advertising than did the *Herald.*

Frantz, in fact, was really trying to make a go of it so that the Colonel in Chicago wouldn't cave in. His staff was convinced that they had a better, brasher, brighter paper, despite slim financial resources. And Frantz knew he had loyal staffers who enjoyed working there more than men enjoyed the *Herald* under Hills, even though Hummel paid them little. But his early editorial opposition to fascism meant that German and Italian resort advertising dried up, though it was an important source of revenue. And whatever he did, as he put it in later years, "people read the *Tribune* surreptitiously and the *Herald* openly in St. Germain."

The *Chicago Tribune* advertising office in New York, using the slogan "Follow the Trend—It's to the *Tribune*," tried to show that the gap in lineage had been closing slowly; Hills supplied the *Herald Tribune* office in New York with figures that showed another story. Sensing the inevitable, the *Tribune* staff prepared a letter for Hummel to send to the Colonel demonstrating that the bad times had hit the *Herald* harder and that he should either buy the *Herald* or else strike a hard bargain. The letter insisted that the *Tribune* was catching up to the *Herald* in advertising lineage, that the *Herald*'s press run drop from 40,000 in 1929 to 15,000 in early 1934 was worse for it than their own drop from 15,000 to 11,000—and that they were now beginning to pull even. Their losses were less, and the fact that they were printed by the *Petit Journal* meant they were much less burdened by fixed overhead costs. If he would only come and visit and see for himself; if he would agree to advance enough money for them to keep going until mid-1935, then surely he would see that a bargain could be struck in which the *Tribune* would have a controlling voice in any consolidated newspaper.

But Colonel McCormick, as always, acted on his own. He came to New York and asked Helen Reid to sell him the Paris *Herald.*

She refused and asked him instead to sell her the Paris *Tribune*. He agreed. After brief negotiations the Colonel signed the *Tribune* Paris Edition's death sentence on October 26, 1934. The price was $50,000. *Tribune* staffers received a required one-month notice, which made it hard for Waverley Root and Frantz to get the staff to continue putting out the paper until its scheduled end on December 1, and led Hills to worry about whether the assets he was to take over then would still be intact. (In fact, Root wrote later, fires in newsroom wastebaskets became endemic in that last month, and sometimes he and Frantz seemed to be the only ones working in the newsroom.) The Colonel didn't bother much about severance pay, and the niggardly Hummel didn't either. As part of the agreement Hummel was supposed to work for the *Herald* for a year, but before the takeover he went on an extended spree, and was not even available to sign the necessary legal documents; McCormick had to send over someone else.

Only one or two provisions of the sale had any visible effect. The major one was that for nine months, dating from December 1, 1934, the newspaper would bear a masthead designation "*The New York Herald* with *The Chicago Tribune*." To Hills' delight, it would then finally become *The New York Herald Tribune*, European Edition (and continue under that title until 1966). Sales, advertising, and subscriptions increased only very slightly. There were only a few hundred *Tribune* subscribers, and many of the advertising contracts were verbal agreements. But Hills figured he would be able to raise advertising rates 10 or 15 percent. Letters poured in after the announcement, asking the *Herald* to continue the *Chicago Tribune*'s comic strips—"Orphan Annie," "The Gumps," "Dick Tracy," and "Moon Mullin"—and Hills did run "The Gumps" and "Moon Mullins" for a short time.

Hills had a very high opinion of Jules Frantz, which he communicated to the Reids. "Under Frantz," he wrote, "the *Chicago Tribune* was improved greatly in an editorial sense, and had it not been for a rotten business department, it would have been quite a formidable business competitor." He invited Frantz to become Eric Hawkins' Assistant managing editor, but Frantz declined and took a position with the *Herald Tribune* in New York, even though a slot awaited him in Chicago.*

As a result of the agreement, however, several able people did come to the *Herald,* among them the cultivated literary editor Robert Sage, who would come back to the paper after World War II. It was a sad event for all concerned, though. The *Tribune* received a small flood of letters of protest, and most *Herald* people felt there was little to celebrate. Then, to Hills' annoyance, the death throes were prolonged. Under the leadership of Waverley Root and May Birkhead, a dozen *Tribune* feature writers and reporters based in Paris, convinced of the loyalty of many *Tribune* readers and conscious of the popularity of many of its features, created a weekly they called the *Paris Tribune.* Hills protested vigorously to *Chicago Tribune* lawyers that their paper used type and subscription lists and appropriated a title all of which belonged to the *Herald,* and that it contained advertisements from advertisers to whom he had promised exclusivity in order to obtain higher rates. The new paper lasted only two months, until the end of January—during which time, to Root's amusement, Hills had to rescind the advertising rate rises—but it seems to have been fun while it lasted.

The demise of the Paris *Chicago Tribune* had one other subsequent unforeseen effect: Hills complained a year or so later when Al Laney left that the floating pool of experienced newsmen he had always been able to depend upon to fill a gap in an emergency simply dried up. After 1935 it was harder and harder to get good men.

---

*Much later, after World War II, Frantz ran into Colonel McCormick at the Overseas Press Club, in New York. He greeted him, reminding McCormick that he had been the last Managing Editor of the Paris *Chicago Tribune.* But the Colonel turned his back and walked away. Frantz had committed lèse-majesté in refusing a job on the *Tribune* in Chicago to take one on the *Herald Tribune* in New York.

To many Americans the *New York Herald Tribune* was a presence to be taken for granted, and its European Edition a familiar and comfortable fixture when they were in Europe. It seemed ubiquitous: they could still find it on central news stands in any major European city. Few of them could have known how low its circulation had sunk, how disastrous was its financial situation, nor that New York kept it afloat to the tune of over half a million 1930s dollars. More of them, however, were aware of its peculiar political stance in those years, for a number of writers called it to broad public attention, and it ultimately led to a clash with embarrassed New York offices, as well as a struggle with the great staff of *New York Herald Tribune* foreign correspondents.

Like its New York parent, the European Edition was unabashedly Republican. In 1932 it agreed editorially with Calvin Coolidge that there should be no change in time of crisis: to elect Roosevelt rather than Hoover would be a "disaster." The new columnist, Lippmann, disagreed; he would vote for Roosevelt, although he was critical of both parties. In Paris, straw votes were inconclusive. At Harry's New York Bar the predominantly male vote was 288 for Roosevelt to 158 for Hoover; at the American Women's Club, a landslide for Hoover. An American woman from Long Island drove a car bearing a banner, "Every Woman in America is for Hoover," to Paris from the boat on which she had just arrived. A Californian in a bar offered to bet 40,000 francs on Hoover.

Despite the diminution of the American colony, the *Herald* again made elaborate preparations for extra editions, for broadcast reports over the Poste Parisien radio station, and for distribution of results to the all-night election parties. It published four special editions, the last one at 11:00 A.M., with, of course, the banner news of Roosevelt's sweep. Wilbur Forrest, from New York, wrote Hills that he thought the election extras a "superb piece of business not only from the news point of view but typographically as well."

In the event, announcing a "Tidal Wave for Change," the front page box reprinted an editorial from the home newspaper calling the election result "a gross injustice to an able President." Nevertheless, the paper bragged a bit about its election coverage and reported that most Americans in Paris seemed pleased by the result. Editorially it lectured Roosevelt to rise above party and avoid "cringing" and "vacillation."

All this could be expected. It seems a part of bearing up and seeing things through in tough times. What was perhaps a bit more surprising was a pair of editorials that appeared on May 22 and October 27, 1932, the tenth anniversary of Benito Mussolini's seizure of power in Italy. The first, headed "Fascism for America," brings us face to face with the most unhappy chapter in the history of the *Herald,* and its major characteristic in the 1930s. Newspaper critic George Seldes, in his *Lords of the Press,* later used the editorial to describe the *Herald*—unfairly—as a paper that openly espoused Fascism for the United States.

It began by describing Fascism in a particular way:

> The social phenomenon known today as Fascism has existed in many countries, in many centuries and under many leaders. Spontaneously, each race has originated a fascism to meet its crisis of the moment. Whatever its special characteristic or name, it has always consisted essentially of a mobilization of moral force. The youth of Japan, fomenting a return to the discipline of their ancestors and the suppression of party government, calls itself fascist. The youth of Germany, ardent to reconstruct the pre-war ascendance and self-confidence of their race, calls itself fascist. The youth of Italy, banded to stem Communism among the workers and sluggishness and ineptitude in the public services, call themselves fascist. . . .
>
> Fascism is the moral equivalent of war. It is not unlike a revival of religion. It does not seek to set up a new form of government, but it seeks to instill a new vivacity and sincerity in those who already govern. It seizes upon the human elements which exist . . . shakes them wide awake, drills and galvanizes them . . . it is a hypodermic injection which will sting flabby muscles until they snap into action . . . to see that those upon whom these duties normally devolve do their work superlatively well.

> The hour has struck for a fascist party to be born in the United States. In the face of the most critical financial situation in the history of the country, Washington presents the amazing spectacle of more special groups seeking to get their fingers in the national treasury than ever before . . . wherever patronage is distributed and crime protected, there is the rumble of indignation among house-holders, the anger and disgust of taxpayers, which presage the gathering of moral forces into overt movement.
>
> Someone will give the signal. It may be a mechanic, coming out of his engineroom, wiping his hands upon oily waste, in despair at the insecurity of his home; it may be a veteran teacher—like Peter the Hermit preaching a crusade. . . . It may be the clean youth and imagination of a Charles Lindbergh. . . . It may be the sagacity and experience of a Henry Ford. . . . In every part of the country men are waiting for the call, and when it is heard, there will be a roar of assent from a million throats.   The elements are assembled for the formation of this kind of fascism in the United States, composed of householders, heads of families and taxpayers. The stage is set.

Whoever the author of this editorial may have been, he had in mind one kind of Fascism, and there were, in the final analysis, many; the tragedy of the idealists who began with this kind of idea was that they ended up with something quite different. And in one sense, of course, he was right. Millions of people in the United States *were* ready to endorse this kind of idea.

The reader might more charitably pass it off as a prediction rather than a call for Fascism unless he had also read the editorial on the tenth anniversary of Benito Mussolini's seizure of power in Italy. Headed "Fascism's Decade," it was an unabashed paean of praise to Mussolini. It described the jubilant demonstrations, the opening of new highways and a great sports center, all to celebrate what it called a "decade of solid achievement."

The editorial went on to characterize the chaos that existed in Italy when Mussolini took office.

> With courage and restraint Mussolini entered this arena. He was not afraid to dare. He stood forth as the type of citizen who is willing

to assume personal responsibility. . . . In his person he became both the spokesman and the banner of the masses. The material accomplishments of Fascism have justified his course. With the merciful ruthlessness of a surgeon he pacified, he unified, the country. . . . Italians can point to a fifty percent larger grain harvest, an unemployment rate of three percent . . . to vast marshes drained and under tillage, to new-born merchant marine and civilian aviation, to scores of new schools and municipal water plants, and to the healing of the breach between the state and the Vatican.

Mussolini never fails to strike straight to the imagination of the common man . . . he knows that what men do will depend upon what they feel, upon what they believe in, upon what stands shining in their inner sight. . . .

. . . The proof of the efficacy of his ideal?

The tenth anniversary of the entry of Fascism into power finds Italy the most stable government of Europe, and Benito Mussolini the most firmly-entrenched ruler of the western world.

All of this is perhaps more startling in retrospect. Many Western leaders of the time admired Mussolini and praised his achievements. The Radical-Socialist Prime Minister of France, Edouard Herriot, sent the Italian leader warm congratulations, and the *Herald* endorsed them in another editorial. In a period when Western democracy seemed to falter in its ability to deal with crisis, people looked to other models. It was the pre–Popular Front time when Communist parties, at the behest of the Russian-dominated Comintern, took the line that not Fascism but socialism and socialist democracy was the real enemy. The older fear of Bolshevik Russia was reinforced as a result, and Mussolini's Fascism, harsh as it was, held its appeal.

But the *Herald*'s attitude persisted in the face of the events of the 1930s, manifesting itself in a continued optimism about the intentions of both Mussolini and Hitler, a reluctance to criticize internal developments in Nazi Germany and Fascist Italy, formal neutrality but great sympathy with respect to Francisco Franco in Spain, and full support for revision of the Versailles settlement in favor of Germany. As a result, Laurence Hills was charged with either being a Fascist or else of being so fearful of losing the large volume of resort advertising from Italy and Germany that he steered the paper into a pro-Fascist direction.

Laurence Hills was a difficult man, and this colored everyone's perception of him. He was easily angered and erratic, prone to hasty decisions and to a measure of hysteria. In the plush years of the 1920s newsmen mocked Hills for trying to emulate James Gordon Bennett. In the 1930s, in addition, he suffered under the pressure of trying to run a paper that was consistently losing money. No one, says one former correspondent, likes a director of a paper that's losing money. In addition the *Herald* depended in part on foreign circulation—though perhaps not to the extent that it had under Bennett—and it was edited in the context of a France that was torn between left and right, where people were ready to attack his paper on short notice. Franco-American relations were again at a low as a consequence of the war debt issue. The Herriot government fell in 1932 when it insisted on resuming payment, with such resultant bitterness on both sides that Hills was asked on a periodic visit to the United States whether it was safe for him to return to France.* In fact, pressures came from everywhere: Ambassador Jesse Isidor Straus not only disliked the paper's policy, but was so concerned about its effect on European opinion that he wanted all items about the embassy or the foreign service submitted to him first along with all editorials on any matter that concerned him. It all made Hills, as one former *Herald* man said, "unreasonable and unpredictable."

In 1938 Hills developed cancer and was out of the office for much of the year, and remained a sick man until his death in 1941.

---

*The *Herald* printed a New York editorial about Herriot's courageous stand and fall on the front page. It condemned the French legislature: "A more costly or destructive saving surely never was undertaken by anyone." A day or so later it printed a report that Senator Kenneth McKellar had suggested in the Congress that visitors from defaulting nations be charged $5,000 for visas to enter the United States. In fairness to the Senate, the suggestion caused considerable hilarity. Next year the French Film Institute tried to get a ban on American films; the *Herald* decried French accusations that America had torpedoed the London Monetary Conference. One bright spot stood out, probable resumption of French wine exports to America with the end of Prohibition!

The illness appears to have changed him: one bureau man who said that Hills could on occasion be mean declared that he became quieter and more reflective, more thoughtful about people. It was in this mood that in July of 1939, sensing perhaps the end of his world, he sat in the golden Paris sunlight on the terrace of the Select, the brasserie at the corner of the rue de Berri and the Champs Elysées, and talked to his former night editor, Al Laney, back from New York for an annual Paris visit. Hills spoke, wrote Laney, of their endless fights in the old days. "He was willing, even happy now, to admit that he had been wrong most of the time. . . . Just recently, he said, he had come to realize that there were men who had loved his paper and the realization had startled him. He wished it were possible now to make his peace with all of them. Without exception, he said, they had not liked him. He said it sadly, without rancor."

Men on the paper found ways to get around Hills. In the late 1920s newsmen developed a file of prominent members of the American community who could be counted upon at a moment's notice to call Hills up and tell him what a fine job had been done in the previous day's paper. He apparently never realized that this became a standard way of putting things in that he didn't like and then pacifying him.

Whatever else one may say, the tone and orientation of the paper reflected Hills' personal views. Fundamental change had become necessary in Western society; "technocracy" fascinated him; and as he once wrote to Wilbur Forrest at the New York paper, "Editorially, we seem to dislike Fascism or Hitlerism as much as we dislike Communism," but when it came to the Spanish Civil War, "personally, my sympathies cannot help but run on the rebel [Franco] side."

New York columnist Leonard Lyons charged in his *New York Post* column on September 2, 1937, "The editorial staff of the Paris *Herald Tribune* is somewhat disturbed these days. Before the paper goes to press each night proofs of the Spanish revolution stories are sent to a member of the Ogden Reid family who resides at the

Hotel George V. . . There the proofs are checked over carefully
and changes made. 'Loyalist troops' is altered to 'Reds,' 'Bolsheviks,' or 'Anarchists' . . . and 'Rebel army' always is changed to
'Patriots.' "

Hills called the charge "the limit of absurdity," though he had,
in fact, told the editorial boys to use "red" and "whites" to distinguish the sides, and as one *Herald Tribune* foreign correspondent
recalls, almost everything that came from Spain came from the
United Press, whose bureau chief had such a strong pro-Franco
bias that the material didn't need much doctoring.

An editorial of October 30, 1938, reflected Hills' views: "The
social policies of the totalitarian countries cannot be dismissed as
valueless on the ground that they rest on a denial of freedom. The
fact which cannot be denied and which is of great political significance is that they make for greater happiness and contentment
among the masses."

In April 1939, now a sick man, Hills spent several weeks in New
York. For the first time, it appears, he came under fire at home. He
was told to stop printing political editorials written in Paris and
use ones sent from the United States. He wrote to Hawkins:

> I do not believe that either Hitler or Mussolini are out to bring
> about a general war and certainly the democracies, I do not believe,
> want it either.
>
> Over here the anti-Fascist and anti-Nazi feeling prevails in every
> part of the country, and an editorial that says even a good word for
> something constructive done in Italy, for example, immediately
> brings a roar from a large element of the population.
>
> I find over here . . . there is a feeling that we have become a Fascist
> newspaper. Of course we have not.

But Hawkins, who tends to explain it all away in terms of the
exposed position of the newspaper, writes, "Like others more
prominent than he in those days, including Winston Churchill,
Hills was impressed by some of Mussolini's innovations in Italy,
such as making the trains run on time. He also had a blind spot

with respect to Hitler and National Socialism." Hawkins himself was happy with the decision that editorials would have to come from New York, but one has the impression that this is because it would tend to keep the paper out of trouble. He devotes little space in his memoirs to the role of the paper in the midst of political turmoil, other than to admit that as a guest of France and as a generally conservative newspaper, the *Herald,* in its editorial pages, had "more of a neutralist tinge than anything else." But he stoutly defends the news columns, "as penetrating and as anti-Nazi or anti-Fascist as might be expected from a team of correspondents that included Joseph Barnes . . . Walter Kerr . . . Ralph Barnes and Frank Kelley . . . John Elliott . . . James [Don] Minifie . . . and Sonia Tomara." But Hawkins' account neglects the fact that the correspondents and Hills became bitter opponents.

Until 1935 the New York newspaper's European dispatches were funneled through London, because of cheaper cable services. That year a reorganization of the European correspondents took place, and the center of operations was transferred to Paris, where the paper could use Press Wireless, a service set up by a newspaper consortium in 1929, which the *Herald Tribune* joined in 1933. The London office resisted the change, disputing Hills' insistence that working from Paris would be cheaper and faster. Eventually New York came around, and foreign correspondent John Elliott (who had left the European Edition in disgust in the 1920s) was assigned to Paris, and put in charge of the European correspondents. In 1937, however, the New York newspaper embarked on a radical course both to distinguish itself from the *New York Times* (and establish what Wilbur Forrest called "journalistic individuality") and to accommodate to the impact of the 1937 recession, which forced the paper to make drastic economies. It moved to larger type with briefer stories, closer editing, fewer pages, and shorter routine treatment of news. Letters to Hills in Paris explained that the *Times'* "long-windedness" was no longer suited to the brisk tempo of the modern world, and would prove "an increasing embarrassment." Nine out of ten readers, declared the *Herald Tribune* managing editor, were not interested in items of record. There was a "change in appetite from newspapers of record to newspapers of live news."*

In line with these changes came restrictions on the foreign correspondents. As Laurence Hills put it, "A good deal of money is being spent unnecessarily. There is a slowly growing habit of not considering beforehand whether the results of trips and expenses are likely to justify the expenditure." There had to be "elimination and condensation of the non-essential in the new form of stories." The foreign correspondents were "used to writing well-rounded out literary stories"; they all filed too many: "long, discursive politically interpretative stories." And Hills, to carry out the tightening up process, was made director of the European News Service of the *Herald Tribune* in John Elliott's place.

From all over Europe the correspondents gathered to protest the move. Don Minifie, from Rome, drafted a general memorandum for purposes of discussion. All the correspondents accepted the unfortunate necessity of drastic economies, he wrote, and associated themselves with "the Home Office's efforts to effect these in the manner which will be the least damaging to the foreign service in view of the high repute which this service has attained in international journalistic circles and the necessity of maintaining the strategic position of the *New York Herald Tribune*." But this should be done in such a way as to preserve to the extent possible the autonomy and freedom of movement of correspondents within their own territories, and—in particular—a correspondent "should under no circumstances be asked to color or bias his dispatches. . . . This is particularly essential for correspondents in totalitarian countries, whose task is already difficult and dangerous, and could only be worsened by injudicious interference." The

---

*Many years later John Elliott dated the beginning of the *New York Herald Tribune*'s decline relative to the *New York Times* back to this decision, with its corollary that the foreign correspondents should file less and especially take care not to duplicate the routine foreign reporting done by the news agencies. A poll among Washington correspondents in 1938 gave the *New York Times* "a great majority of votes as the most accurate and reliable newspaper."

memo went on to deplore the removal of John Elliott, whose "supercession without warning and with no more than a passing phrase cuts at the roots of loyalty and morale throughout the service. . . . If this is the reward that unremitting work, constant care and unswerving loyalty can aspire to, then these virtues are wasted on the *Herald Tribune*."

The correspondents decided not to send a joint manifesto to New York at the time, waiting to see how economies would be applied, but they did draft a joint aide-mémoire which they all signed on December 29, 1937—Ralph and Joseph Barnes, Don Minifie, Walter B. Kerr, and John Elliott. It was strongly worded, and one of the correspondents appended a note to his copy: it reflected "their profound distrust of Laurence Hills, the newly appointed Director of the European News Service. It was galling to all of us to have this notorious pro-Fascist placed over us."

Time magazine published a story in 1939 asserting that Hills kept an autographed picture of Mussolini in his office. Old *Herald Tribune* men do not recall seeing it there. But it may have been a temporary exhibit as a result of an interview Hills had with the Duce in May 1938. Mussolini turned on all his charm, and the communiqué issued by his press office, Hills wrote, "I thought was quite flattering to our own newspapers." He was, it seems, rather easily wooed.

In early August Hamilton Fish Armstrong, editor of *Foreign Affairs,* returned from a European trip and had lunch with his old, close friend, Walter Lippmann, now—with Dorothy Thompson— the most influential columnist on the *Herald Tribune*. Armstrong told him, "The Paris *Trib* is so pro-fascist it would make you sick. You know, it has suppressed columns by you and Dorothy Thompson critical of Hitler and Mussolini."* But it was not Hills who had suppressed them. He was ill and out of the office, and advertising director Hubert Roemer had acted in his stead. Roemer sought approval from Wilbur Forrest in New York: "I have had

---

*Quoted in Ronald Steel, *Walter Lippmann and the American Century,* p. 351

to hold several of [Lippmann's columns] out of the paper here because I do not think that we can snap at the hands that are helping lift us out of the red, and I know that Hills agrees with me in doing so." To which Forrest replied, "You were dead right in keeping Lippmann's more pessimistic pieces out of European circulation." The Dorothy Thompson column, he wrote, "would probably result in barring the *Herald* from Germany and perhaps Italy."

On July 28 Lippmann had a piece he particularly wanted in the paper that Roemer refused to print, "following general policies which Mr. Hills laid down, as well as my own judgement." Lippmann wanted the reasoning in writing, and Roemer obliged. He explained that the paper tried to keep its readers informed through the regular news dispatches that it published.

> But we cannot take the definite risk of antagonizing other nations or in frightening tourists by presuming to tell the former the faults of their regime or the latter by explaining to them through our columns the dangers of an immediate armed conflict over here . . .
>
> I know, and I am sure that you do too, that some of the countries on the continent do not distinguish between the news columns of a newspaper including signed articles such as yours, and the policy of the newspaper itself. . . .
>
> . . . This newspaper's precarious financial position does depend both on tourist readers, on advertisers who want to reach these tourists, as well as on the friendly goodwill or at least on the friendly tolerance of France and its European neighbors. It is very difficult for us to allow ourselves to place the paper in the position of a "political" newspaper.

And from New York, Forrest cabled his approval: "Reid and I agree Hills policy must prevail publication Lippmann articles stop your letter outlining policy excellent."*

* That very month a group of distinguished economists and political commentators including Friedrich Von Hayek, Ludwig von Mises, Raymond Aron, and Jacques Rueff gathered in Paris for a Walter Lippmann Colloquium on the prospects for liberal democracy, and the French government made Lippmann a Knight of the Legion of Honor. See Ronald Steel, *Walter Lippmann and the American Century*, p. 368.

Laurence Hills set the editorial tone, but he would go home at six o'clock at night and Eric Hawkins would be there to put out the paper. It is hard, though, to see anything in the little managing editor's makeup that would have much influence on the newspaper's general editorial stance. He was an able technician and he took orders from Hills. George Seldes attacked him after the war as a supporter of Fascists; friends came to his defense to deny it. Seldes also wrote that Hawkins tolerated resort advertising from Nazi Germany, "swastikas and all." Hawkins wrote a rebuttal in his memoirs, fifteen years later: "The swastika was the German national emblem at the time; the United States maintained normal diplomatic relations with Berlin, and for the *Herald* to refuse advertising that displayed a swastika would hardly have been diplomatic. Furthermore, looking back through the files of these years, I have yet to find any swastikas."

The answer is deliberately misleading: there are plenty of prominent swastikas to be found in the German advertising in the *Herald* of the thirties; the classified listing of state theaters was *always* headed by a swastika-bearing eagle. Even now, it is something of a shock to see the Nazi symbol there.

Many of the editorials of those years were written by a man named Vincent Bugeja, a cultivated and many-talented Maltese known affectionately to the rest of the staff as "Booj," and the subject of countless amusing stories. Bugeja came to the *Herald* in 1920, and would stay almost as long as Eric Hawkins—until 1953. He was a graduate of the University of Malta who became a Jesuit, then resigned to fight the church after Pope Pius X's encyclical against modernism, *Pascendi,* of 1907. Three years under Bertrand Russell at Cambridge earned him a degree in mathematics. After spending the war years in Malta he became chief theoretician for the new Maltese Labor party, was made honorary president for life, and while working for the *Herald* continued to edit a Maltese labor journal and to bother the British governor of Malta.

Bugeja could and did write on almost anything: relativity, mathematics, astronomy, photography, gastronomy, history, or eco-

The newsroom in the Rue de Berri, Vincent Bugeja on the left.

nomics. He wrote well, spoke Arabic, French, Italian, and English, and had a working knowledge of other European languages. When preparations were being made for the 1928 election extra it was Bugeja who defined the election issues; to his surprise he found that none of the journalists except for Barnes had ever voted. The *Herald*'s Christmas magazines featured articles by Vincent J. Bugeja and B. J. Vincent—an obvious pseudonym. He was a member of a nearby nudist camp and another near- nudist camp on a lovely island on the Seine, to which he frequently took staff members.

Bugeja also supported Hills in his views about Mussolini and Hitler. Hawkins writes that Bugeja "felt the Nazis were not bent on war but rather engaged in promoting a new and improved form of Socialism"; *Time* magazine in 1939 wrote that Bugeja called himself a "Communist-Fascist." His were apparently the editorials that were stopped by New York command in April 1939, although no one objected to his being rehired after the war when he turned up in Paris again after four years in hiding.

When Eric Sevareid came to the *Herald* in late 1937, the day city editor was a man named B. J. Kospoth, who had come over from the Paris *Chicago Tribune,* where he wrote art criticism and was viewed as a quiet, self-effacing man, the kind one "could know a great deal about without really knowing anything about him at all," wrote a friend. Sevareid, however, wrote of him that "he was a complete misanthrope who loved but three things—his riding horse, the legend of Napoleon, and Adolf Hitler. When we were alone in the city room, he ceased all pretense of work and strode about, flinging indignant oratory in my direction on the super-human qualities of Der Führer." According to Sevareid, he ended up in a German concentration camp, although someone later received a letter from him as an officer in the German navy.

But the paper also had Sevareid who, as he admits, was largely given his head to write what he pleased, and who conducted a campaign in the *Herald* on behalf of the battered remnants of the American volunteers who had fought Franco in Spain and now desperately needed help in trying to make their way back to the United States.* Another young *Herald* writer, Ring Lardner's son Jim, left the paper in 1937 to fight for the Loyalists in Spain, saying to the newsroom crowd (according to Sevareid), "All you guys will have to meet this thing somewhere pretty soon. I just decided I'd like to meet it in Spain." He was apparently the last of the American volunteers to die in battle, the day before they were withdrawn from the front lines. In other words, there were anti-Fascists aplenty on the staff. But the top levels could hardly be called that.

For its predominantly conservative clientele the *Herald* displayed a clear editorial attitude. In essence, the argument laid out across the years was fairly simple. Western civilization was going through a three-fold crisis, compounded of the threat of Bolshevism, the

---

* To Hills' credit, he recognized Sevareid's merit, as "an all-round excellent newspaperman" who would do as good a job in foreign service as Frank Kelley and Ralph Barnes, who had also started on the Paris paper.

unfairness of the Versailles "diktat," and the weakness of Western democratic society in meeting new, complex problems. The Fascist states stood fast against Bolshevism and demanded a legitimate rectification of the Versailles settlement. They might threaten military might, but it was consistently a mere prelude to diplomatic negotiations which, piece by piece, dismantled the structure of Versailles, thereby restoring a much greater degree of justice and stability. They might not be models for the democratic states, which should, in the final analysis, probably never abandon democracy, yet they provided a legitimate answer to the crisis of the Western soul, and their dose of authority might be just what was needed.

On March 5, 1933, Roosevelt's inauguration stirred the American colony, and the broadcast inaugural speech heard at all the familiar gathering places received much favorable comment. The next day brought two banner headlines: one on the bank holiday in the United States and the other on Adolf Hitler's electoral victory. "Hitler tonight," wrote the *Herald,* "stands as Germany's man of destiny as was France's other Little Corporal somewhat more than a century ago."

The next few days brought a typical *Herald* mix. The social pages noted, "Wiesbaden, Heartened by Hitler's Accession, To Increase Program," while another column read, "Munich Tearoom Chosen by Hitler as Favorite Spot," and extolled the virtues of Mrs. Von Siebert's Carlton Teestube, close to the Brown House, where Hitler and his staff frequently refreshed themselves. "No one should fail to take tea with Mrs. von S." On March 14, however, on page 3, a story on refugees streaming into France from Germany—principally Jews, Socialists, and Communists—reported that border guards had been strengthened to keep out undesirables.

An editorial—undoubtedly written by Bugeja—mused over a problem which had been pondered since Roman times: when a people choose a dictator, isn't that their choice? It was a matter of national character, and abstract ideals of democracy were not applicable. Contrary to Hitler's predictions in a United Press interview, however, the *Herald* predicted that parliamentary government would not disappear in the United Kingdom or the United States.*

Hitler's introduction of the Enabling Act received equal treatment with the introduction of 3.2—low alcohol—beer in the United States; but the German plebiscite of November 12, 1933, confirming Hitler's dissolution of German democracy provoked an editorial a few days later that foreshadowed things to come. "No amount of explaining away," the editorial said, "can detract from the impressiveness of the electoral referendum in Germany last Sunday." Yet on December 11, on page 5, there was a review of a book by Leland Stowe, still the Paris correspondent of the *New York Herald Tribune: Nazi Germany Means War*. In a sense the battle between *Herald Tribune* correspondents and the management of the Paris *Herald* was already joined.

The year 1934 was a pretty terrible one for optimists, and for most everyone else. Austria was in an uproar over the assassination of Chancellor Dollfuss, and Fascism seemed to have claimed another victim; having dissolved political parties, Hitler now crushed the trade unions and in the Night of the Long Knives rid himself of leftist opposition among the storm troopers;† the assassination of Kirov in the Soviet Union was to set off the next round of the Great Purges; democracy virtually disappeared in the few places it still had a toehold in Eastern Europe. Henry Stimson warned that the United States would inevitably be drawn into the next war, which would be worldwide. In France the Stavisky scandal exploded into rioting and shooting in the place de la Concorde, where leftists clashed with the varied right-wing paramilitary groups

---

*Hills noted unhappily that the "troubles" in Germany had temporarily destroyed advertising from there. He was optimistic, though, that it would soon resume.
†The killing of brownshirt leaders occasioned an editorial that must have been written by Bugeja. It spoke of events "reminiscent of some of the bloodiest pages of Gibbon's *Decline and Fall*; nothing was wanting to complete the parallel with the days of Nero, Commodus, and Heliogabalus: a praetorian guard plotting the downfall of the deified Emperor; the leader himself scotching the plot with his loyal cohorts; the slaying of the plotters and the offer of the poison phial to the conspirators; the arrests and the stabbings among orgies of base pleasure."

spawned by the Depression. For the *Herald* this meant the enduring legend of William Shirer covering events from the balcony of the Hotel Crillon when the shooting began, flattening himself on the balcony as bullets splattered over him, and finding a maid shot through the head when he got up again. Two other reporters were bruised in police charges, mobs surged by the *Herald* building— whose lights Hills kept off so that it wouldn't be attacked. "I have never seen reporters run greater risks or do better work than our men here in the last few days, and I thought you would like to know it," he wrote to Ogden Reid.

It is significant of the delicate position the *Herald* occupied in France that it happened to print a profile of the new Minister of the Interior, Eugene Frot, whose first act on assuming office was to fire Paris Prefect of Police Jean Chiappe for having been too soft with right-wing rioters. It was Frot who ordered the firing on the mob, and the *Herald* piece unfortunately referred to him as "the strong man for whom large segments of the public have long been clamoring." A day or so later perfume manufacturer Francois Coty's right-wing group, Solidarité Française, tried to attack the *Herald* building, but the forewarned police kept them off, and Hawkins met with their leaders to make peace.* *Time* magazine subsequently wrote of Hawkins that he was "adept at suppressing what the French wouldn't like," and he himself wrote that he always tried to emulate Bennett's policy of considering the paper to be a guest of the French. "The result was that I was never caned or horse-whipped by angry Frenchmen for real or imagined affronts." And resulting commentary on French politics was very, very bland.

There was, for a short while, some dim, temporary glimmer of light on the international scene. Although 1935 witnessed the rein-stitution of conscription in Germany and then the passage of the Nuremberg racial laws,† the French managed to mend some fences

---

*Ironically, it was Coty who had bought Bennett's Villa Namouna after the Commodore's death. As of this writing, in 1986, the building is once more up for sale.

†Ralph Barnes' reporting of the Nuremberg party rally and party congress produced a single-column front-page story about the Reichstag's new anti-Jewish laws, headlined "Reich Adopts Swastika Flag, Outlaws Jews," but an editorial a day later only commented on how masses reacted at such rallies, observing that "it was impossible not to be impressed."

on the diplomatic front with mutual assistance treaties with Russia—only recently come out of diplomatic isolation when Stalin saw the bankruptcy of the previous Comintern line—and with Czechoslovakia. Even more important appeared to be the Stresa accords that took advantage of Mussolini's interest in limiting resurgent Nazi power by creating a common Franco-Italian diplomatic front against Hitler. In the meantime Britain, in the naval accord with Nazi Germany, had accepted some increase in German naval power. For a short while it seemed that a new balance had been established, matching Nazi Germany's growing power and assertiveness. But the whole possibility of a new structure along these lines broke down when Mussolini proceeded to put into effect his long-cherished plans to create a new empire by attacking Ethiopia in early October.

The *Herald*'s pages quickly filled with war news and reports of diplomatic activity. It had long berated the League of Nations for proposals offering the Duce so little "that he can label them derisory." On October 3 the lead head proclaimed, "Invasion Starts as Duce Demands 'Justice', " and lower down, "Mussolini in Tears, Asks British and French Support," while "Negus Notifies League Italians Have Crossed Frontier."

Its editorial stance quickly became clear. As the British pressed for sanctions in the League and the French, bemused by Stresa, hesitated, the *Herald* asked, "Is Ethiopia a Nation?" An aggression "never envisaged by those who framed the covenant . . . should not be permitted to light a powdertrain across the Mediterranean and blow European civilization to pieces." By October 8 when the League Council declared Italy an aggressor, the *Herald* complained almost angrily that a "so-called nation in the interior of Africa with only the semblance of an administrative government" and an "army made up of white-robed warriors led by chiefs like Sitting Bulls . . . must be regarded as a belligerent nation," and thus be the cause of an American President's having to issue a neutrality proclamation under the recently enacted Neutrality Laws. "Aggression against whom?" it asked, recalling other disputes before the League that had failed to call forth sanctions. It blamed Great

Britain for the vote. "Why must Europe and the world be asked to face the tragic consequences of a strict application of Article 16 [the League Covenant's collective security measures] in this instance?"

In early 1936, with France paralyzed by the social disorder that preceded and followed the election of the Popular Front, while Russia was preoccupied by the purges that took the lives of Old Bolsheviks Zinoviev and Kamenev, Hitler marched into the demilitarized Rhineland, repudiating the Locarno accords as he did so. Again the conflict between correspondents and the paper was clear. Ralph Barnes wrote from Berlin, "The delicate European peace structure was shaken to its foundation today." But the *Herald*, calling for calm, expressed only the view that Hitler should have used the arbitration clause of the Locarno Treaty, declaring that "passions aroused may work havoc with reflection." The loud calls of small Central European countries for sanctions, the stern tone taken by the French press, Winston Churchill's declaration that the League must uphold France or be a farce, all called forth an editorial to the effect that France lost nothing and even gained by remilitarization of the Rhineland, since the action redressed a German grievance and since France received a solemn pledge from Hitler for a twenty-five-year peace pact! The pledge must be taken as sincere for the simple reason that Hitler, like three million French war veterans who want no more war, was a veteran, too. A second editorial a day or so later argued that condemnation of Germany was ill-founded since there had been no discussion of Germany's grievances—especially over the Franco-Soviet pact—just as there had been no discussion of Italy's grievances before the ill-considered condemnation and vote of sanctions by the League.

Those ineffective sanctions came to an end that August, the same month that brought Franco's rising against the Spanish Republic. In September the European powers created that ill-fated farce, the Non intervention Committee, while the United States hastily amended the previous year's Neutrality Act to apply to civil conflict, too. By November, with Franco stopped before Madrid, it became certain that the Spanish Civil War would be a lengthy one; in that same month Japan and Germany joined in the Anti-Comintern Pact, which Italy would sign one year later. In 1937 Japan's invasion of China took on full force; the rape of Nanking in December, designed to frighten the Chinese into submission, revealed an unperceived ferocity among the Japanese that Westerners who had accepted Lafcadio Hearn's portrait of Japan could hardly believe. In Moscow, where the great Stalin Constitution brought the first country-wide, full "free elections" (of a single-party slate), the Moscow trials continued to convince some naive Westerners that most of Russian political and military leadership was really traitorous and pro-Nazi. Marshal Tukachevski and Karl Radek would follow Kamenev and Zinoviev that year; Bukharine, Rykov, and Jagoda would go the next.

The *Herald*—reluctantly—covered it all, but like the audience to whom it appealed and for whom the paper was edited, it also pretended that the world would go on as usual. The year 1937 after all, was the year of the Paris World's Fair, when—if war scares didn't intervene—more American tourists could be expected in Europe than in any year since the onset of the Depression. And so it was that Hills in a speech to advertising agents in New York assured his audience that increased armaments only meant increased pressure for the negotiations that would rectify past error and bring more stability; in Paris a typical *Herald* editorial entitled "That 'War in Europe' " declared:

> Fixed ideas die hard, but when they are repeatedly belied by experience, die they will eventually. The American idea that Europe is on the brink of war has never at any moment been shared by opinion in Europe, for the simple reason that when Europe most feared a conflagration as, for instance, in October, 1935, when Italy invaded Ethiopia, and in March, 1936, when Germany militarized the Rhineland, it was not war that followed but intense diplomatic activity to avoid it. . . . incidents will *not* lead to war . . . but to a diplomatic exchange of views or a round table conference to take the edge off the conflicting issues underlying such incidents.

This will continue. There is no move toward "inevitable European war," merely "jockeying for position at the next diplomatic conference."

In 1936 the *Herald* had covered the American election as usual. Hills himself shared the New York newspaper's confidence that Landon would win, "with everybody in our class of readers hating Roosevelt more bitterly than any Democratic candidate has been hated in recent years . . ." Columnist Mark Sullivan told readers that "disgruntled Democrats" were going to vote in large numbers for Landon. The gayest election night party was, as usual, at Harry's on the rue Daunou, and the *Herald* published its by now usual election extras.

If 1937 was the year of the Paris Exposition, it was also the fiftieth anniversary of the Paris Edition; the paper changed its format that year to modernize headline typography in conformity with the prize-winning New York Edition. Its house ads proclaimed that it was "one American who is always abroad. . . . In all these [fifty] years it has carried the news of America, every day, to its countrymen visiting in Europe and to countrymen living in Europe. . . . Readers can meet it any daybreak in Paris, in London before noon, elsewhere all over the Continent as quickly as fast trains can take it." It recorded the glorious coming and going of the new *Normandie* with a special six-page section. The arrival of the first *Normandie* boat train attracted such a crowd that the platform was virtually impassable for twenty minutes while the mob tried to see the three Russian polar fliers, Marlene Dietrich, and the "Glamour Girls" en route to dance at the Palm Beach Casino in Cannes.

The names and places are all still there as usual—Deauville, Aix, Evian, Serge Koussevitzky, swimmer and movie starlet Eleanor Holmes (all "burned up" over reports linking her name to *Herald Tribune* gossip columnist Billy Rose), the fashion openings in London, the lists of buyers for the new collections in Paris, "Life on the Riviera," "Life in Holland," "5000 Americans Arrive on Five Liners," art, theater, and social news from Brussels, Berlin, and Rome. There, too, are the German travel ads Hawkins could not find when he looked back, years later. Germany no longer "welcomes you regardless of race or creed," as it did in 1934, but its swastika-bedecked ads tell you that "Historic Germany Is an Ideal Vacation Center." "Paris Amusements," "News of Americans in Europe," "Food," "Fashion," "On the Screen," "Where to Dine, Lunch, or Dance," two pages of financial and economic news and tables, all are still there, along with—later in the year—word to the effect that the "Rome Season Hits Festive Peak with U.S. Ambassador's Party."

And of course the Paris Exposition received full coverage. The *Herald-Tribune* had an information booth in the American pavilion, with a registration book to supplement the one it still had on the avenue de l'Opéra. Its annual *Pocket Guide to Paris* could be purchased at either place. And as is true at all international expositions, the American pavilion was late in opening and widely criticized. The *Herald* explained that French laborers refused to work overtime since the onset of Popular Front legislation; American, French, and Chinese university students were spirited in to do the last painting and sweeping under the guardianship of a cordon of Paris police. Americans could telephone in their classified ads to the *Herald* now, though they were told to "kindly make sure you have been clearly understood by asking the operator to repeat your text." Presumably she would not do so on her own, for she was, in fact, an Egyptian princess who held court in the *Herald* building. Books were now reviewed weekly by Frances Fenwick Hills—Laurence Hills' daughter.

The Legion was coming back again, in smaller numbers, for the twentieth anniversary of American participation in the Great War, just about the same time that the *Herald* would be celebrating its own fiftieth anniversary. It all provoked a rash of congratulatory letters extolling the friendly relations between France and the United States and the *Herald Tribune*'s role in promoting them. Even Franklin D. Roosevelt sent one. The paper printed a tourist guide to the United States and a twelve-page supplement on the coronation.

But on July 7 Sumner Welles, the American Under Secretary of

State, made a speech that could well dash cold water on the expressions of Franco-American amity but that brought forth strong *Herald* approval. The United States he said, "will not necessarily and in all cases be on the side of democracy against Fascism." These two slogans "are but a manifestation of the disease from which this world today is suffering." What is the disease? "The policies and maladjustments resulting from the Great War have never yet been rectified. The world is still suffering from the spirit of the Versailles Treaty and the conception of the League of Nations in the mind of the victors. . . . (The League became) to all intents and purposes the method whereby the inequalities, the intolerable moral and material burdens imposed upon the vanquished by the victors might be continued for an indeterminate number of years." "Reason and justice" need to be accepted as guides.

When, in October, Franklin D. Roosevelt made his famous Chicago "Quarantine the aggressors" speech—in the very heart of *Chicago Tribune* land—the Paris *Herald* attacked: why single out so-called "aggressors"? The changes and adjustments to meet the just needs of the have-not nations have been blocked by the idea of the League and maintenance of a permanent status quo. Four months later Anthony Eden resigned as British Foreign Minister in protest directed at the policy of appeasement and now, wrote the *Herald*, "Europe may breathe freely again in expectation of the realization of a new hope." What was the matter with Eden? "*All the trouble which was piling up unnecessarily upon Europe was largely his making*"(author's emphasis). Eden had resisted German and Italian aims without any clear cut program of positive British policy. Eden, who wanted to resist, was the villain—not Hitler, not Mussolini. The *Herald* was happy to note that Lord Halifax had succeeded Eden at Chamberlain's request. Now the English and the Europeans could count on a team that would sharply reverse Eden's course. Halifax, after all, knew precisely what Hitler wanted—since he had talked to Hitler in the fall! And Chamberlain could be counted upon since he "knows what Mussolini wants as a result of an exchange of letters with him." Could one hope for more? Eden, thank goodness, was gone, with his "dogma of despair."

But correspondent Ralph Barnes, with his own more lucid brand of despair, filed a dispatch that found its way into the paper two days later: the German military, he wrote, would be prepared for war by 1940. (Hitler rid himself of those generals who might oppose him in the very month that the *Herald* was celebrating Eden's resignation.) And Joe Driscoll reported from London that Mussolini was about to ask for a share of control of the Suez Canal. (The Fascists in the Grand Chamber had not yet begun their orchestrated cry for "Nice, Corsica, Savoy!") Yet on March 4 the *Herald* wrote about the new French and British military budgets with its own style of editorial despair: "The democracies have ceased to ask when all this expense is going to end, what it is going to lead to, or who is to pay for it all . . . appeals to reason lose all meaning." (And Hills maneuvered to keep Driscoll's alarmist dispatches out of the European Edition.)

Herald readers filled the "Mailbag" with discussion of the issues. Many saw in Fascism a force for order, for the preservation of individual liberty against collectivism, and therefore a response to, and protection against, Communism. Some, curiously enough, asked whether the United States did not have to choose between one or the other, and sought clearer definitions. By the late 1930s there were many repeaters; Ezra Pound's frequent but usually obscene letters could rarely be printed. He generally inveighed against Walter Lippmann, who failed to share the *Herald*'s optimism about the Fascist powers. Another repeater wrote in rhyme: Pauline Avery Crawford, a longtime Paris resident and semi-invalid, who did not have to wait for the racial laws and military expansion to see Fascism for what it was, and who was attacked by others. One letter jeered, "What nettles Pauline Avery Crawford is that Franco seems to be doing very well these days. . . . Back to rocking the cradle!" A letter from "A true American Pacifist," contrary to all evidence, claimed that Franco had gotten rid of *his* volunteers as the noninterventionists wanted. The others hadn't; where were the noninterventionists now? And perhaps more revealingly, a Thomas Gaines wrote to declare that he admired the Czechs and Czechoslovakia, having lived there, but the country had been put together by the victors in World War I from bits and pieces of Germany and Hungary plus added incompatible elements, all in order to weaken the victors' adversaries. Someday self-determination would have to take place. The next year at Munich, of course, it did.

The Moscow trials run through the entire story of these times as another sort of counterpoint that greatly affects the main themes; the main head or the off-lead on the left side of the paper often concerned the trials, and events in Moscow ill served both the Russians in their efforts to forge a common front against Fascism and the historian who attacks the French and British for failing to make common cause with Russia. They provided a fine rationalization for the *Herald*. When the British and French weakly caved in at meetings of the Nonintervention Committee and Russians attacked their appeasement proposal, the *Herald* in turn attacked the Russians for sabotaging the conference by insisting on a hard line against the Fascist powers. Any proposal by, or alignment with, the butchers of Moscow was bound to be suspect.

The Anschluss took place on March 11, 1938: German troops marched unopposed into Austria. That very morning the *Herald* had run an editorial blasting the "aberration" of political thought that asserted "that the best way of keeping peace is for the democracies to resist the dictatorships at all points. . . . By what achievement can they defend their view that resistance—collective resistance if you like—can bring peace. . . . Advocacy of resistance provoked 100% conquests when the conquerors might have been content with 50% as in the case of Ethiopia . . . it provoked a regular Japanese invasion of China. . . . [the idea of resistance has provided] a record of wreaking, a chronicle of self-frustration and self-defeat, completed by formation of the Rome-Berlin Axis and the Berlin-Rome-Tokyo bloc."

The Anschluss, coinciding so beautifully with the *Herald* editorial, provoked a little second thought. The *Herald,* having absorbed what it called the breathtaking speed of events, declared three days later that it was probably inevitable after "Hitler sent his troops into the Rhineland in violation of one of the stiffest clauses of the Versailles Treaty, and was unchallenged by force on the other side." Still, you couldn't blame Hitler for the collapse of the helpless republic created by Versailles; the swift takeover was not Hitler's fault. It was a consequence of the French cabinet crisis and Chancellor Kurt Schuschnigg's error in calling for a plebiscite on the future of the republic at such short notice.

Two weeks of reflection dispelled the moment of gloomy reflection, and all was upbeat once again. After all, Ambassador Joseph Kennedy, arriving in London, announced that "world trade is the antidote for war," and Herbert Hoover expressed his belief that "war is unlikely now in Europe." And the *Herald* was able to explain it all: "The alarmists were proved wrong for the 100th time. . . . Yet these prophets of doom see no reason to desist. . . . The inevitable Anschluss ended an impossible situation." A British-Italian understanding was now possible; as against the League choice of status quo or general war, "the method of settling disputes by direct dealings between the countries concerned had come into its own again."

The *Herald* foresaw trouble over Czechoslovakia later in the year. But "a solution of the Czech-German problem through direct negotiation, avoiding alliances, will be found—without a European War." The one thing to be avoided was any threat of sanctions; ineffective against Italy, they had also served to push Italy into alliance with Germany, breaking the Stresa front and paving the way for the Rhineland reoccupation. Moreover, they only interrupt the bonds of economic interdependence that foster peaceful relations. It was fortunate, the *Herald* declared, that the Locarno powers had no plan ready to deal with the emergency over Austria, since they argued for ten days, and time lost was a gain for peace. In other words—but the reader must be able to supply them for himself—it was better that the Western democracies remain unarmed in the face of Italian and German armed advance, for oth-

erwise they might be tempted to resist. Approvingly it quoted
Cordell Hull on March 19 in his appeal for world order and
condemnation of threats of force both to bring about change and
to block it.*

In late July George VI and Queen Elizabeth visited Paris, and for
four glorious days all the world's troubles were forgotten. Gor-
geous parades, elaborate festivities, fireworks from the top of the
Eiffel Tower, a royal barge trip down the Seine whose embank-
ments were lined with tapestries and marine apprentices bearing
halberds, gold dust in the illuminated fountains outside the Opéra
the night of the gala, the Crillon and the Marine Ministry on the
place de la Concorde draped with cloth of gold and more Beauvais
tapestries—it was all unforgettable, and the *Herald,* for a short
while, was back in its element. But August, September, and Munich
followed.

There can be no surprise at the *Herald*'s reaction to the Munich
settlement in September. It had reported extensively the debates in
Parliament over Chamberlain's refusal to give Czechoslovakia direct guarantees, and endorsed the English Prime Minister's stand
as one that did not "goad Prague to resistance." Peace was saved
again; Chamberlain and Daladier were the true heroes they were
perceived to be by the masses that welcomed them home from
Munich. Cession of the Sudetenland only confirmed the democratic
principle of self-determination, removed another source of the ir-
ritation that dated from the Versailles diktat, and created—finally—a new structure of peace in Europe. A month after Munich,
on November 9, an editorial read, "Judging by the philosophical
calm with which it has been accepted by the Czechs and the Slovaks,
the solution promises to be permanent in a sense which the solution
found by the treatymakers twenty years ago could not be." And
the next day: "The surest ground for hope in the future is that the
justice of these [German and Italian] claims is beginning to be

*Hills sent Walter B. Kerr to Vienna to cover the events, and praised him to Ogden Reid
for doing a superb job. But the Anschluss also took its toll on the *Herald* in loss of sales
and advertising both from Austria and Czechoslovakia.

admitted. The thought of resisting them by war is fading. It is recognized that their legitimate satisfaction makes for a more stable world."*

Of more importance to the *Herald,* perhaps, was the less dramatic establishment in 1938 of German exchange controls that limited the earnings it could withdraw from sales in Germany. There is no record of whether or not the German government used the controls as a direct threat or inducement for the *Herald.* But another case is instructive: Waverley Root, having gone to work for the United Press after the demise of the Paris *Chicago Tribune,* filed a report on January 20, 1938, saying that the Nazis would invade Austria on May 15. (He missed the date, one may note, by only two days.) Goebbels' ministry made all the German papers cancel their UP contracts until the UP fired Root, which it did, whereupon they were reinstated. Root, incidentally, received $1,000 in severance pay, generous for those days, and moved to the Paris *Time-Life* bureau.

But the incident is indicative both of the Nazis' sensitivity to foreign reporting and their willingness to use economic pressures.

Hills, in 1939, ruefully surveying the effect on advertising of the incorporation of Austria and Czechoslovakia, which had both been good countries for business purposes, into the Third Reich, which had not been, reflected, "For many years it has been difficult to do any amount of business with the Germans. . . . If they remain the masters of Central Europe it really puts us in a position of depend-

---

*Mrs. Pauline Avery Crawford, in a poem in the "Mailbag" in the style of "You Are Old, Father William," wrote in one verse:
> You are old, said the youth, so do let me know
> Why, when you've the old cricket bat
> You take an umbrella wherever you go—
> Pray, what is the reason for that?
> In my youth, said the sage, I ruled all the seas;
> On my empire the sun never set; My umbrella
> reminds those I wish to appease
> That I still can keep dry in the wet.

ing almost exclusively on France and Great Britain and Italy for advertising purposes, whereas years ago we had the whole of Europe to till."

It was hard to rejoice during the holiday season in the winter of 1938–39. Peace was preserved in Europe in 1938, but to most people the cost began to be evident. For the persecuted Jews of Germany a year of increasing horror culminated in the Kristallnacht on November 11, anniversary of the armistice. In retaliation for the assassination of a German attaché in Paris, Ernst von Rath, who died of his wounds on November 10, the Nazi regime unleashed a wholesale attack on the Jewish community, and the *Herald Tribune* four-column headlines tell much of the story, cabled by Ralph Barnes: "Anti-Semitic Wave Sweeps all Germany, Synagogues Burned as Police Stand By, Organized Mobs Smash Shops, Homes." In the next few days other three- and four-column heads ran above stories that told of punishments and fines levied on the Jews of Germany, of regulations that forbade their owning businesses, of warnings to foreign Jews not to stir up further trouble, of Jews besieging foreign consulates, of Roosevelt's recall of Ambassador Hugh Wilson. On November 17 an editorial compared the world reaction to the Kristallnacht with how little hue and cry there had been over pograms in czarist Russia. It was now a problem for the rest of the world to help resettle Jews for whom, surely, space could be found in the empty reaches of Africa and South America. (And a story reported the bitter congressional fight shaping up over acceptance of 15,000 Jewish refugees in the United States.)

During 1938, in what was left of Czechoslovakia, the Nazis stirred up Slovak against Czech. In Russia Stalin could look at his decimated officer corps and calculate what the British and French could actually do for him if he were allied to them and Hitler chose to attack Russia. The answer seemed clear: they would and could do little. But he held his counsel. The bleak European winter wore on, and before spring could lift hearts in its usual manner, Hitler seized the rest of Czechoslovakia, and took Memel from Lithuania;

Franco defeated the last remnants of the republic in Spain, and 450,000 refugees poured across the frontier into a France that received them with hostility and concentration camps; Mussolini, not to be outdone, occupied Albania in April, and Hitler denounced the British naval accord and the military security treaty with Poland. In May Hitler and Mussolini formally signed a military alliance. And the French government, "in a high compliment" to Franco, named Marshal Henri Pétain as the first French ambassador to the country whose leader had been his pupil at the French War College in 1926.

The occupation of Czechoslovakia was the crucial event that convinced most European leaders of the inevitability of war and led Chamberlain in England and Daladier in France to abandon appeasement. But it prompted the usual *Herald* stance. The headlines were straightforward: "Czecho-Slovakia Ceases To Exist as State as Hitler Follows His Army Into Prague; Slovakia Invaded; Czech Areas Annexed." But editorially the *Herald Tribune* declared:

> Though European statesmen could not have been unaware what the Czecho-Slovak issue was, it was carefully guarded from world opinion. People were given to understand that what Germany wanted was merely the right of self-determination for the inhabitants of German Bohemia, whereas Germany's real objective was the final breaking down of the encirclement started by the peace treaties and developed in the two decades following the War.

The "ingenious expedient" of a threat of war had again led to a settlement of an international dispute without the actual hostilities as of old. The Germans were asked into Czechoslovakia, so by no stretch of the imagination could their move be called "unprovoked aggression." Two questions had to be asked: "Was German expansion now at the end? Will Germany consider itself satisfied?" Britain had no real interests in Eastern Europe; the countries most concerned by Hitler's latest action should be Italy and Russia. Russia had always been the protector of the Slavs against the

Teutons. Was it not time for Stalin to speak? As for a security pact between France, Britain, Poland, and the Soviet Union, the illusion of collective security should be dead. Such a pact would only contribute to instability: "It will never exercise a restraining influence and it will not be feared." Better it were stillborn. "It is not Germany's plans that have aroused the world's indignation. It is the methods employed."

As for Franco, his success should not be described as another blow, but viewed rather as creating another opportunity for a general European settlement.* To avoid another Munich with its loss of face, the shift in the balance of power in the Mediterranean and the communications problem that had made Mussolini throw in his lot with Franco should be acknowledged and Italian lines of communication in the Mediterranean secured. The "temperate speech" in which Mussolini had asked France to open negotiations over Tunisia, Djibouti, and Suez should lead to actual negotiations so that the gulf between the two countries would not become unbridgeable. As for the several hundred thousand Spanish refugees, the sad stories from John Elliott told of their plight: "No Power Wants 450,000 Spanish Exiles in France." While the French Minister of the Interior declared that France could absorb 50,000 and circularized other countries to see how many they would take—the United States would admit 352 for the year—an editorial asked why, in the light of this, they had been allowed to cross into France at all. There were no stories about appeals for aid, but a letter in the "Mailbag" from Lillian Mowrer, tucked in among others responding to a request on how to cook fennel, pleaded for funds for the Spanish children.

On this note Hills, belatedly back in the United States, after his illness had held up his annual visit, was told to shut up. As his

---

*Dean Beekman of the American Cathedral Church of the Holy Trinity, in a talk at the American Students and Artists Center on the boulevard Raspail, told the assemblage that "the best propagandists in the world today are those on the Left: they have convinced a majority of Americans of the justice of the Spanish Republican side and the injustice of the Franco side."

plaintive letter to Hawkins noted, in New York the Paris Edition had come to be considered virtually a Fascist newspaper, which of course it wasn't. In any event, political editorials would now be cabled from New York, whatever the cost. Management and owners in New York would no longer allow Hills to use all the excuses for appeasement that had for so long animated the governments of France and England and that were obviously still strongly held by so many Americans in Europe. The Reids did not share them, and the *Herald* in Paris would no longer espouse them.

Once again the summer preceding war seemed more brilliant than any that had gone before. Is it retrospect that makes it seem so? Perhaps not; Janet Flanner wrote to *The New Yorker* that

> Paris has suddenly been having a fit of prosperity, gaiety, and hospitality. There have been money and music in the air, with people enjoying the first good time since the bad time started in Munich last summer. . . . There have been magnificent costume balls and parties . . . formal dinner parties . . . alfresco fetes . . . garden parties. . . . The expensive hotels have been full of American and English tourists. The French franc is holding up fine, French workmen are working; French exports are up; business is close to having a little boom. The gaiety in Paris has been an important political symptom of something serious and solid, as well as spirited that is in the air in France today.

On August 6 the *Mauretania*, the *Champlain*, and the *Normandie* docked with a total of 3,300 American tourists, and the *Herald* reported a virtual flood of arrivals throughout the first weeks of August. Norma Shearer, George Raft, Madeline Carroll, and Charles Boyer posed for pictures; so did Edward G. Robinson, who mentioned to reporters that since he had just completed *Confessions of a Nazi Spy* he would avoid travel to Germany. But Germany beckoned: "Through Germany by Mail Coach" ads (with swastikas) vied with stories about important improvements in the facilities at Baden-Baden, where the Grande Semaine opened with a day of racing on August 11. The "Life in Berlin" rubric listed, among others, the Latin Quarter nightclub. The *Herald* printed pictures of American beauties on the Lido, in Venice. Benito Mussolini attended a performance of *Carmen* given in Caracalla's Baths in Rome and received a tremendous ovation. The French railroads announced free transport of an automobile with a five-person return ticket in second class or a *billet de famille* in first on selected lines; Jack Benny and George Burns pleaded guilty to conspiring to smuggle jewelry into the United States for their wives Mary Livingstone and Gracie Allen and were fined and received suspended sentences; and dancer–movie star Vera Zorina announced that she would cross the ocean in the nude: a special shelter built on the top deck aboard the *Normandie* would enable her to abandon herself fully to the sun as was her wont. In Paris, Harry's New York Bar posted a picture of Helen Traubel being inducted into the "Chicago Friends of the St. Louis Browns."

From London Frank Kelley reported the departure of the Franco-British mission for military talks with the USSR aboard the *City of Exeter*. There was little information available on the almost irreconcilable conflict they faced over the issue of allowing Russian troop movements through Poland and Romania in the event of war.

When a *Herald* reader finished scanning the front page and the sports—and there were more *Herald* readers that August than in several years—he found Joseph Barnes' reports on page 3 recording a heightened state of tension along the German border with Poland and what appeared to be the strong possibility of a crisis over the free city of Danzig. Within a few days the German press began to publish more and more stories of Polish atrocities. By mid-August Barnes' reports made the front page. The League High Commissioner for Danzig saw Hitler and Ribbentrop and planned to fly to London. But American news broadcaster H. V. Kaltenborn, interviewed for the *Herald* on his annual European trip, bet 5-1 against a war in 1939. (By this time Washington was fully informed that in early August Stalin had secretly rejected British-French collaboration and was holding discussions with the Nazis over a carving up of Poland, making war inevitable. But the State Department decided not to inform the British and French for fear of revealing their source, an anti-Nazi member of the German mission.)

Kaltenborn professed himself amazed at the new spirit of resolution in England, and predicted that if the Germans attempted a lightning thrust into Poland they would bog down after seizing perhaps a fifth of Polish territory, and the result would be negotiations. Major George Fielding Eliot, another military commentator feeling out the mood in Europe, told the *Herald* that if, indeed, there were a war, it would be a quick and decisive one. If America ever fought again, it would only be on the sea. Never again would American manpower be sent overseas. (He later became a *New York Herald Tribune* war commentator.) Representative Hamilton Fish of New York, visiting the American Legion monument in Neuilly Cemetery with General Pershing, discussed with the *Herald's* reporter his plan for a world refugee center in Central Africa, near Lake Tchad. General Pershing, wisely, seems to have kept his mouth shut.

By August 19 and 20 the trend of German press attacks on Poland and England shared the front page with a picture of Mae West talking to Frank Buchman of the Moral Rearmament Group of the Oxford Movement. William Allen Neilson also appeared on page one as he retired from Smith College, where Mrs. Morrow—the mother of Anne Morrow Lindbergh—was named acting president. On August 21 a three-column head announced that Nazi Germany had signed a trade pact with Moscow; Western spokesmen reassured reporters that it need not affect the military talks with Russia. On August 22 came the bombshell. A four-column head announced that Ribbentrop was flying to Moscow to sign a Nonaggression Pact with Stalin.

Two days later Laurence Hills spoke over the NBS radio system to America from Paris. The pact, he said, "is a blank check given to Germany for the annihilation of Poland . . . it is far worse for

Britain and France than anybody believed possible." And for the first time in the entire month of August a political editorial appeared in the *Herald:* "There is no possible answer save to meet it [the pact] with an even greater firmness . . . or else to yield under circumstances bound to become more disastrous with every increasing of the pressure brought to bear."

The headlines of the next days are like a series of hammer blows. "Break Now Certain; London and Paris Back Warsaw; Hitler Refuses Direct Conversations with Poland." Joe Barnes in Berlin and Ralph Barnes in London reported proposals and counter-proposals and warnings. Once more, there were "Americans Stranded in Europe as Liners Alter Schedules." The *New York Herald Tribune*'s senior editorial writer, Geoffrey Parsons, reported on a tour of Europe and explained Germany's fatal error: the belief that Britain would not fight.

For a few days the world tried to pretend that the end was not coming: "Deauville Remains Animated Despite Departures," read one headline. Sparrow Robertson wrote from there that "notwithstanding the uncertainty of the present time the Deauville sales [of horses] went over very big." Northwestern University, we learn, had high hopes of dethroning the Golden Gophers of Minnesota for the Big Ten title.

But in the face of the speed of events, no one could really care. Hills, for so long the rationalizer of appeasement and the apologist for Fascism, realized his error and, despite previous strictures from New York, wrote a series of signed editorials on the front page. On August 29, in a box entitled "The Situation," he declared, "The issue is the freedom of Poland, the freedom of every nation in Central and Eastern Europe, and ultimately the freedom of France, England, and free peoples everywhere. Americans have already judged the issue. They know where the guilt will lie." And on August 31 he declared, "The U.S. cannot hope to be wholly indifferent."

On September 2, when a banner headline announced the German invasion of Poland, Hills' front-page box made no bones about it:

"The madman has unsheathed his sword and Poland is his first victim." It was in a four-page paper from which advertising had almost disappeared that the British and French declarations of war were announced—and the first U-boat sinking of the war, the *Athenia,* with 1,120 U.S.-bound passengers. One of those passengers, Doris Kent, of Evanston, Illinois, a former writer for the Paris edition, had sent the editorial room a postcard of the ship when she sailed: "Bulging at the sides! But best little boat on the ocean!" She lived to write the story, and the *Herald* reproduced her postcard the day after the sinking.

There are few people left who remember Laurence Hills. One is Harry Baehr, Jr., who went to work for the *New York Herald Tribune* in the 1930s and who, after the demise of the New York paper in 1966 continued to write editorials for the Paris paper until 1979. Another is long-time correspondent Walter B. Kerr. Both share the conviction that Hills was not a Fascist. But in the thirties he was running a paper that constantly lost money. Steamship companies made up the largest single category of advertising (including, of course, advertising for Norddeutscher-Lloyd and for the Italian Line *Rex* and *Conte de Savoia*). Tourism constituted the next largest category, and Italian and German ads made up the largest part of this. Baehr is quite categorical: the German and Italian governments put on direct pressure, and this explains the pro-Fascist bias and the appeasement line. Former *Herald Tribune* reporter Eric Sevareid, in his autobiographical *Not So Wild a Dream*, is less precise: "Our daily editorial wisely looked on both sides of the Fascist question and saw many virtues in the works of Hitler and Mussolini. (We still took in ads from Germany and Italy.)" And there was the great fear of scaring off tourists: summer months' gains diminished the losses of the rest of the year.

But it is doing Hills a disservice to ascribe his editorial policy to commercial considerations alone. Men as diverse as George Bernard Shaw and Winston Churchill found something praiseworthy in Fascism, not simply as an anti-Communist reaction, but rather as a response to new and unforeseen problems in a technological setting that nineteenth-century liberalism had never anticipated. Many made the transition from socialism to Fascism in one easy leap. Hills' own interest in technocracy and his editorial collaboration with Bugeja, a Maltese Labor party theoretician who opted for collectivism of some form, all speak to the view that Hills, fearful of war as so many millions of Europeans were, might well have convinced himself that he was traveling the only possible, reasonable path.

Hills was in wide company when his editorials appealed to the necessity to revise the diktat of Versailles. He may not have appreciated the irony involved. The *Herald,* under Bennett and then his chief aide, Percy Mitchell, was unmerciful in its condemnation of any concessions to the defeated Germany of World War I: the Versailles Treaty erred mainly on the side of mildness and clemency when it should have been even harsher. Yet for the decade of the thirties Hills found the excuse for all Fascist foreign policies in the necessity for revising the unfair peace of Versailles.

Laurence Hills really did not believe that war would come. In mid-1938 when correspondent John Elliott returned to the United States on vacation, Hills wrote to Wilbur Forrest in New York, "I am obliged to smile over this because Elliott is one of those who has persisted in believing in an imminent European War, whereas I do not. I have argued with him but cannot convince him. " He reiterated the view three months later: "If Europe does not see a war this year after the crisis it has been through, I think the chances for a great European war next year are much slimmer. Lippmann has been an awful pessimist and so have been some of our correspondents." As late as August 29, 1939—three days before the Nazi invasion of Poland—he and Geoffrey Parsons, who had returned to Paris from London and Berlin, went to see Ambassador Bullitt, and Hills recorded his view that Hitler still might not move: "I still have some hopes for a peaceful outcome by negotiations."

A sampling of the letters in the "Mailbag" show that many

Herald readers fully supported its editorial stance during these years. What stands out the most is the isolationism of so many of the writers, despite the fact that they lived and worked in Europe. The quarrels of England, France, Germany, and Italy were no business of America's, and the United States, officially, should not judge. And the *Herald,* of course, approved the speeches of a Hull, a Welles, or a Joseph P. Kennedy, who lectured the Europeans on their duty to get along and to do so by instituting free trade! (It was a standard part of British appeasement policy to offer Hitler an economic deal in return for political restraint.)

There was that group of remarkable journalists who saw it as their duty to try to awaken the fearful and usually sluggish and private masses to the potential for disaster: Leland Stowe, Vincent Sheehan, John Gunther, Shirer, Sevareid, the Barneses, and others. More recent scholarship has shown that they often simplified, that they were often unable to penetrate behind the veil masking complex internal rivalries and maneuverings within the countries concerned. Nevertheless, their brand of advocacy journalism shines out when the *Herald*'s editors, like those of so many other newspapers, preferred to drift with the tide, grasp at whatever straw seemed to indicate that the worst was not about to happen, pretend that if one averted one's eyes from the buildup toward calamity one could see life being acted out as though nothing major were going on.

In August 1939 Laurence Hills, a very sick man, realized that he had been wrong. His front-page editorials were a virtual public admission of error. For years he had disagreed with the journalists who reported their own assessments to the American papers. But not so very many people who were wrong at the time reversed their stands in signed, front-page editorials. Laurence Hills did. Now he had to publish his paper in a Paris at war.

CHAPTER 8 1/2

1940

Herald Tribune editorial of March 24, 1940, "The Promises of Spring," articulated what millions felt. As that first winter of war drew to an end it spoke to people's usual delight in the growing warmth, sun, the first green trees, the outdoor sports. "All the phenomena of the approaching season will put in their customary appearance. The tragedy of it all is that few minds will be without a gnawing consciousness that at the front and in many other areas of the world the season of promise has been blacked out. What sort of Spring is portended for Europe, especially?"

For another two weeks people did not know or even seem to care very much. On Easter Sunday the Grands Boulevards, the Champs Elysées, and the Bois de Boulogne were packed. To Sparrow Robertson's pleasure, an immense throng jammed the Auteuil racetrack. Apéritifs were unrestricted for the holiday, and a special dispensation was made of Easter chocolate. The *Herald* carried a regular front-page box that listed Pan American Airways' clipper flights to and from Lisbon; transatlantic air service, established in 1938, continued despite the war. Maurice Chevalier and Josephine Baker appeared together at the Casino de Paris; Greta Garbo laughed in *Ninotchka*. An off-lead on March 31 reported that Bertrand Russell had been ousted by court action from his professorship at City College in New York as a result of a taxpayer's suit.* But the lead that day recorded an ominous warning: "Churchill Predicts Early Intensification of War."

---

*One year earlier the Paris paper had carried a story of an interview with Russell in which the philosopher predicted a European war in 1939 that would result in a Europe in ruins and a dominant United States that could impose stringent progressive conditions on loans

For six months, ever since the German blitzkrieg and massed Russian forces had crushed Poland, Western Europe had endured an uneasy calm that Englishmen called the "Phoney War," the French the "Drôle de Guerre." Churchill, of course, was right. The promises of spring were about to be kept.

Throughout those six months the *Herald* was published by government order as a four-page paper, with many of the customary features missing, and even those four pages were liberally sprinkled with the white holes that marked the heavy hand of the censor. An occasional Lippmann column would be cut in half; an occasional editorial disappeared completely. A front-page box headed "Notice to Advertisers" turned up completely blank. Eric Hawkins joined battle with the censors as he had done twenty-two years earlier, and he seems rather to have enjoyed the job. Net paid circulation had dropped to an average of 6,500 copies a day by the end of 1939—a smaller decline than Hills had expected, because Europeans saw the newspaper as the representative of a neutral United States and a purveyor of uncolored news. The year's loss of over $40,000 was perhaps compensated for by the fact that the building mortgage was finally paid off as well as, on December 1, the last note to the *Chicago Tribune*. At least the rue de Berri building was free and clear.

There were constant problems with communications. The mails were slow and so were the wire services. There was trouble about getting correspondents to the front. After an initial rupture, telephone service to London was restored, so that United Press cables could come from there. As for predictions as to how the war would go, Hills wrote to Ogden Reid acidly, "I have ceased myself to make any predictions whatever."

Advertising largely disappeared; a rather forlorn house ad offered space for rent in the rue de Berri building to those who might conceivably be planning to open a Paris branch or agency; among the building's conveniences were now air-raid shelters in the base-

---

for reconstruction. Such a war could be averted, he had said, if the United States announced its intention of fighting any aggressor, "but that announcement will never be made."

ment. Walter B. Kerr reported on the Russo-Finnish war from the front for the *Herald Tribune* syndicate, and his dispatches were featured in full in the Paris *Herald,* where an editorial predicted the downfall of Stalin as a result of the error he had committed in revealing the Red Army's strength to be a bubble. Hills, on the front page, expressed astonishment that Britain and the United States had failed to break diplomatic relations with the Soviet Union.

Sparrow Robertson continued his usual rounds and his column; political events such as war were beneath the notice of a sports gossip columnist, with some rather strange results. In January he wrote that he had talked with A.E. Tapper of the Chrysler Export Corporation, who had just returned from a Finland where war still raged: "He told me about the beautiful stadium the sturdy little nation had ready for the holding of the Olympic Games that were expected to be held there this year. The complete layout he thought could not be surpassed."

A regular box on the front page of the paper revealed the rather peculiar restrictions that the French government had seen fit to install when it decided to introduce rationing late in the winter. On Sunday there were no restrictions. On Monday no hard spirits could be sold, but wine, beer, champagne, and "soft" aperitifs were allowed. Monday was also a meatless day, although shoppers could buy poultry and rabbit. No "luxury" breads: only ordinary bread, rusks, and croissants were allowed!

On April 10 Churchill's warning came true. The *Herald* reported the full-scale German invasion of Norway and Denmark, two neutral countries that had managed to stay out of the First World War. It marveled at first at how the preparations could have been kept secret; as the debacle unfolded it condemned the misleading, boasting cable reports of Allied victories in the first few days. The war intensified and Hills, in another signed front-page editorial, advocated increased American aid to the Allies—while the paper printed a mind-boggling State Department explanation of why it had omitted to send Adolf Hitler greetings on his birthday: his birthday was

not a national holiday in Germany, and it only sent them to states-
men whose birthdays were, indeed, national holidays!

While the State Department waffled its incredible way through
developing disaster, the *Herald* found room to print an affectionate
and sympathetic obituary for "the last American boulevardier in
France"—Berry Wall, whose passing at the age of seventy-nine was
taken by the *Herald* as marking the end of an era when social
elegance was a virtue, and there was a proper way to handle a four-
in-hand and to mix a salad dressing. He was an arbiter of fashion
in the James Gordon Bennett era; he stayed in Paris through the
bombardments of the First World War, through the upheavals of
the twenties and thirties—unchanged and twinkling in his charming fashion. Now he was gone.

And one week later the savage invasion of Holland and Belgium
marked the beginning of the end for those countries and for France.
Again Hills warned Americans on the front page that neutrality
was no longer a protection, that speed and decisive action were a
factor of incredible importance. (Sparrow, on the back page,
mournfully noted that "owing to the unsettled conditions the racing
card scheduled for this afternoon at Longchamps has been called
off.") Two days later Ambassador Bullitt told Americans to con-
gregate in the Bordeaux area where the U.S. Lines' *Washington*
was ready to sail (and Sparrow advocated the building of handball
courts in European cities; handball was a fine sport that had not
yet caught on here). The next day the ambassador asked anyone
with cars to help take refugees south—while Sparrow noted that
the American Legion Building on the rue Pierre Charron "was one
fine place to meet some of the sporting fraternity to talk over
baseball, horse racing, boxing, football and other sports."

There was now little space in the *Herald* for anything but war
news and notices to Americans. On May 24, by government fiat,
it was reduced to a single sheet, and even then the censor's white
spaces increased. The paper printed Pauline Avery Crawford's responses to Secretary of State Hull's call for Americans to leave the
war zone:

And should I go to old Bordeaux
  to flee the bursting bomb
and wartime woe, how could I know
  the ocean would be calm?
And I demand if I should stand
  and wait a Yankee ship
Upon the strand of far Ire-land
  would I enjoy that trip?
I know full well some deadly shell
  may get me here but I
Must still rebel against the swell
  of waves that hit the sky.

And she stayed in Paris throughout the occupation.

The collapse of the northern front with Dutch and Belgian capitulation and the Dunkirk evacuation brought the war closer to
Paris. On May 30 the *Herald Tribune* printed Sparrow Robertson's
pathetically gallant last column, whose final paragraph read:
"While it is still uncertain if the French Grand Prix will be run this
year on June 30 as scheduled at Longchamps, a number of the
probable starters are having workouts over the gallops at Maison-
Lafitte. The little racing town is one busy place these days."

The ageless Sparrow continued to write his columns, but the
onrush of events and the one-page paper left no space for his gossip.
Few of the personnel responded to the ambassador's call to leave
for Bordeaux, but some sixty-eight men had already been mobilized, and Hubert Roemer, for example, with little to do on the
advertising end, had been writing editorials, working at every sort
of office task morning, noon, and night. Hills, who had had five
operations in the summer of 1938 and another in November of
that year, but who had shown some recovery in 1939, moved to
the Hotel Plaza near the office upon the outbreak of the war. Now
he had just enough men to put out the paper, and it seemed imperative to him that the *Herald* continue to serve as a means of
communication for Americans stranded by the suddenness and
savage rapidity of the German advance. In mid-May he began to

think about what to do if the Germans did the unthinkable: take Paris. Roemer had gone to Orléans earlier, to see if printing there would be possible in the event of bombardment, but no plans had been made, and Hills, in consultation with Ambassador Bullitt, who planned to stay on at the embassy with a skeleton staff, thought he would stay, too; Bullitt promised him the protection of the American embassy. Hills cabled Ogden Reid, who cabled back that Hills should use his own judgment. On May 24 he told the remaining staff that he would stay.

Roemer thought he was all wrong and made his own confidential views known to the treasurer of the *Herald Tribune* in New York. There would not be enough men to put out the paper; the French Linotype operators *all* planned to leave. Hills was naive in believing that he could make a deal with the German military governor. It would be impossible to put out a newspaper which would not reflect discredit on the *Herald Tribune* name; all the press services and distributors were planning to leave when the French government did. "I do not believe that we would be permitted to issue anything except a handbill for the official German news agency," he wrote. "Personally, I would rather be a classified advertising worker in New York!" The French, he thought, after the war— whenever that time came—would look amiss at a Paris *Herald* which obeyed German commands instead of leaving with the rest of the newspapers and keeping its independence on untaken French soil. Hills was being courageous but foolish. He had told the English employees they could leave, and that there would be no stigma attached to French or American employees who left now. But

a good many of the men, however, cannot afford to throw up their jobs and take their families to what they hope is a safer place than Paris itself. All of them are torn between the desire to stay by the paper for which they have worked hard and a natural desire to protect their families and themselves from the Germans who may, or may not, be tolerant because these people have been employed by this American newspaper published in Paris.

What Hills still did not understand, wrote Roemer, was that this was a new type of war and a different kind of regime.

And on June 8, as the Germans advanced closer to Paris, Roemer and three other American employees left in desperation, prompting an angry blast from Laurence Hills. It was apparent that no Miracle of the Marne would save the French capital this time. "The loveliest city in the world has never looked lovelier," said an editorial on the day Roemer left. Reid cabled his sympathy to Hills, but this time chose to make his own decision: "Do not believe Huns will reach Paris this century but if they should you and Mrs. Hills should be elsewhere stop We will not print propaganda and under invasion could not print newspaper stop Think employees their families should be evacuated to French localities their choice our expense under your direction whenever they desire leave best wishes."

Laurence Hills cabled back his agreement to suspend publication when necessary, and his own decision to stay in Paris with his ailing wife. Things were more complicated than Reid knew. Even under the extreme wartime conditions, his lawyer had warned him, he had to do more than move the employees at the newspaper's expense. He had to pay them until August 1, and had a contractual obligation to the tenants so that he had to keep the building open and under proper guardianship even under an invasion.

A day later, on June 9, the French government decided to leave Paris. The German advance was now unchecked. Monday, June 10, Hawkins managed to get out a paper despite an increasing lack of personnel. One column reported the final withdrawal of all forces and the end of the fighting in Norway. Two columns recorded reaction in the United States. The main four-column head told of Mussolini's inglorious and degrading declaration of war upon France and England, while "Nazis Redouble Fury of Drive for Paris." Walter B. Kerr, for the Paris bureau, movingly described the strange exodus from Paris. On the evening of Sunday, June 9, Parisians seem suddenly to have realized that the Germans were about to enter the city. By two or three in the morning the streets were piled high with household goods being loaded into every available form of conveyance—cars, trucks, taxis, wheelbarrows, baby carriages. By Monday afternoon no more bicycles were to be found in the shops. Americans who had stayed behind joined in the exodus. It was calm: on Monday buses and subways were still running, most shops remained open, and people could still even see *You Can't Take It with You* at a movie house on the Champs Elysées. On the twelfth, Kerr wrote, the flight ended almost as rapidly as it had started. Three-quarters of the Paris populace had left. Now offices, cafés, and restaurants were closed. And Kerr speculated about how the hundreds of thousands on the roads south of Paris would live, and who would care for them.

But the issue of June 12 carrying Kerr's final dispatch failed to appear on any newsstand. Hachette had no trucks left for delivery. The paper itself was printed on only one side of a single sheet. It would be the last to appear for four and one-half years. On June 14 German troops entered Paris, eight and one-half months after the outbreak of the war; two days later, Pétain asked for an armistice.

And so, the old Paris *Herald* came to an end—not as bad a paper as some make it out to have been, not as good a paper as it might have been. Its staff dispersed. Most of the English employees made it to England, including Eric Hawkins, who after a complicated routing through unoccupied France, Spain, and Portugal finally joined the *Herald Tribune*'s London bureau. Some were caught and interned. Laurence Hills stayed on and communicated by complicated means through Berlin or Vichy. A night editor named Haffel kept him company, filing some dispatches through Berlin to New York, and Hills' aide and confidante, Mlle. Brazier, a telephone operator, and an elevator girl remained to service the remaining tenants. Without a responsible person in charge the building would probably have been requisitioned, but Hills was assured by authorities that it wouldn't be disturbed. There were still complications about debts and payments to former employees, and Hills continued to nurse the idea that he might resume publication rather than have the *Herald Tribune* lose its position as the only American newspaper in Europe. The machinery was kept greased and in good shape. But it was an idle dream, and when, in January 1941, he transmitted an inquiry to New York through the National City Bank office in Le Puy, near Vichy, about printing a technical journal, a move that would be good for the machinery, he was told firmly that there could be no business operations apart from building rental and maintenance, since a tax loss had already been taken in the United States.

In April 1941 Reid received another letter from Hills dated February 3. Now it was getting harder in Paris. There was little heat, and the pipes and even the ink in the offices had frozen. Hills was preparing for his departure. He would leave Mlle. Brazier in charge, with a power of attorney for the *Herald Tribune* lawyer, Soulas. Admiral Leahy in Vichy and Under Secretary of State Sumner Welles tried to help out, but it was too late. Hills had a relapse and died in the American Hospital in Neuilly on March 28, before Ogden Reid even received his last letter. German permission for Mrs. Hills to leave took longer, but in June she reached Lisbon and then, finally, returned to the United States.

Sparrow Robertson, who never learned to speak French, nevertheless remained in the Paris that was his home. His haunts closing, his Old Pals gone, he found nothing better to do than to come to his tiny, private cubbyhole in the virtually empty *Herald Tribune* building. In the winter of 1940–41, when there was no heat, Sparrow, by this time living in the American Legion Building across the Champs Elysées, nevertheless came to the office to sit alone for hours in the cold and dark. He had a small property in Bois-le-Roi, a hamlet near the forest of Fontainebleau, and Mlle. Brazier begged him to go there, telling him he was only making himself unhappier.

At first he refused. But with the Paris that he knew closed down by German curfew, he finally moved out. He ventured back to Paris to visit old haunts once or twice. On June 10, returning from a last visit, he stepped out of the train onto the station platform and collapsed. Two days later the friends still left in Paris came out to bury him in the Bois-le-Roi Cemetery.

Perhaps June 10, 1941, is the most suitable date for the death of the Paris *Herald*. Sparrow Robertson, even more than publisher Laurence Hills, seems to incarnate the spirit of the paper in the interwar years: unabashedly American yet thoroughly expatriate, in but not of Paris, trying hard to ignore the social, economic, and political upheaval of the times, and acting bravely as though the familiar world would go on forever.

PART III

THE POSTWAR YEARS

CHAPTER 9

The New *Herald Tribune*

EOFFREY PARSONS, JR., the amiable *New York Herald Tribune's* wartime London bureau chief who started up the European Edition again in late 1944, was sure that the United States would be a paramount world power with an all-important world role after victory. A vastly expanded European Edition, when he became its editor, should represent that new American world position. It had the potential to become the true voice of America in Europe, to be read by all influential Europeans who wanted to know what Americans were doing and thinking, to be the symbol of the American Century. And at the same time it could be a model for European journalism, so much of which had been found grievously wanting before the war. It would be a voice for democracy everywhere, and certainly a much better and far more important paper than it had been under Laurence Hills.

By the time of rebirth, though, some of the euphoria of liberation had already evaporated, and the story of the *Herald Tribune* in the years to follow is in good part one of the toll taken by the circumstances of the postwar years: economic distress, political bitterness and polarization, and social disruption. Geoff Parsons made it into a very good paper, but these circumstances kept it from being what he wanted it to become, and it actually came much closer to bankruptcy in 1950 than most people realized. Only Helen Reid's support, government subsidy, a new army audience and heavy cutbacks kept it alive to struggle on in the fifties, resembling nothing more than the Paris *Herald* of the late twenties. In the sixties only adroit maneuvering saved the paper when the American presence in France began to fade, depriving it of its traditional market, and the *New York Times* tried to defeat it in Europe as the *Times* was to defeat the parent *New York Herald Tribune* at home. The *Times* came close to succeeding, but the European Edition's owners persuaded Katharine Graham of the *Washington Post* to join in a common venture, and the *Times* threw in the towel; the *Post, Times,* and *Herald* joined together in 1967 to publish the *International Herald Tribune,* which finally—despite ups and downs—began to be what Parsons had wanted it to be thirty years earlier.

So it has been that, while superficially looking much the same since 1945, the paper has gone through as many changes in these years as it went through in the fifty years after James Gordon Bennett founded it in 1887. Changing world conditions and circumstances were mirrored in the paper itself before it became, in the decade before its hundredth anniversary, what its owners called "the first global newspaper," printed simultaneously in Paris, London, Zurich, The Hague, Marseilles, Hong Kong, Singapore, and Miami, Florida. It was quite an achievement.

Perhaps the trauma attending rebirth should have warned everyone that the future wouldn't be easy. Four years of war had wrought enormous changes. In early 1942, the Axis powers seemed everywhere triumphant, ready to take the Middle East and perhaps India and Australia, to cut off Russia and China, to forge close ties with Latin America. Within a year—at Midway, the Coral Sea, El Alamein, Stalingrad, Kursk—the tide turned in every theater of war, and an inexorable Allied advance began. Millions fought and died as Russian forces advanced on the eastern front. On June 6, 1944, the long-awaited Allied landings succeeded in Normandy, and the Allies broke out to roll across France and liberate Paris on August 24. In America, despite estimates of an eighteen-month campaign against Japan, plans for reconversion and the shipment of large-scale relief to Europe were well under way.

With the liberation of Europe in sight, Ogden and Helen Reid had to decide on whether to reopen the European Edition. Perhaps there was not really any question, but after all, in the thirties the paper had cost them half a million dollars and earned them a certain opprobrium for Hills' editorial stance. A reborn Paris paper would have to pay its way and be more carefully controlled. In the spring of 1944 Helen Reid visited the *Herald Tribune* correspondents in London, where Eric Hawkins told her there was no question but that the paper should resume publication from the rue de Berri. He even had a possible editor in mind: Geoffrey Parsons, Jr., the young London bureau chief whose father was senior editorial writer for the New York paper. The younger Parsons had spent a year in Europe before the war, and had been with the paper in the Midwest and in London for several years. Parsons was ready with his reply when Helen Reid raised the issue of postwar possibilities with him: he wanted to run the Paris *Herald Tribune*. He'd talked to Eric Hawkins about it; he still knew some French from that earlier year abroad; his conversations with de Gaulle had convinced him the French would welcome him. "I was thirty-six years old and it was an easy way to become an editor at a young age," he recalled later.

The Reids talked with others in New York and decided to publish. In August Eric Hawkins prepared to return to Paris to help carry out an agreement to print the army's *Stars and Stripes* in the rue de Berri, once the city was liberated, and Parsons cabled New York to find out what decision had been made. With the Allied troops racing to retake the city, he was eager to go. Reality intruded. Joe Barnes, now foreign editor of the New York paper, cabled back.

Although it is naturally desirable to resume publication soon as possible I think we would need Army and French assurances expense could be kept to minimum during initial period and also that Army would buy copies at cost and deliver. Agree with you it is not too early to start working on all these. We urgently need fuller information on condition building, presses, availability, cost of paper supplies, skeleton staff, communication facilities, all related ques-

tions. General plan under discussion here seems to contemplate Paris
edition tightly integrated with New York edition.

Parsons, ready and willing, was able to reply that same day: the
Army Special Services would help with communications and distribution and were happy to see the *Herald Tribune* reappear.
Apparently there was little fear of competition with the more specialized *Stars and Stripes*. Hawkins took off for Paris to make a first
survey of the situation. The *Stars and Stripes* men, following closely
upon the heels of the advancing armies, had published briefly at
Cherbourg and now were printing in Rennes. Hawkins managed
to find his way there, and he and *Stars and Stripes* editor Robert
Moora followed General Leclerc's Second Armored Division into
Paris by only a few days. Those were the times when American
uniforms in an American jeep brought forth riotous greetings;
Hawkins, as an accredited U.S. army correspondent, was suitably
attired and found himself showered with affection. They drove
excitedly across a Paris that still resounded to occasional shots and
turned into the rue de Berri where, as legend has it, Mlle. Brazier
was waiting to hand them the keys.

It was amazing. The building and the equipment inside were in
perfect shape; only a limited amount of requisitioned metal headline type and a folding machine on one side of the press were
missing. The Germans had gone through the building just once,
taking inventory six weeks after the start of the occupation. In
October of 1941 Mlle. Brazier was able to rent the building to a
French governmental agency, the Services Financiers, Commissar-
iat à la Lutte Contre le Chômage of the Ministry of Labor, and this
seems to have been sufficient to keep the building from being
requisitioned by the occupation forces. Ernest Quillet, an electri-
cian who found another job during the occupation, returned occasionally to keep the presses in order.

In the meantime, Mlle. Brazier had settled debts, paid off claim-
ants, collected rent from the government, and actually turned a

slight profit for the war years.* By September 5 Hawkins was able to cable back that the *Stars and Stripes* could now use the plant, and the first issue rolled off the presses. It looked to him as though most problems could be overcome in short order. The French would authorize enough newsprint to print a daily four-page edition of 25,000 copies. The European Edition, he was sure, could soon resume publication. It ended up taking almost four months.

From London Parsons sent a long and ambitious memorandum to the Reids outlining his view of what the *Herald Tribune* should be like.

> The best paper possible for the European market, it seems to me, cannot be an exact replica of the New York edition...
>
> An adaptation of the *New York Herald Tribune,* published with the understanding that it was aimed at an international public, might actually achieve an international significance beyond anything we can imagine. With the tremendous improvement in communication and distribution which we will have after the war, the Paris *Herald* can be in every capital in Europe on the day of publication with all the news that the New York paper prints . . . there is no question that the Paris edition, given the proper support, could be the greatest paper on this side of the Atlantic and it could be that without a tremendous effort. Its prestige as the most reliable and complete disseminator of news on the Continent would mean that it would have to be read and quoted by all public officials, newspaper men, businessmen and any other groups that realize as they never have before that they must know what America thinks and is doing. . .
>
> With the development of our own coverage around the world it ought to be possible to give our front page a unique value. No one ever consciously attempted to make a newspaper from this point of view.

---

* *Le Matin,* originally the other half of William Alonzo Hopkins' *Morning News,* which Hopkins sold to James Gordon Bennett when Bennett established the Paris *Herald,* ended its long career in ignominy: having continued to publish during the occupation, it was branded as collaborationist and forced to close down. Hawkins learned that there might have been legal problems for the *Herald,* too, if it had published after June 12, 1940, as Hills had wanted to do.

The memo then went on to explore communications problems and suggested that all members of the *Herald Tribune* foreign service, including those in London, file for New York through Paris, thus giving the European Edition a great time advantage. Parsons hoped it would also be possible to establish a regular direct air link between New York and Paris, so that editorial material could be flown over the same day.

Later in September Parsons joined Hawkins in Paris, and it became apparent that Parsons would have some differences with both Hawkins and Mlle. Brazier over how the paper was to be run. The little Englishman and the Frenchwoman had been used to Hills' penny-pinching days and ways. Mlle. Brazier wanted to charge one franc for the newspaper; Parsons had been told from New York that since there wouldn't be much advertising at first, he should charge five. Then Parsons insisted that staffers—Europeans and Americans alike—should be paid American union wages, so that he would not have to recruit the sort of down-and-outers that presumably had staffed the newsroom in the past. The paper was not to run in the red, but it was going to be different, bigger, better, and much more important, and things were going to be done solidly from the start. Hawkins would have to learn that it would no longer be a provincial, poor-paying paper.

Now they were ready and eager to go. The plant was in shape and turning out the *Stars and Stripes.* As one man put it, old French production employees were coming out of the woodwork, looking for their old jobs; Vincent Bugeja had shown up, having ridden out the war in concealment, using a fake Italian ID card; Marcel Tallin, whose father had worked for the Commodore, came back to tackle the problem of advertising, and even "Picasso II"—Van Grasdorf, the photo touch-up artist who had left in the thirties to work for the neo-Fascist *Le Jour* and then joined the Resistance—turned up to take care of pictures. The government newsprint allocation was secure, and the *Stars and Stripes* operation meant that communications with the United States would be eased—and in fact, once the *Herald Tribune* started up, Stars and Stripers brought it features from the United States in their dispatch cases. Virtually all the wire services and foreign correspondents were reporting back to the United States through Paris, so that the news was available. The journalists were ready to put out a paper. But still business complications held it up: negotiations with the Internal Revenue Service in the United States over the tax loss taken in 1940 and with French authorities over profit and loss offsetting all took time.

While these held up the impatient newspapermen, other *Herald Tribune* staffers came to join them. Everett Walker, now assistant business manager, flew to Europe in November, in the first transport plane to land at Orly, to serve as the Reids' personal representative to supervise the paper's reappearance. (He also carried fifty crossword puzzles and solutions in his briefcase.) He was joined by Les Midgeley, described by another newsroom member as the man who really kept the newsroom going in the next few years, by Frank Webb as chief copyreader, Lewis Glynn, an aging Englishman who had hidden out through the war years and now handled the stock reports, various and sundry Stars and Stripers, and pickups from among the accredited correspondents who were all housed in the Hotel Scribe, near the Opéra. One thing remained to be done: construction of "The Wall," a brick partition erected between the *Stars and Stripes* area and the *Herald Tribune* desks to keep the newsroom from utter confusion. It was soon covered with graffiti, and the door in its center allowed *Stars and Stripes* deskmen to come through and help. Some made the transition a permanent one when the war came to an end, and the wall disappeared when the *Stars and Stripes* left in 1946.

The end of the war in Europe seemed in sight when Bill Robinson, advertising manager for the New York paper, made an appointment with General Eisenhower to get the general's final OK and assurance that there would be enough newsprint, gasoline, and transport to distribute the newborn paper. Two days before their scheduled December 19 date Von Runstedt's twenty-eight divisions launched what was to become the Battle of the Bulge. Robinson was sure Ike couldn't see him, but was told the appointment was still on. As he was ushered in he excused himself, saying, "You're moving armies around and all I want to do is start up a newspaper." But Ike laughed, Robinson later reported. "He was the only unworried man I had seen since the Bulge crisis began." "Calm down, Robinson, take it easy," Eisenhower said, and told the newsman that he'd set their two hours aside three weeks ago. "Let's talk," and they did. There would be no trouble with any of Robinson's requests; the newspaper would be good for troop morale. As a result of their conversation, on December 22, with headlines devoted to the Battle of the Bulge, that was raging only 150 miles to the northeast, the *New York Herald Tribune,* European Edition, once again rolled off the presses in the rue de Berri.

How expectations were deceived! In a France liberated from the Nazi yoke, a Paris freed of its jackbooted conquerors, and with a new day dawning, relief supplies should have been pouring back into that cosmopolitan center of the world, and the reemergent *Herald* should have been trumpeting the good news and celebrating the birth of a world freed of Fascism and militarism. Instead, by the time all the details had been taken care of and the paper resumed publication, the elation of liberation had faded in the face of the cold and harsh reality of the coming winter and the fear engendered by the mighty German Ardennes offensive. And for the next four years it would record an amalgam of fading hopes, growing bitterness, increasing political conflict, and painfully slow economic reconstruction in Europe, uncertain leadership in the United States, and anger, misunderstanding, and bitterness between former Allies.

The first number alone contained the germ of almost all of this. The hope and elation were still there, in the announcement of reappearance, with its statement of purpose closely matching Parsons' earlier memorandum, and in the letters of congratulation from Ambassador Jefferson Caffery and General Dwight Eisenhower, who thanked the *Herald* for making it possible to publish the *Stars and Stripes* in Paris. For Ambassador Caffery, the newspaper faced "a new era full of hope." "I am sure," he wrote, "it will continue to be a medium of American information and opinion for all the people of Europe."

The newspaper looked backward a little: the "Mailbag" was reopened with the Old Philadelphia Lady and a letter from "Groucho" on that old favored subject, curbing poodles. A Pauline Avery Crawford poem appeared: "Hail GI Joe and His Jeep." The good lady had remained in Paris throughout the war, harboring resistants in her apartment.* In 1946, finally, she would be given her own weekly column, "Our Times in Rhyme," which she would share with contributors.

The first number of the *Herald Tribune* was a full four pages. It bore a box on the front asking readers to share their copy: the print run was half what it could be with a single sheet two-page paper. It thanked the French Ministry of Information and the French Federation of the National Press for cooperation in supplying newsprint (though production workers from those times remember a good bit of trading of newsprint and general help from *Stars and Stripers*.) Familiar names reappeared on columns: Walter Lippmann, of course, but also Sonia Tomara, reporting on France and the economic crisis brought on by the approach of winter and Joseph Driscoll, whom Hills had tried to banish from the prewar paper, with a saddening article on the sorry state of French hotels he had stayed in—and ducked out of as they came under fire— while he accompanied the American army across France.

Advertisements were few, and Marcel Tallin was able to manage them by himself. For the first number he had garnered a sprinkling of haute couture ads and one from Cartier's. He added Rumpelmayer's Tea Room, Harry's New York Bar, and the old Select, on the corner of the rue de Berri and Champs Elysées, for the second, along with Galignani's Bookshop. From the United States came

---

*Later on she would reveal a dramatic episode in her career of writing letters in poetry to the *Herald:* in the thirties her anti-Fascist efforts had come to be answered rather regularly by another versifier named Douglas Chandler. In 1943, with the Gestapo ensconced across the street and resistants in her own apartment, she came across a precious copy of *Time* magazine smuggled into France from England. As she proceeded to devour every word of it she discovered that Chandler had been indicted for treason in the United States.

ads from Saks, Rogers Peet, and the Waldorf that either greeted the revived *Herald* or promised a better future for returning GI's: "There'll be skiing at Bousquet's when the troop trains are converted," predicted the New Haven Railroad. There was a brief U.S. sports roundup and three columns of economic and financial news, including an eight-inch listing of stocks. The "Mailbag" quickly sprang to life in the next few days with letters of welcome and congratulation, but also with letters on relations between the French and the great numbers of Americans in France. It was a subject that would occupy a large part of the "Mailbag" for the next three years. And there was a mix of news—Americans, world, and local—with warm stories about the reemergence of prewar figures of the American community: Dean Beekman returned to the American Cathedral Church, along with organist Lawrence Whipp, who had been interned by the Germans; Edmund J. Pendleton, organist of the American Church, who managed to hide out during the occupation, would now write music features for the European Edition. Forty members of American Legion Post No. 1 who had been interned by the Germans reopened the building on the rue Pierre Charron, offering its facilities to GI's. Even Gaston Archambault reappeared briefly, with a letter purporting to explain the Old Philadelphia Lady to new readers who might have wondered at her appearance in the first number.

But the Battle of the Bulge, the continued German advances, and then the counterattacks that successfully broke the German drive continued to dominate the paper's first three weeks. In retrospect, the most important stories were not the headline-grabbing ones about military operations but the scattered shorter stories that reflected the *effect* of the surprise German attack. One week before the *Herald* resumed publication, everyone considered the Germans beaten. Now there was a mass overreaction in the opposite direction: column after column reported reappraisals of Nazi strength and the need for an even greater mobilization effort. In the United States rations were tightened, tax cuts were put off, cuts were made in planned reconversion and in exemptions from military service, and stories reported the view that New York might be bombed by V-weapons mounted on German submarines. Most ominously for Europe and for the *Herald Tribune,* spokesmen stressed that all shipping had to be used for the war effort, and little could be diverted to relief.

Two columns in the December 24 issue highlighted the grim prospect. George Slocombe, another prewar veteran, mused about the first Christmas Eve in liberated Paris. *Réveillons de Noël* had always been festive occasions; this one would be cold, damp, and dark. There was no coal and little wine. How soon would things improve? The answer seemed to be given in another story on the same page: the U.S. Department of Agriculture reported that European food supplies would drop sharply in 1945 because of disruptions in the harvest and in transportation. The first years of peace, in other words, would promise *less* food than had been available during the occupation. And the problem was that reaction to the Battle of the Bulge promised to make things worse. When a choice had to be made between relief and reconstruction on the one hand and the war effort on the other, the war effort would now get the support.

Despite the grim picture that could be pieced together from separate stories, the newspaper's tone failed to reflect a full realization of what this reality would mean. Perhaps the newsmen's situation and their delight in Paris colored their viewpoints somewhat. Accredited correspondents were quartered in the Scribe Hotel, where hot water and army rations were available. Others, paid in francs, and without correspondent status, nevertheless were able to eat in army messes and gain access to PX's. Hawkins relates that though he had regained his own apartment, he frequently visited the Scribe to keep in touch with newsmen and to get a hot bath. In 1945, as a result of American businessmen's complaints about lack of State Department help, Ambassador Caffery personally arranged to put the whole California Hotel with its 180 rooms at the disposal of American civilians. Because of its location, across the street from the *Herald* building, the move helped recreate that old tight link between the paper and the renascent American community in Paris.

So it was that in its first three weeks the paper, full of war news and with the grim portent of things to come, nevertheless hit its stride in presenting, locally, a picture of the joy that came with liberation, repatriation, and the pleasure that Americans took in being back in Paris. "Paris Amusements" advertised the new review at the Bal Tabarin: "La Joie Renait"—Joy Is Reborn. Sylvia Beach, of Shakespeare and Company, wrote three columns on how French literature went underground during the occupation. Edmund Pendleton, the organist, wrote on how "Frenchmen fought the enemy with the weapon of Music" and on the bright future he envisaged for music in France. Lewis Gannet wrote two columns on the return of Gertrude Stein and Alice B. Toklas to their home in Paris from their wartime hideout in Culoz, near the Swiss border. Their treasured pictures in their Paris apartment were intact; local merchants greeted them like old friends, and one told Miss Stein his reply to a German who had asked him why the French didn't like the Germans: "Because the Germans are not *rigolo!*" Soon after Christmas the paper began to list auction sales at the Hotel Drouot and exhibits at art galleries. A Pauline Avery Crawford poem on January 4 made light of—but revealed something of the feelings about—shortages:

> More fabulous than fairy dreams
>   To those long wont to cope
>   With Occupation ersatz, seems
>   A cake of U.S. soap!
>
> No warning to the Gestapo,
>   No message to the Pope,
> Availed us then, who had to go
>   Without a cake of soap
>
> With water, water everywhere,
>   Yet we did sit and mope.
> No God was there to hear our prayer
>   For just one cake of soap

But now with peace our soul is fraught;
High is our heart with hope,
Because our GI Santa brought
A CAKE OF U.S. SOAP!

But there was always the grim counterpoint. Slocombe reported the remark of a Frenchwoman in reply to the "indiscrete and unjustified comment" that the French seemed to have all the luxuries denied to other war-scarred countries. "It is true we have the superfluous things. It is only the essentials that we lack." The "Mailbag" swelled with letters about the state of personal relations between French and Americans. Americans complained about French price-gouging and greediness, and Frenchmen—often in sorrow, because the Americans were, after all, their liberators— wrote that the well-fed and well-cared-for Americans seemed to be able to do little but complain, with no understanding of the hardships the French were facing. The American soldier was given an exchange rate that meant his dollars bought little and made French prices seem exorbitant; this contributed to his sense of being taken by the French. Geoffrey Parsons found the situation so bad that he devoted a feature article on the editorial page to explain the rationale for the rate, and why it was important that GI's have explained to them that a higher rate would increase French shortages since it would enable them to buy up scarce French goods.

And then, suddenly, the *Herald* found itself in the same boat as the French. In January, along with the usual quota of stories on the fighting, the crises over Greece, Yugoslavia, and Poland, and the actions of the special courts for collaborators, the paper informed its readers that the French government had ordered cuts in all but essential passenger train service and in domestic electricity and gas, had closed Paris nightclubs, and had ordered that shop windows not be lit at night. The next day a headline read, "Paris Has Hardest Day Since 1939"; the town was blanketed with snow and there was neither heat, light, nor gas during the day. Potatoes had disappeared and all food was in short supply. And the news-print allocations for all papers was cut in half.

For the next five months, until June 13, the *Herald Tribune* published a single sheet of paper printed on both sides, with its price temporarily reduced to three francs. It was obviously difficult to do so soon after the elation of rebirth. Under Parsons, Hawkins, and Midgeley its four pages were tightly edited, informative and spirited. Now everything had to be cut: features, letters to the "Mailbag," advertisements, cartoons, and radio and amusement listings. Smaller type and a tighter format gave the paper a cramped appearance. And on February 6 it voiced editorial disagreement with a speech by Under Secretary of State Joseph Grew to the effect that aid to France should come only after the war was won. In mid-February the paper printed a grim two-column report by Bill Robinson, back in the United States after three months in France, entitled "France Faces Economic Reality." A few days later it published a story attacking an optimistic American report on supplies shipped to France; the French data showed a disastrous lag.

A mid-March amendment to the Lend-Lease Act extension by Congressman Jerry Vorys of Ohio denying any use of Lend-Lease funds for postwar reconstruction led to a sorrowful *Herald* editorial. The move meant that ships bound for France might have to turn back; Vorys' amendment was formally correct, given the original purposes of Lend-Lease, but the *Herald Tribune* regretted the principle.

Over half of the front page continued to be devoted to war news, and much of the rest to diplomacy. The story on the horrifying Dresden air raids gave evidence of the wartime view: Dresden, reported the *Herald,* was a "bastion of the Nazi defenses against the Soviet left flank . . . a center of railways leading into Germany . . . and therefore of vital importance to Nazi defenses. It was a great manufacturing center as well as railway target." V-bomb attacks on London had doubled casualties in the beginning of the year (although specific news of the character of the ballistic missile V-2 would not be released until mid-March). Reports of crises over

Russian relations with the governments of Eastern Europe began to appear on the front page, and the hapless Polish government in exile in London charged Russia and Franklin D. Roosevelt with betrayal of the Atlantic Charter. The Yalta Conference, to which de Gaulle was not invited, featured prominently, and occasioned angry French letters. Roosevelt's soothing gesture of inviting de Gaulle to meet him outside of France on his way home—a gesture contemptuously rejected by the Frenchman—led to more letters and a flap about French censorship of various aspects of the story. Frederik Kuh of the *Chicago Sun,* dean of the diplomatic correspondents, attacked French press censorship as "stupid press muzzling." SHAEF, the Allied military headquarters, he wrote, allowed much that the French forbade; the French censor proceeded to cut fourteen lines of his story! He was answered, ironically enough, by André Laguerre, French government press spokesman in matters of censorship—who would later join the Paris *Time-Life* bureau and then become editor of *Sports Illustrated.*

On Saturday, March 4, after a de Gaulle speech the night before had led to the release of more newsprint, the *Herald* reappeared on four pages, and Parsons wrote that the editorial staff felt "a little bit of the relaxation and comfort that must come to an expansively constructed female when she loosens her corsets." In the restrictive circumstances that prevailed, badly needed news frequently had to be withheld. But in addition to the larger quota of news the four pages allowed, the paper also happily listed fashion openings, amusements, church services, lottery results, and Foreign Service changes and printed a number of features it could not ordinarily run.

In ensuing weeks the paper continued to mix the sense of joy and wonder at the end of Nazi domination with grim reminders of reality. Bugeja wrote columns on the French art monuments that had come through the war unscathed, on the return of French deportees, on how the Pasteur Institute shared its facilities with a U.S. army laboratory unit without compensation. Slocombe wrote about various areas in Paris and how they had come through the occupation. On March 10 the opening of the Paris Stage Door Canteen for servicemen, near the Etoile, featured entertainment by Marlene Dietrich, Maurice Chevalier, and Noel Coward. A modest announcement of the reopening of W. H. Smith and Sons' bookstore, on the rue de Rivoli, foreshadowed better times to come; Josephine Baker reappeared at a benefit concert to raise money for French forces; and Harry McElhone returned to Harry's New York Bar, 5, rue Daunou. But every day also produced stories about shorter rations in the United States, food shortages in the United Kingdom, food demonstrations and riots in France, and the use of scarce foreign exchange by the French government to purchase American grain. De Gaulle greeted the first returned women deportees from Ravensbruck concentration camp, routed through Switzerland and Annemasse, on the Geneva border, as the earliest eye witness stories of the liberated death camps began to filter back. But returned deportees also raided the Printemps department store for clothes, the black market blossomed, and de Gaulle's all-party government seemed unable to produce a coherent economic policy. Local elections showed a decided swing to the left.

The French Ministry of Information released extra newsprint for four pages on the death of Franklin D. Roosevelt, and French letters of condolence poured in to the newspaper, which had room for a few typical ones.

The opening of the San Francisco Conference on the United Nations Charter and the execution of Mussolini shared headlines with the continued progress of Allied armies as they drove across Germany, took Berlin, and met on the Elbe. The now rapidly crumbling front in Europe nevertheless allowed pessimists to predict that the war in the Far East would still go on for a long time. Admiral Yarnell, retired commander of the Pacific Fleet, perhaps set the record: it would take five years to bring down the Japanese. General Stilwell, after inspecting the carnage in Okinawa, estimated it would take two years. And even in Europe, where Geoff Parsons had gone to see the ravages of war in Germany, and where the *Stars and Stripes* had already set up shop and begun to print in a plant near Frankfurt, and where the biggest banner yet had announced "Russians in Berlin," Walter Lippmann nevertheless raised the possibility that joint Western- Russian armies might have to fight for six more months to destroy northern and southern redoubts fanatically defended by Nazi bitter-enders. But even as he wrote, the headlines from May 1 to May 8 chronicled the disintegration of German armies, and the death of Hitler—reported first in the *Stars and Stripes* of May 2, since no other morning newspaper appeared in France, where May 1 was a universal holiday. On May 8 the single word "Victory" spread across the top of the paper in letters two inches high. For the first time since December 1939, reported Bugeja, Paris was fully lighted, and even the big vertical red "Herald Tribune" sign glowed through the night on the rue de Berri. Four pages that day and the next allowed the elation of the moment full play.

On June 12 the *Herald* announced resumption of a regular four page paper, and on June 13 Jacques Soustelle, de Gaulle's press spokesman, declared that press censorship would end by September. The government, he said, would aid creation of a truly free press unlike that which had existed before—"venal and unworthy, reaping profits from its silence and its interested campaigns, quick to calumny and offend, indifferent toward the public good, and which poisoned our political life before giving itself up to the invader."

The *Herald* could now expand again and it did. Advertising still took up little space, so it could publish long stories by Marguerite Higgins on Adolf Hitler; a regular column of international comment by Sumner Welles, former Under Secretary of State; pieces by Russell Hill on the occupation, on Nazism underground, on the controversial ban on fraternization between GI and Fräulein; excerpts from Goering's diary. John "Tex" O'Reilly, one of the frontline war correspondents, wrote a long series on Eisenhower's role in the war. Editorially, the *Herald* voiced continued support for aid to French reconstruction, so vital to Europe, while Bugeja wrote stories on the transformation of the French Communist party into

a nationalist party, emphasizing—at the Tenth Party Congress—
production for reconstruction in cooperation with other parties
and groups in France.

On July 5, for the first time since 1934, the *Herald Tribune* faced
a new competitor: the *Paris Post,* a Paris Edition of the *New York
Post,* edited by Paul Scott Mowrer, former editor of the *Chicago
Daily News.* It was an afternoon paper rather than a morning one,
and sold for three francs as a four-page tabloid. Nevertheless, given
the economic situation of the times, it competed for the scarce
resources available and quickly reached a circulation close to that
of the *Herald*—around forty to fifty thousand copies a day. While
the *Post* depended at first upon substantial military circulation, it
was a serious endeavor. The first copy bore a statement to the effect
that while the new French press was excellent and that British
newspapers now reached the Continent to accompany the reestablished Continental Edition of the *London Daily Mail,* there was
still a need. "Especially from the American viewpoint there is the
well-known and deservedly popular European edition of the *New
York Herald Tribune*—but it is a morning newspaper. We are an
evening newspaper and we think that the large English-reading
public now on the Continent both in and out of uniform should
have a chance to see at least two American dailies."

Moreover, unlike the *Herald Tribune,* the *Post* was a liberal
paper, representative of the United States of Franklin D. Roosevelt
and Harry S Truman—and, indeed, the first number bore a letter
from President Truman wishing the new paper success. It clearly
gave the *Herald Tribune* something of a run. It was, however,
unable to survive the demobilization of American troops, and it
lasted only a year. For the next few years the *Herald Tribune* would
have the European field pretty much to itself. The *Stars and Stripes*
was still rolling off the presses in vast numbers, but it was a
specialized publication. Only later, when it settled down to its
peacetime role of serving U.S. forces assigned to the nascent North
Atlantic Treaty Organization, did it offer serious competition to
the *Herald* for an unforeseen and lucrative market. In 1945, when

planning for the *Herald* took place, no one had imagined that the American army would constitute a permanent potential audience—although as early as March 20, 1945, the *Herald* published a report hinting that U.S. forces might well remain beyond the initial occupation period to remind people that the United States was, indeed, now a great power.*

The world seen through the eyes of the European Edition of those days was hardly a cheery place. The major themes — victory over Japan, collapse of the wartime alliance, the uneven and halting pace of reconstruction—all seemed to converge in the paper's growing coverage of tense Franco-American relations. The first and biggest story was summed up in a two-inch banner headline on a single-sheet extra: "War Is Over." Among the columns was one by Bugeja explaining nuclear fission. But Tex O'Reilly, now on the Paris bureau, noted that there was little celebration in France, since the chief concern seemed to be whether the end of the war might release more American shipping for sending grain, coal, raw materials, and machinery to Europe. The great international conferences—Yalta, Potsdam, San Francisco—all received full coverage, and the *Herald Tribune* played a role in revealing publicly some of the confidential agreements on multiple votes for the Soviet Union and the reparations figure discussed at Yalta. But again, as with Yalta, French absence from the Potsdam Conference provoked more stories than the defeat of the Churchill government in the midst of the conference.

Many items foreshadowed the future. The *Herald* reported on an article in a Communist party theoretical organ by French party

---

*For a while another publication may have offered the *Herald* some competition among Europeans. From D-Day on, the Office of War Information published what began as a sixteen-page weekly leaflet for the French, called *Voir*. It turned into a money-making picture weekly on the model of *Life* and *Look*, sold on French newsstands, and reached a circulation of 500,000. But its profits went into general Treasury funds, so that when Congress cut the OWI appropriations it had to suspend publication on September 15, 1945, even though it had made almost $250,000 in its last quarter of publication.

leader Jacques Duclos, blasting American Communist Earl Brow-
der both for his dissolution of the American Communist party
during the war and for his support for a cooperative Popular Front
policy now that the war was over; seizure of power should never
be abandoned as an option. (And William Z. Foster replaced Brow-
der as head of a reborn American Communist party.) In September
of 1945 stories began to appear about an obscure Annamite nationalist leader in Indochina, variously tagged as Hochinminh, Chi
Mih Ho Chi Ming, and finally Ho Chi Minh, premier of a recently
formed provisional government; confused fighting in Saigon leading to the death of an American colonel brought a banner headline.
The chief French concern evident in the newspaper was whether
and how much the United States would back France in the affair.
American labor leader George Meany took the occasion of an
invitation to address the British Trades Union Council to attack
Russian trade unions as not trade unions at all, and Under Secretary
of State Dean Acheson's criticism of General MacArthur's conduct
of the Japanese occupation brought bitter congressional attacks on
the Under Secretary, producing an editorial supporting Acheson.
The Nuremberg trials shared headlines with the trials of Laval and
Marshal Pétain in France and the Pearl Harbor inquiry in the United
States. On December 16, 1945, the American Church in Paris
reopened its Sunday School; two days later the Paris brothels were
shut down by order of the Municipal Council. General Patton died
and Ezra Pound was declared insane.

In recent years the sad story of the unwilling repatriation of
Russian nationals to the Soviet Union has been fully documented;
but much of the story was to be found in the *Herald Tribune* of
those years—the first columns dealing simply with the huge exchanges of ex-prisoners: Russians, Ukrainians, and Eastern Europeans from the West for French, Americans, and Englishmen from
the camps liberated by the Russians in eastern areas of Germany.
Soon, however, there were stories of Russians hiding out to avoid
forced repatriation, of the dilemma of whether Westerners would
hunt them down to turn them over when other refugees kept

streaming west—and of whether, if the Western Allies did not return the unwilling Russians, the Soviet Union would delay the repatriation of Westerners. On June 17, 1945, the paper printed a report that the Russians had stopped repatriating Swiss nationals until the Swiss resumed repatriation of 9,000 Russian internees, many of whom did not want to return.

Joseph Stalin's election day speech of February 10, redefining World War II as one caused by the persistence of capitalism, and Winston Churchill's Fulton, Missouri, "Iron Curtain" speech were reported in full, along with the widespread negative American reactions to Churchill's call for a common Anglo-American position vis-à-vis the Soviet Union; a *Herald Tribune* editorial condemned the vigor of his tactics. Geoffrey Parsons occasionally skirted the rule about editorials originating in Europe; in 1946 he wrote an editorial page feature arguing that the real issue in March of that year was whether France, under Communist and Socialist leadership, would move into the Communist orbit, with England and the United States turning their backs upon the Continent, or whether it would remain independent.

Helen and Ogden Reid, to their credit, refused to impose a narrowly defined Cold War view upon their *New York Herald Tribune*; the paper's measured view of complex events earned it Republican Representative Clare Booth Luce's epithet of "the *Uptown Daily Worker*." The European Edition under Geoffrey Parsons allowed perhaps even a greater variety of views to be represented in its pages. Early in the postwar period it reprinted a *Nation* column calling for a cleaning out of the conservatives in the Department of State—the Joseph Grews and Jimmy Dunns. An editorial about the arrest of two State Department men and a navy man for passing confidential information on China to a "left-wing" publication decried "red-baiting." William Shirer's syndicated columns persisted in voicing a fear of Fascist resurgence; as the Marshall Plan became a reality, he stressed that Britain and France feared a too rapid revival of German industrial might. If the Marshall Plan was based on rebuilding Germany, its long-range benefit was questionable indeed. Speeches by Maurice Thorez, the French Communist leader, received lengthy coverage; * his talk to the Anglo-American Press Club was reprinted in full. The paper's editorials, while supporting the Truman shift in foreign policy of 1947–48, decried the rhetoric that supported the development of containment, as well as the anti-Communist hysteria it discerned in the United States.

The paper printed both *Izvestia's* as well as the *Daily Worker's* replies to Truman's congressional speech calling for aid to Greece and Turkey, a comment of caution from Lippmann, and Shirer's attack upon the generality of Truman's speech, with his observation that the policy would only work if the United States abandoned Britain's support for reactionary forces and began to work with progressive ones. When it reprinted George F. Kennan's famous "X" memorandum that explained the basis for Truman's containment policy, it subsequently printed Lippmann's reply, in which the latter charged Kennan with laying the groundwork for long-term ideological conflict when the focus of policy should be finding a diplomatic accommodation with the Russians over the issue of Europe. Mao Tse-tung's friend Edgar Snow reviewed Owen Lattimore's *Situation in Asia*; the *Herald Tribune* published Anna Louise Strong's apologetic, pro-Communist account of her jailing in Moscow, and it allowed Richard Wright, the former Communist black author, now living in Paris, to publish a reply.

While correspondents like Seymour Freidin reported on events in Eastern Europe—such as the Communist takeover of Hungary in 1947—in what had become conventional Cold-War terms, Geoff Parsons had a bright young Hungarian economist named Tibor Mende write his own interpretative piece. Mende had been taken on to work on the enlarged financial section; he would much later play a prominent role in the third-world-dominated U.N.

*Including, later, the notorious speech of February 1949, when Thorez declared that as a good Communist he would welcome Russian invaders as liberators if Russia chose to march west.

Conference on Trade and Development. But in 1947 he wrote an apologia for the Communist coup on the basis of the ending of domestic Fascism and play of progressive domestic social forces. A crisis over nationalization of banks, not politics, was the cause of the coup (an interpretation made somewhat questionable by Communist boss Rakosi's boast that he had seized power while Washington slept). Ambassador Jefferson Caffery called in Parsons and told him that he had confidential information—about which he could say little—to the effect that young Mende was a Communist. Parsons told the ambassador that Mende was doing a fine job of financial and economic editing, and that was that.

The treatment and interpretation of the news reflected the reality of the ambiguities and dilemmas of the real world, and not the more simplistic, if necessary, official explanations. Different reporters and columnists provided the differing interpretations. The lively "Mailbag" of those years, too, reflected the fact that Cold War attitudes had not yet fully hardened, and under Parsons' editorial direction it became one of the most important and widely read sections of the newspaper, as Europeans as well as Americans sought clarification of American attitudes within its confines. Letters attacked Truman's policy as too rigidly anti-Communist or even pro-Fascist; some replied in defense of the President; others argued he was too soft on the Russians. Letter writers attacked Congress for destroying American advantage in the Cold War by trying to include Franco Spain in NATO or the Marshall Plan; some pitched in to the extreme line being taken by Henry Luce's *Time-Life* organization over China, now spilling over into a general assault on the Truman administration and on Secretary of State Dean Acheson in particular for being too soft on Communism. Several ridiculed the strong pitch being made by Luce and in Congress for more aid to the decaying Chiang regime. The publication of General Stilwell's memoirs, skillfully edited—some said tendentiously edited—by Theodore White, occasioned controversy over Stilwell's derogatory views about the Chinese Nationalist leader.

On an editorial page a day or so after Churchill's Fulton, Missouri, speech, when a balanced editorial called for friendly firmness toward the Russians, and a sampling of American editorial and congressional opinion largely condemned the Englishman's call for an Anglo-American front, a long letter from T/5 Jerome Minot with the Office of Military Governor, United States, in Berlin complained that the *Herald Tribune's* headline writing reflected a growing anti-Russian attitude to be found throughout the paper. The paper was defended in a later "Mailbag" letter by the head copywriter, Frank Webb. It all made lively reading.

The parent paper, rather than using foreign correspondents for lavish continued coverage like the rival *New York Times,* downplayed its bureaus and resorted to using its somewhat more slender resources in sending correspondents to do special in-depth stories, either singly or in groups. In mid-1947 a team toured Eastern Europe. The group included the new Paris bureau chief, Walter B. Kerr (the man who had written so movingly of the flight from Paris in June 1940, and later covered Stalingrad and Moscow), William Attwood, a 1946 transferee from Washington to the Paris bureau, London bureau chief Ned Russell, and editorial writer Russell Hill from New York. They developed a common format of questions, spent ten weeks in all the countries of Eastern Europe, and returned to Geoff Parsons' Fontainebleau retreat outside of Paris to compare notes and write and rewrite their stories. Their series contradicted some of the growing Cold War stereotypes, reflecting the diversity of conditions in the East, and again letters flooded in, commenting on the widely-circulated and syndicated series. Another time Attwood spent five weeks in occupied Germany, and his thoughtful articles in January 1947 netted him a sheaf of lengthy letters, of which only a few excerpts could be published.

It was a time, hard to recapture now, when Germany still lay in ruins, economic activity remained strictly limited, and a package of American cigarettes could purchase a meal—or a woman for the night. "The German problem" was widely discussed: whether

Germans could ever be trusted, reeducated, democratized, denazified, or not and the replies to and comments on Attwood's articles took every side in the discussion. For a dozen or more years Germans had had only what contact with the outside world the Nazi regime had permitted them, and the first postwar years saw only a slow resumption of communications. The *Herald Tribune* was thus seized upon by many educated Germans as one of the very first links they had with thoughts and ideas from the outside world; other books or periodicals were still scarce and far too expensive. One German letter printed in 1947 pleaded for more extensive distribution of the paper; the *Herald Tribune,* declared the writer, printed three times as much news as any other European paper, was as much the "Voice of Europe" as it was the voice of America. Its objectivity would do much for the education of Germans.

Geoff Parsons' answer to the letter tells much about the difficulties and limitations the *Herald Tribune* faced at this time, which tended to keep it more parochial than Parsons had originally intended. There was no ban on civil distribution in Germany, he wrote. But there was no way to convert the marks received in payment into French or American currency to cover the costs of production and distribution. The approximately 5,000 copies sold in Germany merely served to accumulate marks of no present value; the paper's management was exploring every avenue to overcome the obstacle and widen distribution. But for now nothing could be done. What was true for Germany was true elsewhere. Circulation throughout Europe was limited by currency restrictions, and meeting the inflating costs of production in France was not helped by sales in countries where such restrictions existed—Norway, Austria, Spain, Ireland, Czechoslovakia, and Poland.

In mid-1946, amid all the gloomy news, there appeared on the back page a three-column story about a new piece of apparel—the bikini bathing suit. "The Consensus from Every Angle Is—Wow!" read the head. One subhead said, "Garb Gets Full Coverage, Which Is More Than Can Be Said for the Wearer"; the other read, "*Herald*

Tribune Newshawks Nudge Out Lucie Noel in Zeal To Write Fashions." And an editor's note explained:

> For the first time in history the entire staff of the European Edition and the foreign service of the *New York Herald Tribune* now in Paris insisted yesterday on covering the same assignment. Each was so determined to do the job that, for the sake of organizational morale, they were all assigned to the same story. It turned out to be an exhibition of the world's smallest bathing suit, modelled at the Piscine Molitor. Most of their stories are printed below, although some of them are still writing.

And each story bore its own subhead. Walter B. Kerr, diplomatic correspondent, called his "Big Four Ponder Zones"; Attwood, calling himself atomic energy correspondent, titled his "Experts Poo-Poo Test"; Vincent Bugeja called his paragraph "Glimpses of Long Ago," and recalled his excitement in 1896 at seeing a shapely calf protruding from a bathing suit of the time. Lucie Noel, the fashion editor, merely wrote, "Wow!"

It is this kind of story that the journalists of those days recall with pleasure. When the paper expanded to a fairly regular six pages in 1946 there was more room for the group spirit that began to manifest itself throughout the paper and relieved the gloom of so much of the more serious news. It spread to Frank Webb and his copyreaders: in mid-1947, when a notorious gangster was gunned down in New York, the paper ran a picture of his girlfriend with the caption "Bugsy Siegel's Shapely Friend Shocked at His Untimely End," and Webb, a well-dressed Irishman who wore a pocket watch on the chain looped across his vest, ended up absorbing the more pleasant French habits of indulging in an aperitif and good food and lingering in a café on the way home after work.

The *Herald* crew had a good time putting out their paper. Former war correspondent Tex O'Reilly covered French politics with farfetched comparisons with politics in west Texas, and helped promote the late-night parties that followed lockup of the last edition—and that frequently ended up in the Bois de Boulogne, where

he also pitched for the oft-defeated *Herald Tribune* softball teams.*
A serious and thought-provoking correspondent like Attwood
could produce a dozen hilarious columns about the constant foul-
ups of a tour through French African possessions by reporters in
the party of French President Vincent Auriol (later to be gathered
in a book called *The Man Who Could Grow Hair,* the title of
another series of pieces on a Frenchman who claimed to be able to
do just that). Those who were paid wholly in dollars—the foreign
correspondents—and who received a healthy expense allowance
besides, were the best off. But everyone found pleasure and excitement in working in Paris. In the spring of 1946 publisher Ogden
Reid paid an unexpected visit to the Paris bureau; everyone knew
he was arriving, but not just when it would be. O'Reilly had finished
work, his Canadian WAC girlfriend was sitting with her feet up
on the couch, and the Texan was pouring out whiskey for the
assembling crew. Reid walked in and O'Reilly imperturbably
handed him the glass he had just filled: "Have a drink, Mr. Reid."
"Thanks, I don't mind if I do," said his publisher, and the party
was on.

Yet the high spirits were inevitably colored by the political and
economic circumstances of the times. In late January 1946 Robert
Stern returned to New York to become the New York correspondent of the Paris Edition, where he would channel the flow of
material from the home paper to Paris. His editorial page valedic-
tory—"Farewell to Paris: Mood Indigo"—began by saying, "The
boss said 'write us a light piece about Paris as a farewell gesture.'
Sorry, I don't feel light." He wrote, instead, of his chest tightening

---

*History does record that he defeated the Paris Subway Worker's Union team 17–13 at the
Stade Metropolitain on June 14, 1947. More usual was a game like the one the *Herald
Tribune* team dropped to *Time-Life* by a score of 21–2, billed as the "grudge game of the
century," and preceded by a special limited-circulation in-house edition of the paper, whose
huge headline read "Orgy of Poison Plots, Spies, Sabotage, Reaches Apex Today in Grudge
Game of (Blood) Thirsty Newspaper Nines." Attwood recalls making eight or nine errors,
hitting a single pop fly, yet having reason to hope for the most valuable player award. In
spite of probable lack of reader interest, brief accounts of these games were run on the
sports page. One, written by Herb Kupferberg, extolled "Kupferberg's brilliant contribution
to the exciting game." The night editor printed it, but added a byline at the top: "by Herb
Kupferberg."

as he looked out at the Paris he loved, the familiar beauties of the place de la Concorde, Notre Dame, the Seine at the Ile de la Cité. But what he felt was the anxiety, the despair, the terrifyingly low morale among the workers, the good French bourgeois, the civil servants. Only in a monastery, where monks told him about the work being done by new young recruits, did he get any sense of hope that if and when he ever returned, the attitude he found there might have taken a firm, wider hold.

The story says something fundamental about the European Edition of the *New York Herald Tribune* of those years. Despite Parsons' plans for an international newspaper, despite the fine international coverage in the front pages, its editorial staff rooted it firmly in the Paris milieu in which it was published. It was more than the fact that the paper had reviewers and columnists who dealt with Paris' music, art, theater, or fashions; it was more than having staff like David and Ann Perleman and Vincent Bugeja to cover local affairs. It was simply that Parsons, Hawkins, and the bureau people in addition were all living the strained life of the area and two-thirds of their paid circulation was in France. While the primary function of bureau people was to serve the home paper, they tended to write to Paris deadlines, and like all the people in the other European bureaus, they filed through Paris, simply handing over carbons to the Paris staff. But they also went out on their own and covered French and specifically Parisian events, and contributed their pieces to the paper, which also drew directly from the French press service.

There simply was no division in Paris, as there was in New York newspapers, between city, national, and international staffs. Everyone was living in Paris, and the newspaper—perhaps more serious in its international coverage than in prewar times, and paying less attention to those "names, names, names" that Bennett had decreed it should print sixty years earlier and that continued to appear until 1939—became the American newspaper in Paris, concerned about Paris and reporting both on French political and economic affairs and on Franco-American relations, two sides of the same coin. In

October of 1947 editorial writer Harry Baehr of the New York paper flew to Paris on the first Air France New York to Paris sleeper plane. Once in Paris he did what all the *Herald Tribune* people did: wandered about France writing articles for the Paris paper on what he saw.*

None of this kept the paper from also delivering excellent, broad news coverage.† On the occasion of its sixtieth anniversary on October 5, 1947, it printed excerpts from some of the letters of congratulation it received from President Truman, Ambassadors Caffery, Douglas, Dunn, and Murphy, and Anthony Eden. George Bidault, the Minister of Foreign Affairs, wrote of how it presented "precise and objective news to Frenchmen and friends of France residing in Paris." Geoffrey Crowther, editor of the *Economist,* wrote, "I rather set my face against giving statements to be published, but my respect for the *Herald Tribune* is so great that you may quote me as saying that I find it doubly indispensable—first, for following American news and second, because it gives the best coverage of European news of any paper that I know." But Ambassador Henri Bonnet wrote, "During all these years your paper has been associated so intimately with the daily life and toil of Paris and its people that we have come to think of it as one of our French dailies."

The attention to local detail gave the paper—perhaps unintentionally—a deeply Parisian flavor. Much of it was delightful and funny. But it also meant an intense chronicling of the uneven economic recovery, the frequent setbacks and worsening conditions, the growing American role in European economic affairs, and the resulting incessant tensions and misunderstandings.

---

*He took with him to Paris a hundred-dollar bill tucked into his pocket by owner Jack Bleeck of the Artists and Writers Restaurant on 40th Street, once a speakeasy and the longtime hangout of *Herald Tribune* journalists, who usually referred to it as "downstairs," as in "If you need me, I'll be downstairs." At Bleeck's request the hundred dollars financed a party in Paris such that Baehr has no idea how the paper was ever put out that night.
†In May 1947, the paper claimed that within the compass of its average six pages it carried more international news than any American paper other than the *New York Times* and the *New York Herald Tribune,* and twice as much as either the *London Times* or *Le Monde.*

The first peacetime winter, in 1945, followed the worst summer drought in fifty years. It was a hard one. Robert Stern reported cheerfully on the return of Paris buses, and which ones offered the best ride. But Edwin Hartrick reported on the fuel shortages, the closed nightclubs, and the deserted streets. Sara Lamport reported on the *Réveillons de Noël* in unheated churches. For those with money, she noted, Christmas was cheerful. For those without, it was lean and chilly, and many people did what they had done in August: left Paris—not for resorts, but for the countryside, in search of food and warmth.

The abrupt cancellation of Lend-Lease with the end of the war in the Pacific in August of 1945, although it rated only one column in the *Herald Tribune,* left a bitter aftertaste, coming as it did at the same moment that de Gaulle left to visit President Truman. By and large the American press praised de Gaulle and his mission. But Bert Andrews, in the New York Edition, noted at the conclusion of the mission that the cold truth lay in the behind-the-scenes story; American reconversion would come first, before European relief. When, in September of 1945, Parsons recorded the issuing of the first postwar red *Michelin Guide* to French hotels and restaurants, he noted that it was a saddening catalogue of war damage.

Bread rationing resumed at Christmas time in 1945, and there were French charges that the United States had reneged on wheat shipments. American replies showed that shipments were well ahead of schedule; planned Argentinian ones had failed to materialize. A month later Perleman wrote that 45 percent of French imports came from the United States: all oil, half of all imported food, and one-third of coal; the United States was also supplying France with an enormous number of the so-called "Liberation" locomotives to replace what had been destroyed during the war. France had little with which to pay for any of these imports, yet Frenchmen had little conception of what the United States was doing for them.

On March 2, 1946, Paris lay freezing under fifteen inches of snow.

One major source of local Franco-American friction evaporated when most of the GI's departed, moving their headquarters to Frankfurt, and U.S. forces returned over 3,000 requisitioned hotels, schools, office buildings, hospitals, and warehouses. Yet even the American departure brought anger, and Parsons felt a constant need to try to clear up stories that circulated to the detriment of Franco-American relations. In early August of 1945 he reported on an investigation of French press reports that the U.S. army was burning stocks of food and clothing as it closed out its bases. The embassy, army authorities, and a *Herald Tribune* reporter had all conducted separate investigations; they all concluded that there was no foundation to the stories, and Parsons admonished his French colleagues about "the currently popular French fad of baiting the Americans."

A week later Parsons was to take writer François Mauriac to task for suggesting that the Allies had spared the I.G. Farben works in Hoechst as a result of the influence of American trusts, which also prevented the French from taking necessary action. The record shows, wrote Parsons, that 40,000 tons of bombs were dropped on the Farben works by the American air force; Mauriac was spreading "anti-American and anti-British propaganda." On another occasion the paper reported French apprehension that the United States would deny sales of transport planes to France, while allowing American airlines to purchase them and insisting as a matter of policy on freedom of the skies—thus ensuring Americans of air transport monopoly. Again Parsons tried to answer. Quite clearly the *Herald* had become, for him, an instrument devoted to improving Franco-American relations. In an editorial-page article he demanded that the Department of State be provided with a good information service now that the Office of War Information had been disbanded; without such a service the misconceptions about America could only multiply.

The summer of 1946 brought a measure of economic optimism. French exports spurted, and across the channel—ironically, in terms of what would subsequently happen—British automobile production and exports boomed. The *Herald Tribune* commented that it augured well for the future, since Britain had a head start over all other automobile producers, and under the Labour government labor conditions were stable.

But again, the winter of 1946–47 dashed all expectation. It was perhaps the hardest yet; canals froze and transportation ground to a halt; blizzard after blizzard lashed Western Europe. Rations were cut throughout the Continent; industry ground to a halt; Parisians froze in the dark. Even that summer of 1947, when things looked so much more like normal and the *Herald Tribune* regularly published six to eight pages, with a fattened travel section, France had to stop all dollar purchases, end gasoline imports, and institute two days a week without electricity to rebuild coal stocks for the coming winter. On the front page Jules Grad, one of the former *Stars and Stripers*, registered the drop in the black market franc to 185 to the dollar in May, and to 255 by September. Lucie Noel's lengthy articles on Dior, Givenchy, and Schiaparelli appeared in the same numbers that recorded that Britain had suspended convertibility, cut its imports by 25 percent, and suspended private motoring and any tourist travel abroad, while in France the ration of bread, two years after the war, was cut to *below* the wartime level. The summer editions carried travel ads for Switzerland, Italy, and France; advertisements for hotels and restaurants in Paris, for movies, for books, for French stores, and for automobiles—for sale only to foreigners. But the main advertising revenue derived from the dozens of ads for packages from American shippers, containing nylons, foodstuffs like canned butter, powdered eggs and milk, coffee and chocolate, cigarettes, and automobile tires. Americans with Army Post Office numbers could order them; what it meant was that the *Herald Tribune* was living in good part on ads for goods destined for the black market!*

*There was one contrast. In August the *Herald Tribune* published the first of what would be many supplements on individual countries. An eight-page insert on Belgium, edited largely by the *Herald Tribune* representative in Belgium, Eric Cypres, and written mostly by the Perlemans, reflected the fact that the Belgian economy was booming partly because of its wartime income from uranium shipments from the Congo, partly because a harsh currency reform had worked in getting the economy moving again.

The *Herald Tribune* of those 1947 summer months reflects the profound differences in attitudes that existed in the United States and in Europe. In America there might be temporary shortages in such items as automobiles, for which demand was pent up during the war. But by and large reconversion of an undamaged and war-expanded industrial plant was proceeding by leaps and bounds, and demobilized soldiers were absorbed into the economy with relatively little trouble. Americans were ready to see the same process elsewhere, and American tourists were eager to return to a Europe that would welcome them for their dollar contributions—but whose facilities were still meager.

As a result, the Paris Edition was somewhat schizophrenic. In 1947 it published the first postwar *Travel Guide to Europe,* with articles by all its contributors. The travel section, expanded to two pages on Tuesday, had articles on the reopening of resorts in Austria, bullfighting in the south of France, a "Holiday of the Week" travel suggestion, and resort and hotel ads. The "Calendar of Coming Events" grew in length; so, too, did the number of letters detailing the hardships of customs regulations and border crossings. (An article in "Travel Topics" noted that when an American plane flew to the United States it had to file 528 legally prescribed forms that took at least four hours to fill out: 4 American clearance declarations, 35 landing cards, 35 baggage export certificates, 210 cargo manifests, 42 crew manifests, and 4 stores list. It was about this time, too, that stiff regulations went into effect in France on the cashing of traveler's checks and illegal sales of automobiles, both measures to curb the drain of foreign exchange.) The refurbished *Queen Mary* sailed for France that summer for the first time since World War II and occasioned a full page in the Travel Section; and the sailing of the *Veendam* gave rise to one of those old familiar touches: "Among the passengers are John Jacob Astor and Mrs. Astor," etc. The new regularity of transatlantic air travel by means of the latest Lockheed Constellation and Boeing Stratocruiser airliners led to abandonment of the old "Airline Arrivals and Departures" column.

The resurgence of the American community showed up in the

paper, too, as prewar organizations reappeared. On September 1 Reid Hall, the sixth arrondissement residence for American women students, reopened; Helen Rogers Reid was vice-chairman of the board, Dean Virginia Gildersleeve of Barnard the chairman. In its first year of postwar operation it would house sixty-five students, with the largest group coming from Smith College, led by Mme. Vincent Guilloton. "Paris Briefs" appeared weekly, with notes on meetings of the Women's Sewing Group of the American Church and programs at the old American Students and Artists Center on the boulevard Raspail. A charming article by a young woman named Naomi Barry entitled "Hitch-Hiking Is Easy in France" told how she and her husband had made it to the Italian Riviera in four days. No truck with an empty seat ever passed them by, people went out of their way for them, and everyone talked. (Thirty-odd years later Miss Barry would still be contributing feature articles to the *Herald Tribune*.)

It all contrasted sadly and sharply with the August 1947 economic crisis, when, despite the American tourists, *all* dollar imports had to cease. Strikes that fall and the ban on British foreign tourism boded ill for any Riviera season. The U.S. Congress passed an interim aid bill that helped, but dragged its feet on the Marshall Plan debates. Attwood visited Normandy in January and reported that three and a half years after the Anglo-American landings people in the area were disillusioned, embittered, and pessimistic; their cynicism about politicians was evidently what had led de Gaulle to proclaim his new Rally of the French People. In Germany the meat ration was drastically cut for the month of February, and there was *no* fat ration.

Fortunately, the winter of 1947–48 proved less harsh than the two previous ones. The *Réveillons de Noël* and New Year celebrations were still subdued, Bugeja wrote; night clubs were still closed. But in February some of the electricity restrictions were lifted in Paris. Spring of 1948 brought political crises and taut nerves; war seemed to threaten when a Russian fighter "buzzing" an English airliner on its way to Berlin during the Berlin blockade crashed into it, and the Russian note in reply to British protests was almost unbelievably truculent. The Czech coup, General de Gaulle's call for an American military guarantee of Western Europe, creation of the Brussels Treaty Organization—foreshadowing NATO, with its American membership—war over nascent Israel, a renewed drive by Chinese Communist forces, and an election in the United States that everyone except Harry Truman thought would be won by Tom Dewey were all the focus of attention. Yet spring also brought the promise of a veritable flood of American tourists and of the first more or less back-to-normal summer in France. In April it was announced that all passages on the small fleet of postwar transatlantic liners were booked solid until September 1; the rebuilt *Queen Elizabeth* dropped off 2,300 American tourists on her first call at Cherbourg, and Lockheed Constellations inaugurated the first commercial nonstop New York to Paris flights.

Under the spur of the European Recovery Program the countries of Western Europe created the Organization for European Economic Cooperation, and at The Hague Winston Churchill called for a United States of Europe. The *Herald Tribune's* 1948 *Travel Guide to Europe* was expanded to fifty pages, while the travel section, now under Oden and Olivia Meeker, grew again.

Advertisements in the *Herald Tribune* reflected the improving condition: travel ads displaced the APO black market package advertisements, and in early 1949, as more restrictions were lifted in France, the *Herald Tribune* headlined, "Lights Are On Again in London; End Ten Years of Gloom." It would still be one year before coffee, the last item on the French ration list, would be freely sold, but the black market dollar came to an end in France in April of 1949, and Bugeja reported that the *Foire au Jambon* had returned for Easter Week for the first time in ten years. That summer the overflow of American tourists strained the French currency system. On December 5 Coca-Cola first went quietly on sale in Paris. By the end of the month forty or fifty cafés carried it, raising a hue and cry in both the Communist *L'Humanité* and the independent *Le Monde,* which viewed it as a foot in the door for submergence of the consumer by lurid propaganda.

A month later it was Vincent Bugeja who summed up the first

half of the twentieth century in "An Accounting." Three names
sufficed: Lenin, Hitler, and Einstein. By his reckoning irrational
elements let loose had brought the end of the great liberal era and
produced "violence, strife, fear, oppression, envy and hatred, su-
perstition and fanaticism, abuse of power, and apathy." So much
for the first half of the twentieth century.

    In early 1947 Parsons added an informative and useful section
called the "Monthly Economic Review", under the editorship of
Tibor Mende and an Iranian named Dmitri Abkhazi. In 1948 the
section began to give systematic coverage of European Recovery
Program developments for all fifteen countries involved. But again,
reporting on the ERP produced a spate of *Herald Tribune* editorials, features and letters to the editor about lack of French recognition of what the United States had been doing. When the Russians
shipped France 500,000 bushels of wheat in 1948, the *Herald*
complained that the French knew all about these, while failing to
know or acknowledge that the United States had already shipped
90 *million* bushels of wheat and 390,000 tons of wheat flour. In
January 1949 another editorial denounced the French press for its
dearth of information on American appropriations for the ERP
and for failing to report American food, machinery, and raw material shipments and the provisions for currency arrangements.
Concurrently the paper printed articles about various people's calls
for a better U.S. information service. Geoffrey Parsons, convinced
like many others that independent publications such as the *Trib,
Time, Life,* or the French Edition of the *Readers Digest* could do
a much better job than any official effort, was engaged in a strenuous effort to get government support for wider distribution. But
this story properly belongs in the next chapter.
    In the meantime, in the last years of the 1940s, the paper looked
more and more prosperous and gave its readers an increasing
number of features. By mid-1949 it printed eight full pages a day.
The first three pages were packed with wide coverage to which the

New York paper's still superb foreign correspondents contributed. As they had done with the Iron Curtain series, they frequently operated as a team, doing, for example, an ERP series on all the countries of Western Europe. Parsons ran John Gunther's *Inside Europe Today* serially, and a series on a John Steinbeck–Robert Capa trip to the Soviet Union that provoked a rash of letters: one called it "a breath of fresh air," another "naive . . . and serving no purpose," while a third declared that by printing it the *Herald Tribune* had turned itself into an organ of Russian propaganda which the writer would no longer read. In the New York office a correspondent prepared a "Letter" or "Report from America"—a series of shorts of more than routine interest.

Unhappily, the paper also had to run more and more about espionage and subversion in the United States; Hiss, Coplon, and Senator McCarthy became familiar names to European readers, along with accounts of the Tydings Committee's hearings on the *Amerasia* case and Senator McCarthy's wild charges that Owen Lattimore had been the architect of American foreign policy; even the Alsops were accused by McCarthy of following the Communist line! A Lippmann column noted that Secretary of State Dean Acheson was going abroad hobbled by anti-Communist attacks as no Foreign Minister in any other democracy ever could be. It is quite clear that Parsons' conception of the *Herald Tribune's* role did not mean a downplaying of the seamy side of American life. (Later, after Parsons left, Whitelaw Reid, who had assumed the editorship of the New York paper after his father's death, and worked closely with his mother Helen Reid, lodged fairly frequent objections to what he felt was too critical a way of playing American news in the European Edition.)

All the regular American columnists now appeared: Walter Lippmann's cautious and pragmatic reasoning, the Alsops' and David Laurence's trumpets of doom, John Crosby on American television, a sports column by the great Red Smith, Billy Rose's entertainment-world gossip column, the "United Nations Review," a book column, and the usual crossword puzzle and chess feature.

From France, Bugeja continued to provide erudite articles on scientific affairs while also reporting on such matters as the rebirth of Eugene Jolas' little magazine *transition,* and covering the extended and sensational Kravchenko–*Lettres Françaises* libel trial, in which the Russian defector sued the French Communist periodical for its characterization of him and his writings about the Soviet Union. The versatile "Booj" could also contribute columns about the Two-Mile Waiters' Race and the *Semaine de l'Amabilité,* in which Parisians were exhorted to be amiable—for a week, at least. Eugene Jolas was then briefly recruited to do an art, literature, and theater column, "Across Frontiers."

A new "Mostly About People" feature that would have a long and varied career began in April 1949 with lengthy interviews, anecdotes, and brief takes, all written by different staffers. Even Parsons got his hand in on that one during a Big Four Foreign Ministers' meeting that took place in Paris following the end of the Berlin blockade. A newcomer, Robert Yoakum, interviewed French dockworkers to see if men belonging to a communist-dominated union would actually unload American weapons destined for the French army and NATO. Some would; some wouldn't. "On Paris Screens," Paris After Dark," and Slocombe's worthwhile book reviews, Gil Robb Wilson's column "Air World," a regular "European Opinion on World Events" feature drawing from newspaper editorials—all lent a sparkle to the paper. It prompted someone to write in to cheer for all the fine columnists but to declare, "Sparrow is missed! . . . Ed, go bird-hunting!"

French racing results, the winning numbers in French lottery drawings, and, of course, French fashion news added to the local feeling of the paper. Lucie Noel, who began a career with the European Edition in 1935 as assistant to the then fashion editor and rejoined the paper in 1947 after a stint in the U.S. army, became required reading for both resident and visiting American buyers, as well as an arbiter of fashion for both Americans and Europeans who read the *Herald.* A United Nations General Assembly meeting in Paris would get full coverage, but the Marcel Cerdan victory over American boxer Tony Zale got almost as much; Cerdan was a French idol and singer Edith Piaf's great love. A Herb Kupferberg piece on the British Automobile Show, on which the British placed so much hope for firmly establishing the British lead in world automobile exports, got prominent display; but so did the stories about French Communist leader Maurice Thorez's fiftieth birthday celebrations. It was about this time that a house ad proclaimed

More pages
More Columns
More stock reports
More features
More news!
More for your Money!

Despite its fine international coverage, the European Edition was once more and still the Paris *Herald*, with a coziness and familiarity that would, for a while at least, be greatly enhanced by one of its newest columnists, a chubby young man in horn-rim spectacles named Art Buchwald.

Buchwald's story is probably familiar to most readers. Ten dollars to a chance drunk in the street persuaded the drunk to become his short-term "father" and give permission for him to enroll in the marine corps at the age of sixteen during World War II. He served as an underage marine in the Pacific for seventeen months, went to the University of Southern California for three years on the GI Bill, then, after receiving an unexpected veteran's bonus, hitchhiked to New York and crossed to France on one of the early student ships. Once in Paris he enrolled in the Alliance Française and attended one class in order to continue getting his GI Bill living allotment, supplementing it by selling his foreigner's gasoline ration coupons on the black market. He lived on the Left Bank, of course, in the Hotel des Etats-Unis, run by Polish refugees, where he helped out in the campaign of another lodger, Garry Davis, self-styled Citizen of the World.

The French clamped down on the gas coupon racket and Buchwald turned up at the *Herald Tribune* one day early in 1949, where Eric Hawkins turned him down; Parsons had told Hawkins that the paper's financial situation was tight—how tight, no one really knew—and that he couldn't hire anyone. But Buchwald demonstrated the initiative that had served him well in the past, and that would serve him even better as the years wore on. When Hawkins was absent for a while, he bearded Geoffrey Parsons, who explained that since all editorial personnel were to be paid at the Newspaper Guild scale, he couldn't take on anyone else. But Buchwald argued that because he was writing an occasional column for *Variety,* a single column at twenty-five dollars a week would be enough—and Parsons decided to try him, giving him the "Paris After Dark" or "Paris Screen Talk" columns, where he could review movies, night life, and a restaurant of the week, and bring in a little advertising. Buchwald needed a good bit of help on the first ones, but when, after a few weeks, he told Parsons that *Variety* could no longer use him the editor succumbed, and let him do two columns, thus bringing him up to guild standards.

Soon Buchwald and Bob Yoakum began doing the "Mostly About People" column together. It was one of Buchwald's early contributions to this column that pointed him in the right direction: a sketch about a visiting fireman who wanted Buchwald to take him to see "the real Paris." The fireman rejected the bare bosoms of the Folies Bergères as something you could see in any burlesque house back home, and the tournedos Rossini in a fine restaurant as showing that the French don't know how to cook, since they forgot the ketchup, finally he was left by Art in a low-down Apache dive: "*This* is the real Paris!" Other sketches followed, larded in among the movie and restaurant reviews; "Garçon, my *café* won't *filtre!*" identified him with those thousands of naive visiting Americans trying to cope with Continental mores and difficulties, and he was off and running, ultimately to become the Paris *Herald Tribune*'s most valuable property. He developed an interview technique that caught visitors off-guard and made the most of opportunities that developed.

Buchwald himself recounts the incident that made him famous.

The Paris RKO Pictures representative told Art that the movie *Joan of Arc* was opening at the Paris Opéra with a personal appearance by producer Walter Wanger; if Art would give it a good review, he'd get a pair of tickets to the next movie. Buchwald, instead, wrote a barbed account about their conversation, and the next day an angry Wanger, speaking at the American Club of Paris, called the *Herald Tribune* movie critic "immature and inadequate." A wire service representative asked Buchwald for his comment, and the latter replied, "In France when a producer doesn't like what a critic says, he challenges him to a duel. If Mr. Wanger will send his seconds we can discuss weapons!" The wire services carried the reply, and the *France Soir* headline proclaimed, "Two Americans To Fight for the Virgin of Orléans."

The pages of the newspaper soon carried advertisements for a first book by Art Buchwald, *Paris After Dark,* mainly a collection of his restaurant and nightclub columns. It was the brainchild of another staffer, Jim Nolan, a promotion and advertising man, who couldn't sell the idea of publishing it to Parsons and his general manager, William Wise. But the two agreed to give it free publicity and distribution. The book became a huge success; Nolan, after several printings, sold his remaining rights for a good dinner at Maxim's and a Richebourg 1934—the most expensive wine he ever had, he claimed, since the book went on selling and selling.

Everyone was having fun. The paper ran a series of letters in the "Mailbag" on writers and books that had mentioned the *Herald Tribune.* People came up with Arnold Bennett's *The Loot of the Cities,* Gertrude Stein's *Everybody's Autobiography,* Hemingway, Fitzgerald, Edward Everett Hale, Erich Maria Remarque, and two books by P.G. Wodehouse, although the letter writer couldn't remember which ones. By the summer of 1950 the former *Chicago Tribune* and *transition* editor Robert Sage had taken over the travel pages, which he would make into one of the paper's best features during the next decade, when the real flood of American tourists began again and the American colony in Europe grew to its 1960 peak. Already the section was thick with ads.

Until the Korean War broke out in July, the European summer

promised to be the best since the end of the war, and by all rights the fattened *Herald Tribune* should have been in the best shape it ever had been. From that two-page period in early 1945 it had weathered successive postwar crises, overcome the foreign exchange problem, increased to a regular eight pages carrying a substantial volume of advertising, and was now distributed throughout Western Europe. The United States government, through the Mutual Security Administration, bought 10,000 copies a day, and the creation of NATO had brought an infusion of American troops to Europe, with the possibility of greatly increasing military circulation to the officers and their families at the new NATO headquarters outside of Paris. The 1950 *Travel Guide* was fatter than ever, Paris was gay, and everyone was having a good time. Then, quite suddenly, something happened to Parsons' marvelous paper: right in the middle of the summer season, with all its American tourists, the European Edition shrank to six pages, half the features disappeared, and Geoffrey Parsons himself soon left. Old readers started to complain to Helen Reid about the changes in their beloved Paris *Herald*.

In fact, what had really happened—though few of the staff ever learned the whole story, and few readers ever heard anything but gossip—was that the paper had been mismanaged into deep debt and into the possibility of paying large penalties for having violated French law. The accounting department had fallen into such complete chaos that the full extent of the disaster took time to ferret out. Once more, as in the thirties, the Reids were put into the position of having to advance several hundred thousand dollars to the European Edition. Helen Reid had to decide whether or not she could actually save the paper. She decided she could, but only drastic and painful surgery and extensive retrenchment would do it. It was a close shave. It brought to an end what the new general manager called "the era of wonderful nonsense."

CHAPTER 10
The Debacle

IT WAS NEVER at any time an easy job to put out and distribute the European Edition in those chaotic postwar years. The early paper shortage that forced production of a single sheet for six months was a minor difficulty compared with the continuous effort required to keep income abreast of spiraling costs in the face of rapid inflation. In late 1948, when Parsons raised the price of the paper to fifteen francs, a story apologizing for the latest increase noted that production costs had jumped a 100 percent in twelve months; only an increase in advertising and job printing would fill the gap between income from sales and the increased costs. The ever-present exchange controls were more than a constant irritant: most costs were incurred in France, but if income from sales abroad couldn't be transferred back to France, then the sales outside of France to that great market Parsons had envisioned at the outset were of little use. Legal requirements for money transfers were both complex and in constant flux, and seldom related to reality, so that there was constant temptation to avoid the law. Not too many people were willing to change dollars at fifty francs when they could get three or four times as many out on the street.

Bill Robinson, who had come for the start-up in December 1944, stayed in Paris until early 1945, supervising the business side of the paper. Mlle. Brazier acted as business manager under his direction. When he left he convinced a friend, Ken Collins, to leave his job as advertising manager for Macy's in New York to replace him as general manager in Paris. Collins, who had spent the war years in the air force, was an old acquaintance of Parsons' from Harvard days.

When Collins left the paper in late 1946, he brought in as the new general manager, in what became generally known as Collins' legacy to the paper, his old air force deputy, William Wise, a big, expansive, and outgoing man with grandiose ideas which, in his way, he shared with Geoffrey Parsons. For a while, at least, they seemed to get along fine. One thing they did, in 1948, was to retire Mlle. Brazier, who was placed on the "inactive payroll" at $200 a month, charged to the New York paper "during the whole term of her life."*

Communications were a constant problem. In the first year *Stars and Stripers'* delivery of features from New York helped, and so did the *Stars and Stripes* distribution system to the troops. (At one point, though, some stickler enforced regulations prohibiting army delivery of unofficial publication. Eisenhower complained that he wasn't getting his *Herald Tribune,* and someone else resolved the problem by having a number of generals subscribe to fifty copies apiece, which could then move through army channels.) By 1947 the paper could inform its readers that it received full Associated Press and United Press wire service coverage, full service from *New York Herald Tribune* correspondents all over Europe filing through Paris, and Agence France Presse coverage outside of Paris, and that it had a correspondent in New York who skimmed all the material coming in there to send it directly to the paper in Paris. The system didn't always work well, though, despite improvement as time wore on. Sometimes news service machines spewed out scrambled communications; Press Wireless, the radio link that provided American editorials and news, was often disrupted, and even contact with London frequently proved difficult. In a letter back home from Finland, correspondent Bill Attwood wondered what his stories could possibly look like by the time they reached New York:

---

*She was still receiving payment in the early 1980s, and managed to sustain her reputation a few years earlier when she gave circulation director Francois Desmaisons "the tongue-lashing of his life" for mistakenly leaving her off a revised free subscription list.

What happens to my words in the course of their trip to New York shouldn't happen to third class mail. First I take down a skeletonized story to the Helsinki telegraph office and give them to a woman who speaks no known language. She files them to London, where they are delivered to our London bureau. An Englishman then reads them off rapidly by phone to Paris, where they are recorded on a machine. An Australian woman named Thelma Ball plays the records back and types them out. [At this point copies were retained for the Paris Edition. But the rest of the process is of some interest!] She gives them to a French teletype operator who speaks no English. He sends them to the Paris Press Wireless office where another Frenchman sends them to New York. At forty-first street a copy girl takes what's left of the story and gives it to the cable desk. They recopy it and shoot it to the copy desk, which proof reads it, puts a head on it and sends it to the composing room, where a linotpyer has one last crack at the poor mangled prose.

Of course, once Thelma Ball had typed copies from the record in Paris, one copy went directly to the copydesk there, and then to Richard Beecher's staff of French Linotype operators. But everyone agrees that though the Linotypists didn't know English, they were good, and proofreaders caught most of the errors.

And Geoff Parsons, many felt, was a fine editor for the circumstances. He was never one to spend much time in the newsroom in his shirtsleeves, putting the paper together; this he left to the reliable Hawkins and the able and energetic newsroom head, Les Midgeley. He wrote only occasional editorial page features, and he spent much time in conviviality. He liked to live well; in 1946 he married an American actress, Dorothy Blackman Tartière, widow of a downed French air force flier, and in the process acquired a handsome old apartment on the Ile St. Louis. He and his wife, "Drue," had a retreat in Fontainebleau where they often entertained important visitors. As one former employee put it, Geoff would say, "Don't disturb me, I'm having René Pleven out to my place over the weekend." There were other employees who said that he had political ambitions, that he was trying to parlay his position and his friendship with such Americans as Averell Harriman into the ambassadorship or some other high office. But few denied that he inspired those putting out the actual paper, that he fought for good working conditions for them from New York, and that, most important of all, he conducted the necessary negotiations that permitted them all to issue the *Herald Tribune* in the confused postwar milieu that existed, where the growing American presence through the Marshall Plan and the North Atlantic Treaty offered opportunities that nevertheless required intensive negotiating.

He may have been too lavish in his use of expense accounts. When the *Herald* put out a supplement rich with advertising to celebrate the glorious maiden voyage of the refurbished *Ile de France* in July 1949, Geoff Parsons, of course, sailed on her to do some negotiating in the United States. He borrowed from the paper and allowed employees to borrow; when general manager William Wise became a member of the board of directors in an organizational reshuffle upon the occasion of Ogden Reid's death in 1947, it turned out that Wise owed the newspaper thousands of dollars— a debt he was supposed to liquidate since French law forbade a director from having personal debts to his company. And Geoffrey Parsons still owed the newspaper substantial sums when he left in 1950.

Circulation manager Charles Spann made prodigious efforts in the immediate postwar years. A Czech who had been in the Resistance—and who, in his last years, fatally stricken with leukemia, received blood transfusions so that he could continue coming to the paper—he managed to find ways to compensate for the loss of military circulation as the American demobilization proceeded apace in 1945–46. From 31,000 in 1947, circulation had climbed to 47,000 two years later. But the problems were immense. Circulation was thinly spread out across all of Europe and was therefore costly; a high proportion of unsolds would be an intolerable burden, so that making the paper available to occasional readers in isolated or remote areas was impossible. The exchange controls and inflation took their toll. Nevertheless, through careful scheduling of railroad and truck transport, Spann could tell sales representatives in 1949 that the paper was on sale in over 6,500 hotels, kiosks, and bookstores in some 1,600 towns in twenty-six countries, with subscriptions reaching people in another ten. (One racket cost it dearly in those tight days: chambermaids, hotel porters, railway attendants, and others were apparently reselling a large number of already purchased and discarded copies. The paper itself appealed to readers to tear off the logo once they were through with the paper in order to prevent such resale!)

Parsons and Wise tried to burst the bonds circumstances seemed to have imposed upon the new European Edition. Collins had already made one effort, commissioning a survey in England to see whether the *Herald Tribune* should start up an English Edition. Perhaps the shade of James Gordon Bennett was hanging around; as a consequence of a negative recommendation, Collins contented himself with an only partially successful promotion campaign to increase both circulation and advertising. All through 1947 and 1948 Wise and Parsons engaged in planning and negotiations not only to deal with the vexing matter of blocked currencies, but to do it within their rather grandiose conception of transforming the *Herald Tribune* into a multilanguage, international newspaper whose circulation would reach into the hundreds of thousands. They were spurred on by the conviction—frequently repeated by Parsons to those whose help he was seeking—that the *Herald Tribune* was the best newspaper in Europe, carried more international news than any other, and that it could do a better job of propagating the diverse American views of world affairs than any official, and therefore suspect, publication could.

By early 1947 several key people high in the Truman administration were already buttonholing Congress about the currency problem. The State Department was spending $3,000 a year on *Herald Tribune* subscriptions to distribute to European leaders; it raised its offer to $60,000, which Wise told department officials was still too low. In consequence, in September and October of 1947, American embassies carried out a survey of how many copies of the *Herald* they could comfortably and usefully distribute to officials, editors and publishers, libraries and schools, and arrived at a figure of 10,000, at a cost of $200,000.

In late 1947 Parsons managed to get in to see Secretary of State George C. Marshall in London, although Marshall had a policy of not meeting with individual newsmen. Parsons told Marshall that when Whitelaw Reid had toured Europe upon succeeding his father as editor of the *New York Herald Tribune,* "he got almost tired of hearing. . . that 'the European Edition is the best paper in Europe' " Marshall seemed to be in agreement; the State Department could not do the sort of job the *Herald Tribune* did. But as Parsons talked to him, it became evident that the Secretary of State was unaware of the blocked currency problem and of efforts being made in Washington to resolve it. When Parsons then told Marshall about all this, as well as about plans for several foreign language editions, contingent upon the present edition getting back into the black— which in turn depended upon Washington helping out with the blocked currency problem—Marshall asked him curiously if the whole idea wasn't to get the European Edition out of the woods! Parsons reported that he told the Secretary of State diplomatically that this was putting the cart before the horse; government help would certainly have that effect. But the point was to get the unofficial voice of America and Americans out to all English-speaking Europeans. At present it couldn't be done.

Six months later, in June 1948, Congress agreed to appropriate money to buy the blocked currencies, reimburse American publications in dollars for amounts they had earned, and add the foreign currencies to the "counterpart funds" Marshall Plan countries were setting aside for development and reconstruction purposes. (*Time, Life, Newsweek,* and other publications benefited as well as the *Herald Tribune.*) But according to Parsons, the move was too late: a year before the German currency reform in mid-1948, he wrote, there might have been a market for seventy-five to one hundred thousand copies. But the reform with the concomitant revival of German production and revaluation of the mark, brought with it a revived German press, too, and the results were therefore negligible. Everyone else at the paper thought he had been far too optimistic.

On the other hand, the Marshall Plan ensured that the U.S. government would, indeed, carry out the project of purchasing the 10,000 subscriptions of the *Herald Tribune* for European distribution, and until the mid-fifties it continued to buy several thousand subscriptions, although the number declined steadily. By 1950, therefore, almost one-fourth of the *Herald Tribune's* paid circulation resulted from U.S. Mutual Security Administration subscriptions; another 5,000 copies were sold to service personnel in Germany; circulation through normal channels therefore still totaled only 25,000 to 30,000 copies. (In one memo in late 1947 Wise had estimated that they needed to sell 150,000 more copies to get the paper into the black!)

Parsons continued to work on his big projects, one of which was for a French language weekly edition of the *Trib*. In one memo he listed those who favored such an edition: former Secretary of State James F. Brynes, former Ambassador Bullitt, Ambassadore Caffery, Averell Harriman, Senator Lodge, Ambassador to the United Kingdom Lewis Douglas. A Frenchman like planner Jean Monnet, the man most responsible for French reconstruction, told him, "Of course you ought to do it. How can I help?" There might be objections from the French press to a foreign daily paper supported by non-French funds, but they wouldn't apply to a weekly, and Parsons explored the details of production of such a weekly at great length with Eric Hawkins.

In another memo, prepared some time in early 1948, entitled "The *New York Herald Tribune* Project for Europe," Parsons cited current paid circulation of about 30,000, which he confidently expected would rise to 100,000 once currency restrictions were lifted later in the year! He proposed that $3,700,000 be appropriated to cover initial expenses for a year in producing first a French language weekly, then one in Italian and one in German. Circulation of these could be expected to reach 850,000 within a year, and to double soon after that, thus reaching a readership of at least

3,400,000 people, figuring that each copy would be read by at least two people. But all of the editions would soon be self-sustaining; they would very soon be able to begin paying off the initial loan in foreign currencies. In fact, he calculated that there would be a possible gross profit the first year of $150,000.

But while Geoffrey Parsons and William Wise were building castles in the air, no one was minding the shop. The fact was that despite all the maneuvering and negotiating, despite Spann's success in opening up difficult distribution channels, Geoffrey Parsons' vastly improved "product," substantial increases in advertising, and the now frequent supplements—"bland, kind, and expensive," wrote Jim Nolan, in a memo to Parsons and Wise in December 1949—the newspaper had begun to lose money. For its first two years, 1945 and 1946, it had made a modest profit, thanks in part to printing the *Stars and Stripes*—10 million francs (roughly $80,000) the first year, and a nominal 400,000 the second. In 1947 and 1948 it lost close to 20 million francs each year. In 1949 William Wise circulated a memo to all services to mark completion of his first three years on the paper. In it he noted the progress made in circulation, advertising, and size, and the increase in job-printing income, and he wrote, "Three years ago, the newspaper operated at a loss. Today, thanks to your efforts, it is *not* operating at a loss . . . Our role has been, and will continue to be, to permit Geoffrey and his editorial group to produce the best in journalism. Your efforts and the faith and confidence of the owners of the newspaper, have made, and will continue to make, this possible." The faith and confidence of the owners were shaken, however, when the audit showed that the loss for 1949 had actually soared to 66 million francs!

The first concrete indication of trouble—apart from the actual rather substantial losses for 1947 and 1948—came in early 1949, when someone discovered that the warehouse where stocks of *Herald Tribune* newsprint were supposed to be piled up was actually empty. It turned out that Emile Ribet, the production manager who reported directly to Wise, had sold and loaned out newsprint right and left. People who remember him as an able technician but no manager assumed he got caught short, but the audits showed that Ribet had pocketed millions of francs; some companies had loaned him newsprint for which he had never paid, and when his checks to one woman bounced, she placed an attachment on the *Herald Tribune* bank account that was only freed when an amount equivalent to her claim was placed with the French Treasury with no admission of responsibility. Insurance covered some of the losses, but for years the paper had to carry a reserve on the books to cover possible claims.

Ribet dropped out of sight. The affair shook Parsons and Wise, who found a replacement of an entirely different caliber, André Bing, a German refugee from the Nazis and hero of the French Resistance, who would become one of the key figures of the fifties and sixties. Bing, with fifteen years in the printing business, was appalled at the lack of accountability within the various services. When he looked into the job-printing situation, about which Wise had boasted and which was, presumably, crucial in making up the deficit created by the newspaper itself, he immediately found that it was operating at a deficit. Charges to clients were far too low, the presses and stereotype room were overstaffed, and the composers and proofreaders were receiving 20 percent more than the French norm even for dealing with the French-language job printing.

Wise, who had just allowed Parsons to expand the paper to a regular eight pages, authorized Bing to proceed with reorganization, and asked all services to be more careful about expenses, but it was simply too late. Bing soon discovered that for eighteen months the paper had failed to pay the French government its portion of Social Security taxes for the entire personnel; the paper had in effect been using the money to pay its running expenses, which explained Wise's claim that the paper was in the black. In addition it soon developed that the *Herald Tribune* had also forgone paying income tax on that portion of the salaries of editorial personnel that they received in dollars in New York; the general arrangement was that they got half their money in Paris and the other half in New York, but under French law, income tax was owed on the entire amount. Bing persuaded Wise to bring in new auditors—the prestigious international firm of Price, Waterhouse, and Company—who estimated that the paper might well owe a total of 13 million francs (roughly $300,000) on these two items alone, not to speak of possible *triple* penalties!

To add to all of this, it turned out a little later that the paper had also been violating French exchange control laws. By formal agreement the American company, in New York, made collections for the French company—from American advertisers in payment for space in the Paris Edition, from the State Department for subscriptions, from *Stars and Stripes* for its sales of the European Edition in Germany and on army posts elsewhere. On the other hand, it spent money for the European Edition, purchasing Finnish newsprint, ink from American suppliers, occasional pieces of machinery to supplement or repair the rapidly aging equipment on the rue de Berri, and direct payments to the Paris paper to cover the large operating losses it incurred in the late forties. The American company's disbursements on behalf of the Paris paper exceeded receipts by $600,000 over a seven-year period. On a much smaller scale, the Paris Edition provided similar services for New York, making some collections and some disbursements. The point was that these bookkeeping operations, which resulted in a large dollar debt by the Paris Edition to the New York company, bypassed and violated French controls over currency exchange, and in the early 1950s they required complicated negotiations to avoid both penalties and recurrence of the violations. (When the whole matter came to light and negotiations ensued between the paper's lawyers and the French authorities, the latter proved both helpful and lenient, with a resolution being negotiated at little real cost to the newspaper in 1954.)

And finally, as a sort of anticlimax, in 1951 the new publisher, Buel Weare, discovered that since 1947 Wise had failed to register either the newspaper or the *Travel Guide* with the Bibliotheque

Nationale, as required by French copyright law. He hastened to rectify the situation.

André Bing could do something about the overstaffed and inefficient production end of things, but he could do nothing about the accounting department. The Price, Waterhouse 1951 audit recorded dryly that "toward the end of 1949 and in early 1950 the accounting procedures of the Société Anonyme [the *Herald Tribune* corporation] fell into a deplorable state, and it became necessary to proceed to a complete reorganization . . . [that] took effect July 1950. Numerous errors were noted, some of which concerned previous year . . . [reflected in current account]."

Wise, who in June of 1949 had distributed that curious memorandum about how well things had gone under his three years of management, was simply overwhelmed. He and his wife liked the life in Paris so much that his first impulse was to try to cover matters up and protect his job. He didn't do a very sophisticated job of that, either: he stuffed bills into his desk drawer until things simply got worse and worse.

At the end of 1949 Helen Reid and Bill Robinson, now executive vice-president of the New York paper, got the word. Their first reaction, in October, was to tell Geoff Parsons to cut editorial salaries by 4 percent, and then to reduce the editorial staff itself. There were twenty people in the newsroom at the time, and it was an unhappy Parsons' painful task to call several of them in to be dismissed. Within a year there would be only twelve. But Helen Reid realized that the situation obviously called for more when she was forced to advance the European Edition several hundred thousand dollars. In early 1950 she sent over the *Herald Tribune's* chief accountant, William Fitzsimmons, to find out what was going on. Wise apprised all and sundry of the visitor's imminence. Fitzsimmons arrived in late March, planning to stay right across the street in the dependable California Hotel for some ten days. In the accounting department they called him "Felix the Cat" as he prowled and poked around. It helped not at all that Fitzsimmons found that Wise still (illegally) owed the paper a personal debt of $5,000 and

that others, Parsons among them, also owed it varied sums. One
of the first consequences of his visit was a meeting of all heads of
services called by Wise on April 11 to discuss possible economies.
On April 12 Wise "resigned." (He apparently received a night letter
of dismissal at 2:00 A.M. New York didn't always keep the time
change in mind—or perhaps was showing Wise how to save
money.)

The second consequence was that Helen Reid realized from
Fitzsimmons' first report that she would have to decide whether or
not to try to save her beloved Paris paper from the financial and
legal morass into which slack management and accounting had led
it. Despite problems with her *New York Herald Tribune,* which
was not doing as well as it should, she resolved to keep the European Edition afloat. She plucked a former army lieutenant colonel,
Buel Weare, from the *Herald Tribune* syndicate and rushed him to
Paris on a week's notice, where he was named president of the
European *Herald Tribune,* on April 14. Weare was a Midwesterner,
a Princeton and Harvard Business School graduate, formerly with
the *Des Moines Register and Tribune.* A small, dry, precise, man,
whom the French employees immediately dubbed "le colonel," he
was the antithesis of the big, bluff, loud-talking, expansive Wise.
Some people who knew him well thought of him as a generous
man, but one who left all his warmth outside the door when he
came in to the office. Those who remember him only from the
office in the Paris days think of him as the coldest man they ever
had to deal with. He moved the general manager's office downstairs
to where he could better supervise operations, got himself cordially
disliked by all those who had lived through the easygoing, high
expense account days of Wise and Parsons, and acted to save the
paper. The way it was still being run when he arrived, he felt,
justified the most rigorous measures.

The first thing Weare did was to ask Price, Waterhouse not only
to act as auditors, but to come in and install a new accounting
system. The second thing he did was to order the cashier and
accounting departments to stop handling personal transactions for

the personnel: the order mentioned the heavy volume of such activity and the burden this placed on the offices involved, but the real reason was the tangle of personal finance with the newspaper's accounts and the opportunities the situation offered. William Wise had authorized outrageous expenses and loans, and for some unfathomable reason had put the wife of the French Minister of Tourism on the payroll. It is a measure of how badly things had been done that Weare's stringent economy measures put the Paris Edition back in the black well before the end of the year, and Weare reduced the losses to only 11 million francs for the whole of 1950. The profits he managed to rack up in subsequent years—37 million francs for 1951 and 47 million for 1952, for example—were applied to reducing the debt, which had reached 140 million francs when he took over (roughly $400,000). By promptly instituting a regular program of repayment to the French authorities, negotiated with the aid of the advertising director, Marcel Tallin, whom he made vice-president of the *Herald Tribune,* he avoided what could have been triple penalties.

Eric Hawkins might refer contemptuously to Weare's "penny-saved-penny-gained devices," and other journalists followed suit; one recalls finding Weare working in his overcoat because he had turned the heat so far down. But Weare had found a cozy situation in which, in his view, everyone was being allowed to get away with murder while the ship foundered. Personal loans, extravagant expense accounts, overmanned machines, and a style of getting along that was developed during the days when black market dollars went far had all contributed to the debacle, even if the main cause was the lack of attention to the requirements of French law. In early June, after clamping down on the size of the paper and the beginning of reorganization of accounting, Weare wrote to Robinson: "The next reorganization should be in the editorial department where we must change from a Cadillac to a Chevrolet operation. It is very painful to write this, but Geoff Parsons just can't make the grade. He is sweet and kind about everything I ask him to do, but his laxness and irresponsibility make it impossible for him to do any kind of an operating job . . . he is in no position to lead his editorial men in a different direction."

A month later he wrote back a general report, in which he qualified Spann, the circulation manager, as "honest and able," and Tallin, the advertising manager, as "competent, industrious and trustworthy"; and he wrote, "I have respect and liking for André Bing, our mechanical superintendent." But, he went on, although "heaven preserve the line between editorial and business, I am on both sides of it now and can't help myself. We have a lot of capable high-grade men in the news room, who will always do creditably, given any kind of help from a playing captain. Their morale is understandably low" because the only editorial management done in the past had been by Eric Hawkins—"and that has been paralyzed by Geoff."

Weare tried putting Parsons on regular editorial hours and in charge of the editorial page in an attempt to save him. It didn't work, and a month later they had a final talk. Parsons, who wrote his father that he was trying to get along with Weare, that he was now working over a fourteen-hour day, was doing the whole editorial page, and was on hand every night for the final edition at 11:30, protested to Weare that he could not be held responsible for Wise's mismanagement. Even outside auditors, A.V. Miller, the New York paper's treasurer, and Fitzsimmons, the accountant, had not spotted what was going on. But Parsons, Weare thought, had long ceased to be a working newspaperman. He still owed the newspaper such a large sum that it virtually dictated the nature of the final separation settlement. Helen Reid had known that the outcome was inevitable, but it was still a shock when Weare called her from Paris to tell her that in spite of his efforts to get him into a harness on the editorial page, Geoff had to go. And it led to no little bitterness with the senior Parsons, still chief editorial writer for the New York paper.

Parsons would continue to maintain that he had been held responsible for Wise's mismanagement, and that Wise had been foisted on him by Ken Collins and Bill Robinson. But he had been

warned about what was going on by people who resented the way
Wise threw his weight around and who distrusted his judgment.
Subsequently, with Averell Harriman's help, Parsons became a
NATO information officer back in Europe, and ended his career
as a European representative for Northrop Aircraft.

And so, finally, Eric Hawkins became the real editor of the
European Edition, although he was frequently harassed by the
publishers who came and went during the next decade. In the fall
of 1950 the longtime *Herald Tribune* foreign correspondent Walter
B. Kerr came to Paris as the Reids' personal representative, with
the title of European editor for the New York newspaper, responsible for European news gathering for both the Paris and New York
editions. He ran the Paris bureau in the rue de Berri building, and
conferred with Hawkins every day, but it was the latter who did
the editing. As Kerr put it, "I went home at six. Eric came at four
and stayed until midnight."

The economy moves, naturally, strained relations with the production workers, too. The postwar years had been hard on everyone, but by European standards workers at the *Herald Tribune*
had done well. There were some twenty different contracts for
various categories of workers, but they had an informal coalition,
the Groupement Intersyndicale d'Ateliers, they were covered by
collective contracts with the French Press Association that provided
extensive social benefits, and they participated in an elected worker's committee, the Comité d'Enterprise, whose rights under French
law included nonvoting representation on the board of directors
of the corporation.

Until 1950 there existed something of a cheerful in-house atmosphere. In the winter of 1947–48 Mrs. Reid had sent a monthly
CARE package to each of the 226 employees, who paid for them
at the official exchange rate of the time. The proceeds went into a
fund, the Fonds de Solidarité, to be used for cases of unusual loss
or hardship—to send the children of a sick worker to the country
for two weeks, to help out an employee with an aging, ailing
mother, to reimburse a telephone operator whose purse had been

snatched as she was returning home at 6:00 A.M. During a four-week newspaper strike of 1948 *Herald Tribune* employees continued to work, on the basis that the *Herald Tribune* was not a French newspaper.

Once financial realities caught up with the paper, the picture changed. Bing's insistence that the composing room tighten up produced the Comité d'Enterprise decision to employ an outside auditor for the first time (at the company's expense, as provided by French law). As the C.E. minutes put it, members decided to do so "in the face of the hardened position of management so they can verify the accounts of the house and know whether yes or no this enterprise is on the edge of catastrophe as the Directors are pleased to say each time the C.E. asks for something." The C.E. representatives on the board then took the position that the debt to the New York company should be converted into shares in the Paris Edition. When Weare, a year later, succeeded in turning a substantial profit of forty million francs, all of which was being applied to reducing the accumulated losses of previous years, they repeated the demand, asserting that since the losses of the previous years were due to incompetent management, the moral responsibility rested upon the New York stockholders who had appointed Wise. If the newspaper was now making a profit, the workers should have a share in it.

To the workers, profits would mean funds for the use of the Comité d'Enterprise. To management they would have meant payment of French taxes as well as absorption of the loss. So Weare continued to pay off the debts, the Comité became more militant, and in years to come relations between production workers and management were never the same. White-collar workers charged production workers with unfair domination of the Comité and walked out on it; the Comité delegates were to make constant demands to upgrade the shabby facilities at the rue de Berri, for more control over hiring and firing procedures, for extra pay for overtime. André Bing would later tell one director that the workers were never as unhappy as they made themselves out to be; as one

Comité member put the matter, "Our strength has always resided in an attitude of confrontation."

In the second half of 1950 Buel Weare did what Helen Reid wanted him to do: save the European Edition of the *Herald Tribune*. The journalists who suffered under his ministrations all have epithets of varying vigor for him. But he looked at them with an equally jaundiced eye. In late 1951 the regular members of the editorial staff—reduced from twenty in 1949 to eleven now—asked Weare for a blanket increase in pay. Geoff Parsons, they argued, had established American standards of payment at the outset in order to maintain American professional standards; it would be a major tragedy if they were allowed to decline.

Weare flatly refused their collective request, and his counter that each man would be individually treated on his merits led them to complain to New York. Were the 1951 profits to be taken out of the pockets of the editorial employees when unionized production and office workers received regular raises under French collective contracts? From Bill Robinson Weare received an agonized memorandum: in New York it was customary to give unorganized employees the same benefits as those in unions. Unless he had persuasive arguments to the contrary, shouldn't he raise the journalists' salaries by the same percentages the French workers were getting?

The little colonel had been getting other flack. In December of 1950 Helen Reid had written to him that she had received complaints from Paris, among them one from the daughter of former Senator O'Gorman, and she quoted it:

"The paper is definitely sliding down hill since Mr. Parsons went out and a strict economy program under Mr. Weare was instituted. For three or four years I have been here it had the reputation of being the best paper on the continent . . . the best single piece of propaganda our country had. Now it is the subject of lamentation."

In the face of this complaint and of Robinson's agonizing about salary levels, Weare let New York have it. He had been put in charge. Three people were very good and had either recently received or would receive merit raises. The "invaluable" Art Buchwald had seen his pay triple since July 1950. Robert Sage, the old *Chicago Tribune* man now doing the travel pages, had recently gotten a pay raise and would get still more. This left five men, one a major disappointment, and four on the copydesk, all of whom were competent and were being liberally paid. Two of these five were the real force behind the movement for a blanket pay increase, and the paper could get along very well without them. The French workers and office staff had started from a much lower base and needed the increases they had received. Hawkins and Kerr concurred in Weare's conclusion that the Americans, all of whom received two to four times what their opposite numbers on French papers were paid, and who received half their pay in dollars on which they were getting a 25 percent premium (because of a restored black market differential), had all had a favored position as a result of the policies followed in Parsons' time. That time was, Weare had told the newsmen—using a phrase that obviously rankled—the "era of wonderful nonsense," and it was now over.

Somewhat later he scrawled on the bottom of the memo, "end of it."

CHAPTER 11
The Fifties:
The Best of Times, the Worst of Times

VETERANS OF THE FIFTIES on the Paris *Herald Tribune* like Art Buchwald remember it as a great time, when everyone had fun putting out the paper from a marvelously crazy newsroom. They recall a bunch of oddball characters, or moments like the one when Art finally decided to smash all the rickety, much-mended chairs and pile them in the middle of the newsroom, so that someone would be forced to buy new ones. Buchwald himself remembers with amusement how surprised prominent people were who came to visit the eminently well-known and widely distributed newspaper: only a handful of people in the cluttered newsroom put it out, and during most of the decade it had only one reporter. But certainly all the important Americans who came to Europe in increasing numbers read it, the Mutual Security Administration subscriptions meant that most European governmental and business leaders received it and took its existence for granted, and everyone knew and recognized the "Golden Girls" in their yellow sweaters who hawked it on the Champs Elysées in front of the American Express offices, and on the boulevard Montparnasse.

Eric Hawkins was now sole editor, permanent secretary- general of the Anglo-American Press Association, Chevalier de la Légion d'honneur, a legend in his own time who gave the paper an aura of solid continuity. In 1955, on the occasion of his fortieth year with the newspaper, he was given a surprise party upstairs in the *Herald Tribune* cafeteria and a dinner in the Pré Catelan restaurant in the Bois de Boulogne, where Art Buchwald acted as master of ceremonies and Ambassador Douglas Dillon presented the little Englishman with a scroll and a plaque reproducing the front page of the May 8, 1915, issue. As Hawkins reflected on these golden years in his memoirs, he wrote that in the last half of the fifties the paper entered on the most prosperous period it had known since the time of James Gordon Bennett.

He was all wrong, a fact that illustrates how divorced from the operations of a paper the newsroom personnel—even the editor—may be. Buel Weare's unwelcome ministrations put the paper into the black in the early fifties, but it was a highly precarious prosperity, and despite the paper's subsequent expansion and appearance of substance it was back in the red by 1958, and would continue to lose money for another decade. Parsons had had a vision of what the paper could become: a serious, multilanguage, world newspaper aimed at elites throughout Europe, designed to cement European-American relations within the framework of a new distribution of world power. He failed, and the story of the fifties is really one of how his four successors floundered as they tried to define a new role, find a new audience for the paper, steer it in some new direction, and make it into the profitable enterprise everyone else seemed to assume it was. Each claimed to have laid the basis for future success, but despite European and American prosperity, the growing influx of Americans, the increase in size, and the razzle-dazzle promotion stunts of these years, circulation in 1960 was only a little higher than it had been ten years earlier: an average of 49,000 copies a day. The paper was attractive and often lively, but it had lost many of the European readers it had had in the forties, and resembled nothing so much as the parochial American-in-Paris paper of the interwar years, differentiated chiefly by the better news coverage modern communications offered it.

At the end of the decade, when it faced forthcoming competition from the mighty *New York Times,* production manager André Bing addressed a memo to the newest director, Philip Weld. "For fifteen years," he wrote, "the European Edition has been the only real 'European' newspaper heralding . . . the future economic unity of Europe. Having thus contributed to prepare the market, it will now be facing growing competition." The major problem, though, was that the circulation costs of a newspaper of this type and its limited market meant that "this newspaper . . . seems to be condemned, in a market of 250 million consumers which it somewhat helped to create, never to attain the normal status of a profitable investment." And he went on to suggest that the company branch out into other Europe-wide investments such as newsprint mills, advertising agencies, or distribution companies in order to have profitable ventures to provide backing for the inevitably unprofitable yet prestigious *Herald Tribune* itself.

It was a clear indication of how difficult the decade had been, and how bleak the future of the newspaper as such still seemed.

Buel Weare, the first of the four directors, annoyed Hawkins in many ways, but especially in his insistence that the paper could not expand in size. If advertising were to grow, Weare made it clear in a memo, it would be at the expense of features and the news hole—the space allotted to news; an expansion in the size of the paper itself would cost too much, since it inevitably led to higher costs in paper, printing and shipping. The editorial staff first appealed this to New York in 1953, when American tourists really came back in full, but the treasurer, Barney Cameron, wrote back, "You must remember that our experience with a larger paper a number of years ago did not pay off in larger circulation," by which he meant, of course, Parsons' late forties product.

Weare's constant conflict with the editorial staff over space was further exercised by the little man's passion for order and precision, which ill-accorded with the usual newsroom spirit. There are still amused recollections of his orders that all desks be cleared by the end of the working day, of his putting locks on the cabinets where

the copy paper was stored—and giving up when he carefully calculated that he was losing more in locks being broken by the
newsroom staff than he was saving in paper.

Of somewhat more importance is that all through the fifties the
paper's always delicate editorial position as an American paper in
a European milieu brought it under pressure—sometimes from
unexpected sources. Helen Rogers Reid wrote to Buel Weare and
to Walter Kerr in August of 1950, "The home paper wants to keep
better informed on editorial decisions than has been the case in
recent years . . . there was responsibility on both sides of the Atlantic for not having insisted on closer cooperation with our editor
and managing editor and for that reason I reiterated the policy—
adopted when the European Edition resumed publication after the
war—that the New York paper will continue to direct its editorial
and news operation both of which had never been adequately
practiced."

Whitelaw Reid, editor of the New York newspaper since the
death of his father, perhaps inspired by his mother's letter, fired
off a number of memos to Paris objecting to the nature of headlines
and the way in which the news was played. Among others, one
memo pointed out that in a single day the paper had played up the
defection of a Reuters correspondent to the Russians, the attempted
suicide of a GI about to be arrested for a sex murder, a report by
the National Council Against Conscription stating that "the U.S.
is paying lip service to disarmament," another AP story concerning
an appeal to the President to stop drinking—and the editorial page
had a *Dallas Morning News* cartoon entitled "Now, Be Good Little
Boys," showing Uncle Sam handing a gun to a struggling pair
consisting of an Arab and a Jew. His memorandum concluded,

> This is really not a bad crop for one day. What it really comes down
> to is that each one of the items listed above could be justified by
> anyone inclined to do so on the grounds that it is either legitimate
> news or that freedom of the press is attacked by any attempt to

suppress news or political comment. However, once again, we have a perfectly clear case of cumulative effect which is detrimental to the U.S. and quite gratuitous. This goes on day in and day out and gives the *Herald Tribune* what amounts to a permanent bias against the good name and political prestige of the United States.

In another memo on another crop, he concluded with a general blast: "The current editorial policy of the European Edition of the *New York Herald Tribune,* particularly with regard to choice of headlines, selection and playing up of sensational news stories (usually A.P.), and choice of political cartoons, results whether by design or negligence, in constant and unfavorable distortion of U.S. policies and of the character of the American people."

There were pressures from sources closer to the paper, too. No one has ever said that the 10,000 Mutual Security Administration subscriptions directly affected editorial content. But at about the same time that Reid was writing from the United States, the embassy in Paris complained that the *Herald's* treatment of the fighting in Korea reflected badly on American fighting abilities.

Weare and Hawkins took the criticism seriously, and Weare responded with a five-page analysis. He took a week's worth of headlines that had come under criticism, compared them with the New York Edition, the *New York Times,* and the Continental Edition of the *London Daily Mail,* and wrote to Hawkins in conclusion: "You might tell them at the Embassy that your staff knows that this paper has certain diplomatic functions. We know that the day may come when we'll have to be more discreet—in the national interest. But not yet. North Korea isn't going to whip the U.S. If we do a straight job now, we are going to have the pleasure of ending up with a victorious flourish which will be a credit to both our troops and our journalism. *Et voilà.*"

In May 1953 Weare returned to New York when Ogden Reid, Jr., Whitelaw's younger brother, known throughout the *Herald Tribune* organization as "Brownie," came to spend a brief and

rather tumultuous year as general manager of the European Edition, fresh from four years on the New York Edition, where he had
made his mark by coauthoring with Herbert Philbrick several series
of articles that revealed his major concerns: one group on American
military unpreparedness, another on "The Threat of Red Sabotage," and a weekly series called "The Red Underground." One of
the reports he received on his arrival tells something about the
general way in which the editorial staff tailored the news play to
particular purposes: "On May 30, 1953, the New York editorial
on Eisenhower's press conference answering Taft's go-it-alone
speech was front-paged. This was done in order to dramatize to a
rather skeptical Europe that the administration and the Republican
Party, as it is currently constituted, are not prepared to abandon
their allies."

The same report noted that the editorial page attempted to have
a really representative sample of American newspaper editorials
from all parts of the country,

> to help important people and their governments visualize the com-
> ponents of reasonable American thinking . . . help them understand
> the make-up of Congress and the different points of view with which
> President Eisenhower has to cope . . . .
>
> In the issue of June 10, 1953, the space under the cartoon was
> devoted to a series of editorials on the question of Red China and
> the U.N. When public opinion crystallizes in the United States on
> particular issues, this procedure can be repeated.

It was, in a very real sense, an explicit continuation of Parsons'
early view that the paper had to perform two tasks: provide as full
a presentation of the news as possible, while at the same time
explaining American policies and realities to the French, and protecting newsmen like Robert Yoakum, who was threatened with
expulsion over articles about, and interviews with, North African

nationalist leaders.* (Yoakum recalls frequent pressures from the Quai d'Orsay—the French Foreign Office. Walter B. Kerr remembers occasional protests, but nothing he could interpret as pressure. Yoakum got around the cautious Eric Hawkins when he wanted to counter some alarmist Alsop columns on the imminence of a Soviet attack through stories based on interviews with American diplomats in Eastern Europe. He simply didn't tell Hawkins what he was doing or what was in the stories.)

It was not a particularly propitious moment for Brownie to bring his own particular concerns to the European Edition. A month after he took over, on June 20, 1953, the day of the Rosenbergs' execution as atomic spies, the production unions mounted a fifteen-minute strike against the paper. (It was a tribute to the mounting authority of production manager André Bing that he was able to talk them out of the full-day strike decided upon at a mass meeting.) Buchwald recalls that among the first things Brownie did was kill one of his columns on McCarthy (which the now-departed Yoakum got printed back home in the *New Republic*). He also ran occasional Philbrick columns on the Communist menace in the United States, and full texts of Dulles' Cold War rhetoric which, as the editorial room people saw it, cut deeply into the news hole, since Brownie wouldn't allow a larger paper. Reid claimed later not to remember the incident, but newsroom personnel recall his pulling out a picture of Einstein that they planned to run on the pacifist scientist's seventy-fifth birthday and—dramatically—stopping the presses to bury an Adlai Stevenson speech that had been prominently displayed on the front pages. There was certainly no editorial

*Despite his unhappy separation from the paper, Parsons continued a lifelong interest in how it was run. In 1954 he wrote to Helen Reid from NATO headquarters in the Palais de Chaillot begging her to drop David Laurence's column. It was so far against what Ike and the *Herald Tribune* stood for; Laurence was not a decent person like the exasperating old Mark Sullivan, nor did he represent the respectable right. He was a member of the "pompous and pseudo-respectable McCarthyite fanatic fringe" and thus especially out of place on the *Herald Tribune*.

on the Senate's censure of Senator Joe McCarthy. (What Buchwald claims irritated *him* the most was Brownie's insistence that he take down a poster of Stalin whose hand held a pasted-on bottle of Coke!)

Brownie left in 1954 to attend to the finances of the New York paper, and then to oust his brother Whitelaw and try to put the *New York Herald Tribune* on a sufficiently solid financial footing that he would be able to attract investors.* He left behind him his assistant, Sylvan Barnet, who thus became the third director of the fifties. (Art Buchwald declares that the editorial staff didn't pay much attention to them as they came and went. To Willett Weeks, who arrived in time for the farewell dinner for his predecessor, Barnet, Art said, "Well, we'll be giving *you* one of these soon!" Weeks, well aware that the staff would resist change imposed by someone they viewed as temporary, let it be known that he planned to stay until he retired.) Barnet was a highly successful salesman whom Bill Robinson recruited as the European Edition's sales representative in New York in 1949. What he could sell at the outset was essentially aimed at GI's in Europe, but the imaginative Barnet convinced a French government still worried about its balance of payments and the dollar shortage that unless it admitted imports of such American luxuries as Philip Morris cigarettes, Four Roses Whiskey, and Coca-Cola, it wouldn't be able to attract American tourists. He then, of course, was able to secure their advertising in the European Edition.

Barnet would have numerous suggestions for the editorial content of the paper during the two years he was there, and it was he who persuaded Brownie in New York to allow the paper to expand

---

*Brownie's subsequent career took a curious course. Eisenhower named him ambassador to Israel after he sold the *Herald Tribune* to John Hay Whitney in 1958. A skeptical Senator Fulbright grilled him at length about his qualifications; Reid declared—among other things—that he didn't know whether he would have voted to censure Senator Joe McCarthy. He later became a Democrat, worked with Martin Luther King's Poor People's Campaign, and after a stint in Congress served as commissioner of environmental affairs in New York. He and his brother maintain a minor stake in the *International Herald Tribune*.

again (though he was not able to persuade him that they should buy the next-door building on the rue de Berri when it was offered to them for the equivalent of $50,000). But in terms of the political context of the times and its influence on the paper, it is most notable that he stressed to Hawkins the need to use the increased space in the paper to print more American news and selected texts of American officials' speeches and documents, "which make us valuable to U.S.I.A. [Information Agency]" The Mutual Security Administration subscriptions were already beginning to decline in number, but they were still essential to the European Edition, and Barnet didn't want to lose them.

When Barnet returned to New York to work with Brownie Reid he was succeeded by Willett Weeks, who, like Weare, was a graduate of the *Herald Tribune* syndicate.* Barnet and Weeks had to weather the Suez affair in 1956, when Dulles' and Eisenhower's strenuous opposition to the Franco-British-Israeli invasion of Egypt brought a sharp drop in the *Herald's* Paris circulation as it printed editorials from New York supporting Eisenhower's policies. Weeks then presided over the paper during the last years of the decade, when the French political situation became more and more tense as left and right polarized over the Algerian War, and Paris became the scene of frequent demonstrations and riots.†

In fact, by 1958, when the Fourth Republic collapsed, Willett Weeks had had grilles installed over the display windows on the

*Weeks got his job by placing an ad in the *New York Times* "Situations Wanted" column. When Mrs. Reid heard about it she was not amused, and gave orders that no one else was to be hired in the same manner.

†Art Buchwald, in a 1978 column about the paper's move out to the suburb of Neuilly, reflected on how good the old location had been: "What made the rue de Berri offices so interesting was that they were so conveniently located near the Champs Elysées where most major political demonstrations were held. All a reporter had to do was stroll a block to the Champs, watch the demonstrators throw café chairs and tables at the police, and report on how many rioters were clubbed over the head by the gendarmes. One time a colleague, Robert Yoakum, came back from a left-wing demonstration with his head bloodied. He said he had been whacked by a policeman for just standing on the sidewalk. 'Why didn't you show your press card?' Eric Hawkins, the managing editor asked. 'I did,' said Yoakum, 'that's when he hit me.' "

ground floor, and had increased other security measures. André Bing contemplated the possibility of printing the full press run in Rome, where, for a short while, a Mediterranean Edition was already being printed. And for the first time since the end of World War II the *Herald* became again the target of direct government censorship, as the death throes of the republic stirred the news staff into unaccustomed activity. Banner headlines about the crisis in Paris pushed news of the Russians' sputniks, the Lebanon crisis and American intervention, and Nixon's stoning in Venezuela into the background. While the cautious and balanced editorials from New York drew a grateful letter of praise from Weeks, local coverage flourished, just as it had back in 1934, when the Third Republic had come under attack.

At the time de Gaulle announced that he was ready to accept power, American servicemen were warned to stay away from Paris, and newspapers were warned not to publish anything inflammatory.* On May 22 Willett Weeks wrote to Brownie Reid in New York, "We are extremely fortunate to have here Eric's intuitive grasp of how the French and Algerian news should be handled. So far we have had no complaints on any score from French authorities. Yet I do not feel that our readers have been deprived of any of the essential news that has found its way into our office." Four days later the European Edition was seized for publishing one of correspondent Barrett McGurn's dispatches from Algeria, although a censor at the Associated Press had passed it, provoking a protest by the Paris Press Association and from Weeks, who calculated that the seizure had cost the paper over a million francs.† There

---

*In the middle of the crisis one story would still note that 400,000 Parisians were planning to leave the capital for the four-day Pentecost holidays on 244 special trains, and as if to emphasize the background of stable, continued economic growth against which the political crisis was unfolding, the paper recorded that on May 27 the Eiffel Tower would be illuminated indirectly by spotlight for the first time, if the unions were not on strike against de Gaulle's threatened takeover.

†Weeks received an apology from the government for another seizure a year later, when the *Trib* printed an account of government stoppage of a number of *L'Express* carrying an interview with an Algerian leader. In this case the *Trib* had not carried the substance of the interview.

were more blank spaces as the time for decision neared; circulation increased by 35 percent in Paris and 15 percent outside. The headlines told the story well, starting on May 14: "Army Takes Over Algeria Provisionally; Junta for De Gaulle in France"; then, "Paris Rightists March on Assembly from Etoile; De Gaulle Says He's Ready To Take over"; "De Gaulle Approved as Prime Minister, 329–224; He Asks Six Months of Emergency Powers." Finally, on June, 3, "De Gaulle Wins Reform Powers 350–163."* By the time of de Gaulle's investiture on June 2, to banner headlines in the *Herald Tribune,* Joseph Alsop himself was there to add his imprimatur of approval, and the New York paper's editorial reprinted in Paris wished de Gaulle well in establishing a government firmly in control of both foreign and domestic affairs. (No one seems to have remembered that in 1951 the paper had reported a speech in which he repudiated the whole structure of the North Atlantic Treaty Organization, insisting that all bases and communications in France should be under French control.)

In the meantime, in contrast to what Geoff Parsons had hoped for back in 1945, the paper had developed into something quite like that of the late twenties. On the front pages the Fourth Republic might be crumbling, but in the back of the book pretty Maggie Nolan would be writing one of those dreadfully "sophisticated" "People" columns about "celebrities," with subheads like "The Arty-Smart Set" "Around the Whirl in the Rain," "As If You Didn't Know," "How 'Un-Cannesy' Can You Get," "On the Line from London." Until 1958 the paper still listed arrivals who had registered at the American Express office (though no longer registering them at the rue de Berri). In one of his last columns for the *Herald Tribune* Bugeja had written a piece in June of 1953, "Paris Defies Rain for *Grande Semaine*":

*On June 5 the front page also bore the news that Harry McElhone of Harry's New York Bar had died of a heart condition. He had bought the bar back in the post–World War I years of the Third Republic, run it through the Fourth, and just failed to see the birth of the Fifth.

> There was a time, say 40 or 50 years ago, when the phrase *Grande Semaine* conjured up visions of fashion displays on the race course, parades of private carriages on the Champs Elysées, private dinner parties, open air dances and suppers in the fashionable restaurants of the Champs Elysées and the Bois de Boulogne and, of course, the Bal du Grand Prix at the Opera . . . .
>
> Economic and social changes following two World Wars . . . killed all that. But some of the former halo about the *Grande Semaine* has remained, in a diminished form.

Yet only one year later reporter Alain de Lyrot would be writing that the *Grande Semaine* had been fully resurrected and that Paris abounded with what had not been seen for ages: gray silk toppers. It was symptomatic. Ten years after the war the French were better off than they had ever been before. The wealth was beginning to spread. From bicycles Frenchmen had switched to motorbikes, and now were beginning to buy cars in record numbers. In 1955 the *Herald* recorded the debate about allowing parking along the side aisles of the Champs Elysées, and the gates were opened that would turn Paris into one enormous parking lot. Americans came to visit and live in ever-increasing numbers, and the *Herald Tribune,* despite New York, began to grow again in size to accommodate all the local news and features, as well as one rather unaccustomed addition, comic strips.

The comic strips were a result of an element no one had foreseen earlier: the continued presence of hundreds of thousands of American soldiers in Europe years after the end of World War II, and the further influx resulting from growth of the NATO infrastructure. To seek out this unexpected market and compete for it with the *Stars and Stripes,* Buel Weare created a special edition of the regular European Edition with added features: a full page of comics and another of sports and army-related news and stories.

Walter Kerr was strongly opposed: he argued that there would be a lack of balance, with almost as much space given to comics as to general news. It would irritate current readers, detract from the policy of putting out a paper that reflected the aims and standards of the New York Edition, and suggest to Europeans a waste of scarce and expensive newsprint. Finally, referring to Weare's suggestion that the last page bear a copy of the front page masthead so that news dealers could display the paper with the last page uppermost, Kerr wrote, "I hate to think of any display where the *Stars and Stripes* and the *New York Times* will be selling news and we will be selling comics."

But Weare, still in the process of paying the debts incurred in the forties, determined to go ahead. The special edition, known familiarly as either the Army or Bulldog Edition, appeared on November 5, 1951, the first of the many attempts made during the 1950s to go beyond the confines of the usual newspaper and seek income from some broader venture, and it lasted until May 1955. It was a bone of contention; some argued that it was too expensive for the slight gains in circulation it represented, while others thought there would have been losses without it. Other new competitors entered the field—publisher Mel Ryder's *Army, Navy,* and *Air Force Times,* each aimed directly at the armed services. Under Brownie Reid's direction a new man charged with military circulation, Paul Gendelman, conducted a series of surveys to determine just why servicemen bought one or the other of the competing papers. Despite Gendelman's enthusiastic recommendations for ways to improve military distribution, the coup de grace came in 1955 when the *Stars and Stripes* went on sale early in the morning at French bases as it had always done in Germany, cutting heavily into the *Trib's* military sales in France. As a result, in May 1955, Sylvan Barnet closed the chapter on the Army Edition, consolidating the two versions by adding some of the comics and special features to the regular edition.

The comics, as a result, were one legacy of the Army Edition, and their incorporation into the paper turned out to be a deadly serious business, worthy of highest managerial attention. Some strips would have to be dropped when the consolidation took place, but which? In each case, it was an agonizing decision, provoking agonizing response. If the paper was trying to appeal to cosmopolitan Americans rather than to military personnel, different strips would have to be used: "Moon Mullins," "Smilin' Jack," or "Joe Palooka" might be dropped—among others—but "Pogo," "Peanuts," and "Dennis the Menace" would have to be added. (Styles change. "B.C.," "The Wizard of Id," and "Miss Peach" were later additions. In an attempt to retain at least some military subscriptions Weeks took care to move "Beetle Bailey" to the top of the page in 1955.)

Sylvan Barnet, who engineered the change during the eighteen months he was general manager, bore the brunt of jibes at the American Club when the first numbers came out with the comics on the back. But six months later, he recalls, people would say to him, "Dennis was great today!" At a dinner one night Eric Hawkins sat next to Mme. Henri Spaak, wife of the great Belgian and European statesman; to him she declared "If you drop Donald Duck, I'll stop reading the *Herald!*" "Penny"—never a favorite with GI's—was dropped at one point and Henri Bonnet, France's first and longtime postwar ambassador to the United States, called to say that unless "Penny" was restored, Mme. Bonnet would not allow the *Herald Tribune* in the house. At another dinner party Mme. Pibul Songgram, wife of the Thai strongman, turned from the party on her left to Barnet and said, "Tell me, Mr. Barnet, do you think Rex will ever marry June?" The reference, as aficionados will know, was to the soap opera/comic strip "Rex Morgan, M.D."

The first readership surveys conducted in the mid-fifties showed the comics to be the second most read part of the newspaper, after the international news. Much later, a new editor, B. J. Cutler, moved the sixteen remaining comics to an inside page; comics on the back would perhaps help sell the paper to soldiers, he reasoned, but many people were shy of being seen reading the paper in the Metro, with all the comic strips visibly proclaiming the childishness and frivolity of their reading habits. By 1985 there were only nine strips left, but the heritage of the fifties and the Army Edition lived on.

Spann's successor as circulation manager, Paul Gendelman,

would never forget the beckoning army audience. Successive directors turned down his recommendations for special columns aimed
at army wives, for a *Herald Tribune* "Military News Letter," for
an elaborate, homey, Saturday supplement, for a *Herald Tribune*
buying club. Willett Weeks, Barnet's successor, responded to one
of Gendelman's suggestions in a revealing manner: "The truth is,
I think, that our intellectual content is a little high for enlisted
personnel. There is no reason why we should grade down the paper
to try to get these readers, but I do think a column dealing with
activities among the military brass might help us solidify ourselves
among the officers. I am going to see if I cannot sell Eric on this
idea."

With the exception, therefore, of a small minority of army personnel, the armed forces as audience were largely lost by the *Herald
Tribune* to specialized publications. Barnet looked elsewhere, to
the growing potential of American travelers in Europe. The great
transatlantic ships were back in force, supplemented by the surge
in scheduled transatlantic air travel, and Robert Sage's sophisticated travel pages suggested to Barnet what he wrote to Brownie
in New York: the *Herald Tribune* must be preeminently a *travel*
newspaper, indispensable to all the new American tourists. With
Brownie safely back in New York, it was also possible to eliminate
the Philbrick "menace-of-communism" columns and the full half-
page texts of Dulles' speeches; with the increase to eight pages after
consolidation of the special edition, there was considerably more
room even after giving almost one page to comics. But Barnet
pleaded for even more: to Barney Cameron, back in New York, he
wrote that the restricted regime of the early 1950s, combined with
Brownie's desire to publish all those speeches and communiqués,
meant that the paper was "over-heavy on international news . . . .
Little space was given to sports, almost none to finance other than
stocks, and even more serious, we were no longer doing an adequate
job on travel, our main category of advertising . . . . There was not
enough light material in the paper to balance the very heavy political and international news up front . . . . Increasing advertising

was eating into the news columns, making the paper much too tight."

Increased travel features were the key to the Americans in Europe; increased financial news was "the key to gaining more European readership," essential to keeping circulation up during the winter months when tourism fell off. Cameron allowed the paper another two pages, although he denied the eager Barnet the financial editor he'd asked for, and Barnet went ahead with his expansion of stock listings, commodity prices, mutual funds, and other financial listings. He badgered Hawkins about getting all this in.

Hawkins' main virtue was reliability: he could be counted on to get the paper out regularly and on time—an imperative for a paper with international distribution, that had to make train, truck, and airline schedules with precision or else lose sales. He hardly ever took vacations; the paper, the California Bar across the street where he took his one after-work drink, his wife, and his lady friend were his life. But in the eyes of the directors who came and went, although he was excellent at the task of getting out the paper on time, he was also an unimaginative man, best at taking orders. As he aged he also stood more and more on prerogative. He got touchy and resented suggestions. So directors like Barnet and Willett Weeks chafed at the difficulty of making the substantial changes they deemed necessary for the paper.

Barnet was convinced that the paper was its own best promotion, and he bombarded Hawkins with memoranda. "A lively picture each day above the fold on the front page will do more for circulation than any promotion we can think of," he wrote to the editor in the fall of 1955. "I think we should make a special effort during these days in which our circulation normally drops off, to have good action pictures and at least one light story each day on page 1 above the fold" (where it would show on display racks). Barnet and Weeks worked with Bing to try to get an improvement in the pictures; the equipment used was antiquated American stuff that they thought the French workmen weren't using to best advantage, and there were problems to be solved with picture suppliers. But they also had to get Hawkins to accept a front-page layout that would emphasize the pictures. They pushed the Englishman continually to brighten up the front page, to use shorter or larger and better headlines, along with the better picture display. It took a bit of pressure from Reid, too, but by 1957 Weeks would write to Frank Taylor, Executive Vice President of the New York paper, that the results, finally, were noticeable. "For the first time our Circulation Department proclaims it has a really saleable product and this admission serves to deprive them of any excuses for not continuing our gains." (But three years later Paul Gendelman, the circulation manager, would still be writing a memo to Weeks' replacement, Gloucester, Massachusetts publisher Philip Weld, with exactly the same concerns: better pictures more prominently displayed on the front page, larger headlines, and more international emphasis in the news stories. And Weld would write home that under the aging Hawkins the *Trib*—as more and more people called it—was "the dullest newspaper I have ever seen," until luckily the International Edition of the *New York Times* "chose to steal that honor from us!")

Barnet and Paul Gendelman did much to mark one aspect of the newspaper in the mid-fifties. Barnet was preeminently an imaginative salesman; Gendelman, brought in as assistant to the ailing Charles Spann to promote army circulation, became circulation manager when Spann died. The two of them managed to stuff the paper with innumerable continuing puzzles and contests—"Coinword," "Bonanzagram," and "Faces and Places." It is hard to calculate how many readers these brought in, but the response was certainly impressive: in one week there were 10,500 entries for a single "Coinword" puzzle. In a manner reminiscent of James Gordon Bennett himself, the paper held a regular travel story contest with daily, monthly, and annual awards, and offered Pan American round-trip tickets to Paris and Rome and eight-day vacations in Rome and Geneva. Contests were designed to run on during the summer so that tourists would be sure to buy the paper every day. (And in a memo to new publisher Weld in 1960 Gendelman would still be riding this hobby horse, recommending more puzzles and contests.)

It was Gendelman, too, who created the Golden Girls in 1957—attractive girls, mostly Sorbonne students, German, Scandinavian, or English (French girls wouldn't do it and Americans thought it didn't pay enough)—to hawk the newspapers along the Champs Elysées, in front of American Express, along the boulevard Montparnasse. They were all equipped with a yellow pullover emblazoned with "Herald Tribune" in black, and if they didn't sell too many papers, they were a marvelous promotion stunt, soon extended to the Riviera and elsewhere. When the *New York Times* got around to establishing its International Edition in Paris in 1960 it sent out young male street vendors, also prominently identified across their chests; rather stuffily it huffed, "We want to sell the paper for what it is, not for who's selling it." The Golden Girls got further publicity when the late Jean Seberg played one in the Godard new-wave movie *Breathless,* starring Jean-Paul Belmondo.*

If Barnet and Weeks spent considerable time on the content and look of the *Herald Tribune,* and went along with Gendelman's circulation promotion stunts, they also followed in Gordon Bennett's footsteps in seeing that special occasions were used for promotion. When Eisenhower or Nixon was in Europe, he was always hand-delivered a specially wrapped and addressed copy of the European Edition. When the *New York Herald Tribune* sent over an especially high-powered team to cover the 1955 Geneva Conference and the meeting between their boy Ike and Khrushchev and Bulganin, the Paris paper used a charter plane to fly 500 copies to Geneva by six-thirty in the morning so that delegates could get a roundup of the news earlier than from any other English language newspaper. Just as in the old days, the 1952 and 1956 elections brought forth numerous special editions, a *Herald Tribune* elec-

---

*Weeks was concerned when he heard about a movie in which a *Herald* vendor got involved with a hoodlum. Wouldn't it bring the newspaper into disrespect? Should they do anything about the use of the *Herald Tribune* symbol? But Thomas Quinn Curtiss, the paper's film critic, reassured him: the way the film was being made, it would probably never be shown in any major movie house!

The most famous "Golden Girl" of all: Jean Seberg in Godard's movie, "Breathless." (Associated Press)

tions results service that could be reached by calling Western Union, and the posting of election results in several locations around Paris.

And then, of course, there were the columnists. Many came and went, especially the stringers with social notes from other cities. Some were old-timers: Pendleton on music; Yvonne Hagen on art and artists; Lucie Noel, who still covered fashion with illustrations by Flozanne and was helped, later in the decade, by Hebe Dorsey, who would eventually replace her; Sage on travel. There were the syndicated columnists from America—Lippmann, David Laurence, Roscoe Drummond, Walter F. Kerr on Broadway theater, Hy Gardner's celebrities column which began in the Army Edition, and John Crosby on television; Barnet, for some reason, was sure that Europeans were vitally interested in the development of American TV. Then there were some of the newer ones: the young lady whose initial column in the forties was on hitchhiking to the south of France, Naomi Barry, who wote "At Home Abroad," on shopping, restaurants, places to go. In a real sense, the problem of her columns underlined the uncertainty of the European Edition's 1950s market: to Barnet she was "tops," but Gendelman, looking for increased circulation outside of Paris, thought she was much too parochial. Both Barnet and Gendelman kept looking for social columns from London and Rome to attract circulation outside of Paris. Thomas Quinn Curtiss reviewed films and theater then; he continued to do so in the 1980s, still living below the Tour d'Argent—which reputedly served him most of his meals and had on its three-star menu "Eggs Thomas Quinn Curtiss." Could one be more of a Paris and *Herald Tribune* fixture?

But by the late fifties it was Buchwald who had become the star of the paper, and many people still feel that in those up and down times he did much to hold the paper together—to lighten the general atmosphere in the newsroom and keep everyone sane in his own somewhat insane fashion. There was no question about his importance to the European Edition. Everyone read Buchwald; his *Paris After Dark* had gone through many editions, and others of his columns were immortalized in subsequent volumes. Barnet and Weeks got him syndicated: the first American newspaper in which this quintessential American in Paris appeared was in Fargo, North Dakota!

By the end of the decade he appeared in over 150 newspapers. No one on the paper made the kind of money he did. When American tourists in Paris wandered up the Champs Elysées and— looking down a side street—saw the "Herald Tribune" sign, they would often turn down the street and come in to ask if they could talk to Buchwald. As he put it, it was a time when anybody who was anybody in America took to coming to Europe, and when they came, they read the *Herald Tribune;* it was an ideal showcase in which to build his reputation, worth ten times as much to him as being in an American newspaper in America. Even if the legends were not all true, the Paris *Herald Tribune* had a legendary quality to it, and it rubbed off. Yet his relations with New York were always touchy; when he wanted to cover American elections, the New York office didn't want to pay his way; it skimped in various other ways, trying to make him pay the full salary for his secretary, so that the incredulous Weeks and then director Philip Weld wrote desperately back to New York to protest that Buchwald was *the* star of the paper, and had to be kept happy. As Weld put it, "I meant it when I said that the worst blow this paper could suffer would be any disruption of the harmony that exists between Art and the paper . . . please don't let anyone in New York fuss him unnecessarily . . . New York must agree he is our only real star. I treat him as Casey Stengel treats his twenty-game pitchers!"

But if Buchwald occasionally raised a fuss about his treatment, he also went his merry way in Paris, interviewing celebrities, writing columns like his famous one explaining Thanksgiving ("La Fête du Merçi Donnant") to Frenchmen, and—when he was attacked by Eisenhower's press spokesman for writing "unadulterated rot" about a press conference on the President's illness—retorting in print that he wrote only "adulterated rot!"

At one point the dean of the American Cathedral Church decided to play his new carillon every hour on the hour from 9:00 A.M. to

9:00 P.M. Buchwald, now married and living close by, filled the "Mailbag" with antibell letters, signed by Micheline de Bois, Pierre Robespierre, Robert de John, all to the effect that God could, after all, call the faithful to worship more quietly or at least more occasionally. Buel Weare, director at the time, was a deacon at the cathedral, and came around to the newsroom to ask if there had been no probell letters. The next day the "Mailbag" published one that read, "Dear Sir, I don't know what all the fuss is about the bells. They have never bothered me. [Signed] Giulio Ascelleri, Rome, Italy." By Hawkins' decree no more bell letters appeared, but according to Buchwald, the bells stopped except at noon and on Sundays. It was, he later wrote, one of the few crusades ever carried on in the European Edition. (Fifty years earlier, in 1908, Bennett's *Herald* foreshadowed Buchwald by publishing a letter bemoaning the morning din of chruchbells, inevitable even when one is sick. "The devil woos his disciples gently to come to theaters, etc. through the columns of your and other journals and very successfully; why cannot the church do likewise?") Until 1961, when he was given his own separate office, the funny man worked in the newsroom, where the paper from the wire services receiver would drape itself over his desk as the girl tore it off to distribute it around the room. The grumpy old *Stars and Striper* Jules Grad would eat his late supper on Art's desk, just to show that everyone was still equal—until Art's secretary finally put a stop to it.

Lucie Noel, the perfect little lady, would sail in and out of the newsroom accompanied—during the showing of the new collections—by the New York newspaper's Eugenia Sheppard, who would fly over for the openings; Lucie Noel scolded the French designers in print for "the Sack," telling them that if they persisted in ugliness, Paris would lose its spot as the fashion center of the world. The rest of the crew in the newsroom would mock the two ladylike fashion writers, although their function was supremely important; Hebe Dorsey, hired to help out when fashion openings overlapped, was younger and jazzier. She married one of the copy-

The Paris *Herald Tribune*'s biggest star, Art Buchwald, shares a laugh with sixties editor Bernie Cutler.

writers who had been around forever, Frank Dorsey, a man supposed to have come over during the Spanish Civil War, and who
probably would have been in trouble back in the United States.
Julian Jacobson, a big-nosed, bald man with his rimless glasses
inevitably askew, had left his bookstore in Brooklyn to work for
the European Cooperation Administration in Marshall Plan days,
and now worked on the copydesk, but tried to get himself fired so
that he could collect the severance pay and open a bookstore in
Spain—which he finally did. In 1959 Art had to share his own desk
for a while with a new young, redheaded, girl-chasing, copywriter
sporting a weedy beard, named Richard Roraback, who would go
on to do sports and then put his own personal stamp on the
"People" column.

While Buchwald was waiting for inspiration to strike he would
frequently shoot dice with Roraback, and Eric Hawkins would
come out to watch; but Hawkins' secretary had to be cautious
about barging in on the aging editor in his own office, in case he
had a young lady in there with him. He was known to one and all
as a ladies' man. And while the newspaper was being put together
the staff would debate Proust or Stendahl or when to drop "Mr."
for "Mons." or "Herr" or "Sr." It was all a lot of fun, despite the
dirt, the din of the presses doing job printing down below, the
frequent heat and the smells, and the pose of amateurism and
expatriatism that virtually one and all maintained—except, perhaps, for Roy McMullen, the somewhat staid head of the copydesk.

McMullen was one of those 1946 recruits to the paper—a former
glider pilot waiting for a discharge and hanging around, whom
Parsons took on. (It was McMullen and Bugeja that Les Midgeley
wanted to have along to edit a nice four-page paper in America
such as the one they had put out in Paris in those marvelous early
days.) He stayed all through the 1950s, arguing with Hawkins over
the fairness of banner headlines of Cold War issues, over whether
the Russian sputnik should get two columns or more: Hawkins
didn't want to give the Russians too much credit, but McMullen
told him they'd have to have banners the next day. (The smaller

American satellites in February 1958 occasioned a special edition.) Hawkins, the Englishman living in Paris since 1915, was biased toward news about Paris and France; the cosmopolitan McMullen wanted more international material.

And looking over their shoulders, and worrying about the bohemianism of it all, were the directors—Weare, cutting down their space, Reid, making them put in the anti-Communist material and taking out stories about people he suspected of Communist sympathies, Barnet, asking for more U.S. news along with more travel, finance, and columns from outside of Paris, and Weeks, slowly coming to the conclusion that the key to the paper's future lay not in Paris, but in the entire Common Market area.

The building they all worked in was dilapidated; Buchwald wrote much later that he didn't think it had ever been painted inside since the paper moved in. It was a pardonable exaggeration; when Weeks became director he oversaw a minor renovation of the inside of the whole building. (And when André Malraux, de Gaulle's Minister of Culture, insisted on the cleanup of all Paris, the *Herald Tribune* was forced by law to scrub down the whole exterior of the building. By the time they got around to it, 21 rue de Berri rather stood out like a sore thumb among the other buildings that had already been cleaned.)

If Buchwald was the most widely read and laughed at, he also provoked controversy and legal suits that the paper helped him fight; his columns were translated into French and published in French newspapers, and there were Americans who charged that as he poked fun at French practices and customs, he helped poison Franco-American relations. (Incredibly enough, his present outside office in Washington, D.C., is papered with hate mail.) But to the French weekly *L'Express,* describing him as "mi-Hamlet, mi-Falstaff," he was "le Comte Artois de Buchwald, une institution Franco-Americaine." And he enjoyed himself, the people in the newsroom enjoyed themselves—while the directors tried to hold the whole rickety structure together against increasingly heavy odds.

More than any of the newsroom personnel or readers knew, it really was a question of holding the whole rickety structure together, and the four directors were involved in a variety of activities in trying to do so. Part of the difficulty lay in undoing the effects of the spree of the late forties, especially regularizing complicated exchange control matters; the newspaper was deeply involved in international exchange, French law was complicated, and matters had been let slide and eventually had to be negotiated. There were also issues of compliance with French labor law that had to be resolved. Then, too, the rue de Berri plant had been ambitiously conceived back in the late twenties, so that until the 1960s it had to depend upon contract or job printing in order not to stand idle too much of the time, and this posed both problems and opportunities. As constituted in the 1950s—either in the spare six-page guise imposed by Weare, or in the fatter, healthier-looking format of the end of the decade—the newspaper alone could not stand on its own two feet.

The four directors pursued, in turn, the army market, Mutual Security Administration subscriptions, and the possible publication of other newspapers and magazines, and tried vainly to expand circulation and distribution of the *Herald Tribune* itself in hitherto untapped markets. Most of the effort expended on all these matters had little to do with the actual production of the European Edition, although starting with Barnet, the directors tried to spruce it up and revitalize it in order to capture new markets. But all of the effort was vital to the continued health of the paper, even though many of Willett Weeks' attempts at securing other essential sources of income came to nothing.

In Barnet's two years as director the Mutual Security Administration subscriptions were still important, though beginning to wind down. Buel Weare had never been very happy about depending either on these or on sales to the military, feeling that both were only temporary palliatives. Nevertheless, they had provided the margin of profit in the early fifties, and he had pursued both energetically. In mid-1952 his hard work paid off in a 75 percent renewal rate for the MSA subscriptions.

The new Eisenhower administration complicated matters when it took office in 1953. Only elaborate lobbying succeeded in keeping the program under the MSA when a transfer to the more niggardly State Department threatened—potentially disastrous, since State was under strong attack by McCarthyites in Congress. Congressman Rooney had already declared the program a subsidy to the press, causing Barnet to fume: "A sad thing that purchase of mental bullets is considered a subsidy, whereas the purchase of tanks is not considered a subsidy of the company that manufactures them."

Weare curtailed his vacation in Ireland to fly back to Paris and beard Frank Dennis, the chief of the Office of Information of the MSA, who was highly receptive, and cabled Washington that European leaders trusted the impartial news presentation of the *Herald Tribune,* a sudden cut off of which would have a bad effect. The government, he declared, got a high value for every cent spent on the subscriptions. Some cuts were inevitable, of course, as the whole Marshall Plan spirit wound down and European recovery took on its own élan. For 1953, nevertheless, the MSA ordered some 7,500 subscriptions. By 1954 the number was down to 5,200. In 1956 it dipped below the 5,000 mark, and the whole program was phased out by the end of the decade. While it lasted it was one key to the paper's health.

Regularization of the paper's status under French law remained a nagging concern for all the directors in the decade of the fifties. Weare arranged a scheduled repayment of illegalities with respect to Social Security and income taxes in 1951, although the possibility of penalties still existed until Willett Weeks finally liquidated the matter by making the final payments in 1957. The multiple exchange control violations were more delicate. In the early fifties the *Herald* had numerous illegal currency deposits scattered throughout Europe, as well as the illegally incurred debt to the New York office. Again, Weare was able to negotiate a quiet accord that avoided both penalties and sanctions. Exchange controls and import restrictions nevertheless continued to involve successive directors. In 1957, with pressure on the franc, the French government restricted imports of precious Finnish newsprint. French newsprint allocations proved insufficient, and in the crucial month of August Weeks had to restrict the number of pages the paper could print. He petitioned the French authorities to allow him an exemption; the *Herald Tribune* had imported paper since the late forties, summer was its biggest season, and it had a fundamentally different market from French newspapers. But the crisis passed and the restrictions were lifted.

Later in the decade, and then in the 1960s, the paper again found itself in violation of French law, and in one case in the rather expensive need to regularize matters. When Gendelman established the Golden Girls as vendors, everyone knew they would be in the nature of casual labor that would come and go. It was decided to take the risk of being in violation of the matter of working papers and not register them, with all the paperwork and the complicated through minimal social charges this would entail. The newsroom personnel, of course, all had their papers—more or less—but again the calculated risk was taken not to enroll them in the *retraite des cadres*—the retirement fund for professionals. The successive directors and André Bing felt that few would stay long enough to begin cashing in on this. But in 1963 when the venerable Robert Sage died, after many years first on the Paris *Chicago Tribune* of the twenties and thirties and then the *Herald Tribune,* and Mrs. Sage, perhaps unwittingly, sought to cash in on the *retraite des cadres,* the whole unwelcome issue came to light, and provision had to be made, including retroactive payments into the retirement fund for those who had been there a long time.

In one rather unexpected way, the international nature and distribution of the European Edition paid off as of 1952 when the French government, to stimulate exports, began to refund taxes on the value of goods exported, and extended this to newspapers produced in France and sold abroad. Weare and Reid were delighted, of course. For 1952 the refund amounted to the considerable sum of 10 million francs (close to $30,000). In 1953 it rose to almost 15 million francs, and in 1954, despite a government decision that it should not be given on the whole sum earned abroad, but on that sum minus expenses incurred in foreign countries, it still amounted to over 5 million francs. By the end of the decade, after de Gaulle's devaluation and the strengthening of the French balance of payments, the refunds came to an end. While they existed, though, they certainly helped the balance sheet.

And while the balance sheet was in the black, from 1951 through 1957 (1954 was a bad year, but matters improved again in 1955), the French company paid the New York office on a rather complicated basis for services rendered, in order to keep the French company from showing too much profit. Primarily this was to avoid French taxes and some of the resulting social charges the paper would have to pay out of profits. It was also a way of avoiding building up franc balances when the possibility of devaluation and consequent loss remained a constant threat. In those years civilian sales and advertising revenue did climb sufficiently to offset the declining military circulation and loss of government subscriptions. But the paper stayed in the black until 1958 primarily through two other revenue-producing operations: job printing and the creation of special sections.

Ever since André Bing's reorganization of job printing in 1949, it had turned a substantial profit. In the decade of the fifties the *Trib* printed half a dozen other publications: the largest-selling French daily sporting journal, *Sport Complet,* the French satirical newspaper, *Canard Enchaîné,* and an odd assortment of left-wing publications. In the late 1950s, when rising costs had again overtaken revenue, the job-printing situation offered an opportunity that Weeks and André Bing explored at length. The three aging owners of *Sport Complet* offered to sell it to the *Herald Tribune,* and the offer was an attractive one. *Sport Complet* had long rented offices in the rue de Berri building, so that administration could easily be shared. The New York office reacted cautiously and slowly and brought in an outside auditor. Weeks and Bing held discussions with the managers of *Stars and Stripes* and of Ryder's *Army, Air Force,* and *Navy Times* on the possibility of printing in the rue de Berri plant, or of doing Ryder's *American Weekend* as a forty-page supplement for the *Stars and Stripes,* or of actually publishing and printing a Sunday insert called the *Armed Services Family Magazine* and even possibly taking over editorial direction of *Stars and Stripes.*

Nothing came of any of these discussions, and late in 1959 the *Sport Complet* deal fell through, too. To Barney Cameron, the *Herald Tribune* treasurer in New York, Weeks wrote mournfully that something might have come of the deal "had we gone ahead with the purchase of *Sport Complet* earlier this year as recommended."

In the search for income from other ventures, Weeks did manage, for a couple of years, to publish something called the *Business News Letter,* a biweekly, eight-page affair that drew on the resources of the *Monthly Economic Review* (which Weeks at another point considered selling as a separate publication). But again, after considerable effort, the enterprise met with failure. With a little over 200 subscribers it began to break even by mid-1960. Weeks, however, received instructions to discontinue the newsletter when it became certain that the *New York Times* was entering the field in Paris. The *Herald Tribune,* he was told, should strip for action.

For Weeks, however, the moral of the whole futile story was not that the *Herald Tribune* should stick entirely to its last. In December 1959 he wrote to Barney Cameron in much the same terms that Bing later wrote to Philip Weld. "Without these two supplementary sources of income," he declared, referring to the job printing and the now dead and gone U.S. Information Agency subscriptions, "the European Edition is not so constituted as to produce a profit." If it couldn't find other profitable publications, either it would have to embark on a drastic retrenchment that would invite in other newspapers, or it would have to expand its circulation in order to get more advertising revenue. But the problem of circulation expansion always remained the same: expansion would have to take place outside of France, and that always meant heavy increased shipping and distribution costs, plus the inherent problems of supervising and checking up on the actual distributors and on the sales points. Gendelman's circulation department had several roadmen—one of them, Francois Desmaisons, eventually became circulation manager after Gendelman.* But there was always the threat to cut down on them as a way of saving money—for a while, in 1954, there was only one instead of three.

Weeks did make one major attempt in late 1957 to expand circulation in the Mediterranean and Middle East more efficiently than could be done from Paris by creating a special Mediterranean Edition printed in Rome. It was not small-scale endeavor: it meant setting up an Italian company, dealing with new currency problems, different labor laws, and insurance,and compensating for the effect on diminished use of equipment and manpower in Paris, as well as persuading a reluctant New York office that the project was worthwhile. Eventually, after the initial transitional stages, the new edition would have an editorial office in Rome, with its own editor and a slew of desirable local features: Italian financial news, local pictures, movie and events timetables like those in the Paris Edition, art and personality notes, and Vatican news. In the beginning, in December 1957, the Mediterranean Edition simply consisted of a third edition set up in Paris that carried extra Roman material in it, predated and with the mats flown to Rome to be printed there under contract. By mid-1958, with more material supplied by a stringer attached to the Rome bureau of the New York paper, 11,000 copies were being printed, and Weeks professed to be satisfied with the results so far, although revenues were lower than budgeted and expenses higher. But the July Lebanon crisis that

*The rue de Berri building and salaries were not the only places where the shoestring nature of the operation showed up; in 1958 Gendelman asked Weeks, if, at a cost of $800 plus trade-in, they couldn't get two new Simca Aronde cars for the road inspectors. Until now they had been driving Renault Quatre Chevaux, the tiny, tinny cars Renault had introduced to France during the postwar years of scarcity, and the inspectors complained justifiably about having to drive them all over Europe!

brought American marines wading ashore on the chic beaches of Beirut cut into sales, and in October New York management made the decision to kill the Mediterranean Edition in the light of Middle East unrest.

Military circulation declined, job-printing income fell off, the lure of other publications never brought results. But one source of income developed in those days did help, and it has stuck: the special section. Three years after the *Herald Tribune* started up again after the war, when newsprint availability eased, and when the refurbished *Ile de France* set sail for the United States in 1949 (with Geoff Parsons on it), a special section hailed the event. Another celebrated the Holy Year (though that one was marked by continual problems of web breakage during the printing run), and another hailed the accomplishments of the Marshall Plan after the first year of its full operation. The flavor of these sections is perhaps best expressed by Robert Yoakum in a 1978 column of reminiscences about his years on the *Herald Tribune:*

It is night. The time is July 20, 1949. Two young men—Jim Knight, city editor of the *Trib*, and I—were in the last hectic stages of getting out a "souvenir supplement" on the liner *Ile de France*, which had been rebuilt and was about to be launched on the Atlantic run.

The preparation of newspaper supplements is not the most rewarding experience in journalism. It involves writing feature stories to accompany advertisements—in this case, 12 pages of advertisements—and the trick is to write at length so as to fill up space.

To fill those 12 pages with information about one ship took a lot of imaginative stretching. We never used an Anglo-Saxon word when the longer Latin equivalent was available. We wrote a long and numbingly boring article about the shipyard that rebuilt the ship.

We wrote five paragraphs under the head, "Chef Prepares Kennel Menus for Cats, Dogs." And four paragraphs under "Fresh Flowers Decorate Ship on Every Trip."

The supplement had to go out that night, folded into the regular paper, and the deadline was coming up fast. Imagine our distress, then, to learn from the head of the composing room that there was a hole on page seven.

"How the hell could there be a hole?" Jim asked in alarm.

"Damned if I know," I replied. "You hold on here and I'll write something."

But what? With only minutes to go I rushed upstairs to my desk in the city room, grabbed a World Almanac and a sheet of statistics issued by the French Line, and began to write one of history's most inconsequential comparative statistics stories. Readers throughout Europe—those few who reached page seven of the supplement— would learn that:

—The 19,350 sheets of the *Ile de France,* if knotted end to end, would reach the entire length of New York City's five boroughs.

—The ship's 244,400 pieces of linen, if spread out, would occupy an area of 2,325,024 square feet, or 10 acres more than the Tuzigoot National Park in Arizona.

—The ship's 14,825 plates, if stacked up, would reach a height of 492 feet, or two feet higher than the Time and Life Building in New York City.

—The alcoholic drinks carried on the liner (in other words, not counting the 3,420 quarts of mineral water) would amount to one-third of a second's flow over the Kaieteur Falls in British Guiana, based on the mean annual flow.

Jim Nolan, a self-described business innocent who secured a rather hazardous job as promotion manager in 1948, but whose primary function was to sell advertising space in the New York Edition to Europeans, dreamed up the Marshall Plan Supplement and went around telling governments that they should buy advertising space to publicize their accomplishments in order to persuade Congress of the effectiveness of the plan. "Parsons and Wise," he wrote, "promised the greatest supplement to appear in any newspaper, something we could really be proud of—seventy percent editorial and the *Trib's* best writers analysing the current state of the Marshall Plan and its members. In the event it was so ghastly (and about thirty percent editorial) that I had to steel myself to send out justifications to the advertisers." Nolan was also eventually deputized by Marcel Tallin to go and get payment from the delinquent French government office that had contracted for advertising space, and when he went to the right office at the Quai d'Orsay, he was taken into a locked room where he was handed 1,000 thousand-franc notes from a drawer, from what he assumed was probably some sort of anti-Communist slush fund. He carried them back across Paris to the rue de Berri in his briefcase with some trepidation. (He also married the girl who laid out the supplement for him and pulled together the raw materials sent in by government offices. Later, as Maggie Nolan, she wrote the gossipy "People" column.)

The tradition was broadened in the 1950s. Sylvan Barnet, while still advertising representative for the European Edition in New York, dreamed up the special sections on American port cities; in 1952, for example, there were supplements on Brazil, Switzerland, the United States Lines, the Saar region, and one for Christmas. That year the supplements brought in a net profit of 14 million francs, the job printing some 18 million, and the Mutual Security Administration subscriptions about 45 million—a total of over 76 million francs—and the export tax refund added another 10 million. Since net profit for the *Herald Tribune,* S.A., was 47 million francs, without these sources of income the paper by itself would have been 30 million francs or about $100,000 in the red. In 1953 the supplements typically brought in 25 percent of total advertising income. Newspapermen on the *Trib* were derisive about the supplements; current special sections are far from the sheer puffery that they were at their origin. But now, as then, they continue to provide an important margin of profit to the newspaper.

Hope springs eternal in the human breast. The announcement in August of 1958 that John Hay (Jock) Whitney, Eisenhower's ambassador to the Court of St. James, had purchased control of the *New York Herald Tribune* and its Paris subsidiary from the Reids stirred much excitement. Whitney's grandfather, after all, had once edited the *New York Tribune,* and had occupied the same ambassadorial position Jock now occupied. And Whitney's forebears had been James Gordon Bennett, Jr.'s cronies at the Jockey Club. It all seemed to fit. Whitney was one of the wealthiest men in the United States, and an early supporter of Eisenhower as a member of the liberal wing of the Republican party. The *Herald Tribune* in New York certainly needed the boost Whitney could give it. So, of course did the European Edition, always much shakier in those years than it appeared to be on the surface.

Only three years earlier, when the expansive Sylvan Barnet finally overcame the Weare–Ogden Reid hold-down era and oversaw a substantial recovery from a poor 1954, he was nevertheless asked by Reid to prepare a schedule of possible savings for the European Edition that would have included elimination of the second edition, a reduction of personnel in advertising and circulation, and, once more, a reduction in the size of the paper. Reid didn't find it necessary to order that any of these measures be taken, but he did follow Barnet's suggestion that they drop the correspondent the Paris paper had in Washington, attached to the New York newspaper's bureau there.

When Willett Weeks arrived to replace Barnet in late 1955, he, too, came with instructions to keep costs down, and one of his first steps was to cut stock listings. Soon convniced of his mistake, he gradually restored them. But a year later, while Reid was still trying hard to make the New York paper pay, Weeks prepared yet another contingency money-saving program entitled "Suggested Program for Operation of European Edition under Adverse Economic Conditions." It was not intended for immediate implementation, but merely to have on hand for a moment when it might become "impossible to predict a profit situation over a substantial period of time," and it listed some twenty-nine detailed steps that could be taken, in increasing importance. In the summer of 1957 Weeks was urged by Barney Cameron to trim expenses in order to balance the budget, and Cameron, who asked Weeks to cut down on stringers, objected to a move the Paris director considered highly important, the hiring of Jan Hasbrouck to help with the "Monthly Economic Review" and to write a weekly column on European economic integration.

The year 1958 threatened to bring the first loss since 1950, and shortly before the Whitney acquisition Weeks raised subscription and single-copy prices in several markets, restricted returns by distributors, eliminated a number of vendors, cut out shipments to several marginal markets, and looked closely at the possibility of cutting out the second edition by simply doing more "replating" of the first as well as possibly cutting out his recently established Mediterranean Edition.

Then, three weeks after institution of the economy moves, came the exhilarating news of the Whitney purchase. Whitney and several of his associates joined Ogden Reid in Paris to look over their new acquisition, and Weeks showed them around and presented his plans for the future. In honor of the occasion, a week later *Editor and Publisher* printed a story about Jock Whitney's new Paris acquisition, headed "HT's European Edition Prosperity Is Exciting."

The article recounted all the problems and costs of circulating an international newspaper, noted the high return rate of 30 percent compared with American newspaper return rates of 8 or 9 percent, and the fact that a typical issue contained only about 25 percent advertising compared to 60 or 70 percent for American newspapers, and discussed some of the problems of censorship to which it had been subjected, as well as those of running a multilingual staff in the rue de Berri building. But the whole tone was highly upbeat, stressing the increases in advertising and in civilian circulation, noting the presence of the Mediterranean Edition, and declaring, "As American political weight continues to increase on the international scene, so does the future of the paper seem to open wider and wider."

The upbeat tone of the article reflected Weeks' own sense of what might be done with the European Edition. Since Parsons' failure the paper had become a parochial Paris product, and lost

"Jock" Whitney looks over his new acquisition, with Managing Editor Eric Hawkins to the left, Production Manager Andre Bing between them, and long-time composing room foreman Richard Beecher on the right.

much of its European readership. Weeks now envisioned a whole new role that might get it out of the impasse. To Frank Taylor, executive vice-president of the New York paper, he wrote that its future lay in servicing the nascent Common Market: "This paper could become the information center for all of the people in Europe . . . concerned with the possible effects of the market." And he recommended the hiring of an editor and reporter whose sole concern would be to give coverage of European developments. He didn't get them, though he got Jan Hasbrouck for a weekly column on Common Market developments. Then, in late 1958, when news came of the Whitney purchase, he wrote to Barney Cameron that with only a modest increase in spending, circulation could be increased by 100 percent. Gendelman had prepared a plan that, he confidently asserted, would raise circulation past the 100,000 mark

within three years, and Weeks used it in preparing a report for the
Whitney people divided into two parts, "Present Status" and "Future Possibilities."

Under "Present Status" Weeks noted that the paper had an
average circulation of 48,000 in seventy-one countries, with (incorrectly, as it turned out) half going to Americans and half to
Europeans. In 1957 the paper had paid charges of $50,000 to the
New York paper, and showed an additional profit of $45,000.
"The European Edition," he wrote, despite the economy moves he
had just been forced to make, "is from all points of view in the
strongest position in its history . . . . Financially, the paper is sound,
though the possibility of severe year-to-year fluctuations can never
be discounted in an enterprise that reacts so sensitively to international events . . . . In intangibles, the prestige of the paper has
never been greater nor—insofar as such things can be gauged—
has its readership felt more goodwill towards the paper." And he
noted that recent refurbishing of equipment meant that there were
no pressing needs in this domain. But the paper did need an understudy to Hawkins, and a business manager to aid the director,
who simply had too many ancillary duties outside the paper to
properly investigate all the departmental and interdepartmental
problems brought to his attention.

Weeks then listed the moves that Gendelman had suggested to
increase circulation—increases in direct mail promotion, in allowing more unsolds, in increasing the number of girl vendors by 25
percent, a three-year moratorium on price increases in the paper,
a development effort in marginal markets in Asia, Africa, and
Europe where the cost of transportation at present inhibited any
sales effort, a broader general media promotion effort, increased
pages devoted to news, the hiring of a features editor and another
reporter ("We have only one reporter—a ridiculous situation for
a paper of this size"), and increased distribution of sample copies.
(In only one area enthusiastically pressed by Gendelman did he
balk: a heavy effort aimed at the military market that would—
once more—include more comics and special pages of material

designed for military personnel.) There would be increased temporary and capital costs, but "it is felt that increased circulation, to be achieved by the above devices, is the great break-through that would lead the European Edition to a new level of prestige and profits."

Weeks had already given Hawkins a long memo on what might be done on the editorial side to contribute to the expansion program: better book review coverage keyed to European availability, more space for art reviews, perhaps a column on recordings, improved women's coverage, more space for food, wine, and restaurant reviews, more bylined articles by the *Trib's* own staff, and an increase in the sampling of American editorials, which had seemed to be decreasing lately. It was all an ambitious contrast to the actual measures that Weeks had been carrying out since his arrival.

In early January a board of directors meeting in Paris approved a part of the program, but only a part. Only a little while later, however, in July 1959, Weeks was writing back in anguish to Avery Brundage, a new Whitney representative on the board in New York. He was now being asked to hold down losses and defer expenses, only months after the start of the expansion program. It was true that gains had been less than expected, and the costs of returns higher. But short-term losses had been lower, and now he was being asked to avoid the projected $22,000 loss for the year. Did a loss of $22,000 really appear so important to New York that the whole expansion program had to be jeopardized? The forecast was healthier now than four months earlier. Could New York not realize how morale would be on the European Edition if the long-run expansion plan were cut back six months after its inception? As he pointed out to Brundage in a later letter, part of the problem was costs incurred in bringing over three new people—John Wachob as advertising director, to replace Marcel Tallin, Nat Kingsley as the long-discussed and much-needed second man to Eric Hawkins, and Doris Sanders as promotion director, along with the unbudgeted costs of bringing over three new people for the board meeting.

Weeks had always resented what he felt was the penurious and cautious "old guard" around Reid at the *Herald Tribune;* when Brownie came over for periodic visits accompanied by Frank Taylor and business manager Barney Cameron, he was subjected to a grilling about every penny. The Whitney team's visits were far more agreeable. Yet once again the upshot of the whole major expansion program was a plaintive quarrel with New York over figures and costs of this magnitude (and a small further irony lay in Weeks' being asked upon his return to New York, in May 1960, why his move had cost so much). What Weeks and many others simply failed to realize was that Jock Whitney faced a far worse financial situation than he had foreseen when he first acquired an interest in the *New York Herald Tribune.* At the start of 1958, for example, management estimated losses for the coming year at $1.2 million; by mid-year the estimate was raised to $3 million. Money was available not so much for expansion as simply for saving what existed; Whitney was willing to pour a lot in, but clearly expenditures had to be watched much more carefully than people had thought when they first learned of Whitney's purchase of the paper. Just as clearly, Whitney's people did not feel that increased expenditures for the Paris Edition were justified by its prospects.

Perhaps they were being a good deal more realistic than Weeks and Gendelman. Weeks' vision was bold, but before its time. The "exciting prosperity" that *Editor and Publisher* wrote about was clearly illusory, and the 100,000 circulation that Weeks aimed at in three years would seem to have depended on a marked change in the nature of the paper, in the conditions in which it was circulated, and in technology: twenty years later facsimile transmission would finally lead to the breakthrough he sought. But it did not yet exist.

In short, the 1950s were a time of great uncertainty for the European Edition—a time of recovery based on stringent economies and a short-lived program of government subscriptions and army purchases, of a gradual supplanting of these by civilian subscriptions and sales, but a time, also, of a scrambling for alternative sources of income, of expedients to save money, and of plans for ambitious future growth that came to grief. Just as in Parsons' time, the newspaper grew in size and resumed its old guise of an American in Paris—while it aimed at being more international. In late 1959 Weeks and Gendelman faced an unpleasant reality about the *Herald Tribune's* readership: it came as something of a shock to find out from the latest readership survey that while advertising and promotion had been publishing the paper's readership as roughly 48 percent American and 52 percent European, it was, in fact 65 percent American and 35 percent European.* The figures were extremely important. The rebirth and surging growth of Europe inevitably meant a changed relationship with the United States. The American presence in Europe would undoubtedly be relatively reduced, and for a *Herald Tribune* stuck in an unprofitable rut, this could be a disaster. Weeks sensed this and, like Barnet, suggested a "European" solution for the *Trib;* but the readership survey showed that so far, the makeup of the newspaper did not in any way help it to reach out for that solution.

Most of the newsroom personnel, enjoying the Paris of the fifties, seem to have been oblivious to the precarious financial situation of the newspaper and the rather desperate measures management kept trying to take to improve the financial base; most would probably have endorsed Eric Hawkins' mistaken view that the decade had been a sort of onward and upward march to prosperity. Most didn't give a second thought to the effect America's changing position would have on the newspaper. But by the end of the decade they at least all knew that the *New York Times* was about to arrive on the scene, and the *Herald Tribune* European Edition now faced its greatest challenge yet.

---

* *Editor and Publisher* had used the fifty-fifty figure, given it by Gendelman, and commented on the prestige the paper obviously had among European leaders in all walks of life, despite its high price.

CHAPTER **12**

The Battle of the Boulevards

𝕴N 1960, following two years of the first American postwar balance of payments deficits, American gold reserves dropped by an alarming $2 billion. The new Kennedy administration responded with several policies. To reduce government expenditures abroad, it closed half a dozen American military bases in France—a move that by André Bing's estimate automatically cost the *Herald Tribune* 4,000 sales a day. To reduce American tourists' expenditures abroad, the administration cut tourists' duty-free allowances drastically—at about the same time that German tourists in France started to outnumber American and British tourists taken together. Americans began to avoid a hostile and unwelcoming Gaullist France, Americans resident in Paris prepared to leave in droves, while American multinationals established their new offices in Europe in Geneva, Frankfurt, and London—but not Paris.

The result was predictable: French retailers reacted rationally to all these developments by switching tourist-oriented advertising to German publications. The "Auto Market," which had sometimes filled two-thirds of a page of display and classified advertising in the *Trib* in the 1950s, virtually disappeared as Renault and Peugeot cars that had once been duty free for a family of three or four now faced substantial customs payments. Retail shops and places of entertainment and even Paris real estate advertising dropped sharply. The *Herald Tribune's* economic base began to shrink drastically. At the time no one could be sure of whether the drop was temporary or represented the start of a long-term trend. But the change came at precisely the time that the *New York Times,* long represented by a limited edition distributed from Holland, prepared to switch to full production and distribution of an International Edition in Paris.

Printer's Ink called the ensuing campaign the "Battle of the Boulevards." The *Times'* decision to spend large sums to start up its International Edition in Paris and overcome the European Edition of the *Herald Tribune* was based on the lure of the Common Market and its influence in tempting American companies to overcome the common external tariff by moving into production in Europe. The *Times* could deliberately aim for a European image, at becoming a second newspaper for Europeans. *Times* plans called for a 75 percent European audience within three years. Willett Weeks had seen the future of the European Edition in these terms, too, but despite all that he had tried to do, the paper remained the Paris *Trib* to most people, and the disturbing 1958 reader survey had shown a failure to retain or regain the European readership it had had for a while before the resurgence of the postwar European press.

The first solid piece of information came from a French technical journal that reported the *Times* was planning to transmit whole pages from New York to Paris by the first transoceanic teletype setting system (knows as TTS). Weeks, who had once looked briefly into using some such step for decentralized multiple printing centers for the *Trib* in Europe, wrote to New York that the move was technically possible but the cost would be "overwhelming . . . prohibitive." It was, one must suppose, the habit of penny-pinching on the *Trib* that made it impossible to envisage expenditure on this scale and therefore led him to conclude at first that the *Times* was more probably going out of business entirely in Europe. Still, the stories of a possible *Times* move continued to come thick and fast, and consideration had to be given to the European Edition's defenses.

In New York, Whitney had ended a period of uncertainty for

the *New York Herald Tribune* when he chose a young, likable, and successful small-town newspaperman to edit the prestigious New York newspaper—Robert M. White II, editor and publisher of the *Mexico* (Missouri) *Ledger*. White himself wrote of the occasion, "When I took over the *New York Herald Tribune*, it clearly had been on a death trend . . . I was the fourth Chief Executive Officer in a period of a few years. That kind of administrative change obviously shakes an institution to its roots." He knew that he would be devoting most of his time to the New York part of the job, and would have to deal with Paris rather summarily. On a quick trip to Europe to see Jock Whitney, he made a brief visit to Paris where he met Willett Weeks for the first time, and got the impression Weeks was anxious to return to the United States.

As a result, upon his return to New York he invited another small-town newspaperman acquaintance to dinner—Philip S. Weld, publisher of the *Gloucester* (Massachusetts) *Daily Times* and the *Newburyport* (Massachusetts) *Daily News*—and asked him whether he would consider taking over the Paris *Herald*. Weld, a New Yorker, Harvard graduate, and newspaperman of wide experience, was an adventurous type who had led guerrilla units behind the Japanese line in Burma during World War II; his wife Anne had studied at the Sorbonne.* Weld's major stipulation was that he would go for only eighteen months. But first he and his wife would go for a week to look things over under the guise of checking out the need for new mechanical equipment. Once in Paris, Weld talked to Weeks, who seemed frustrated by the job's demands, met the aging Eric Hawkins, a relative newcomer named Nat Kingsley, Bernie Cutler, the *New York Herald Tribune's* former Moscow correspondent now running its Paris bureau, and all the heads of services. Only a stop to see the Whitneys in London led Weld and his wife to the conviction they should take the job, and even then with one proviso: Weld would be allowed to retire Hawkins immediately. Whitney agreed, and announced the changeover on March 16, to take place six weeks later.

---

*Weld capped his sporting career in 1980 when he won the single-handed Observer Royal Western transatlantic sailboat race from Plymouth, England, to Newport, Rhode Island.

Willett Weeks got a big send-off, with a "Weeks Flees the Country" in-house special edition and a going-away party where the secretaries, young and old, performed in a conga line wearing Golden Girl *Herald Tribune* sweaters, and Buchwald lauded Weeks as the man who had put a light in the men's room where, he said, the existing dim bulb had been installed by Buel Weare to keep people from sitting on the toilet to read!

The night before Weld was to take over he dined at Geoffrey Parsons' elegant apartment on the Ile de la Cité. Despite his treatment by Helen Reid ten years earlier, Geoff Parsons was determined to do something for his old paper. He had invited Amory Bradford, a lawyer and general manager of the *Times,* in town presumably to make the final decision about opening up the *Times* operation. It was an opportunity for Weld and Parsons to make a final effort to persuade Bradford that the *Times* shouldn't do it, and they tried hard. Paris, they told him, was like a small-town newspaper situation: there still wasn't room for two American newspapers at once. Weld offered to take him over to the rue de Berri the next day to show him the books; Parsons added something about his own chastening experience. If their plans were all part of an attack upon Whitney and the *New York Herald Tribune,* Weld said, then, of course, the *Times* was bound to go ahead. But it would cost everyone millions, and there was no guarantee of who would win.

The talk of the evening meant that rumor was now fact, and it hardened Weld in his determination. A battle was going to be fought and the decks would have to be cleared. And so, on Saturday, May 30, he called Eric Hawkins into his office for what the older man thought would be a talk about personnel. Instead, Weld told him he was going to be retired effective immediately; the staff was informed the next day, and two days later the paper published a public announcement.*

Hawkins didn't take the dismissal lightly. A few years earlier,

---

*There was no proper picture of Hawkins in the files to illustrate the notice, and when he was asked for one, he refused: his wife couldn't read English, but if she saw his picture, she'd ask what it was all about, and he preferred she not know. On his last day he couldn't put the paper out; he left the office and Kingsley did it for him.

fighting any discussion of his inclusion in the *retraite des cadres,*
he had told Sylvan Barnet he intended never to retire, and even
now, as he maneuvered for higher retirement benefits, he declared
that he had intended to go on being editor for five more years.*
Some people were shocked. It seemed like too brutal an end to an
era that had begun, after all, on the night of the sinking of the
Lusitania. Surely an editor-publisher could have kept Hawkins on
for another year as managing editor. But Philip Weld was a man
in a hurry, sure that Hawkins' continued presence would be an
obstruction to desperately needed change. He did, in fact, sweeten
the bitter pill in various ways. Hawkins was named "Editor Emeritus" and given an office in the building (although Art Buchwald
pointed out that "no one knows what an 'Editor Emeritus' is, nor
what he does, except get the *Herald* free every morning for the rest
of his life").

In New York someone had had the happy idea of putting Hawk
to work on writing his memoirs as a sort of informal history of the
paper, with the aim of getting them done by 1962, when the *Trib*
would be celebrating its seventy-fifth anniversary. Hawkins kept
busy, too, with affairs of the Anglo-American Press Association,
of which he had been secretary-general "cum laude" for twenty
years: on his eightieth birthday the association gave him another
testimonial luncheon, complete with special issue of the *Herald
Tribune,* attended by Ambassador-at-Large Averell Harriman, in
Paris to negotiate the Vietnam peace, and Henri Bonnet, and em-
ceed by Geoff Parsons. The de Gaulle regime promoted him to
Officier de la Légion d'honneur. Perhaps the highest accolade was
paid him by the California Hotel across the rue de Berri, when it
affixed a plaque at the corner of the bar where he habitually took

---

*No one could challenge his devotion to the paper. A calculation in his own hand shows
that during the fifties he took just six weeks' vacation in 1952 and six more in 1955. His
own modest salary was a useful argument for keeping other newsroom salaries low. And
though most people thought he grew in the job, he always remained penurious. The director
of the *London Observer* news service once asked Nat Kingsley if he couldn't get Hawkins
to increase the fee paid for the service. Kingsley replied that Hawkins still thought in prewar
terms. "Yes, but pre–World War I?" was the rejoinder.

a single drink on his way home. It is still there: "Hawkins' Corner." In 1969, after telephone calls from his lady friend on vacation in the south of France failed to rouse him, *New York Herald Tribune* correspondent Don Cook and Hawk's secretary, Mlle. Surevitch, found him dead of a stroke in his apartment.

A few days later Richard Roraback wrote a tribute to him in the paper: "A rare bird, Eric Hawkins: a tough old buzzard of a boss who commanded loyalty and reaped affection; a pint-sized peacock who managed simultaneously to be a ladies' man and a man's man, with no visible diminution on either score at the age of 80; a James Gordon Bennett owl who was a living education in the best of old-style journalism and who could say with a perfectly straight face: 'You don't work for the *Herald* for money; you work for the *Herald* because you love it.' "

As for the vital matter of a successor, Philip Weld had already picked one during his earlier visit: Bernie Cutler, former Moscow correspondent, now head of the Paris bureau. Cutler, Weld thought, was tough-minded, in touch with the times and with modern newspapering as the aging Hawkins no longer could be. His standing among members of the Paris press corps and in New York was high: "He could write like a dream," said Weeks, who had promoted Cutler's syndication. He would be abrasive and step on a lot of toes, Weld knew, but the *Trib* needed someone tough and honest to shake up and shape up the newsroom, and a lot of toes would have to be stepped on. Cutler could do it.

Cutler's choice was something of a surprise. As Weeks had written earlier, when Cutler was transferred from Moscow to head the Paris bureau, "Cutler totally lacks the necessary experience in editing to be useful as a standby for Eric Hawkins . . . His sole interest is in being a damned good reporter." Besides, Weeks had brought over the former managing editor of the *Herald Tribune* news service, Nathan Kingsley, as a tentative second man to Hawkins. Kingsley's understanding that he was coming as Hawkins' successor to work with him over a transition period meant a certain amount of ill-feeling that was never dispelled, and Kingsley and

Cutler never got along well (although Weld thought that they "teamed ideally"). And there exists a general consensus that Cutler was an extremely able editor who did much with little, but that he was, indeed, a tactless and abrasive man, harsh with his staff. The newsroom atmosphere was certainly never again one of cheerful anarchy as it had been under Hawkins in the fifties.

There was bound to be a clash with newsroom personnel anyway, whether Cutler or Kingsley became editor. Both of them were appalled at what they found in the newsroom. Apart from a small core of professionals like Roy McMullen, it was composed, they thought, of amateurs—"of snide, knee-jerk anti-Americans," said one—who put out a sloppy and tendentious product. Clannishness, Kingsley wrote, was "intensified by a history of lack of professional competition, a practice of recruitment of people often with very limited professional experience . . . and a low salary scale." Once Hawkins was removed, several of the newsroom staff were eliminated. Weld, Kingsley, and Cutler may not have agreed on everything, but they agreed on this necessity, even though French law on severance pay made it an extremely expensive proposition— but "one of the soundest investments we can make," Weld told Cutler.

Naming a new editor and ridding the newsroom of deadwood were the important actions Weld took with respect to the editorial side of the paper, along with reinstatement of a New York correspondent to improve the nightly file from the home paper. As the time approached for the launching of the *Times,* White wrote to him from New York, "How lucky we are and how right you are to have the timing we have on the Eric Hawkins change." On the business side, though, Weld was equally proud of what was a much less controversial change. He had come for only eighteen months, and someone else would have to be named to succeed him during the decisive next few years. Since World War II there had been Robinson, Collins, Wise, Weare, Reid, Barnet, Weeks, and now Weld. In January 1961 Weld persuaded Jock Whitney to turn the job over to André Bing, who took the position of general manager in June, acting as publisher in all but name, with authority over, and responsibility for, all departments of the newspaper except editorial content and policy. He would appoint all department heads except the editor, approve all department budgets including the editorial one, and where financial or space considerations conflicted with editorial plans, his would the final decision. It was the first and last time that anyone but an American had been given such authority.

Letters and cables of congratulation poured in. Bing had the respect of everyone who knew him, as a master of the detail of the newspaper, a tough, decisive, fair bargainer, and a gentleman to all. The "cyclistes"—the messenger boys—remember him as someone who *always* raised his hat to them as he passed by. Comité d'Entreprise spokesmen remember—with immense respect—their bargaining sessions with him. One of the heads of service whom Bing promoted recalls him with the comment, "Ça, c'était le Grand Chef!" There is little question but that major credit belongs to Bing for seeing the newspaper through a period that included the death of the parent *Herald Tribune* in New York, a basic change in Franco-American relations, the decline of the American market in France, and the heavy hand of competition from the *New York Times*. Before Phil Weld left he sent Jock Whitney a letter of understanding following two weeks of discussions with Whitney and Walter Thayer, Whitney's long time associate who was now president of the newly named Whitney Communications Corporation. The letter summarized the financial policy to be followed by the European Edition, and included two remarkable key statements: "It is more important to hold down the deficit than to try to match the *New York Times*. If this runs the danger of allowing the *Times* to close our lead more easily than we'd prefer, New York understands and accepts the risks."

Whitney wrote back cheerfully, "We do not believe that holding down the deficit is necessarily incompatible with staying in front," and in a five-year review, prepared in October 1965, Bing quoted the earlier letter from Whitney and remarked, "We've tried to justify his confidence." Everyone felt he did.

Roland Pinson, Bing's second-in-command, moved up to become assistant general manager.

There were other changes in personnel in the early sixties. When Cutler was plucked from the Paris bureau to be made managing editor and then editor at the time of Weld's departure, someone was needed to head the Paris bureau. The bureau, whose prime job was to gather news for the New York newspaper, had always served as an important direct source of news for the Paris paper; its members usually wrote to Paris deadlines and often acted as the European Edition's reporters. Weld pleaded with New York for haste in filling Cutler's position as bureau head, and was relieved when the experienced Don Cook was named in August as chief European correspondent, based in Paris, and authorized to re-arrange and coordinate the work of the other correspondents to take advantage of economies offered by the jet age. But Cook remembers it as a time when the once great *New York Herald Tribune* staff was being decimated: the Bonn and Rome offices closed, and only one man was left in London when Cook moved to Paris—where he never had enough travel funds anyway to justify his being called chief European correspondent. And he and Cutler never got along, so that the all-important relations of the European Edition with the bureau suffered badly. In fact, when he left in 1965 for the *Los Angeles Times,* no one replaced him for six months. It all meant that the European Edition, after 1960, had to rely much more on news services than it had in the past—and again, at the worst possible times.

Cutler took advantage of the months between hard news of the *Times'* arrival and the actual start of publication to begin making some of the changes he thought were necessary. At Weld's sugges-tion, he moved the comics inside, off the back pages. He increased

American coverage elsewhere, and was rewarded in his view when the 1962 reader survey showed that the chief complaint about the paper was lack of American news.

Along with a stream of inside news on *Times* plans and contacts came information that the *Times,* paying out tremendous sums, would carry complete New York Stock Exchange and American Exchange tables, along with bond and commodity reports. This worked out to very nearly three full pages—a quarter of the paper and of the transmission time, and a clear indication that the *Times* was taking to heart what Weeks had long suggested for the *Herald Tribune:* an orientation toward the growing financial and economic integration not just of Western Europe but also of the whole Atlantic area. The *Trib* responded, doubling its own stock and bond coverage two days before the *Times* appeared, and of course Cutler denied that the *Times* had anything to do with it; the plans had long been under way. Still, it gave the *Trib* just one page to the *Times'* three, and Cutler continued to make a virtue of what filled the other two pages: the comics, better sports coverage, entertainment in Europe, and more feature columnists, in which the *Herald Tribune* still excelled.

Cutler soon returned to the practice of spacing out features on particular days, and anchoring them in the same place in the paper, so that news as well as columns would appear where readers might expect them to appear. "History in the Making," banished by Willett Weeks, returned on Mondays to match the *Times'* two-page "News of the Week in Review." Two days a week there appeared a "Mostly for Women" page, where Hebe Dorsey on fashions in Paris vied with New York's Eugenia Sheppard. (Fashion was always touchy. Hebe Dorsey made one remarkable but understandable error in those years: reporting on a costume exhibition she referred to a celebrated turn-of-the-century "cocotte," Cléo de Merode, a beauty indelibly associated with the Belle Epoque, Maxim's, and King Leopold II of the Belgians. To Hebe Dorsey and everyone else's surprise Cléo de Merode—still alive sixty years later—wrote to the *Herald Tribune* taking exception to the appellation "cocotte," and her letter was duly printed on the "Mostly for Women" page, while Bing wrote a letter of apology to the director of the Centre de Documentation du Costume. And the American Emba Mink Breeder's Association scolded Hebe Dorsey for suggesting that mink was a good buy in Scandinavia, and then reporting that the Empress Farah of Iran wore "a floor-length white Ermine cape from Dior's" to the Paris Opéra, when it was in fact mink. This one brought almost everyone—Cutler, Walter Thayer in New York, Bing, and Wachob—into the investigation; it turned out that Dior had misinformed Miss Dorsey, who couldn't after all, "finger an Empress' cape!")

"Clementine Paddleford in Your Kitchen" was displaced by a new constellation, one of whose stars would soar: Beck, Child, and Bertholle, whose *Mastering the Art of French Cooking* the *Trib* serialized. Then there were columns on restaurants, art—all the features of women's pages of those days. The Saturday-Sunday number featured film and theater criticism, book and music reviews, and lengthy listings of events. The *Herald Tribune*, in other words, remained richer in European and specifically Parisian features than the *Times* would ever be. It also had the comics, banished to an inside page, but read regularly by 65 percent of readers—a larger percentage than read U.S. news, editorials, and columns, European news, and sports!

The *Trib* had always excelled at putting out special editions, in part because everyone considered them excellent promotion vehicles, and in October 1962 there was a happy occasion for one—the paper's seventy-fifth anniversary. The powers that be made everything they could of it to remind Europeans that—as against possible upstart competitors—there had been a *Herald Tribune* European Edition for fully seventy-five years, filling its task of serving Americans in Europe and Europeans who wanted to know American thinking and American events. Jock Whitney came over for a luncheon for French officials and publishers; Walter Lippmann spoke; French radio and TV and French publications covered the event. And on November 29 a gala performance of *Le*

"Golden Girls" waiting in the wings to deliver the 75th anniversary edition to the Gala audience at the Comédie Française.

Bourgeois Gentilhomme at the Comédie Française, with helmeted Garde Républicaine ushers, elegantly bound red memorial programs, and a select guest list had as its high point the intermission: dozens of Golden Girls streamed down the aisles to hand out copies of the twenty-four-page 75th Anniversary Edition. It was an elaborate preparation. Jock Whitney's picture appeared on the front page with one of Buchwald and one of James Gordon Bennett, Jr. There were reproductions of historic front pages, stories about great scoops of the past, and, of course, dozens of advertisements taken by European publications to salute the *Herald Tribune* on this auspicious occasion. And in the midst of the festivities Jock Whitney was made a Chevalier de la Légion d'honneur. Let the *Times* try to match that!

The *Times* was, in fact, ready to match a lot, and *Tribune* personnel kept a careful watch on its operations. From London sources came word that the *Times* planned to spend $3,500,000 the first year, and had budgeted $500,000 for promotion alone. Weld determined that the *Trib* would husband its own meager $40,000 budgeted for promotion for a counterattack. The *Times* would give a higher commission to kiosks and would charge advertisers less. Gendelman reported to Bing that the *Times* aimed at net paid sales of 35,000 at the end of three years (which, in the event, it did reach); the *Herald Tribune* bureau head, Don Cook, claimed to have won $100 from the *Times'* Sydney Gruson, who was willing to bet that the *Times* would equal the *Herald Tribune's* circulation at the end of a year.

Bing and Weld were kept fully informed on the *Times'* press run and returns on forms printed for the purpose, along with the *Times'* sales availability at various sales points, advertising lineage, revenue, and relations with particular advertisers. Weld knew the *Times* would be handicapped in attracting advertisers by a smaller circulation at first. If the *Trib* could keep a relative lead long enough to retain a major portion of the advertising, it could survive, despite the danger that the prestige of the *Times* in the United States gave its salesmen strength there that would not be commensurate with actual circulation figures in Europe. Gendelman noted that it was easy to keep the finger on the production-run button and then cite inflated figures: "The *Rome Daily American*," he wrote to New York, "once or twice a year runs off 30-35 thousand copies and immediately dashes down to the Embassy in Rome to make sworn statements." In fact, the *Herald Tribune* itself used impressive stamped statements from the embassy in Paris, and sold advertising on the basis of its average print runs.

Then Weld discovered that there was a French equivalent of the American Audit Bureau of Circulation—the highly respected and trusted Office de Justification de Diffusion (OJD), an organization jointly owned and financed by advertisers, advertising agencies, and newspaper publishers. In 1961 the *Trib* had its first OJD audit, and Weld wrote triumphantly, "We now carry this emblem of purity on our masthead!"

The battle of circulation figures would be carried out on several fronts: the *Herald Tribune* people accused *Times* advertising salesmen in 1961 of using the press-run figures as though they were net paid circulation. A series of charges and countercharges appeared in the trade journal *Advertising Age*—which, in turn, noted dryly that the *Herald Tribune* had never gone to the Office de Justification de Diffusion until the *Times* appeared on the scene.* But the *Trib* people took satisfaction in the fact that the *Times* put off being subjected to an OJD audit at least twice, until April 1963, when it turned out that it had a net paid circulation of 31,797 to the *Herald Tribune's* 50,624.

It was not just circulation data that was in dispute. Bing kept an ad in readiness in case the *Times* published one on comparative advertising lineage in Europe. As he put it, it would not be a "wash your dirty linen in public" ad, but, like the one on circulation, be designed to cut short any further misleading statements from the *Times,* which would be boasting about lineage "sold at fancy rates or at no rates at all . . . to keep the leadership we must fight when it is necessary." Besides, Wachob had informed him that the *New York Times* had put advertisers up to complaining about poor reproduction and printing in the Paris *Times* so that they could ask for free reruns and the *Times* could then report increased lineage published! Later, in July 1964, the *Times* did publish a house ad giving figures on advertising gains in the *Times* and losses in the *Tribune.* Bing, evoking a French law of 1882, formally requested of the *Times* that it publish a letter from the *Trib* with its own contrasting computation of advertising lineage for both papers. As

---

*On another occasion the *Times'* general manager wrote to André Bing to protest a conversation John Wachob had held with a member of the International Edition staff; Wachob had said the *Times'* general manager's kids at school were telling their friends they were leaving at the end of the year. So, asked Wachob, when is the I.E. going to fold? Such a rumor could do substantial damage. Bing replied on the next day that all members of the staff had been instructed not to repeat rumors of this nature. Certainly, he assured the *Times* man, this one had not started at the *Trib.*

he expected, the *Times* people turned him down, but he was confident that the threat of legal action under an obscure French law had alerted them to the dangers of publicly publishing unilateral claims of this nature, and that they would avoid doing so in the future.

From the start, for the first year, Bing kept a tally for Weld of extra expenses incurred as a result of the presence of the International Edition. For the first couple of months he calculated that the enlarged news hole and increased cable transmissions were costing the *Herald Tribune* $10,000 each month; the augmented stock list alone amounted to $250 a week.

The *Trib* had to stop postdating copies to be shipped afar and tagging them as the "Special Express Edition," since the *Times* planned no postdating. It might, Weld figured, cost them 2,500 copies a day, but not to abandon the practice could lead to charges of mislabeling and a loss of prestige. The *Trib* had always saved some money during the winter months when the tourists were gone by actually cutting back on the size of the paper; in the face of the *Times'* competition it could no longer afford to do so. Press times would have to be more strictly observed than in the past, in order to match distribution schedules even more rigidly; a delay of an hour in reaching Rome, for example, could be counted on to cut sales by 10 percent. The *Trib* could ship off its first edition at 1:30 A.M., an hour and a half before the *Times,* tied by its New York transmission times. This meant, in many cases, being able to make early French trains that the *Times* could not, so that it could beat the *Times* on newsstands in France outside of Paris, and in Belgium and Switzerland. On the other hand, the *Times* sometimes contained later news: American sports results and the kind of Washington news that breaks late in the day. As a result, the *Tribune* often had to go to a third or fourth edition, keeping an editor late on the job, and, of course, costing more money.

Distribution always remained a fundamental part of the battle. Once it got going the *Times* was supposed to have eight roadmen out supervising circulation—when at times in the fifties the *Trib* had cut down to a single man. It was, in fact, this single man whom Weld and Bing made circulation manager in April 1961, a few months after Paul Gendelman left: François Desmaisons, a Frenchman who had become fluent in English when he was a Free French liaison with the British during World War II, and who had worked on *Herald Tribune* distribution through armed forces channels during the fifties. Desmaisons' intimate knowledge of both the channels and the people involved helped immensely. But he had to add expensive roadmen, and in major cities outside of Belgium, Switzerland, and France, the two papers arrived at roughly the same time, using identical forms of transportation.

Success in distribution depended upon regular press times, composing room action, and newsroom promptness in "locking up" the pages. Weld made one change in all innocence. To improve the flow in the composing room he installed an illuminated board with lights for each page, to be lit up as the mat for that page left the room. It was promptly dubbed "le phare"—the lighthouse—by an amused composing room team, who, he came to realize, were a law unto themselves and would continue to do things strictly in their own way, as they felt on any particular night. But Cutler did his part to ease relations with the composing and press room people by reducing chaos in the newsroom and feeding the pages down to the composing room more smoothly—despite the resultant resentment among the somewhat anarchic newsroom personnel.

Cutler also stood firm in preserving the general appearance and layout of the paper. In New York, when White left and John Denson became editor, the desperate competition with the *Times* there took the form of gimmickry in format and layout, and New York accused Cutler of stodginess in not following suit. He insisted, however, that the traditional appearance of the European Edition was one of its biggest assets; changes would be only incremental.

In at least some areas the *Times* and the *Trib* cooperated from the start. In New York Bob White sought and got assurances from the *Times* people about their discussions with the French production unions, making sure they would not set costly precedents in the matter of manning their machines. On the issue of possible sharing of TTS transmissions of stock tables, the discussions proved abortive. But both accepted the desirability of identical newsstand prices throughout Europe. As time wore on, managerial personnel did occasionally discuss possible changes in advertising rates, and Desmaisons and his counterpart sometimes agreed on matters such as not using or dropping expensive charter flights. When the *Times* flew to Spain the *Trib* also had to, it cost them both too much, and neither gained; Desmaisons got the *Times* to abandon charter flights.

And, of course, in Harry's New York Bar and over good Paris food and drink, the newsmen and others talked shop and exchanged bits of gossip—and sometimes went back to the store and put information down in a memo. Thus André Bing learned that the *Times* lost a staggering $1,700,000 in each of its first two years—compared with the $102,000 in 1961 and $155,000 in 1962 that New York had had to advance Bing and Cutler for their operation of the *Trib*. In early 1963 Bing and his counterpart at the *Times* lunched together to discuss an impending price rise in French newspapers and to agree on their own price rise in France and elsewhere in Europe, thus carrying out the spirit of what an earlier *Times* general manager wrote in his letter of congratulations to Bing in 1961, "and be assured that in those areas where it is important to both of us to present a united front you will have my cooperation."

In one important area the *Times* had an immediate and lasting influence on the *Herald Tribune:* the pay and general legal situation of newsroom personnel. Everyone knew that the *Times* was going to pay more, but *Times* men promised in New York that they wouldn't raid the *Tribune* newsroom. Ever since Parsons' difficulties in the late forties the *Herald Tribune* people had complained about their pay scales, beginning with the attempt to circumvent Buel Weare by appealing to New York to overrule him. All through the 1950s the succeeding general managers managed to fend off demands from the newsroom, continuing Weare's policy of dealing with the employees individually and avoiding collective bargaining. Weld's arrival and the advent of the *Times,* with its higher salaries, increased the pressures. Weld held the line until he left, telling the staff in April 1961 that a raise was quite impossible, and he didn't mind the resulting hostility.

But times had changed. The past irregularities had saved the paper a lot of money over the years. The newsroom crew could legally ask for the French-mandated, thirteenth month's extra pay retroactively; on the other hand, because they worked a five-day week, they could not ask for the French vacation schedule. Bing felt they were after French benefits to be added on to what were essentially salaries and working conditions close to American standards. Newsroom personnel countered that they received the lowest American salaries paid in American organizations in Europe, while *Times* men received a good 25 percent more. Bing finally concluded that if the paper acceded to most of the newsmen's demands, in the long run it would not cost too much; the paper could tighten up on individual raises and on dismissals, recruit less costly help, and avoid the almost automatic adjustments for devaluations that had been given in the past. And when he and a newsroom personnel negotiating team signed an agreement in May 1962—setting the scale avoided ever since Parsons' time, but without any retroactive payments or recognition of the Newspaper Guild—he noted that the agreement at least protected the paper from costly lawsuits that it probably would have lost.* In 1964 the

*The *Herald Tribune* did constantly face lawsuits. Lucie Noel, displaced by Hebe Dorsey, brought suit to collect severance pay based on employment as fashion editor since the forties, when she was described as such by Parsons in a column in the paper, even though she was actually paid by the contribution. Bing, who fought all such cases hard because of the nature of French law, insisted she had been put on the European Edition payroll only in the late fifties. She was also after thirteenth month pay retroactively, a precedent designed to chill the heart of any manager. To make it more of a family matter, she shared the services of the same lawyer with former promotion manager Doris Sanders, also busy suing the paper. It was, incidentally, precisely to avoid some of the binding conditions of French law that most contributing feature writers were paid by the column rather than being put on the payroll. John Wachob, fired in 1964 by Walter Thayer, president of Whitney Associates, over policy differences with respect to North African supplements, sued to gain severance pay that would include his five years of service on the New York paper before he came to Paris in 1959. He protested, too, what he called summary and unfair dismissal. In a sad and dramatic twist he died of a heart attack suffered during a meeting between him, his lawyer, André Bing, and the *Herald Tribune* lawyer.

newsroom personnel were also finally, as required by law, included in the retirement fund, the *retraite des cadres*. Once more the French legal authorities were lenient: a small settlement of some $15,000 in back payments, and immediate rectification of the situation by enrollment of present personnel avoided all penalties.

And so, finally, thanks to the *Times*, the *Herald Tribune* found itself paying newsroom personnel on the basis of a regular scale, and in full compliance with French law on personnel matters—the Golden Girls excepted, of course. It was, in a sense, another step in full professionalization of the paper, another move away from the informal and penurious fashion in which it had previously been run. It did not, incidentally, stop several people from moving over to the still-better-paying *New York Times*, among them Thomas Quinn Curtiss, the longtime movie and theater critic. Wachob himself had been negotiating with the *Times* at the time of his death in 1965. And ironically enough, the *Times'* general manager during much of this time was Walter B. Kerr, the former *Herald Tribune* correspondent.

Kerr was there primarily to rectify an egregious error made by the *Times* that probably saved the *Herald Tribune:* the use of TTS to transmit a paper conceived and edited in New York, whose Paris editors therefore didn't control the contents, and which, as Kerr said, resulted in a paper that was cold, gray, with no human quality, none of the "personality" of a paper that allows it to live. Moreover, TTS transmission cost much too much, just as Weeks had foreseen, and when radio channels were used rather than cable, the results were often garbled (so that, as someone wrote, the International Edition had no need of a crossword puzzle, the paper served as one itself).

Trib personnel remember some of the more memorable consequences of the *Times'* attempt to virtually reproduce the New York front pages: on the day that the *Herald Tribune* featured a banner headline about de Gaulle's rejection of British entry to the Common Market, the *Times* headline told about New York being blacked out by a power failure. Editorial flexibility allowed the *Trib* to

print late-breaking European news that the *Times* didn't have—
results of a crucial vote of confidence in the National Assembly,
the death of Eichmann, and so on. The *Times* used valuable space
for regional American news of little interest to European readers.
"Independence," Weld had written in 1960, "represents the strongest weapon in our counter-attack." And it was.

In 1962 and 1963, however, a series of events triggered a fundamental change. A long, costly strike in New York led to cost-
cutting by the Paris *Times;* an expensive Western Edition of the
Times in California flopped; and on June 20, 1963, following the
unexpected death of *Times* publisher Orville Dryfoos, the young
and somewhat inexperienced Arthur Ochs "Punch" Sulzberger
became president and publisher of the New York paper, where he
soon began to make personnel changes. One result was that *Times*
management reassessed the Paris effort and decided it could both
improve the editorial product and save money by abandoning the
TTS transmission for all but stock and bond quotations, and allow
its Paris editors the autonomy the *Trib* enjoyed. Shortly after the
changeover, in 1964, Bing wrote to New York,

> The *Times* is now trying to do what, for their own good, they should
> have done right from the start . . . given editors a lot more autonomy
> . . . printing only a few minutes later than we do . . . [the paper] is
> undoubtedly improved editorially . . . transport and transmission
> costs have gone down. In short they are now trying to use the
> formula which has made our life possible for so many years. If they
> had started that way earlier, we would have a serious problem by
> now. Changeover now will take time for readers and advertisers.
> But in the long run, with tremendous editorial resources and the
> unique network of correspondents, the *Times* will be a much more
> serious competitor than the one we have been facing up to now.

A year later, in August of 1965, he was more emphatic. Cutler
and Kingsley—who left in 1964—had done wonders: they had
improved the wire services being delivered to the *Trib;* they had
added the highly useful London *Observer* news service to AP, UPI,

and Agence France Presse; they had forced the rewrite men to do better, so that stories seemed fresher. There are those who will argue that in the face of the *Times* competition the newsroom team pulled together as it never had before. But the decline of the once great *New York Herald Tribune* news service and its staff of foreign correspondents could not be compensated for: "Our inferiority in the field of foreign news has become a real handicap," Bing wrote. "Readers and distributors keep telling us so, and a look at our recent circulation figures in some countries, and the little we know of competition's results, confirms it."

In 1961, the first year of *Times* competition, there had been a sharp drop in both circulation and advertising; daily net paid circulation of over 58,000 in 1960 declined to 49,000 the next year, although circulation remained stable in France itself. Advertising continued to decline for the next few years, though circulation began a slow recovery and surpassed the 1960 mark by 1965. But the rate of increase slowed down that year, and Bing wrote that the reason was the *Times'* coverage of European news, "because of their network of European correspondents we no longer have . . . Readers and advertisers keep drawing our attention to this." In February 1965, when Don Cook left the Paris bureau to join the *Los Angeles Times,* and was not replaced for several months, the absence of a correspondent in Paris hurt badly.

In late 1965 the *Times* made a deal with *Figaro* to move operations from its rue de Lafayette plant to the *Figaro* plant on the rue d'Aboukir near the Bourse. It was an expensive switch, and to Bing a significant one: once the International Edition was installed in the *Figaro* plant it would be even harder for it to end operations— "another reason why time is not necessarily working in our favor."

And then, besides, the international situation began to make itself felt. In July 1962 Bing reported an alarming drop in advertising in response to the first American restrictions on duty-free entry for tourists' purchases: the *Times,* he noted, had suffered a similar drop. Airline mergers were bad news: they meant fewer airline ads. So was the increasing use of charters: charters didn't place display ads in Europe, but only in the United States. In 1960 American tourists purchased 11,500 *Herald Tribune* copies a day in the summer; in 1962, only 5,500. In mid-1963 the *London Economist* published a story to the effect that American tourists spent less, went to fewer cities, and stayed outside of major centers, spending their time in small pensions and bed-and-breakfast facilities—and obviously buying little. André Bing wrote in 1964, "In the eyes of advertisers, American readers, be they residents or tourists, are simply no longer worth five or ten readers of other papers." In other words, the wealthier Americans, generally on a buying spree in a cheaper Europe, had enabled the *Tribune* to charge that much more to retail advertisers than European papers could. This was simply no longer true.

International magazines like *Time* and *Newsweek,* and an "increasingly sophisticated European press," attracted international institutional advertising like Imperial Chemicals, Krupp, General Electric, International Harvester, or Bethlehem Steel. Only improved financial coverage would enable the *Tribune* to break into this rich field. And the *Times,* wrote Bing, "assisted by their powerful machinery at home, selling advertising at whatever price and conditions the market can bear, has obviously influenced our results." In 1965, to improve and reorganize the advertising department, he hired a new director, Richard Morgan, a cosmopolitan, expatriate American educated in Europe and the United States, who understood from the start that he would have to restore and diversify the *Tribune's* advertising base by seeking whole new categories of advertising.

In late 1965 Bing calculated that the *Times* had lost close to $10 million to the *Trib's* million in the space of five years. He quoted Laurence Hills' memorandum of thirty years earlier: "Under present conditions it seems that one American newspaper is possible as a public service institution for American interests in Europe; two newspapers, from the standpoint of regular business principles, were impossible."

"Things have not changed much after thirty years," he wrote.

To what purpose had the money been spent? The *Trib* had survived and the competition had been hurt. In the second round of the competitive battle, after the *Times* reorganization, inflation had really begun to tell: "Salaries, social charges, and transport expenses keep growing at a quicker rate than revenue. The competitive struggle makes each sale more expensive." The situation could be accepted temporarily on the grounds that the competition was suffering more than the *Trib*. But in the summer of 1965 the *New York Herald Tribune* office calculated that the *Times* now surpassed the *Trib* in classified lineage; the *Times* itself calcuated that while it now had 71 percent as great a circulation figure as the *Trib* (using OJD figures), its overall advertising lineage was actually 40 percent greater.* "The battle," wrote Bing, "is one in which there can be victory or defeat—but not a draw." One or the other of the papers would disappear, or a merger would take place, whose terms would be determined by hard bargaining and depend on the competitive position of the papers both in Europe and at home.

The first merger discussions took place in the summer and fall of 1963 and, as nothing more than a preliminary skirmish, established the desirability of merger. But neither party felt strong enough to negotiate its own terms, and each felt for the moment that time was on its side. So, over the next year, Walter Kerr went ahead with the project that he thought would strengthen the *Times'* bargaining position—autonomy—while Bing and Cutler fought to keep their leading position. In early January of 1965 Bing's assistant, Roland Pinson, completed a study of what it would cost to strengthen the paper in the field in which everyone now agreed the *Times* led: the stock and bond tables. The result was rather dismal. To do what the *Times* did would require an initial outlay of

---

*The *Trib* people continued to dispute this. In January 1966 Richard Morgan, Wachob's replacement, provided Bing with calculations to show that *Times* figures were inflated by roughly a third through including advertising lineage in special sections repeated from New York special sections. Without this, Morgan figured, the *Herald Tribune* still had 10 percent more advertising despite a 40 percent higher rate. Besides, he told Bing, the *Times* had resorted to ridiculously high commissions and even bribes to sell ads for Spanish and Portuguese special sections.

$250,000 for machinery and $250,000 a year in operating costs and the addition of extra pages to the daily paper. But another opportunity opened up at the same moment, producing a considerable flurry of excitement. This time, it concerned the *Wall Street Journal.*

There had long been rumors that the *Journal* might open up a European Edition, and it had, in fact, explored the possibility of starting up in Frankfurt, now rapidly becoming a European financial center. What the *Journal* now proposed, however, was some sort of joint venture with the *Herald Tribune,* and Bing was delighted. The *Journal* would add both financial coverage and foreign correspondents, and make complete stock tables possible. The only thing to avoid, Bing wrote, would be "giving the impression that the move is part of the present wave of American take-overs in Europe and that the European Edition would become the mouthpiece for big American business."

The flurry of excitement faded. Barney Kilgore, president of Dow Jones and publisher of the *Wall Street Journal,* later told Turner Catledge, managing editor of the *Times,* that, given the present operation of the *Herald Tribune,* a joint *Herald Tribune/Wall Street Journal* operation wouldn't pay off. He still liked the idea, but now could really only envisage it in terms of a three-way association, involving the printing of a merged newspaper somewhere outside of Paris. Said Catledge, "Perhaps you're the most objective since you have no losing operation there," and Kilgore replied, "I'm strictly objective: I've never even been to Europe!"

To rectify at least one part of its weakness vis-à-vis the *Times,* the European Edition then turned to a new news source, adding the *Los Angeles Times/Washington Post* news service for a six-month trial period in late 1965. The *Washington Post,* under the brilliant but mercurial Philip Graham, had sought to break out of its rather parochial existence in the 1950s, establishing its own first foreign correspondent in 1958. The *New York Times'* attempt at an expensive, short-lived Western Edition then stimulated the *Los Angeles Times* to form a news service with the *Washington Post,*

and the joint service began to establish a network of foreign correspondents. Bing had "great hopes" for the new arrangement:
from the *LAT/WP* communications center in London the *Trib*
would receive everything their reporters filed from Europe, Asia,
Africa, and the Near East.

In the meantime, Ivan Veit, vice-president of the *New York Times*
and publisher Sulzberger's close counselor, spent a summer week
in Paris inspecting the International Edition operations. His report
was discouraging. Morale was "unbelievably bad," relations with
New York were "wretched," advertising had no real expansion
plan, and "as we are now performing, we cannot succeed and don't
deserve to." In New York, he said, it is assumed that anything with
the name "Times" on it is better, but while the International Edition
was in some respects better, in overall quality the European reader
"will not perceive any great superiority . . . It was disconcerting to
hear frequently from *Times* [N.Y.] devotees that they like the 'Paris
Trib' as well or better." Kerr, of course, had his own side of the
story, and his own complaints. Everyone agreed, after all, that the
1964 change made on his own initiative had led to a much better
paper.

André Bing kept track of the troubles at the International Edition,
and New York let him know when the desultory talks with the
Times resumed in late 1965. But now the situation in New York
affected the negotiations: the management of the parent *New York
Herald Tribune* finally gave up their long battle to remain competitive with the *New York Times,* and entered into their own labo-
rious nine-month-long negotiations with the Scripps-Howard and
Hearst interests to create something called the *World-Journal-Tribune*—or WJT or "widget"—a merger of the *World Telegram and
Sun,* the *Journal American,* and the *Herald Tribune.* The key to it
all was that by 1966 the *Herald Tribune* attracted roughly 10
percent of advertising lineage in New York, the *Journal American*
and the *World Telegram and Sun* about 7 percent apiece—and the
New York Times 43.6 percent. Jock Whitney had been putting
almost $4 million a year into the *Herald Tribune,* and that just
couldn't go on.

Ultimately, the negotiators secured an agreement and announced on March 22, 1966, that publication of the *World-Journal-Tribune* would begin a month later—failing to take into account that they would not be able to reach agreement on severance payments for the nearly 1,000 American Newspaper Guild employees who were losing their jobs. And so, the day before publication of the merged newspaper, pickets appeared outside the three buildings, to begin a strike that would last until September 12. The result, as New Yorkers know, was a failure: the *WJT* lasted only eight months, coming to a sudden end on May 6, 1967. The great old *New York Herald Tribune* and the two other newspapers disappeared forever.

In the meantime, Jock Whitney and Punch Sulzberger met in July 1965, and the former made it clear that he was keeping the European Edition out of the merger talks he was conducting with Hearst and Scripps-Howard in New York, and that the only sort of deal acceptable in Paris would be a fifty-fifty one, despite the *Herald Tribune's* weak position in New York. In December the interested parties all sat down for lunch, and Walter Thayer told Sulzberger that if it hadn't been for the *Times'* International Edition, the Paris *Trib* would not only be making a small profit, but undoubtedly would have moved out of its cramped quarters in Paris, probably to Frankfurt. The important matter developed in this conversation, however, was that the issue of control of the newspaper would be the sticking point; Thayer remarked that he couldn't think of a suitable formula, Whitney said that they'd give it more thought. *Times* representatives insisted that if Whitney wanted management control, the *Times* would have to have editorial control. Nor was the *Times* willing to concede managerial control for more than a limited period. (At which point a further minor complication ensued when Lord Thompson of Fleet Street, publisher of the *Times* of London, indicated he might have an interest in buying both papers and combining them. He came back to the charge once more a year later, but again nothing came of it.)

Then, with the newly merged New York newspapers ready to appear on April 25, 1966, the New York strike intervened, weakening Whitney's hand on the Paris negotiations. From Paris the

Times negotiators heard a spate of encouraging rumors: François Desmaisons was reported to have told people at *Le Monde* that it would all be over in six or eight months, thanks to the blow in New York; André Bing was said to have told friends, including the circulation manager of *Figaro,* that it was already all over, and that he couldn't care less, since his severance pay would reach $100,000. And *Trib* columnist Naomi Barry was supposed to have stopped by the *Times* to offer her services because of the uncertainty at the European Edition. "We don't need her," said this report, "but she's usually well-informed and worth talking to!" The rumor mill, of course, ground out two sets: Bing, after commenting that the *Times* again overestimated the gains from a merger, also reported to New York about this time that the *Figaro* people were far from happy about how their deal with the *Times* was working out!

In July the *Times* got a disturbing set of messages from different sources. From Washington came a memo that there was speculation the *Washington Post* was ready to buy the Paris *Herald Tribune.* It seemed logical, "since *Post* anxious for some time to become better known as an international newspaper and also to improve their image overseas." The *Times'* lawyer called the *Herald Tribune's* lawyer, Jacob Javits; what was going on? Javits told him that since the *Times* people remained adamant about the issue of control, and in view of their draft of proposed bylaws, there had indeed been conversations with the *Post,* not on a *Post* purchase of the European Edition, but on a possible joint venture in which the *Herald Tribune* would retain management and editorial control. Nothing, however, was settled.

A week later Thayer, declaring that the *Times* discussions were at an impasse, told their lawyer he was going to Paris to look things over. Remember, the *Times* man told him, with us you will turn a loss into a profit. What will you and the *Post* get out of a deal?

Thayer stirred things up by confirming to reporters in Paris that there had, indeed, been long conversations over a merger of the two Paris papers. Sulzberger, upset, felt compelled to reassure the Paris *Times* staff that though there had been tentative and confidential talks, there had been "no visible progress." And Thayer, on returning, found himself accused by Sulzberger of violating "minimum standards" by not disclosing negotiations with a third party while he was still talking to the *Times,* as well as failing to keep word of the conversations confidential as everyone had agreed they should be.

Thayer replied briefly that since the negotiations had reached an impasse there was no longer any reason not to talk to anyone else. As for confidentiality, the negotiations were common gossip, and his public statement had been in reply to a *Times* reporter who said he was aware that there had been talks. For a year they had negotiated in good faith. He hoped their differences could be considered a matter of differences over interpretation.

And then, on August 5, Whitney and Katharine Graham, who succeeded her late husband Philip as publisher of the *Post* in 1963, announced jointly that the *Post* had bought 45 percent of the *Herald Tribune,* European Edition. Once the details had been settled, it would be called *New York Herald Tribune/Washington Post International.* "It will," said Whitney's announcement, "give us the opportunity to enlarge and broaden the editorial coverage of our Paris paper and to enhance its present position in the European market," and went on to mention the *Washington Post's* thirteen correspondents in eleven different bureaus, its collaboration with the *Los Angeles Times* in a wire news service, and its ownership of *Newsweek* magazine, all of whose resources, it implied, would be at the disposal of the Paris newspaper, whose circulation, it stated, "is nearly fifty percent greater than that of its closest rival."

It was true that Katharine Graham and her husband Philip had long been interested in some activity abroad that would enhance the reputation and influence of the *Washington Post.* Walter Thayer has it that one evening in the summer of 1966 he was invited to dinner at Art Buchwald's, in Washington, and, finding himself seated next to Mrs. Graham, turned to her and said, "Why don't you buy into our Paris *Herald Tribune?*" to which she replied,

"What a fine idea! Why don't you talk to Fritz Beebe [the chairman of the board] tomorrow?" And the result, within two weeks, was the *Post–Herald Tribune* agreement. The background to this (historic) conversation, of course, was the lengthy negotiations with the *Wall Street Journal,* but especially those with the *Times,* which had stalled over the issue of control.

In Paris, the newsroom personnel went about their business with only rumors of negotiations and deals in the background. Bing was discreet, and the newsroom people had their job to do: put out the newspaper every day. There were changes in personnel: Art Buchwald left for Washington in 1962, to try for further fame and fortune, concentrating on political satire rather than the primarily nonpolitical subjects he wrote about in Paris. He gave himself two years, having asked for a leave of absence in case he fell on his face. But he obviously did not, and soon wrote back happily that each Washington column produced ten times as many responses as he received for a Paris column. They missed him at the *Trib:* the sometimes befuddled, sometimes innocent, often wryly satirical American in Europe, with whom other Americans could identify, and whom Europeans enjoyed for his view of Europe. Six months after he left, John Crosby came and put in a year, but it was not the same, and Crosby left in October of 1963. Buchwald still thinks they need someone at the *Herald Tribune* to play the kind of role he played on the paper in the 1950s.

Dick Roraback, the thin, red-bearded young man who had started on the desk, then did a sports column called "Another Point of View," and finally ended up with the "People" column, helping fill the gap. *Herald Tribune* people remember him as fairly crazy; he drank a six-pack of beer every night as he worked, and lent the "People" column a personal style it has not had since he left in 1972. Kingsley left, too, at the end of 1963. He loved the excitement of those years, despite the strains, and despite not getting along well with Cutler. When the composing room personnel gave him a going-away party, they told him, "Tu es un emmerdeur, mais un emmerdeur sympathique!"—which may be freely and politely translated as "You are a nuisance, but a likeable nuisance!" He considered it a high accolade.*

The history of the *Herald Tribune* should provide anyone with enough evidence to show that Franco-American relations have rarely really followed the pattern set by symbols like Lafayette, the Statue of Liberty, or General John Pershing striding down the gangplank in 1917 to declare, "Lafayette, we are here!" The de Gaulle years were among the more difficult ones, and Bernie Cutler was not as diplomatic as Eric Hawkins.

De Gaulle's attack upon American policy and the American presence in Europe was consistent and multipronged, in line with his vision of a Europe of nations united from the channel to the Urals, i.e., excluding England and America, but including a European Russia whose presence—after détente became entente—would be less of a threat than that of the United States. His government was pervaded by an authoritarian attitude toward all the mass media, and for perhaps the first time the Paris *Herald Tribune* found itself attacked for distortion and bias in its reporting of political events in France by the government in power. Cutler's attitude, in response, was that the paper should not hedge in reporting de Gaulle's moves or recording his intentions any more than it would hedge in reporting unfavorable developments in the United States.

There was hardly an all-out attack. Kingsley recalls no instance in his five years on the paper of a message or serious attempt to influence the paper by either the embassy or the Elysée Palace. Cutler felt "no direct pressures from the de Gaulle government." Both recall occasional complaints about misunderstandings, tele-

---

*And Kingsley remembers occasions like the night of President John F. Kennedy's death, when the question of space was resolved by the composing room foreman, Lucien, who suggested omitting the comics, thereby both giving them more room and changing the paper's tone; or the time he told Lucien to move a headline and the latter balked, saying "No, it looks better where it is," and then, when Kingsley insisted, saying, "Listen, I went to school for this, did you?"

phone calls from officials they knew at the Quai d'Orsay—the French Foreign Office—to the effect that a story was exaggerated or unfortunate, or a column out of place. On one occasion, in April of 1964, an Alsop column attacked de Gaulle's worldview and referred to "extreme eccentricity, repeatedly revealed, as when Alain Peyrefitte [de Gaulle's Minister of Information] genially suggested that Belgium, not being a true nation, had better be divided, with its Francophone half returning to France and the rest going to the Netherlands." The conservative *Figaro* reprinted the column the next day with a disclaimer at the start, calling its judgements "excessive and without nuance." The following day both papers published a reply by Peyrefitte, who declared that after searching all his utterances, he "formally denies allegations of Mr. Alsop, whose methods do not add to his reputation."

In August of 1965, during the French presidential campaign, Cutler printed reporter Ron Koven's story that de Gaulle had told American envoy George Ball of his intention to put all NATO bases in France under French command—a move that would force them out. Peyrefitte told reporters as he left a cabinet meeting that the *Herald Tribune* story proved Henri Bergson correct when he said that man's capacity to fabulate was still alive and well.*

Cutler was somewhat more careful about cartoons: he chose not to print a Mauldin one picturing de Gaulle in the middle of an American army cemetery in France with the caption "Yankee, Go Home." In September of 1966, though, a Herblock cartoon appeared showing the general inspecting the world floating in space in front of him at waist level, with the legend "And He Saw That It Was Not as Good as if He Had Done It All Himself." (It happened that de Gaulle was visiting Southeast Asia at the time, where he blamed the United States for the "unjust and detestable" Vietnam War in which a great nation was ravaging a small one.)

Reporter Ron Koven, however, was—as Cutler put it—"in the

*The move was, in fact, made in the spring of 1966, well after the election and its rather embarrassing runoff.

front line, in a way, in daily contact with French officialdom, and they tried to intimidate him in a way that they would not try on an editor more removed from them." At one point, accompanying the de Gaulle party during the presidential campaign of 1965— during which de Gaulle repeatedly spoke of "the two hegemonies" and of the pre-1914 alliance with Russia—Koven filed a story whose lead referred to the derisive whistles de Gaulle received from a crowd of workingmen in Angers, where unemployment was heavy, and their refusal to join him in singing the "Marseillaise" at the end of his speech. Other newspapers—*Le Monde, Le Figaro, L'Humanité*—reported the incident, but deep within their stories or, as did the *Times,* somewhere inside; Koven and Cutler gave the incident a lead on the front page. And the next day, as the presidential motorcade reassembled, one after another of the Gaullist Ministers stopped to tell Koven that his piece was not very appreciated, that he had gone too far. The Gaullist *La Nation* printed a front-page editorial to the effect that Koven was the only one who had seen the incident, and deserved a palm for imagination. It was intolerable, the editorial went on, that a foreign newspaper implanted in French soil should print such a piece. When Koven filed a story about Soviet complaints that the French at the Laos peace conference were playing the Chinese game, he was told that it was too bad one could declare a diplomat persona non grata, but not a reporter; he took it as another warning when he was told that, of course, the government would never close the newspaper—with the "but" implied.

Hervé Alphand, formerly French ambassador in Washington and now secretary-general of the Foreign Ministry, told a meeting at the Quai d'Orsay that Koven was the spearhead of Ambassador Harlan Cleveland's anti-French campaign, and the word got back to Koven. When the reporter prepared to leave Paris and return to the United States, he went to see Alphand, who told him, "I've always received you when you asked, but you have systematically deformed everything you've seen."

André Bing dealt with one other case of French government

harassment—of a different sort. The French Tourist Office in Canada distributed a pamphlet to Canadian tourists on their way to visit France, full of tips on how to behave in France—and how to avoid being taken for a U.S. citizen instead of a Canadian. Among these was one to the effect that you should avoid walking around Paris with a copy of the *Herald Tribune* tucked under your arm. In Washington Buchwald received a copy from a Canadian friend, and proceeded to write a typical Buchwald column about it. In Paris André Bing read the column and asked Art to send him the pamphlet. He delivered a formal protest to the Ministry of Tourism, and a spokesman for the Ministry, apologetically declaring that it was really all in fun, nevertheless promised to stop distribution. The *Herald Tribune* was saved from attack on at least one front.

The European Edition of the *New York Herald Tribune* made it through the years from 1960 until December 5, 1966, by the skin of its teeth. On that day it became the *New York Herald Tribune/ Washington Post, International.* The parent paper, of course, didn't make it. If it hadn't been for the intervention of the *Washington Post* there is reason to doubt that the European Edition would have long survived its parent, or that the eventual necessary merger with the *New York Times* would have maintained the *Herald Tribune's* identity. Whitney certainly intended to keep the paper going, and perhaps, after abandoning New York, he might have been willing to continue to put money into Paris. Walter Thayer declared that there was no question of abandoning it. After all, the *Times'* losses continued to be heavier than anticipated. But so did the *Tribune's,* and as Bing pointed out, the circulation trends were troubling, and the French milieu had changed radically.

The *Herald Tribune* still had a reputation and tradition in its favor. Temple Fielding, in his 1964 *Travel Guide to Europe,* had this to say: "Wherever you roam on the Old Continent, the Paris edition of the *New York Herald Tribune* will be your faithful informant and companion. This international publishing landmark, today a sprightly 76, is now far zippier, fresher, and more readable than any other English language newspaper abroad. From Bergen to Lisbon to Athens to Davos to Ruritania, direct your concièrge to deliver it to your room daily. To my Nancy and me, and to thousands upon thousands of news-starved Yankee wanderers, it's the best 10¢ investment in Europe."

When the popular French film actor-director Jacques Tati made his comedy *Playtime*, whose theme was essentially that despite modernization of Paris, there still must be some hope that Paris might remain a human city of people in their own "quartiers," he was quite willing—for a small consideration—to have a lighted "Herald Tribune" sign in the background of several scenes and a sweatered Golden Girl selling the paper in another. But Fielding and Tati weren't dealing with changes in demographics, advertising patterns, or flows of financial and economic information, all of which had put continued existence of the *Herald Tribune* as it had long existed in doubt.

The *Post* deal meant that it got a new lease on life, and would also remain essentially the *Herald Tribune,* drawing on tradition and reputation. It was certainly a time for celebration. But not for everyone: as one part of the deal there would be a new editor and a new publisher. On August 29, 1966, came the announcement that Murray "Buddy" Weiss, an old *New York Herald Tribune* hand, would take Bernie Cutler's place, and Rober Taylor Mac-Donald, a former McKinsey and Company management consultant who became general manager of the *New York Herald Tribune,* would come to Paris as publisher to take active control from André Bing, who would retain the title of general manager.

It was a blow for Cutler, who was always aware of negotiations, but not of their details. He admits to having been harsh with the staff, and to not having been much of an administrator. Yet all the newsroom personnel came to the going-away party at Harry's New York Bar. Philip Weld had put him and André Bing in charge, and promoted François Desmaisons to chief of circulation. The three men had worked closely together; they had renewed the newsroom personnel, installed a degree of professionalism lacking earlier, revamped much of the makeup of the paper while retaining its familiarity, reoriented and improved its general coverage, and found a way to compensate for the decline of the *Herald Tribune* news service. They had increased its stock listings and financial coverage and brought about a recovery in circulation in the face of the continued and improved competition of the *Times,* finding new, though frequently more expensive, markets. They had held the deficit way below that of the *Times'* International Edition.

And all this had been during a time when the American presence in France had begun to diminish and change drastically, when much of the traditional market had begun to dry up, when Franco-American friction and bitterness had increased as a result of de Gaulle's own views and of the stepped-up Vietnam War. At the time that Cutler left, Claude Bourdet, editor of the leftist *Nouvel Observateur,* was leading a movement to boycott American products: "When a Frenchman drinks a Coca-Cola he is participating with the Americans in the War in Vietnam," declared one of his posters.

Despite the death of the home newspaper, the team of Cutler, Bing, and Desmaisons had kept the Paris Edition in sufficiently good shape that Katharine Graham found it a worthwhile investment. But the people at the *Post,* knowing that the deficit had reached a rate of $300,000 a year, and that the *Times* had to be beaten, insisted that the new joint paper needed new leadership. So Cutler went to the Scripps-Howard chain, first as a roving correspondent, which kept him in Europe for three years, then to Washington as chief editorial writer, and finally as Scripps-Howard editor-in-chief.

A newsstand purchaser might very well have failed to notice the change in the logo on the front page on December 5, 1966, when the *New York Herald Tribune,* European Edition, became the International Edition of the *New York Herald Tribune* with (in smaller letters) the *Washington Post.* The paper still looked and read much like the same old *Herald Tribune.* In part this was

Katharine Graham and Jock Whitney show off their new joint venture in December 1966.

because Whitney remained the senior partner in the new venture, and in part because everyone assumed the virtue and necessity of retaining the traditional appearance of the paper. Ben Bradlee, managing editor of the *Washington Post* and an old Paris hand, in Paris for an inspection trip in mid-October, reported back that few European advertisers or readers knew of the *Post* and its importance in Washington, despite recent expansion of its overseas bureaus. The *Herald Tribune*, however, was well known as a French institution ("The *New York Times*," he recorded, "is definitely not.") And the big Paris bash planned in celebration for early December should emphasize "the permanent rebirth of the Paris paper more than the arrival of the big noise from Washington."

The team chosen to run the merged paper would also ensure that it retained a *Herald Tribune* flavor. Buddy Weiss was an old New York employee who had started as a copyboy for the *Trib* in 1946, and on his way up the ladder to managing editor served for a while as the New York correspondent for the European Edition, responsible for overseeing the flow of stories from the New York Edition to Paris. When the *World-Journal-Tribune* negotiations got under way he moved to the *Boston Herald and Boston Traveller,* from which Bradlee and Katharine Graham did not find it difficult to woo him. Buddy Weiss would bring with him something of what had always made the *Herald Tribune* in New York or Paris a special kind of club to those who worked there. (And, Bradlee concluded in his report of October, "Weiss is going to be great!")

Bob MacDonald, on the other hand, was a strange quantity to many of the journalists. A tall, soft-spoken Yale and Wharton School of Finance graduate who looked rather like Jimmy Stewart, he had come to Whitney Communications in 1961 when Whitney called in McKinsey and Company, the international management consulting firm, to prepare a five-year plan to put the *New York Herald Tribune* back in the black. Old *Tribune* hands derided the move ("The *Herald Tribune* is a newspaper, not a business"), and the plan was sidetracked by the 114-day strike a year later. Nevertheless, MacDonald, who had some journalistic experience, stayed on to become executive vice- president and general manager of the New York paper. In this capacity he had come to know something of the European Edition's operations, since André Bing reported to him regularly; the Whitney people thought his knowledge of the advertising market in the United States would be especially helpful. He was also a known quantity to people at the *Washington Post.* It took little convincing to get him to go to Paris for eighteen months, with the proviso that once things were running smoothly he would return to the United States and act as publisher from New York.

Weiss would stay on as editor until 1979, MacDonald as publisher until 1977. But the two men would preside over a major change in the nature of the paper, as great as the change from Bennett's day to the twenties, or from the thirties to the postwar period. Once more, it would be the need to adjust the paper to evolving economic, political, and social circumstances in the world in which it was distributed, along with new technological developments in transportation, radio transmission, and editing and composition, that would dictate the paper's transformation. But other newspapers failed in the face of the changes; Weiss, Mac-Donald, their staff, and their successors ensured the *Herald Tribune's* success.

Changes had to be cautious and incremental. Patterns of advertising, circulation, production, and editorial content could hardly be transformed immediately, and alteration in any one was linked to alteration in the others. And there was one extremely important factor to keep in mind: in 1955 only about half the readers were American; in 1965—and in 1967—readership was two-thirds American. The new team might want to reach out to a growing English-speaking, cosmopolitan audience of "influential Europeans," but they could not ignore the large percentage of American readership scattered now throughout Europe. Their problem was to gain the former without losing too many of the latter. In addition, in the early months planning for the future had to be done on the assumption that the competing *Times* would be there indefinitely. And, as had always been true for the *Herald Tribune,* international events would have an unforeseen but enormous influence on what the new team would do.

Much, therefore, remained familiar in the first months of what was formally called the "Whitpost venture." The old *Herald Tribune* columnists were still there: Hebe Dorsey, sounding a little like someone out of Bennett's time, writing about "Deauville: Baccarat, Beaches and Brummels"; Naomi Barry, on the elegant Le Mas Restaurant in Corrèze, "A Gourmet's Mecca in France's Heartland"; Mary Blume on French restaurant critics Gault and Millaut's tour of the United States and on their pleasure at much that they found. Dick Roraback began doing the "People" column and occasional general reporting, and lent the column a particularly screwy, personal touch full of spoonerisms. Five years later, though, when the real changes came to the paper, he would become something of a misfit and leave, after a long drawn-out squabble over severance pay.*

Until the Cutlers left, B. J. Cutler's wife, Carol, continued to write art criticism; Alexis Lichine contributed a wine column, and Wolfe Kaufmann replaced the renegade *Times*-jumper Thomas Quinn Curtiss on Paris theater and films. There were still the familiar Parisian stories: a Mrs. Daniel Wildenstein had named her handsome three-year-old colt "Herald Tribune," and when some objection was raised, she pointed out that there were horses named "Match" and "Paris-Jour." Although the travel section had already shrunk to a single page on Thursday, there were still columns of "Life on the Côte d'Azur" and "When in Italy" ads. But now, too, there were the less familiar bylines of *Post/Los Angeles Times* correspondents and columnists: Anatole Shub on Communist affairs, the versatile Karl Meyer, Robert S. Elegant on the Far East, the Detroit military affairs writer S. L. A. Marshall, political commentators David Broder, and Roland Evans and Robert Novak. Ben Bradlee set up a separate office in Washington, headed by an old *New York Herald Tribune* editorial writer and Washington correspondent, Fred Farris, to provide *Washington Post* copy to

---

*Roraback made history before he left, though. In 1971 it suddenly hit him that a hundred years earlier Bennett had sent Stanley to find Livingstone, and he told Weiss they ought to do something about it. When Weiss replied that *Post* or *Times* people in Africa could write something about it, Roraback hit the ceiling: "*Washington Post* people! *Times* people! You're going to have a story in the *Herald Tribune* about Stanley and Livingstone with a *New York Times* byline?" Weiss saw the point and told Roraback he could look into what a trip in Stanley's footsteps would cost. Roraback came back with the discouraging news that the 2,400 miles would cost thirty cents a mile. "Jesus Christ! Thirty cents a mile!" was Weiss' reaction, and Roraback went off and brooded.

Then he came back to Weiss with a typed sheet headed "James Gordon Bennett to Henry Morton Stanley," followed by Bennett's "Draw a thousand pounds; when that is finished, draw another thousand pounds, and when that is finished, draw another thousand pounds, but find Livingstone!" Below that was another heading, Murray M. Weiss to Richard M. Roraback: "Jesus Christ! Thirty cents a mile!" Below that he wrote, "The history of a great newspaper." Weiss took the note, read it, went in to MacDonald, and came back ten minutes later to tell Roraback he was going. The result was a series of articles beginning on the front page on November 9, 1972, run alongside the original Stanley articles; some were serious reflections on what Roraback saw, some were parodies, and some were simply genuinely funny in their own right. But it was a last gasp for Roraback.

the Paris paper geared to meet Paris deadlines and needs. The *Post/ Newsweek* communications relay center was shifted from London to Paris so that the *Tribune* would have direct access to copy as it went from all over Europe to Washington.

One of Weiss' first changes was to revamp the format of the "Business and Finance" pages in early October. In fairly short order he decided that the *Trib* had to spend the hefty sums of money Pinson had calculated it would cost for the complete stock tables if they were to win the competition with the *Times*. Six new Linotype machines equipped with Teletypesetting equipment had to be ordered, scheduled to go into operation at the end of May 1967, and it is indicative of the original attitudes MacDonald and Weiss brought with them that MacDonald, for one, had doubts about the machines. "I still don't think that full stock tables will add much to our readership," he wrote to New York, "but I think it will slow down the *Times'* growth if not actually cost them some circulation." Still, he did think that more space to business news would help out; he authorized an expansion to a regular twelve pages in April (while the *Times* was still stuck with ten, since Sidney Gruson, now publishing the *Times* International Edition, calculated that a move to twelve would just cost too much). Both MacDonald and Buddy Weiss had toured Europe seeking out ideas, reactions, and new stringers to contribute occasional pieces from other European capitals, and MacDonald became convinced that with some further changes, "we can increase our appeal to English-speaking Europeans." It was the first time that he had articulated what would be the major theme for the future.

In one move that saddened some older readers of the paper, in January 1967 MacDonald closed down the "Monthly Economic Review" and phased out the old *Herald Tribune Travel Guide to Europe*. It had not been profitable in recent years. To save money it had been printed on newsprint on the *Trib's* press, so that it was bulkier than the many newer competing guides, and advertising had become harder to attract. (At one point, to everyone's embarrassment and surprise, Andrew McElhone visited the rue de Berri to complain that Harry's New York Bar with its long-running *Herald Tribune* ad had never been mentioned in the *Guide* since the *Guide's* postwar resumption!)

There was at least one last big public relations job in Paris when the actual merger took place in early December. It was not quite up to the 1962 seventy-fifty anniversary celebration with its Garde Républicaine at the Comédie Française, but it still focused on the image of an American in Paris. A fat twelve-page special section published on December 6, when the paper bore its new masthead, featured articles by former President Eisenhower, Walter Lippmann, and Raymond Aron on its front page, along with the final chapter from John Steinbeck's new book, *America and the Americans*. Inside, other big names—Senator Fulbright, J. Robert Oppenheimer, John Kenneth Galbraith, and George Ball—made their own contributions on the general theme of Europe-U.S. relations, while historians like Sir Dennis Brogan and Golo Mann and Europeanists like Robert Marjolin and David Ormsby-Gore represented Europe. Art Buchwald, now in Washington, starred with his account of his 1950s crusade against the church bells of the American Cathedral Church.

The *Washington Post* mailed out 3,000 copies of the edition to government executives, members of Congress and the diplomatic corps, and civic and business leaders. The flood of letters in return should have gratified Katharine Graham in her decision as much as it did the *Herald Tribune* staff. Many mentioned relying on and enjoying the *Herald Tribune* during tours of duty or government or business service abroad, expressing pleasure at the new association or referring to the event as a milestone in publishing history and in the development of the world press. Allen Dulles wrote that he was "delighted to see the great traditions of two great papers combined and carried forward. I feel that this newspaper will play an important role in forming public opinion on vital questions of foreign policy," while Under Secretary of State Foy Kohler, asking whether something couldn't be done to pattern gross U.S. newspapers after what he called "your slim, readable Paris product," expressed a "real debt of gratitude to you for not allowing the European Edition to go the way of its New York parent."

Which was much to the point. The collapse of the New York paper and the moves made in Paris between the fall of 1966 and the spring of 1967 to keep the paper competitive with the revitalized *Times* International Edition were both expensive. When Whitney stopped publishing in New York it meant that the Paris paper had to pay for a number of services it hadn't before. The work of getting U.S. advertising increased with the disappearance of the New York paper and its advertising staff. The volume declined sharply, while the *Times* International Edition continued its gains. To maintain past advertising or seek out new, the *Trib* tried to improve overall circulation figures by increased distribution to high-cost areas like Africa and the Middle East. The effort to provide a more attractive paper than the *Times* by adding more pages produced all the usual higher outlays for paper, printing, and transportation. Together with the decline in military circulation as NATO bases moved out of France, this meant that the paper lost close to half a million dollars in 1966; it went into debt by another half million between January and May of 1967. In April of that year MacDonald wrote that any conclusions about the future should be postponed until the effect of the increased stock tables could be measured.

Yet MacDonald was less fazed than this indicated. Some of the money went into capital investments that could be expected to pay off in the future. Jock Whitney seemed determined to keep the European Edition going: his marching orders to Weiss and MacDonald were to win in Paris. And Katharine Graham was willing to spend large sums to establish her paper's position in Europe: by May of 1967 the *Post's* contribution amounted to $450,000.

Sulzberger knew that Whitney and Graham wanted to force the *Times* into a three-way partnership in a single newspaper, and that they would give Buddy Weiss and Bob MacDonald full backing, including the cash which had been in such short supply. His public reaction to news of the *Post*-Whitney agreement had been optimistic; there would be no abandoning of the International Edition. "We can handle the losses," he had declared. "We'll just keep getting better." But he had acted decisively with another one of those administrative changes that had marked his still-short tenure as publisher of the *New York Times.* He named Sydney Gruson, his former foreign editor in New York, as new publisher of the International Edition, moving him to Paris at just about the same time that Weiss and MacDonald went to the Paris *Trib,* telling him that the time for decision had arrived. Gruson was to give the job six months and then make a firm recommendation concerning the future—and he did.

In early April Gruson reported formally to Sulzberger that as far as he could see, deficits would only increase in the future, never to be brought down to the $500,000 a year figure considered to be the maximum sustainable pretax loss. Advertising and circulation would improve; they would actually hit the 50,000 target he had set for circulation in 1967. The product, he thought, would continue to improve, too. But the situation would not. The *Herald Tribune–Washington Post* deal meant that in essence, Whitney had won: the *Times* could only come in as a one-third partner and could never expect the business or editorial control it had wanted; fusion would have to be on terms that would essentially preserve the flavor and look of the *Herald Tribune.* The time had come to talk merger, and the issue now was simply that the merged paper should not detract in any way from the quality and prestige of the *New York Times,* and the key was the number one job—the editor-publisher or whatever he might be called. But this was the moment. "The merged paper will have to come some day," he wrote. "I think it is unwise and wasteful of us not to make every effort to see that the day is sooner rather than later."

Gruson told all this to Bob MacDonald over lunch, and MacDonald immediately called Thayer in New York. "You'll never believe the conversation I just had with Gruson," he told him, repeating its substance. Within a month after Gruson's letter, the two parties reached a draft agreement; only on May 16 did Sulzberger inform the staff in Paris that the paper would be closed down within a week.

There were innumerable details to iron out: legal arrangements with the French authorities, the disposition of redundant employees (*Times* employees were promised consideration as the *Herald Tribune's* staff expanded, but there were still quarrels over this months later). Tangible property had to be disposed of, contracts be reassigned, and so on. On the ownership side a new "H.P.T. Joint Venture" replaced the "Whitpost Joint Venture." The *Times* would now share proportionately in costs and profits and provide its own material free of charge, the way the *Post* did. The new paper would pay for the *New York Times* news service, however, just as it payed for the *Los Angeles Times/Post* service. Management decisions would be taken jointly; in case of disagreement Whitney and the *Post* would have the right to final determination with the exception of certain matters on which unanimity would have to prevail—large-scale borrowing or capital expenditures or a change in name or nature of the business.* Most *Times* people in Paris would be laid off with severance pay, but a few would be coming over to the rue de Berri. Did this mean that some *Trib* people would have to leave, after having helped achieve victory? There were people like Thomas Quinn Curtiss, the film critic, who had jumped from the *Tribune* to the *Times* for twice the pay, and who was rumored to be coming back. Loyal *Tribune* people wanted to know whether, after receiving severance pay from the *Times,* Curtiss would now be paid what he had received at the *Times,* while some of them received much less or got the sack. How were such issues to be resolved and by whom?

The whole matter came to a head just as the new paper was to

---

*By 1971, when the paper had begun to make such substantial profits that the partners no longer used it for the tax advantages offered while it was in the red, the partners decided to go back to the premerger formula of a French corporation or "Société Anonyme" (S.A.). The three partners now became the stockholders—MacDonald relinquished a position as partner—but most important, the *Times* insisted that a two-thirds vote of the board of directors suffice for naming an editor, and that any single member of the joint venture could ask for MacDonald's retirement.

be put out. Walter Thayer and Ben Bradlee were in town for the occasion, and they joined the beleaguered Weiss and MacDonald in the negotiations with the newsmen, who, on a night of confrontation, took refuge in one wing of the building while Weiss and his managing editor George Bates virtually put out the paper single-handedly. The angry *Trib* newsmen felt they were going to get the short end of whatever deal would be worked out, but in essence the management told them that any who wanted to could take his severance pay anytime within the next thirty days and leave; individual contracts would be negotiated with the rest. There were enough transients who might leave under these circumstances to make room for the few *Times* men coming back. In one sense it was an opportunity to get rid of deadwood by making better offers to those Weiss and MacDonald wanted to have stay. And so, after some acrimony, it worked out largely that way, although neither all those they wanted to leave took off, nor did all those they wanted to keep actually stay. And there continued to be some animosity over the returnees, who had made their packet at the *Times* International Edition while it was in existence.

On May 22 the new partners signed a final, formal agreement, and on May 23, out of the venerable plant on the rue de Berri rather than from the *Times'* offices on the rue d'Aboukir, the first—slightly jumbled—number of the new *International Herald Tribune* appeared with the phrase "Published with *The New York Times* and *The Washington Post*" under the logo, thanks to Katharine Graham's loss of the coin toss that put her paper's name second. It was the six-year-old International Edition of the *New York Times* that disappeared, while the European Edition of the *New York Herald Tribune* lived on in a new incarnation—and with a new name which, to some, seemed somewhat mouth-filling. Said Art Buchwald, "*International Herald Tribune?* By the time you finish pronouncing it you've missed your plane!"

CHAPTER **13**

The *International Herald Tribune*

THE FIRST FRUIT of merger was an unforeseen, unexpected, and explosive rise in circulation. André Bing, convinced during the period of competition that there was a large overlap in readership between the *Times* and the *Trib,* told MacDonald that the combined paper would have a circulation of around 70,000. Perhaps he had deluded himself because he was trying to convince advertisers that they should stick with the *Trib* rather than split their ads. But Desmaisons essentially agreed with him. It was therefore an extraordinary surprise when five months after merger net paid circulation hit 96,000—"We are undoubtedly being read more today by influential Europeans throughout the Continent than both papers were before," MacDonald wrote to Whitney—and when a year later it passed the magic 100,000 mark; magic to MacDonald, and to advertising director Richard Morgan and his staff because of what it symbolized to advertisers, but magic and exciting also to all those who put out the *IHT* in terms of general expectations about the future.

The unexpected surge meant a wild ride for Roland Pinson's production people, more advertising as the enthusiastic Morgan took advantage of the rise, and a necessary increase in the size of the paper. By 1971, when circulation had soared to 120,000 a day, MacDonald had increased the paper from a regular ten pages a day to sixteen. A few months later the partners accepted his suggestion that advertising offices be opened in Chicago and Los Angeles, to supplement the five-person sales office housed in the *Newsweek* building on Madison Avenue in New York.

Each decision to increase the paper's size involved careful and complex calculation: compactness has always been viewed as one of the *IHT's* virtues; increased weight meant increased transportation costs, of unusual importance to a paper so widely distributed; increased pages meant more paper, ink, composers' and printers' time. These considerations also led MacDonald to authorize Weiss' hiring another man to help financial editor and columnist Carl Gewirtz on the increasingly important financial pages, and another deskman to coordinate the flow of material from the States and to build up further the existing network of stringers. Even more, all of the expansion brought a strain on the aging plant at the rue de Berri. On May 5, 1969, an eighteen-page regular issue meant that for the first time since the move to the building in 1930, a part of the press run had to be printed at a nearby plant, Les Imprimeries Parisiennes Réunies, from molds from a double set of mats, and shipped from there. MacDonald reported to the owners that despite an occasional press run of more than 150,000 copies, the existing facilities could probably handle the expected growth of the next three or four years. But the time should be spent on making plans for new facilities.

It was exciting. For the first time in a decade, in November 1967, the paper began to show a "paper-thin" profit, and as it widened MacDonald was able to plow it back into the paper, to expand and improve it. He worried about what joint control might mean, but not having to ask for money from the owners created an increased sense of independence: he and Buddy Weiss were largely able to inform the semiannual meetings of the board of their plans for the next six months. It did also mean that changes and expansion would come only as the paper generated enough funds to make them. And there were some differences with—and within—the board. At the outset there was a clash over what seemed a small matter that led, nevertheless, to considerable correspondence. This was the matter of bylines on stories, and it portended another, more basic conflict over the "personality" of the paper.

MacDonald and Weiss were concerned that the paper had too

many story credits in it. "As it is," MacDonald wrote to Walter Thayer at Whitney Communications, "we project to our readers too much of a hodgepodge of material supplied from extraneous sources . . . and look like the *Reader's Digest*. It is unquestionably *not* in the interest of the *Herald Tribune* to be used as a vehicle for journalistic commercials." Ben Bradlee at the *Post* was willing to support a determined drive to remove virtually all the story credits, and the Whitney people hoped that with the view from Paris supported by two of the three partners, the *Times* people might cave in. But Sulzberger and Gruson stuck to their guns. Gruson wrote, "I think we should seek the strongest possible representation in the paper through our news coverage . . . the reader should be aware of the source . . . Our identity is subsidiary in the name of the paper and in the staff running it. The identification of our staffers with the paper's full name on news stories is practically the only way we have of putting our impact into the paper."

And in 1969, when Monroe Green, the advertising vice-president of the *Times*, toured Europe, he made much the same point in reporting his impressions of the paper:

> The newspaper generally speaking, is still the Paris *Herald* or Paris *Herald Tribune* to transients, residents and business people alike. There is occasional curiosity about relationship of the *New York Times* and *Washington Post* to IHT. Very few know that NYT is part owner. Most view *Times* by-lines or credits much the same as a reader of a newspaper in a U.S. city which subscribes to NYT News Service . . . [But] the signed pieces and news credits help the *Times* at least as much as larger space on masthead, etc.

The bylines and story credits stayed. In 1974, when Whitney sent over a young, former Nixon speechwriter named Lee Huebner on an inspection trip, to see how the newspaper was doing and what direction it might take, one thing that he noted was the degree of frustration among journalists rewriting stories over the fact that the *Post* and *Times* people got all the credits.

The other thing he heard was more important, a constant refrain:

the news service and *Times* and *Post* stories were written essentially
for an American audience back home. You could rewrite them in
Paris, but what was still lacking was news specifically gathered and
written for the *IHT* as a newspaper that aimed at a growing *international* audience. It was more than a refrain, it was a chorus. It
came from MacDonald, who told Huebner that if he had the
money, the first thing he would do would be to expand the paper's
own news sources. (Circulation promotion and facsimile printing
came second.) Gewirtz told him, "The two men in Washington
(manning the *Herald Tribune* desk at the *Post*) represent exactly
what the paper needs elsewhere," in Brussels, the seat of the European communities, in Frankfurt, the growing European financial
center. Weiss embroidered on the same theme: he would like five
or six roving correspondents, like *Newsweek's* Arnaud de Borch-
grave. The biggest problem was in science and medicine, where all
they got was U.S. news. Dick Morgan, when he was willing to
speak cautiously and off the record about editorial matters, told
Huebner the same thing. Then correspondent Jim Goldsborough—
the *IHT's* only full-time political writer at the time—made it the
theme of an article he wrote for the *Columbia Journalism Review,*
when he took a sabbatical year off as Edward R. Murrow fellow
at the Council on Foreign Relations. The paper could get by as it
was now, he argued, but when it faced real competition on the
same order, it would have to develop its own sources.

Former *Herald Tribune* correspondent Don Cook argued that
Weiss and MacDonald could have exerted more pressure back
home in the early seventies to get the desired correspondents. But
he himself pointed out in an article in a 1978 *Saturday Review*
entitled "Trench Coats for Sale: The Eclipse of the Foreign Correspondent" that it cost over a $100,00 to keep a correspondent
abroad, and that only three American newspapers now had more
than a handful—the *New York Times,* the *Washington Post,* and
the *Los Angeles Times.* Still, he blamed the shortsightedness and
penuriousness of newspaper chains that could afford to send more.

The Paris *Herald Tribune* had never had much of a staff of

reporters since World War II. Sometimes deskmen were sent out to do stories, and as long as the *New York Herald Tribune* had a bureau in Paris, its people often acted as reporters for the Paris Edition. But by the early 1960s there was no one in the bureau for a time, and then it closed down. Cutler brought in twenty-six-year-old Ron Koven to supplement Jim Goldsborough, but Koven left and Goldsborough was once more the sole reporter until he, too, left in the late seventies, to be replaced by Joseph Fitchett. Only in 1979, when a new team of publisher and editor arrived, were there any additions to the reporting staff.

The point was that the board—and especially the *Times* representatives—opposed any move to increase the *IHT*'s own news sources all through the decade of the seventies. *IHT* correspondents, it was argued, would only duplicate what *Times* and *Washington Post* people were already doing, with little incremental benefit. Sydney Gruson, who didn't want to seem interfering, but who kept an eye on matters for the *Times* and had a number of suggestions about the paper, was emphatic about only one thing: the *IHT* should not add to its reporter-writer staff to develop its own personality. It should rely primarily and capitalize on the output of the two parent newspapers. When Ron Koven left for Washington in June 1969, Gruson asked why, in fact, they should even bother to replace him. He was in favor of plowing profits back into the paper, but not for replacing Koven, and he called the problem of identity "pure garbage." The *IHT*'s identity lay in being able to draw on the finest news services in the world, those of the *Times* and the *Los Angeles Times/Washington Post*. In contrast to the old days, after all, when the job of putting out the paper involved an act of imagination, padding out the skeleton cables, now it was the opposite one of selecting only a small part of all the copy that poured into the newsroom for three of the most important American papers plus the news services.

There were some other general points of friction, too. *Herald Tribune* men sometimes felt that the *Times,* in contrast to the *Post,* was too concerned with protecting its exclusives and tended to treat the *IHT* as a "news service client" rather than as its own international edition, despite naming an *IHT* liaison at the *Times,* Natalie Layzell. In late 1972 both MacDonald and Fred Farris, from the *IHT* Washington bureau, pressed *Times* people on this issue, arguing that if the *Times* let them have exclusives a couple of hours earlier than they were getting them now, they still wouldn't "blow" the exclusives by printing them in the *IHT* too far ahead of time. The people at the foreign desk of the *Times*—who also said they got a lot of flak from their overseas people who wanted to see their copy in the *Herald Tribune*—argued that they would have to consider stories individually: some would be so sensitively exclusive they wouldn't release them to the *IHT* until the *Times* was actually out on the street, but in most cases they would try to be as cooperative as possible. In the meantime, Farris worked out a quiet arrangement with the Washington bureau of the *Times* to get copy directly from the people there.

There was always to be some degree of friction, too, over *whose* material appeared in the paper, although Weiss seems to have been exempt from pressures. Certainly, as the paper expanded, he and MacDonald discussed expansion of financial and commercial news, the number of features, and so on. But the selection from the immense volume of news transmitted to the paper, and the play it received, was essentially up to Buddy Weiss and George Bates, his managing editor. Nevertheless, *Times* and *Post* men were acutely aware of whether their stories or someone else's had appeared. Fred Farris, the *IHT* man in Washington, with his office space on the editorial floor of the *Post,* regularly pinned up a current copy of the *IHT* behind his desk, with stories originating in the *Post* outlined in red for *Post* journalists to see. Gruson, at the *Times,* not only kept an eagle eye on *Times* material in the paper, but also prodded MacDonald about his failure to use some *Times* columnists, especially Tom Wicker. (Weiss used James Reston, Cy Sulzberger, and Anthony Lewis, but balked at some of Wicker's columns on Vietnam.)

But it was MacDonald who absorbed the shocks, just as it was he who would write a soothing word to some American traveler writing in to complain bitterly about the "liberal bias" throughout the only important American newspaper available in Europe. Richard Morgan, in advertising, was afraid that the heavy coverage given to Watergate in the early seventies would alienate some of the conservative readers and advertisers both; his ad salesmen, for whom the newspaper itself was the best selling tool, felt that the news content was too American anyway. MacDonald himself shared their view that Watergate coverage was too heavy and felt that *Times* and *Post* reporters had been allowed to introduce too much ideological and personal bias into their stories. But everyone paid attention to the proverbial separation between the editorial department and the other services. MacDonald fended off criticisms and left Weiss to his own sense of what was paramount, including his view that the paper had to change from its earlier decided emphasis on U.S. news to increased international coverage in order to attract a far more international readership.

Legend has it that one of the first things MacDonald did was to get rid of the Golden Girls—the Champs Elysées, Montparnasse, and American Express street vendors—in order to stress that the paper was no longer designed for American tourists abroad but was, instead, becoming a serious financial paper for the new transnational and multinational elites of the Common Market. In fact, the Golden Girls didn't disappear until March 1969—two and a half years after the advent of the new team—and even then, MacDonald disbanded them "with a great deal of reluctance." They were getting harder to recruit—there had actually been newsboys as well as girls in the last year; François Desmaisons, in circulation, thought of them as part of a great tradition and a still-useful promotion device (and still regretted their loss fifteen years later).

Richard Morgan, the advertising director, was delighted they were gone. He was himself a second-generation expatriate: his father had fought in the First World War and remained in Paris, and Morgan was born outside of Paris, baptized in the American Church when it stood on the rue de Berri, educated in Paris and at Eton and Harvard—with the result that he felt at home anywhere, a citizen of the world. He brought this attitude to his work at the *Herald Tribune,* which he saw as a potential global newspaper; he was a strong exponent of multiple facsimile editions scattered throughout the world—Frankfurt, London, Beirut, Tokyo—and the United States. In the Cutler days, when he came to the newspaper, the rather lax and languid advertising staff under Wachob could hardly give advertising space away, and still relied on the rapidly drying-up Paris retail and American tourist-oriented trade. But the *International Herald Tribune* with its incomparably rich news sources could now reach a "quality market" the old paper rarely did: the new, influential, prestigious citizens of the world who were, presumably, more and more like Morgan himself.

In 1969 the paper launched an advertising campaign based on the catch phrase "the Significant Europeans," each ad of which pictured a prominent professional or business person: "He reads two newspapers every day," his own national one, of course, and the *International Herald Tribune* as a second. "Significant Europeans read it for what their own local papers don't give them: worldwide perspective, exclusive business news, complete Wall Street prices. It's the *one* international daily in all of Europe." And while these ads appeared in European national media, in the United States Morgan used testimonials by U.S. advertising executives in advertising trade publications. The future, Morgan felt, was promising, expanding, almost unlimited. People in his office bandied around projected circulation figures of 150,000, 200,000, more. Twenty-five years later, Geoffrey Parsons' earlier vision appeared to be coming true; what Willett Weeks had wanted a decade earlier now seemed possible, because the newest technologies in communication linked financial and other markets in ways they had never been linked before, and gave the newspaper the potential of being distributed in novel ways to serve the newly linked markets.

When the *IHT* merger took place, the *Tribune* staff raided the *Times* quarters to bring back some of the plush furniture the *Times* directors had bought, and the rue de Berri building was remodeled and repainted inside. The *Times* teletype machines were added to the new ones MacDonald had so recently purchased, and Weiss began using various *Times* features and columnists as well as its enormous volume of international and domestic news. In October 1968 Weiss dropped the *Times*' summary "News of the Week in Review," with the argument that it contained the kind of summary to be found in weekly news magazines, and was unnecessary to daily readers. And he substituted a beefed-up weekly stock section that included the year's highs and lows along with a wrap-up of the week's transactions on the New York and American stock exchanges. The response was such—the Duke of Windsor telephoned in his congratulations and mentioned that he was dropping his subscription to *Barron's* as a consequence—that five months later MacDonald and Weiss put through further changes in the financial listings, requiring the move to a standard fourteen-page paper. Again the stock listings were rearranged and expanded. Most important, Carl Gewirtz set to writing a weekly feature on the Eurodollar bond market that became one of the most popular features of the paper and made Gewirtz's reputation among financial analysts. "Insights and Sidelights," restored as a weekly feature in November, was now expanded, with stories on, for example, Russian-Chinese relations, growing links between the United Kingdom and Bonn, or the Apollo space program. Weiss got an expanded news hole for the rest of the week, and Morgan got more space for the increased financial advertising the paper was now beginning to draw. Others got the headaches: Desmaisons was handed a heavier paper to deliver and Pinson a bigger one to produce.

A few years later, when the first facsimile printing went into operation in London in 1974 (and when another price rise went into effect), MacDonald expanded the financial section and tables even more. Clearly, the impact of computer and satellite communications on the creation of a supranational market had made itself felt. "Pogo" and "Li'l Abner" disappeared from the comic strips. The weather in some thirty-odd other towns was added to the reports for Paris, London, Berlin, Rome, and New York—shades of James Gordon Bennett. Obviously, the weather reports were not for the same sort of cosmopolitan elite Bennett was concerned with; yet in a very real sense they symbolized a return from a more parochial orientation to one that reflected a greater international integration.

From the vantage point of the eighties, the pattern, the moves, the new nature of the paper, all seem clear to those who participated in the change. It was by no means as clear at the time, and day-to-day events did much to shape what happened. In 1966 MacDonald had not believed that expanded financial tables would help very much; in 1968 he decided against using the Dow Jones/AP financial services—which he took on three years later. Richard Morgan, like Weeks before him, focused on the cosmopolitan growth of a united Europe; yet in the sixties the European movement faltered under de Gaulle's blows, and Gaullists argued that they had simply exposed the weak bases of Europeanism. It was mainly the unexpected circulation increase of the first six years that led people to adopt Morgan's point of view—that the Golden Girls–Paris *Trib* image had to go, that circulation of a truly international, business-oriented general newspaper could continue to soar, now that the right direction had been found.

Yet again, as in the past, events constantly falsified expectations. Net paid circulation doubled in those first six years. Outside of France it had soared from forty to one hundred thousand. In 1972 MacDonald wrote that planning for the future should be based upon an expected circulation increase of 7 percent per year, and advertising salesmen were told to sell on this basis. Instead, by 1975, circulation had dropped by 10,000, back to 110,000. Earlier euphoria evaporated in the face of political upheaval in Italy, Spain, and Portugal, Nixon's devaluation of the dollar in August 1971, renewed inflation, oil price rises, and the resultant necessity of price increases for the newspaper.

Over the years MacDonald was forced to go from eighty centimes in 1968 to two francs fifty in 1975, thereby—among other things—curtailing an extensive effort at creating a youth market in French schools that had produced 7,000 subscriptions in 1970, and dropped below the 2,000 mark a few years later. Even a single event like the collapse of Bernie Cornfeld's sprawling, shaky Investor's Overseas Services could hurt the paper. Cornfeld had virtually invented the offshore mutual fund—mutual funds of American stocks sold overseas to tap an investor pool that had never been touched. For a while its immense success spawned a rash of imitators and a large volume of advertising: in March 1969 IOS could buy a full half-page ad in the *IHT* for its IOS Venture Fund. But the downfall of the whole mismanaged enterprise meant a sharp loss of one type of advertising revenue, and a new activity for the advertising department, which would now scrutinize advertisements for such funds and charge them for their daily listing on the financial pages. In 1976 newsprint prices rose 40 percent; air controllers strikes and mail walkouts in France and elsewhere cut deeply into circulation, illustrating what MacDonald called "the fragility of our market," now more and more dependent on international distribution.

The rise in sales outside of France placed an enormous burden on Desmaisons' distribution service. In November 1969 MacDonald launched the first of a series of flights with chartered planes colored in the traditional *IHT* yellow and black. The first flights, to Scandinavia, were followed by others to Germany, Switzerland, and one to Italy shared with the French newspaper *Le Figaro*. The charters meant early morning delivery in dozens of new locations since they allowed earlier commercial airline connections from the major cities they served, and breakfast-time delivery, as Desmaisons could testify, meant thousands of sales otherwise lost. The flight to Italy, for example, arrived in Milan at 3:45 A.M. instead of 9:25 by commercial airliner. From Milan it could be dispatched to other northern Italian cities in plenty of time. In the meantime the charter flew on to arrive in Rome by 5:30 A.M. instead of the previous 9:55.

The charters were the occasion for a large-scale advertising and circulation promotion campaign: a paper airplane made from an *IHT* illustrated a typical ad—"Now the Trib *flies* into Sweden early every morning!"—published in major Swedish newspapers and magazines. Frequent reference was made in publicity handouts to Bennett's pioneering use of delivery trucks in Paris, the great red Mercedes to Normandy in 1905, and the first use of commercial airline delivery to England inaugurated by Laurence Hills in 1928. The charters appeared to have helped with the circulation increase of the early seventies: at the end of less than a year of operation sales were up 25 percent in Scandinavia and Germany, 20 percent in Switzerland, and in six weeks they jumped by one-third in Italy.

But the ballyhooed flights to Italy lasted only six weeks. They began the day after the *Herald Tribune's* on-again, off-again competitor in Italy—the *Rome Daily American*—had started to print full stock tables, and the *Daily American's* owner-editor charged on page 1 that the *IHT* charter flights were designed to force it out of business. (MacDonald, reporting to the owners in New York, wrote that the timing was "quite by accident.") The *RDA*, as people called it, was one of several, often shoestring, English language competitors the *Trib* faced in various areas of the world. Begun in 1946 as a sort of postwar *Stars and Stripes* by three former GI's, it had changed hands several times. Heiress Doris Duke once worked in its newsroom at a typewriter for thirty-five dollars a week. One owner was a retired New York banker, Landon Thorn, husband of Countess Mara, and *RDA* owners had approached the *Herald Tribune* several times since 1962 either with offers to sell or to share stock transmission or distribution costs. The offers were interspersed with threats: to invoke antitrust legislation against the 1966–67 *IHT* merger, to invoke Italian law against tobacco advertising to keep the *IHT* from being distributed in Italy, and finally, and successfully, to get the Italian director of air transport of the Ministry of Civil Aviation to revoke the charter landing rights.

André Bing fought, but to no avail. The charter cancellation was a real loss, and for a few years, at least, the expanded *RDA* cut heavily into *IHT* Italian circulation: in January of 1972 MacDonald estimated the loss at 4,500 copies a day.* The charter flights were an essential interim step while MacDonald investigated the possibilities for international facsimile transmission. They were only one of several moves Desmaisons made to reach previously untapped or scanty markets.

On July 1, 1968, sixty copies of the *IHT* went on sale in tourist hotels in the Soviet Union, the first American non-Communist newspaper to be sold there in forty years. The *IHT* jointed *Le Monde,* the *Times* of London, and the *Neue Zuricher Zeitung* as the only non-Communist papers sold in all of Russia. In Poland, where earlier repeal of International Media Guarantees had cut sales, it was available in public reading rooms, though not on kiosks. Hungary and Romania allowed fairly free distribution, though it circulated only in small numbers; in Romania, where French influence remains strong, *Le Monde* sold 1,200 copies to the *IHT's* 50, but Desmaisons hoped for substantial improvement. Circulation increased in Czechoslovakia during the Prague Spring.

---

*There are really two footnotes to the whole matter of the *RDA.* One is provided by Thomas Powers, author of *The Man Who Kept the Secrets: Richard Helms and the CIA* (New York: Knopf, 1979). Powers worked as reporter, and editor at the *RDA* in the mid-sixties, when its paid circulation, he writes, was one-tenth of the 32,000 it claimed, and he figured that it was primarily a tax loss for wealthy Americans. But he was told at the CIA that the agency covered 40 percent of the *RDA's* losses.

What he does not mention is that in the early seventies it looked as if it might really offer serious competition to the *IHT.* New purchasers improved it greatly, expanded its sales to Spain, Portugal, and Greece, threatened to move further into Europe, and to make it a financial newspaper with real clout. An old *Washington Post* man with good government connections was listed as associate publisher, and the new owners included a retired air force general, an Italian-American businessman named Antinucci, and a "mysterious international banker and financier"—Michele Sindona. Sindona, it may be remembered, is the man whose shady financial empire later came crashing down after the failure of the Franklin National Bank in Brooklyn, who was "kidnapped" and then returned to New York, where he was convicted of fraud and jumping bail to avoid his fraud trial—and whose trail led to the Vatican, the Mafia, and the highest levels of the Italian government. In 1973 and 1975 new owners again offered to sell the *RDA* to the *IHT.* It has since suspended operations.

But the Warsaw Pact invasion nipped it in the bud. Desmaisons would nevertheless not abandon efforts to increase circulation in Eastern Europe, nor his efforts elsewhere, as one letter from South Africa attests. It came from the chief reporter of the Johannesburg *Sunday Times,* and he complained jocularly of finding the very day's *IHT* in Madagascar, a day-old one in Luanda, Angola, and a two-day-old one in the tiny town of Luso, in the zone of civil war fighting. "I feel as though some Javert is editing the *Herald Trib,*" he wrote. "Somewhere, I must escape. Kindly advise where, to my home office!" In late 1969, after an intensive tour of Africa, Desmaisons negotiated sales rights in nine countries where the paper had not been sold before: Ghana, Zaire, Uganda, Malawi, Rhodesia, Mozambique, Tanzania, Zambia, and Ethiopia.

Throughout the decade Buddy Weiss directed editorial policy without editorial conferences, usually making up the front page himself, sitting at the newsroom desk in his shirtsleeves, eating his proverbial peanut butter sandwiches, his dog at his feet. Because he took such a direct hand in makeup, forgoing surveys, avoiding editorial conferences, he appeared not to be concerned with new directions. For years there was an in-house joke about the luncheon Buddy was going to have someday, to share ideas about the flavor of the paper. When Lee Huebner visited the rue de Berri in 1974 on behalf of the owners, he had a sense that the news staff had little idea of what audience they were editing for. Yet Weiss, on his own, did guide the *IHT* toward what he called an "Atlantic viewpoint," and in one interview he articulated it:

> With . . . a multicultural audience we can decide what we're going to publish on a much different standard than might be the case if we were publishing in New York. We can assume that our readers are among the best-educated and best-informed. Therefore we can publish, and do, more American and international news than 95 percent of the American press.
>
> Our news policy must be different from that of a newspaper

Editor Murray "Buddy" Weiss, who steered the paper in a new direction, checking a linotype page make-up in the Rue de Berri.

published in America or say, Britain. Even the most internationally minded newspaper will usually lead its page with a local story—a subway-fare increase, a public-school riot, a work-to-rule slowdown on suburban trains outside London.

None of these, no local story is of interest to our readership. We have to find our identity in other ways.

One small incident gave an early indication of his thinking: the American Library in Paris asked MacDonald to print a tag line on the weekly best-seller book list: "Most of these books are available at the American Library in Paris, 10 rue Camou, 7ème—the largest collection outside of the U.S.A." MacDonald thought it would be OK. Buddy Weiss vetoed it. The tag line would contribute too much to maintaining the Parisian image he had already decided to try to get rid of. The shift to an international viewpoint would never be easy. Unforeseen events in Paris and Washington would have much to do both with the play of the news and how Buddy Weiss would determine the play. May 1968 is one case in point, Watergate another.

Shortly after merger, while dramatic international news filled the front pages, a staff writer, Richard Howe, wrote an interesting story headed "Money-Minded French Youth Not as Yé-Yé as Feared." Interviews with almost 300,000 young French people between the ages of fifteen and twenty-four found that most thought their lives would be improved by more money; 70 percent between the ages of sixteen and twenty-one earned their own living. They were, on the whole, "serious, highly security-conscious, and quite capable of handling the France of tomorrow." Their chief weakness, it seemed, was unwillingness to take a risk. They should give little trouble.

Exactly one year later the new *International Herald Tribune* spent most of its time chronicling the widespread 1968 revolt of that same French youth. In April and early May the establishment of Special Drawing Rights by the International Monetary Fund gave way to President Johnson's decision to de-escalate in Vietnam and to abandon office. Ron Koven's coverage of the Paris preparations for Vietnam peace talks received banner headlines, and somewhere on the front four or five news pages, Columbia University riots in New York shared space with Ralph Abernathy's "Poor People's March on Washington." An ad for a new Mercedes 220 that could be bought for under $3,000 accompanied a page 3 story by Jim Goldsborough that an outbreak of rioting at the Sorbonne had led to the first closedown of the university since the 1930s.

On May 6 a slick-covered French travel supplement bore a soft-focus photograph of a *Herald Tribune* salesgirl in a yellow sweater selling to lazing young people on a Paris quay, and Naomi Barry wrote about how to follow the yellow roads (on Michelin maps) "for the casual France." But the next day the lower half of the front page was filled with accounts and pictures of student rioting, and for the next week each front page bore one or two columns on student protests, while the rest of the page featured headlines on American primaries (and Robert Kennedy's first win), the start of the peace talks in Paris, developments in Czechoslovakia, and the course of continued fighting in Vietnam. On Friday, May 10, Naomi Barry praised a ten-franc prix fixe meal at Les Copains on the Left Bank—though it's a little hard to tell how she got there and back, since the same paper reported heavy street fighting. The lead continued to be on the Paris peace talks, but a May 13 story on the next day's sympathy strike in support of the students (with a box to the effect that there would therefore be no May 14 edition) covered half the front page; Ron Koven had a story on the government's reaction.

A few days later as students occupied theaters and threatened to take over the TV stations, and as more workers joined the movement (and de Gaulle contemptuously continued to tour Romania), a banner head read, "France Approaches Paralysis," and Naomi Barry switched to reporting on the striking workers at Boulogne-Billancourt while Hebe Dorsey told readers that the social calendar had been thrown into "diamond-studded chaos." On May 25 the banner read, "Paris Explodes Into the Worst Violence Yet Following Plans by de Gaulle on Referendum." Goldsborough and Koven seemed to have been everywhere in Paris and written about everything. And Roraback interspersed his sports column with paragraphs on the fighting along the boulevard Saint-Michel. The next day's issue carried a review of Jan Myrdal's new book, *Confessions of a Disloyal European,* calling it "an indictment of all that we are." Naomi Barry apparently felt it wise to get out of Paris, for her account of a ten-dollar lunch at the famous Restaurant de la Côte d'Or in Saulieu reported that with so many Paris restaurants closed the Côte d'Or was jammed. The irrepressible Hebe Dorsey suggested that the future of Paris couture might well depend on the outcome of the current crisis.

The tide turned, and the *IHT* recorded it. Goldsborough's story on May 31 accompanying a front-page picture of pro-Gaullist demonstrators filling the Champs Elysées from one end to the other

read, "Gaullists Recapture the Streets." Still, de Gaulle had to
abandon his projected referendum and dissolve the Assembly; but
the Gaullists did make sharp gains when the elections took place
late in June. A full-page American Express advertisement on how
it could help stranded travelers foreshadowed the summer drop in
tourists. And in the meantime the *IHT,* for two sad days in early
June, moved events in Paris inside while it devoted the front page
to the assassination of Robert Kennedy. Two months later, when
the *Apollo* made its first moon landings, temporarily refurbishing
a tarnished American image, a press run of 178,000 copies of a
special issue celebrating the landings received special distribution
to hotels and newsstands and to a temporary crew of fifteen street
vendors, while 250 copies were flown to Romania, where President
Nixon was visiting, for distribution from the embassy (since the
Romanian distribution authorities refused to make any special
effort).

The new *"International" Herald Tribune* was obviously overtaken by the crisis in the city in which it was published; later, in
the early 1970s, when the United States was preoccupied by what
came to be called "Watergate," the *International Herald Tribune*
reflected its peculiarly American nature. In Weiss' judgment Watergate merited day-after-day front-page treatment, while the rest
of the paper demonstrated the extent to which it had become more
cosmopolitan. Thomas Quinn Curtiss, back from the *Times* International Edition, reviewed films in Paris and Michael Gibson did
art; David Stevens, another ex–*Times* International Edition man,
reviewed music, traveling to festivals all around Europe. Stringers
from other parts of Europe contributed more—on the London
theater and ballet, on art in Brussels and Bruges, on birth control
in Spain. Souren Melikian created a regular feature on the international art market—principally as reflected in London, but in the
rest of Europe, too. And William Weaver, reporting on music in
Trieste in 1974, wrote that the festival of operetta there—with
Lehar, Strauss, Kalman's *Countess Maritza,* and Benatzky's *White
Horse Inn*—reminded you of the fact that Trieste had once been a

part of the Austro-Hungarian Empire. Classified advertising, many of whose older, more parochial categories had virtually disappeared, now bore such weekly rubrics as the one entitled "International Executive Opportunities." With Roraback gone, the "People" column, with a less personal touch, was signed "Samuel Justice." It was, in fact, rotated among deskmen—so that when someone inquired for Samuel Justice or asked who he was, the response could be "There ain't no justice." The Saturday-Sunday number, with its art, music, and theater features from all over Europe, seemed particularly cosmopolitan.

But when the Judiciary Committee of the House of Representatives voted to recommend the first article of impeachment against President Nixon by a vote of 27–11, a banner headline told the whole story; a week later the banner heads grew, culminating in the one on Friday, August 9. "Nixon Quits" and the Saturday-Sunday "Ford Is U.S. President." The stories were direct from the *IHT* outpost in the *Washington Post* newsroom, bearing Fred Farris and Bob Siner bylines. Europeans expressed their puzzlement over the whole affair, and other services in the newspaper—advertising and circulation—had their own fear that the Watergate coverage was hurting their expansion efforts. Herblock's August 8 cartoon of a United States dragging an unseen figure out of the White House door, its feet dug in, hauling on a tape coming from a reel, provoked letters of protests. But Buddy Weiss was not to be moved by expressions of reader disapproval.

American election specials had always been something of a specialty since Laurence Hills' days. In 1960 the exuberant circulation director, Paul Gendelman, arranged that the vendors on the Champs Elysées parade a donkey in the case of a Democratic victory or a circus elephant if the Republicans won, with plenty of photographers on hand. From a purely logistic standpoint the Kennedy victory came as a great relief! But the *Herald Tribune* had always been Republican under the Reids, and continued to represent the Eastern liberal wing of the party when Whitney bought it. In 1964, when the European Edition published the New York

Edition's front page editorial on its own front page—"We Choose Johnson (rather than the conservative Arizona Senator Goldwater)—it went on to say, "Travail and torment go into these simple words, breaching as they do the political traditions of a long newspaper lifetime."

In 1968 the new management made elaborate preparations to report the elections returns, with Radio Luxembourg giving continuous all-night coverage, periodic reports and analyses by Ron Koven direct from the *IHT* offices, and a gigantic reception at the new Pan American Airways Building around the corner on the Champs Elysées. While 3,000 people were invited, 6,000 showed up; three editions were planned, and five actually printed, with a total press run exceeding 154,000 copies.* But for the first time since Bennett, the paper officially supported neither candidate. Instead it reprinted editorials from the two parent newspapers. When the *New York Times'* "Humphrey for President" editorial appeared, and a letter writer challenged the paper's choice, the *IHT* served notice that it had, in fact, endorsed no one. It has not done so since.

There was perhaps one other rather unnoticed change accompanying the transformation of the Paris *Herald* into the *International Herald Tribune:* Weiss allowed his editorial page editor to cut the "Mailbag" drastically. In the past it had reflected the diversity of the American community in Paris; lengthy arguments would occupy it for weeks on end—sometimes on questions of politics, sometimes on minutiae of household details, problems of living in Paris, or questions of etymology. There were dialogues in verse, protests about the paper's editorial stance, philosophical disquisitions. But Weiss' *International Herald Tribune* had little space for this kind of thing. Letters continued to pour in. But to print them, remarked the editorial page editor once, meant relin-

---

*The preelection straw poll at Harry's New York Bar proved correct again, as it had in every election since 1924. The composing room personnel tried to take advantage of the big plans to influence negotiations that had been going on for some time. The situation turned into a poker game between them and Pinson. Pinson won.

quishing space that could be given over to columnists with something more important to say.

Two years after merger with the *Times,* MacDonald reported to the board of directors that a "growing number of French businessmen are beginning to recognize the *Tribune* as an important European daily rather than a paper for American tourists." This represented "a significant change in attitude." The end of the Golden Girls "means the end of a great tradition, but it is a normal consequence of the fact that we have become much more of an international newspaper in Europe rather than one aimed principally at the American tourist." Three years later, in 1972, back in Paris after a stint in the United States, MacDonald reported to the board that he considered the beginning of the new year to mark the end of a four-year program of base building and of investment in staff, in distribution, and in the paper itself. The investment would now pay off in expansion.

It didn't quite happen that way, as the events of those years produced the unforeseen lag in advertising and in circulation. Yet, apart from a period of a few months, the paper continued to make a profit, and 1976 brought a reversal of the decline. By 1980 the OJD circulation figure finally exceeded that of 1972. The readjustment of sights in the mid-1970s meant there was a little less of the boundless optimism produced by the first years of merger; people's expectations were a little lower, but everyone still counted on a slow expansion that did, in fact, take place.

There was one recurring theme all through these years, when members of the staff talked about the *IHT.* No one else had ever tried to do what they were doing—to create a genuinely international newspaper. How could you measure success? Against what other newspapers could you measure it? The answer, of course, was that there were no others. The paper was unique, and so was the effort. If then, in the mid-seventies, a readership survey showed that 58 percent of the readers were *still* American, was this a failure or not? There were attempts to discount the survey: Americans were more likely to answer questionnaires. But it was disturbing to those in management and advertising who were trying to create the image of a newspaper being read primarily as a second newspaper by European influentials. If net paid circulation continued to hover around the 120,000 mark, instead of reaching several hundred thousand, as Richard Morgan and others had predicted, was this a failure? Other European newspapers were doing badly, but they were not in the same boat.

Buddy Weiss—"by the seat of his pants," as one editorial writer put it—successfully steered the presentation of the news into a more international direction, and oversaw the major changes in the financial pages. The principal problem really became what to do with the mix of features in the rest of the paper—what was called "the back of the book"—if the newspaper was to appeal to and attract the hoped-for new audience. Two sections were relatively untouchable: the comics and the largely American sports page on which Americans abroad relied so much. There were other features: Hebe Dorsey had become a well-know name in the fashion world, and Thomas Quinn Curtiss continued to review films from his Left Bank quarters. In 1974 another of the thirty-odd stringers became a full-time general feature writer: Mary Blume, who by most accounts had become the best writer on the paper.

It was the rest that was controversial. The features editor, Betsy Bates, found many of the *Times* and *Post* features too American to be very useful, and grumbled about the book reviews from the *New York Times* that were too oriented toward American readers. There were always complaints from some European readers that Art Buchwald and Russell Baker and the comics were incomprehensible, the sports page too parochial. There needed to be some sort of genuine international features focus with stories on Germany, Italy, and Spain: the American-in-Paris past was hard to overcome when no one was sure about what the increasingly widespread readership might want. The somewhat frenetic Betsy Bates had her own rather vague formula: the *IHT* was "an international newspaper edited for Europeans with an American bias," but this formula was not always helpful in trying to fill space in the back of the book.

Still, there was always testimony to the general excellence of the editorial direction Buddy Weiss had given to the paper. Typically, in *Campaign,* a British advertising trade publication, columnist Clive Irving lauded the *IHT.* It was one newspaper, he wrote, that had found the formula to deal with the long-term explosive rise in costs of newsprint, labor, and energy. Since the merger, when the *Herald Tribune's* original purpose as a paper for American expatriates had lost its validity, making it look like "an overdraft for life," it had become "the first pan-European English language daily for a premium readership." Its merit, for Irving, lay in the values it applied to the news, the breadth of the material it could draw on from the parent publications, and the column of Russell Baker. But more:

> Because the *IHT* is edited neither as an American province in Europe nor with the blinkered vision of any one European national loyalty, it somehow places the world in a far better balance than any other paper I know. Though edited by Americans, it also sees America with unusual detachment and knowledge . . . Despite its weaknesses in financial and industrial coverage and in retaining an idiomatic American aura in its makeup this is one newspaper rescued from death and given an emergent market by luck, judgment and hard-nosed commercial decisions owing nothing to ancient interest. What a lesson.

CHAPTER 14

Modernization

Anyone searching to launch a daily newspaper like the International Herald Tribune in Europe today would find Paris to be among the least attractive cities to establish headquarters and business operations in, and the two most deterrent factors would be costs and labor climate.

R. T. MacDonald, in his 1976 "Facilities Review"

WAY BACK in 1955 Sylvan Barnet sought Brownie Reid's permission to buy the town house next door to relieve overcrowding in the antiquated rue de Berri building. Brownie said no. In 1958, when Whitney bought the *Herald Tribune,* Bing and Weeks reported that the space problem was now bad enough to hurt morale. "The day is surely going to come when we will want to move from this building," wrote Weeks, citing also the twenty-five-year-old presses, ancient Linotypes, antiquated stereotype and photoengraving equipment, and the fact that the building was "not well located for our purposes, though in a very fashionable and expensive neighborhood."

No one could deny that the site was rich in history and folklore, and awash in nostalgia. In December 1963, when André Bing tried, unsuccessfully, to persuade the Municipal Council to rename the street the rue John F. Kennedy, he pointed out that it had always been associated with Franco-American amity. Thomas Jefferson had lived on it when ambassador to France in the 1780s; the American Church had been built at No. 21 in 1850; the rue Washington and rue Lincoln were nearby. In 1969, when a movie version of *Tropic of Cancer* was filmed with Rip Torn as Henry Miller, the director wanted a sequence on Miller's work for the old Paris *Chicago Tribune,* and used the rue de Berri building as the setting. Numerous father and son teams had worked in the rue de Berri— the Tallins, the Jauretts—as well as several husband and wife teams. Bosses had married their secretaries there; bars in the neighborhood—the Select, the Berri Bar, the California—had been favored or boycotted.

The "tappeurs," as management called them,—the various neighborhood or Parisian organizations seeking funds or contributions, or selling tickets—had come around year-in, year-out. "What has the 'Amis des Champs Elysées' done for us?" asked Bing in one memo. Would continued membership be of any help to advertising? Some "tappeur" requests were inevitable—membership in the American Overseas Memorial Day Association and the American Chamber of Commerce, attendance at the *Nuit du Centenaire du "Figaro"* at the Opéra, dinner for the Presse Diplomatique Française. Some were sheer mild blackmail: contributions to the galas of the Ministry of Labor, the Paris Firemen, the Gaz de France, the Préfècture de Police, and so on. But this was all part of being in the middle of the Paris that was the real home of the old European Edition of the *New York Herald Tribune,* and the rue de Berri seemed indelibly associated with the paper.

The site was, however, increasingly inconvenient. The 6:00 A.M. deliveries of great rolls of newsprint hampered early morning automobile and pedestrian traffic. Until the cheap 1946 wiring job was replaced, the newsprint elevators broke down occasionally, leaving twenty tons of newsprint blocking the sidewalk of the busy, narrow street. No one at the elegant California Hotel across the street appreciated the sounds of the trucks pulling out in low gear at 1:30 in the morning after the arduous task of loading the packages of finished newspapers. Bing saw to it that the men worked as quietly as possible, and made sure to warn the hotel when oil had to be pumped into transformers from trucks parked in the street at night as well as having it done before the tourist season began. In 1970, for the first time, the elderly ladies in the house next door began to complain about the noise of the presses at night. And the parking problem simply worsened across the years, as workers shifted from bicycles to cars.

The increasingly international distribution of the paper called the location into question, too. Half the print run may have been distributed in France a decade or so earlier, but by 1970 only one-fifth of the papers were sold in France, and in the decade of the sixties the American colony resident in Paris declined by three-fourths, while the number of Americans living in Germany and the United Kingdom more than doubled.

Distribution in France by the Nouvelles Messageries de la Presse Parisienne (NMPP) was relatively simple. But the Middle East, North Africa, the Scandinavian countries, United Kingdom, Italy, and Greece were all served by air freight, with planes leaving at varying times of the morning for different countries and regions. Each flight had to be chosen so that its time of arrival could be best coordinated with further local shipment to the thousands of sales points. Some areas were served by different planes on different days, so that each day required a separate routing. Keeping track of it all and adapting to changing schedules was no mean feat. In addition, trucks leaving the rue de Berri at 1:30 A.M. sped through the night delivering papers to Brussels, The Hague, Amsterdam, Rotterdam, and—on the longest run of all—Frankfurt. In Frankfurt papers were transshipped to planes for Austria and Turkey. The truck runs were hazardous high-speed adventures; during the winter snow, ice, and fog hampered the drivers, and late arrival in Frankfurt, for example, meant late distribution and missed planes for other areas. In December 1969 a driver was killed, and it was a relief to Desmaisons when the charter flights were instituted in 1970.

In the early seventies another complication emerged. The *IHT* still printed two editions; the first was critical, since it was the one that supplied the growing market outside of France. Because of the stock transmissions from New York the presses couldn't start until 11:30 at night, and the first edition had to get out in time to make the various means of international transport. But the plant could only print 100,000 copies by 2:00 A.M., and the first edition demand reached that figure in early 1972.

What this all suggested was that France, and especially the rue de Berri in the heart of the Champs Elysées district in Paris, was no longer the ideal location for printing the *International Herald Tribune*. As a result, MacDonald initiated the first of a series of studies on future production of the newspaper, while the board of directors set up a Special Projects Committee to work with him on the matter. Technology had changed since the time that Willett Weeks had looked into the nascent process of facsimile printing before he left for New York; he had concluded then that the cost of transmission over French PTT lines would be "staggering." A year later Bing clipped an article from *Advertising Age* to the effect that the Tokyo *Asahi Shimbun* had completed a facsimile link between Tokyo and Sapporo, enabling it to print by the offset process 500 miles from where it had its main press run. If it were at all possible, satellite plant printing from facsimile transmission would both relieve circulation problems and reduce the strain of printing so many copies at the Paris plant. But transmission across international borders might pose insoluble problems.

André Bing brought in consultants. The first canvased a host of possibilities and concluded that the *Trib* would probably have to move out of Paris unless, indeed, it was able to secure the cooperation of two or more national postal services for international facsimile transmission. Another consultant, less sanguine about such an unprecedented arrangement, suggested a huge, new, central Paris printing plant. MacDonald, himself a member of the International Press Telecommunications Committee, looked into the European space satellite program with a view to satellite transmission, but concluded that the program was a mess. He also considered—but rejected—deliberately limiting growth of the paper; to do so would give too much scope to new, potential competitors, now that English was becoming the primary Common Market commercial language.

There seemed, in the early seventies, little scope for increasing revenue by price rises. International advertising was too precarious. Decreasing the number of "unsolds" was always an alluring way of dealing with rising costs, but it was no solution. "We know," wrote MacDonald, "that IHT readers are an extremely mobile group. Thus most sales points sell only a few copies to readers many of whom change every day. Therefore it is inherently difficult to maintain availability of the paper throughout its circulation market—particularily in the face of rising demand—without incurring a high percentage of unsold copies."

Facsimile transmission inevitably emerged as the most plausible of the alternative solutions to the *IHT's* problems of widespread distribution, the congestion, inconvenience, and increased expenses associated with complete production at the rue de Berri, and the need for increased revenue in a time of generally rising costs. Rome, London, and Frankfurt all seemed good candidates for the first attempt. But the *Rome Daily American's* success with the Italian authorities chilled interest in Rome, and Frankfurt, despite all its attractions as a growing financial center, had to be dropped when its transmission rates proved too high. London, after much backing and filling, looked best, particularly after its long-delayed entry into the Common Market. Arduous negotiations followed with French and British authorities, printers and distributors, and equipment manufacturers, and on March 11, 1974, the *International Herald Tribune* was able to open the first international facsimile link. Offset presses began to role at the firm of King and Hutchings in the London suburb of Uxbridge at 11:50 A.M., only minutes after those in Paris.

It was a real triumph for the newspaper and also for Roland Pinson, the self-made man who had begun as André Bing's secretary a quarter of a century earlier. Bing, indefatigable but long a sick man, was forced to retire in 1972, and died of a heart attack in April 1973; MacDonald promoted Pinson to technical director in his place. It was Pinson who completed the negotiations with the French postal, telegraph, and telephone authorities and the British

General Post Office, and managed to carve out cramped space for installation of the new equipment at the rue de Berri. A young man named Alain Lecour, formerly one of Desmaisons' circulation inspectors, installed and took over the operation of the Uxbridge end of things. In today's typical international fashion the transmitters were British-made Muirhead machines; the modulator-demodulator devices that scanned a proof sheet in Paris, transformed the light and dark areas into binary language for transmission, then decoded it in England, were French-built. The printing firm of King and Hutchings was situated near Heathrow Airport, so that copies could receive quick shipment to Scandinavia, northern Germany and the Low Countries, as well as Scotland and Ireland.

The whole move proved extremely providential: the 1973 war in the Middle East had just led to quadrupled oil prices and a concomitant rise in the cost of jet fuel, with the result that continued charter flights would have been unduly expensive; French postal authorities also pushed through an unanticipated rate increase at about the same time. Together with printing and transmission costs lower than forecast, all these developments meant that within nine months, according to MacDonald's calculation, the operation saved the *IHT* over $500,000, considerably more than he had projected.

As a true international "first," the new operation provided an immense public relations opportunity, of which the promotion people took full advantage. In England there were advertisements in major papers and in the trade press; there were posters, special mailings to newsagents, stickers for windows and cash tills, distribution of thousands of display racks and vendor bags. Free copies of the initial runs were distributed on trains and to retailers, and the event received coverage in the press and on radio and television. By the end of the year circulation in the United Kingdom increased by almost 50 percent. (Most of the promotion was aimed at a relatively elite, well-heeled audience, but there was also the suggestion that distributors try to arrange with Kentucky Fried Chicken to put *IHT* sales racks in its 150 U.K. outlets. Kentucky

Fried Chicken managers, unfortunately, replied that the kind of people who eat Kentucky Fried Chicken were probably not the kind of people who read the *International Herald Tribune*.)

The operation started auspiciously. Uxbridge, however, would constantly be plagued by strikes, by an unwillingness of English pressmen to accept the principle that production for sales abroad should not be affected by a strike directed at local conditions or political causes. Desmaisons frequently had to resort to expensive charters and long truck trips while the Paris press again ran off the full production run. Nevertheless, the Uxbridge operation clearly demonstrated the feasibility and desirability of facsimile transmission and its use in other areas where the labor climate was better appeared likely to produce much better results. (A later examination of the possibility of faxing to Zurich revealed that in seventy years there had been one printers' strike of one hour—to add to which Lintotypists in Zurich worked forty-three hours a week to Parisians' twenty-five, took four weeks' vacation to the Parisians' seven, and had never insisted on minimum manning requirements for newspaper production.) Uxbridge was the first major step in the long-discussed process of production modernization, and it presaged many more.

Once again, though, Robert Burns was proved right about best-laid plans of mice and men. When the first intensive efforts and negotiations took place in the early seventies, they were based on the assumption that the *IHT* faced an inherently expansionist situation reflecting inclusion of England in the Common Market, and the increased use of English as an international language in an increasingly integrated and constantly expanding world economy, where soaring numbers of cosmopolitan businessmen and financial officers manned growing numbers of multinational enterprises based on the development of instant transnational communications. Pretax profits had jumped from $250,000 to over $1 million.

In June of 1974, when Lee Huebner made his general inspection trip on behalf of the board, the atmosphere was very different from the heady days of the early 1970s, and soberer yet in 1975, when

Huebner accompanied yet another board delegation and wrote the report on its six-day investigation. He began by citing the spirit and sense of dedication of the employees, in the face of unique challenges, "unbelievably archaic facilities," the fact that the production technology had been outmoded decades earlier and that the manning requirements were highly excessive even for the outmoded technology. And labor unrest in Paris was about to lead to even higher costs. The paper's "great traditions, dedicated staff, consistent editorial quality, loyal readers and advertisers, and its outstanding reputation," Huebner wrote, were trememdously valuable resources, but they now simply had to be matched by renewed production facilities if their potential was to be realized. Outside consultants had not produced the required results, and the visitors determined that modernization plans should be worked out in-house. The *main* source of savings for the *IHT* would lie in the area of composing, where some seventy-six men now did a job that a handful could do after modernization.

MacDonald was given the go-ahead to do a full-scale, in-house "facilities review," while the board set up a Facilities Review Committee to work with him. The soaring costs of production and distribution had been absorbed by the recent price increases, but the price increases could not continue without crippling circulation. Limited circulation would mean further loss of advertising. The situation had, in fact, become critical; the paper could only be saved now by modernization.

This was the theme MacDonald played when he completed the draft of his report several months later. In the late sixties the issue had been how the *Trib* should be produced to accommodate to a predicted rapid expansion; now it was a question of what changes would save it in the face of the adverse trends he listed once more in his report: the world-wide recession triggered by the oil price increase of late 1973, inflation rates significantly greater than any previously experienced, the overnight doubling of the price of newsprint, the resultant decline of advertising lineage, and the aggressive pricing policy he had unwillingly been forced to follow to protect the profit margin. Dramatic as it might sound, his facilities review was therefore in the nature of a "survival manual." And action—suggested by all the foregoing—was now dictated by the "rapidly deteriorating labor situation in the Paris press, leading to every-increasing union rigidity." It was a far cry from the projections of five years earlier.

The mid-1970s union situation to which he referred was, in fact, *dramatique,* a French word that implies more than its English equivalent. MacDonald did not exaggerate when he tried to impress upon faraway American owners just how bad the situation had become. Most of the events centered around the *Parisien Libéré,* whose owner, Emilien Amaury, had determined to face the issue of modernization head-on, and proposed dismissals of over 200 printing personnel in March 1975. In short order the unions occupied the *Parisien Libéré* plant, and Amaury moved his printing to Belgium. There, however, sympathetic Belgian unions blocked him, while French workers declined to deliver the paper in France. Amaury, having left the conciliatory Paris Publishers Association, equipped a plant outside of Paris, and manned it with non-Communist Force Ouvrière workers. On June 13 the house of André Bergeron, head of the Force Ouvrière, was bombed; a day later Bernard Cabanès, senior editor of Agence France Presse, died from a bomb blast presumably designed for the *Parisien Libéré's* senior editor of the same last name.

While other publishers watched Amaury's attempt to evade union restrictions, the Paris printers struck sporadically both to keep the publishers from following suit and to try to get them to put pressure on Amaury. The *IHT* was shut down on several occasions, and MacDonald was unable to get a special status for non-French circulation. On September 26 the strikers invaded the Paris stock exchange at its peak trading hour, and in the ensuing chaos two men, including a police commissioner, died from heart attacks. Ten days later a hundred printers occupied Notre Dame Cathedral for four hours, tolling the great bells and hanging long banners from the towers.

In the meantime another publisher muddied the waters politically: Robert Hersant, owner of a string of provincial newspapers, who bought the conservative Paris *Figaro*. Hersant had suffered condemnation to ten years curtailment of civil liberties in 1947 for wartime collaboration and for having led a pro-Nazi organization. Subsequently amnestied, he served in the National Assembly. But his purchase of the *Figaro* led to a brief journalists' protest strike; a year later, when he bought the mass-circulation *France-Soir*, previously owned by Hachette, the journalists there followed suit. The struggle over automation had now taken on a distinct political coloration.

In February 1976, 2,000 *militants* besieged the meeting of the Publishers Association, which reached an agreement with the unions that no jobs would be lost as a result of automation. Labor unrest continue through the next few months, however, particularly since the general economic situation had provoked the government into adopting a wage restraint program. The *Parisien Libéré* affair ended only with a government-imposed settlement in August of 1977, with large indemnities and job transfers and reinstatements for the personnel involved.

In the midst of all this, MacDonald had therefore recorded what he felt had to be done in his "Facilities Review": leave Paris. Housing most—if any—of the paper's operations in Paris simply was no longer viable, particularly in the antiquated and inefficient ruc de Berri quarters whose sale, now that the area had become an extremely high-rent one, would bring in a considerable sum. A move to the outskirts involving modernization would simply invite union retaliation. It was economically sounder to remain within France rather than to try to move to Belgium, Holland, or Germany, where costs would be high, labor troubles might be just as great— as Amaury's move to Belgium had shown—and start-up would be unduly expensive. Bordeaux, Marseilles, Brittany, and a half-dozen other locations were either too far or didn't have interesting facilities. In Lyon, however, L'Entreprise de Presse #I, among the largest and most modern photocomposition and offset printing establishments in France—jointly built by *Le Progrès de Lyon* and *Le Dauphine Libéré*—could offer exactly what was wanted. The best alternative would be to move the headquarters, editorial offices, and composing room to Lyon, while establishing a facsimile printing operation outside of Paris (the Lyon establishment might be able to provide backup printing in case of need). Circulation and advertising offices would stay in Paris, and another facsimile printing operation would be set up in Zurich.

Moving any part of the operation out of Paris would undoubtedly cause a strike, along with occupation of the rue de Berri building; it would be wise, therefore, to move virtually the whole production facility in one fell swoop. As icing on the cake, the French government provided political support and employment incentives for decentralization. Lyon was a cosmopolitan center with excellent transportation connections to the rest of Europe and offered an attractive enough urban atmosphere to keep good editorial people. The cost of living was 25 percent lower than in Paris, Lyon had its own stock exchange and good banking facilities, and incentive employment grants there would total half of what would be needed for severance settlements in Paris. By remaining in France the *IHT* would avoid trouble with the NMPP, its French distributor. Everyone agreed that a facsimile link to Zurich was essential, but moving the whole enterprise there as some had suggested—business, editorial, and production—would not result in enough savings. It was going to be the board's decision, but if it were up to him, he would begin preparations for the move to Lyon immediately, since the complexities of French law would mean considerable delay: consultation with the worker representatives and required Ministry of Labor approval of the "Social Plan"—the plan for what would happen to each and every worker when the move was made—would take several months. In order to forestall a strike it was therefore essential to organize the move secretly ahead of time—to have the Lyon enterprise order the facsimile transmission equipment, to make arrangements and install equipment in Zurich, and if possible to arrange for facsimile printing in a plant outside of, but near, Paris. All of this would take precious months *before* the legal steps were initiated, and these would stretch on, too.

And in the meantime, as MacDonald stressed, the *Wall Street Journal* threatened again, while the London-based *Financial Times* had made plans to open an international facsimile operation in Frankfurt—one of the originally preferred locations for the *Herald Tribune*. Either of these would pose a more serious threat to the *IHT* than anything that had gone before. And, indeed, when the *Financial Times* began its facsimile edition in Frankfurt in December 1977, it turned out to be—as one *IHT* report put it—"more of a frontal attack than we expected." The owners were willing to take heavy losses to establish their base; the *Financial Times* had a staff of twenty-two in Frankfurt, including six editorial personnel, so that five or six pages of international news were done locally to be added to those transmitted by facsimile processes. (And by late 1978 *IHT* market research showed the paper to be "more influential in our area than had been previously supposed.") Even so, moving the *Herald Tribune* out of Paris to Lyon was a big step, and board members wanted to be certain. They sent Lee Huebner and a consultant, John Prescott, to Paris to review the report with MacDonald.

Huebner, who had first met Jock Whitney and Walter Thayer through the moderate Republican Ripon Society he had helped organize, had written a doctoral dissertation at Harvard on the mass media, and was now a partner in Whitney Communications, where he had familiarized himself with a wide range of techniques being used in different circumstances. Prescott, an independently wealthy newspaperman, former president of the *Washington Post,* and a longtime member of the *IHT* board, had years of experience in newspaper production and in particular in labor relations. The two men held a round of meetings with MacDonald, Pinson, and the paper's lawyers, and MacDonald's "Facilities Review" was redrafted to reflect some of their changes and challenges. They both still retained some reservations, though, when the review was presented to the board. Sulzberger and Gruson seemed ready to accept the Lyon recommendation, but Prescott and Huebner's report of their brainstorming sessions with MacDonald made the Whitney and *Post* people hesitate. The board was about to communicate its hesitation to MacDonald, when the beleaguered MacDonald resigned.

There was more to his resignation than the board's unwillingness to back him fully on the move to Lyon, and the sense he had of intrusive interference by the various board committees and delegations. He had been considering leaving for at least two years, for personal reasons. On the other side there were board members who felt MacDonald had been too slow in moving on modernization, and had had to be prodded into beginning and carrying out the facilities review. They needed someone experienced in the new technologies. The board began to search for MacDonald's replacement—and sent Lee Huebner back to Paris again to make a more intensive on-the-spot investigation. MacDonald had given six months' notice, so that while the urgency remained, there was also the dilemma of whether to make a move that would leave the new publisher faced with a *fait accompli,* or to try to postpone a final decision, using the excuse of a change at the top. There was much to do and to be looked into, and the energetic Huebner threw himself enthusiastically into the task, with MacDonald's full cooperation.

A touch of bad publicity complicated their task. In October 1976, the Paris *Metro,* a brash young publication more or less modeled on successful "underground" American weeklies, and founded on the notion that the international version of the *Herald Tribune* had left the field open for an English language newspaper about Paris, published a rather derogatory article by one William Dowell called "The Graying of the *Herald Tribune,*" replete with much nostalgia about what it had been like in the old days. This in turn was picked up by *New York* magazine, where the editors planned to run an article to the effect that MacDonald's resignation indicated the possible demise of the *IHT* by the end of the year! MacDonald had managed to get some of the material in the *Metro* story toned down a bit, but the *New York* one could have been much more harmful. The fact was that the second half of 1976 had seen a remarkable recovery from the bad times of the last few years, and MacDonald so informed *New York* magazine. The result was a reference to MacDonald's leaving what the *New York* story now called the "ailing" Herald Tribune—a minor if useful improvement. After the story's appearance MacDonald assembled the whole editorial department to reassure its members that the paper was doing better than in some time, that his departure was almost entirely family-related, and business-related only in the sense that if he stayed on now, it would have to be for virtually the rest of his professional career. Whatever happened, he told the group, the editorial offices were highly likely to stay in Paris.

Huebner visited both Lyon and Zurich and soon determined that legal and financial complications were, if anything, even greater than technical and labor ones. Despite enormous French tax payments and penalties if the newspaper left France, Zurich began to look more attractive. He found the Zurich printing establishment willing to go to great lengths to accommodate the *IHT;* reports had already appeared in Swiss and German papers that the paper would be coming to Zurich. Then when he stopped off in Geneva, on the way home, he found that the *Tribune de Genève* was equally ready to accommodate the *IHT*. Its managers argued that French-speaking Geneva, with its international location, was an even more logical spot, and the fact that the *Figaro* was ready to launch an International Edition there proved what they argued. (And it occurred to Huebner that competition between Zurich and Geneva might well help in obtaining those difficult Swiss work permits.) Geneva authorities were ready to do anything they could, though there was a problem about the size of available presses.

The plot thickened. In a long conversation with François Desmaisons, Huebner discovered that the circulation director was dead set against either Lyon *or* Zurich—and certainly against Germany, which had again been mentioned. Desmaisons thought the *IHT* should stay in Paris if at all possible, though he could reluctantly accept a move to Geneva or Brussels, both of which were French-speaking. Then it turned out that Buddy Weiss thought that London would be the best place for relocation! (Later, when MacDonald's successor actually prepared to move to Zurich, Buddy remained convinced that the move wouldn't work.)

In Paris Huebner heard yet another point of view: *IHT* management was taking too "Anglo-Saxon" an approach toward French government and the "informal and exception-ridden nature of Latin legal arrangements." The French government would not like to see the *International Herald Tribune* leave Paris, and could, in fact, make things hard for the paper if it did (such as seizing assets to guarantee strikers' unmet claims). But it could also, if properly approached, be induced to make it easier for the paper to stay. There was plenty of room for give and take, in the form of investment guarantees, relaxation of certain exchange control requirements and taxes, an assurance of the necessary permissions for restructuring and laying off workers, relocation incentives for a move to an area of Paris like La Défense—the new, half-occupied office area across the Seine from Neuilly, to the west of Paris itself. It might be helpful—in trying to work out these matters—if the board of directors had perhaps one or two French members. At least one firm decision resulted from Huebner's investigation: the board discarded MacDonald's favored Lyon suggestion.

By the end of 1976 board members found the publisher to whom they would entrust the modernization move; Bob Eckert, the fifty-six-year-old president and publisher of the *Binghamton* (New York) *Sun-Bulletin* and the *Evening* and *Sunday Press,* and until 1971 president of the *Hartford* (Connecticut) *Times.* Like Philip Weld, seventeen years earlier, he was not a big-city publisher, and his French would never be more than rudimentary. But he and his assistant, Larry Sackett, were familiar with the newest techniques and technologies. After a short, preliminary visit he came over in January 1977 to begin to learn the ropes from MacDonald who left, finally, in February. And Eckert was quickly convinced that the move to Zurich should be made: in his first two or three months in Paris the *Parisien Libéré* affair led to eleven days' work stoppage. Requests that the *IHT* be allowed to publish for international distribution was refused. "The *IHT*," Eckert was told, "will be treated the same as other Parisian dailies." To the board he wrote, "There will never be acceptance of us by the unions as an international newspaper published in Paris."

Eckert was quintessentially American in approach, and this frequently led to clashes with the predominantly French personnel on the paper. He and Larry Sackett, trying to shake up and change procedures, would say, "We do it this way in the States," and to his exasperation the often unstated reply was "But this is France." He felt he got results by being a bit of a bull in a china shop, but one result was considerable mutual animosity. He thought the Comité d'Entreprise was on balance a useful institution, though he considered it—correctly—his adversary.* But he was appalled to find that the paper had to provide space, for which it paid rent, to the Comité for its offices and that he had to pay the Comité personnel for time spent on Comité business. He was startled to learn how little control management had over hiring and firing at all levels. A Buchwald, as he put it, couldn't be hired now. It is said that one of Eckert's first lessons in French labor law came when, in anger, he wanted to fire one of the top maintenance men who refused to put American-type toilet paper in the men's room in place of the usual slick French stuff, and he was told of the enormous severance pay to which the man was entitled because he'd been employed for thirty years—for each of which he would receive one month's pay! Not too long after he arrived in Paris Eckert told Roland Pinson that he felt much more at home in Zurich than he

---

*A typical cover of the Comité's own internal publication, *Tribin,* carried the word "Non" decoratively arranged 1,003 times to make the point that its leaders felt they had been refused a share of the cake when 1978 turned out to be a good year. Eckert was hardly pleased when Comité members later insisted on attending board meetings in New York, as they were entitled to do at the paper's expense, to raise not only fringe-benefit questions, but also issues of the newspaper's management, such as elimination of the proofreader staff when photocomposition was adopted. After all, they argued, they wanted to be able to take pride in their product.

did in Paris. The toilet paper was perhaps only one factor. When the required thirty work permits came through for Zurich, Eckert, now eager to make the whole move, began to secure the necessary equipment.

Then, at the June board meeting, Eckert got the word that the board did indeed want him and Pinson to try to negotiate what MacDonald had felt was impossible: an agreement with the unions for modernization in the Paris area, keeping Zurich open only as an option. What this meant was that to get French cooperation the two men would have to bargain in good faith to work out the problems *within* France, while at the same time—to reduce the evident risks of a prolonged and potentially disastrous strike or slowdown—actually prepare to publish *outside* of France, in Zurich. The fact that the setup in Zurich, ready for completion by September 1, would be used in either case for facsimile printing (apart from some of the equipment, including the computer and the video display terminals) enabled them to do both—to bargain in good faith to stay, while genuinely preparing if necessary to move. Zurich was, indeed, a strike-breaking option.

It was not the way Eckert would have liked to proceed, but he was willing to go along with it. It was important that the French government as well as unions in Switzerland and Britain not see the *IHT* as a fugitive from French law, that the French not be provoked into hostile action, that the possibility of continuing to distribute the 17 percent of the newspapers sold in France be kept open. The strike which so many expected would result from presentation of the Social Plan to the Comité d'Entreprise would allow the *IHT* to legally begin composing and publishing in Zurich, but in such a move the contracts in Zurich might bind the paper for a year, while the strikers might desist in Paris, thus requiring the paper legally to pay them. The Comité might also refuse to meet to *hear* of the plan, in which case the paper might well be stymied unless some way were found to get around the tactic. And there was always the possibility that if, in response to a strike, the paper made the move to Zurich, distribution records and computer programs and accounts might be seized by the strikers in Paris; it was imperative that these be immediately duplicated and safeguarded.

Complications seemed endless, extending to matters of capitalization, taxation, and incorporation in Switzerland as either a subsidiary of the French company or as a corporation owned directly by the American partners. As Huebner wrote at one point, not only had there been too many different people involved in trying to work out the matter, but it was far more tangled than they had expected when they first set out on it. "There are so many moving parts to it," was the way he put it.

Nevertheless, one conclusion to the June discussions was that the French government should not be caught by surprise when the plan was presented to the worker representatives. Walter Thayer, chairman of the board, joined Eckert and the *IHT* lawyers in making a presentation to high officials in the Ministry of Labor, people close to President Giscard d'Estaing (who was known to read the *IHT* every day), explaining the paper's situation to them and telling them what would have to be done if the paper was to stay in the Paris area. Eckert believed that this was crucial, that the government in fact passed the word on to the unions that it wanted the paper to stay in Paris, and that they would have to reach a settlement.

But it was Roland Pinson who carried out the actual negotiations with the unions, and as far as he was concerned, the real possiblity of Zurich, where the preparations made for editing, composing, and printing were made fully known to the union representatives— and Eckert's and Sackett's obvious preference and determination to go there if they could—was the sword of Damocles that brought agreement. He and Prescott presented union representatives with the detailed plan whose preparation Prescott had supervised at a first meeting in late October.

In essence, Pinson explained, the paper would go to what was called third generation modernization. News from the various wire services would go directly into a central computer; editorial room personnel would both edit stories on video display terminals and, as they did so, compose them so that they would come out "hy-phenated and justified," ready to be pasted directly onto page grids, from which plates would be photographed. The *IHT* would transmit these to Uxbridge and to Zurich, but would also contract to print a third of the whole press run in Paris, on another newspaper's press. In the process, of course, Linotypists, stereotypists, and pressmen's and mailroom personnel's jobs would be eliminated. Of the hundred and forty-odd now employed, the paper would need only about one-fifth. There would be various ways to work matters out: some personnel would be retained; the general Paris press accord of July 1976 envisaged voluntary early retirement without loss of benefits for people in their upper fifties, plus a system of preretirement benefits. Some press personnel would find jobs at the printing establishment with which they would contract for Paris printing. And finally, there would be some who would receive the legally required severance pay plus an additional sum the *IHT* was willing to pay. Editorial personnel would go through the retraining required for use of the video display terminals (VDT's).

The workers' representatives responded two weeks later in a hot meeting to the effect that modernization might be necessary but must entail *no* unemployment, and demanded to meet with representatives of the board. As yet, there had not been the explosion MacDonald had predicted earlier—neither threat of a strike, nor occupation of the building. Eckert thought the approach to the Giscard government helped; others thought the fact that the Communist newspaper *L'Humanité* also faced the need for modernization meant the the Communist party would not back the Communist-led unions in their resistance to the moves and thus weakened their opposition. But Pinson remained convinced that it was Zurich that did it. The unions had been hurt by the *Parisien Libéré* affair; they did not want to see a newspaper leave, realized that a move to Zurich was not an idle threat, and knew that retaliation against the paper if it did leave would gain them nothing.

Pinson was perfectly willing to have an owners' delegation come talk to the unions. The board sent John Prescott, who simply let them know that because of the paper's unique international circulation, because of the absolute necessity for late news and late stock tables, and the rise of international competition, the owners were convinced that the paper's survival was at stake. Modernization in the form of electronic editing and printer subcontracting was essential. The alternative was to leave France. The workers should stop questioning the process, and instead start talking about the details of the Social Plan. The owners, he assured the union representatives, fully realized that they had responsibility for all the people who worked for the paper, but they also had responsibility for its survival. The solution chosen might eliminate a great many jobs, but it would protect more jobs than any other solution would.

Hard, precise bargaining followed which resulted in assuring substantial severance pay for some workers, jobs elsewhere or early retirement for others, and retention of some thirty workers at the paper (twice as many as Eckert thought were needed for the job). The *IHT,* in return, got a very large degree of flexibility in using workers by French standards. On January 11 the Social Plan was presented to the Ministry of Labor representative, along with the corresponding lists of those who would leave and those who would stay, and she indicated that approval would be swift. Six weeks later the exhausted negotiators signed the final accord.*

The move from the rue de Berri was incredibly complicated. A modern, glass-and-steel building out in Neuilly owned by the Prudential Company was found after a considerable search. It had several floors available along with an underground garage, and it was conveniently located in a most unpicturesque setting on the avenue Charles de Gaulle, a broad, multilaned east-west highway that stretched from the Porte Maillot to the Pont de Neuilly. The building was also on the last Metro stop and had air-conditioning and a transplanted Englishman to maintain it (and a security-conscious East German trading mission out back, which eventually

---

*There are stories to the effect that the union leaders who made the final determination about who would stay made sure that all the activists were kept on.

built an outside staircase to the machinery on the roof so the mission personnel wouldn't have to let the Englishman working in the offices of an American newspaper go through their part of the building). Much of the required equipment had already been installed in Zurich, with the result that some of the training had to take place there; then the material had to be transferred back to Neuilly.

During January and February the computer and typesetters, the camera and film-processing facilities, were all installed and their users trained. Then links to news and picture services were arranged and hooked up to the computer. The advertising and editorial personnel were trained in their new roles, and finally, while the paper was still being published at the rue de Berri, editorial equipment and supplies and the facsimile equipment were transferred and tested in Neuilly. The first number came out of Neuilly on Monday, March 27, allowing the weekend for the transfer. The basic steps in modernization had taken place, and after all the research on alternatives, the *International Herald Tribune* was still, if not in Paris itself, at least in its suburb of Neuilly.

On the night of Friday, March 24, 1978, the last number was produced on the rue de Berri by the Linotypists, stereotypists, proofreaders, and pressmen, and shipped out by mailers. Only a few pressmen and mailroom personnel would still be carrying out their functions two days later, over at the plant of *Le Matin,* on the north side of Paris. The smells of ink, oil, lead, sweat, the roar of the press, the clacking of the Linotypes, the pinup-studded locker rooms, the rolls of newsprint—all would be gone. The cluttered newsroom would no longer resound to the sound of typewriters. Even deskman Sim Kantin's magisterial invention would be replaced by a computer printer. Kantin—the last man to be hired by Eric Hawkins—had come up with the simple expedient of a string with a paper clip at the end of it in order to avoid sending the aged copy boys two floors down to bring copy back up to the editorial room. The device had served for fifteen years. Now the building which had inspired it, and from which the paper had been issued since 1930, would be sold to a French pension fund combine for some $2 million dollars.

There was, of course, a party that last night once the paper was done. The Weisses have a picture album of the event. It got rather soggy; one well-known correspondent supposedly had to be saved from throwing himself into the roaring printing press, while another deskman threw up all over it. Peggy Sunde Weiss, formerly a secretary, now Buddy Weiss' wife and coordinator of special supplements, came across one of the printers, Robert Devogel, wandering around virtually in mourning. She tried to confort him: they all felt that way, even if they weren't losing their *métier*. On an inspiration the two removed the French and American flags that always flew alongside each other on the second-floor roof above the entrance. Buddy Weiss took the French one, and the desolate printer, facing an unwanted early retirement, clutched the red, gray, and blue American one to him and left. He had it laundered and hung it in his living room. But his heart failed him soon after, and when the Weisses went to his funeral—postponed so the *Herald Tribune* people could be there—the flag was draped over his coffin, to be buried with him. The *Herald Tribune* and the rue de Berri had been his life.

Once the move was made Eckert found himself with more hard bargaining, this time over the newsroom working conditions, where the deskmen claimed that video display terminals posed potential health hazards and argued that they were now, in effect, composing as well as editing the paper. Several newsroom people left at the time of the move. Among those who stayed, a lot of ill-feeling came pouring out, much of it directed at the heavy-handed Eckert, who stood accused of every kind of parsimony in pursuit of the bottom line. Eckert, however, had a sense that much of the hostility was really the result of earlier mismanagement within the editorial room.

There was no doubt about Weiss' genius at getting out a well-

The newsroom at the Rue de Berri with Buddy Weiss on the right.

The new newsroom in Neuilly.

edited newspaper. Without any ruler, as his admirers said, he could lay out the whole front page in nothing flat. He had been at the *Trib* for ten years when Eckert arrived; in 1974 he had suffered a stroke, and his managing editor, George Bates, took over for him while he was out. At that time MacDonald was surprised to find out how much Bates did *not* know about things he should have known about; Buddy, the editor who had never held an editorial conference, did not seem to communicate very well. Weiss' penchant to be completely the shirtsleeve layout man left Bates' role rather ambiguous, and by the time Eckert arrived two years later he found Weiss and Bates at complete loggerheads; within two months Bates left after a violent blowup. MacDonald had frequently spoken to others of the need to get Weiss to think in terms of policy issues, broader executive questions. "For several years," he told one visitor from the United States, "this paper has not had an editor." One deskman-cum-sportswriter who liked Weiss immensely nevertheless reported that Weiss would let men write their whole stories and then, as he put it, "shit-can" them—in part because of another failing, an inability to say no to people. He was "too nice a guy," said another one of his colleagues; he couldn't lay off those he should, he had a hard time coming down on anyone who deserved it—or in providing editorial direction to those who worked under him. Some thought Buddy refused to allow junior people to advance, or refused to use stories reported and written by rim people on the desk. No one was allowed to write for Paris *Metro* while it existed—neither desk people nor stringers. And some thought he hadn't stood up to the board over the issue of adding correspondents. There were those who would defend him against all these charges; he was a very likable man. But the newspaper, presumably, needed more than that.

It was almost inevitable that Weiss and Eckert would clash. When George and Betsy Bates left, Eckert, concerned with the many criticisms over features and lack of any strategic features planning, tried to be helpful about replacements, and Weiss charged him with interfering with personnel decisions in the editorial domain. And the proposed move to Zurich stood between them, too. Buddy didn't think it would work at all: he shared Pinson's view that circulation in France would suffer, didn't think the printing establishment was up to the job, and planned to stay only six months at most if the move were made. Weiss thought that morale problems existed throughout the newspaper, largely as a result of Eckert's obvious desire to go to Zurich and to show the owners a good profit. When the Zurich move was still in the works, with the business offices expected to stay in Paris, Weiss asked Eckert where he planned to be himself, and Eckert told him: Zurich—where the editorial offices and composing room would be. From then on, Weiss felt, it would have to be him or Eckert. And when the move was finally made to Neuilly instead, and Eckert—in what otherwise would have been a perfectly normal move—located the publisher's office on the same floor as the editorial offices and newsroom instead of upstairs with the business offices, he was sure of it.

There was one final incident. Ever since the 1967 Middle East war, Arab states had prohibited distribution of copies of the *IHT* containing the occasional Israeli ads published in the paper. Since there were so few, the paper, like other U.S. publications and with full knowledge of the Israeli advertisers, took to substituting house ads for the Israeli ones in the copies destined for Arab countries. In 1977 Zionist offices in London asked Weiss for an explanation of policy, and Weiss wrote mistakenly that the *IHT* no longer took Israeli ads. The *Washington Post* received and published a copy of the letter and members of the board were deluged with adverse comments, despite Eckert's letter of disclaimer.

In essence, Eckert, who had already decided that he himself would leave in six months, told Walter Thayer he felt he could no longer deal with Weiss. In December 1978 Eckert told Weiss he would have to go; in January 1979 Weiss met with the board in New York. It was a bitter blow, hardly softened by a severance payment in the six-figure range. When he returned to pack up in Paris, he refused to go back to the office to make the rounds, but many from the paper came to say good-bye at the Weisses' apartment.

So by early 1979 MacDonald was gone, the paper had moved to the sterile but far more functional setting in Neuilly (where, declared a longtime secretary, the spirit of James Gordon Bennett had clearly not moved with it), and now Weiss was gone, too. MacDonald and Weiss had worked in tandem, prepared the way, guiding the paper through radically changing world circumstances.

In February the board named a new editor, a relatively young Associated Press foreign correspondent named Mort Rosenblum. There were a half a dozen candidates, but Eckert had pushed strongly for Rosenblum, who had spent a dozen years in Africa, Southeast Asia, Latin America, and then as head of the Paris Associated Press bureau in the rue de Berri building, where he'd gotten to know the *IHT* people and their goings-on. Like other correspondents all over the world, he had come to regard the *International Herald Tribune* as a sort of house organ that he could trust and rely on when local newspapers exhibited their obvious biases, and its heritage had great meaning for him. He thought the paper had slipped in recent years, and he wanted both to build on what Buddy Weiss had done and correct the course.

Eckert left as planned in June of 1979, six months after Weiss. Perhaps no one carrying out modernization could have been very well liked; as one stringer put it, "Eckert was sent over to do his job: make the move without losing one day of publication or advertising, pare the staff—and he's done it." But many of the *IHT* personnel felt the move could have been done with less resultant ill-feeling and damage to morale.

The board's new choice was none other than Lee Huebner, by now thoroughly familiar with the *IHT's* overall operation. He came fresh from a stint as publisher of Whitney Communications' *Oil Daily,* but he obviously had a running start so far as the *Herald*

Tribune was concerned, and he was full of enthusiasm for the future. He had a reorganized staff to work with: Roland Pinson—who had come to the paper as a simple secretary over thirty years earlier—was named associate publisher on May 17, 1979; René Bondy, the young director of finance, took on additional responsibilities and also became general secretary; Larry Sackett, Eckert's assistant, became director of operations, charged in particular with planning projects involving the use of computers, expansion of technical facilities, and new business opportunities. By the time Huebner arrived, Rosenblum had already launched a four-page special section called "Weekend"; it was rather hastily conceived and begun, Huebner thought, and didn't bring in the extra advertising revenue needed to cover its costs. But Huebner also brought with him the conviction that the paper should, finally, increase its own stable of writers, and over the next few years secured the board's agreement to the long-coveted extra reporters, giving the editor a flexibility in assigning reporters to special stories aimed at the *IHT* readership, as well as a much-needed expansion in international business news.

In addition Huebner initiated an early edition designed to get the paper to places like Rome and the Riviera earlier than they had arrived in the past, and to places like northern England where it hadn't really been worthwhile to try to distribute at all. He shared with many staffers the conviction that the paper, now that it had gone through the pangs of modernization, needed much greater promotion. People who were exposed to the paper liked it; a readership survey on editorial content confirmed this (and Art Buchwald still turned out to be the most popular single feature, just as he had been in the late fifties). But so many potential readers had never even seen the paper, and Huebner, who pulled together promotion, marketing, public relations, and special projects into a single department, had high hopes that increased bulk sales to airlines, hotels, schools, and corporations might also help increase the exposure.

Eckert, at Morgan's and Sackett's urging, had agreed to the

introduction of color advertising, designed to capture a market previously restricted to weekly news magazines. The production process was remarkably complex: the four-color ads had to be printed weeks earlier in a plant in Montpellier, in the south of France; the newsprint rolls were then trucked to the *Le Matin* plant in Paris, where the black and white print was superimposed as the newsprint ran through the presses a second time. An electronic scanner kept the two printings in alignment. The first night—the day before Huebner took over—the web kept breaking and production was a nightmare, and the new publisher found himself walking into quite a scene. But he was, himself, convinced of the necessity for color, the problems were resolved, and he supervised the introduction of color to Zurich and Uxbridge, and ultimately to all the new printing plants.

But it was also Huebner who sent editor Mort Rosenblum packing after two short years. In the winter of 1979 Huebner had prepared a statement for the board on challenges facing whoever would be Weiss' successor. The strength of the *IHT*, he had written, lay in the quality of its hard international news, its tight editing, the professionalism of its display. But it lacked the sophisticated business coverage of the type offered by the *Wall Street Journal* and the *Financial Times*. The features' mix had grown largely out of the personal interests of the contributors and the accident of their availability, and the whole features enterprise needed to be lifted out of its "stepchild" status. Sports coverage needed to be broadened to include more European sports, and the editorial page needed a broader mix of international opinion. Somehow, too, the thirty-odd supplements done each year should be seen by the editor as more of an opportunity than a burden.

Rosenblum had seen to some of this, particularly in the area of features and business news. But Huebner's statement had gone on to say something about personnel and morale, and the ghetto psychology that might be inherent in the situation of the newsroom personnel at the *IHT*. It had been aggravated in recent years by a lack of opportunity to originate stories or to feel a sense of professional progress, by the lack of bylines or a sense on the part of newsroom personnel that other professional colleagues ever saw their paper—as well as the problems inherent in the modernization process. What was lacking was strong and consistent editorial leadership; a new editor should be a diplomat, a leader, a healer, sensitive to the problems of motivating able people under circumstances quite different from those at most American newspapers. This, Huebner concluded, was what Rosenblum had been unable to do successfully, and the board accepted his judgment.

For a few months early in 1981 a Rosenblum appointee, Walter Wells, originally an editor for the *Richmond* (Virginia) *Times Dispatch* and then assistant national editor for several years at the *New York Times,* became acting editor. Then in late 1981 a new sorting-out of editorial responsibilities took place, reflecting both experience with Weiss and Rosenblum and the views Huebner had articulated in his 1979 statement. Philip Foisie, a twenty-five-year veteran of the *Washington Post,* became executive editor. He was the man responsibile for expansion of the *Post's* foreign desk and creation of its network of foreign correspondents, and he had been on the *Herald Tribune* board of directors briefly when the *Post* bought in, in 1966. He would now have overall responsiblity for the *IHT's* editorial operations, while Walter Wells—in a move that balanced *Post* and *Times* representation—became editor, responsible for putting out the daily paper and directing its staff as Weiss had done. Wells and the director of the editorial and opinion pages reported to Foisie; so did the director of special reports, whose operation would be more closely incorporated into the everyday editorial operations of the newspaper. In effect, Foisie would now do what MacDonald had long felt Buddy Weiss needed to do, but for which he didn't have the time or inclination, and what Mort Rosenblum had been unable to do solo either: give systematic thought to the overall direction in which the newspaper should go, and see to it that the day-to-day operations fit into that direction. As a team, Foisie and Wells might be able to correct some of what seemed wrong under previous regimes.

The late seventies and early eighties were tough years for international publications. The *International Herald Tribune* weathered them better than most, well enough to be able to finance a variety of moves, of which the most important was certainly the installation of a facsimile satellite printing operation halfway around the world, in Hong Kong, enabling the paper to promote itself with much fanfare as the world's first and only global daily newspaper. Huebner announced the move on May 14, 1980, and the first number was printed as scheduled on September 15. It was, as Lee Huebner put it, "a miracle of modern technology," and prompted publications like *Advertising World* to start off their stories about the achievement with predictable references to the late Marshall McLuhan's "global village."

The Hong Kong enterprise was the culmination of an effort begun nine years earlier, during which Foisie and several others conducted negotiations for a joint Asian venture with the *Asahi Shimbun,* one of three Japanese newspapers with English language editions. The negotiations foundered in 1978 over such issues as the name of the joint paper and the matter of editorial control— at about the same time that the *Wall Street Journal* made its own entrance on the Asian scene. The woman proprietor of the *Sing Tao* newspapers of Hong King, Sally Aw Sian, was already faxing over slow-speed lines via a truck-sized satellite in orbit over the Indian Ocean all the way to London. Willingness of telecommunications authorities to rent high-speed lines to the *IHT* on a part-time basis made *IHT* operations via the same satellite possible, and the *IHT* Pacific Edition came into being, with transmission from an antenna in Brittany to the satellite 23,000 miles over the Indian Ocean, and from there to a ninety-foot antenna on Hong Kong's Stanley Peninsula, where the signal was transformed into a photo negative to be sent to the *Sing Tao* printing plant in Hong Kong. From there air shipments ensured same-day arrival in all major cities in the area instead of at the end of three or four days, as in the past. Sales in Asia soared from the 2,000 mark to 13,000 within a few months and reached 25,000 by 1985. In short order several

The printed-in-Hong Kong IHT arrives on the newsstands in
September 1980.

hundred copies started going to the People's Republic of China for sale in hotels in Peking, Shanghai, and Canton.

The Hong Kong Edition was an undeniable success: it began to turn a profit by early 1982, a year and a half ahead of schedule. As a result, with satellite transmission techniques well established, the search for further suitable facsimile sites continued. Each had to be based on a weighing of several factors: the cost of establishing and operating new sites against the savings brought by reducing production and distribution from older, existing sites, while taking into account revenue gains from possible increases in circulation and advertising. In 1982, on October 4, ninety-five years to the day after Bennett began the European Edition—and with much fanfare—Huebner inaugurated a second Asian satellite-linked facsimile operation in Singapore. Two more followed, at Ryswyk, outside The Hague, in 1983, and at Vitrolles, near Marseilles, in 1984. The former would improve service to northern Europe and the latter would serve the Mediterranean area and, in particular, Spain and Portugal, whose market potential seemed previously to have been underestimated. (The possibility of transmission to all facsimile sites in Europe by satellite transmission rather than by cable promised further reduced costs and less expensive establishment of even more facsimile operations in what remained the *IHT's* primary market area—Western Europe.)

Suggestions for other new facsimile sites came in from all over the world—from Rome, Athens, Cyprus, Beirut, Cairo, Bahrein, Kuwait, Lagos, locations in Asia and Latin America. In the light of a new "index of desirability" developed at Huebner's request, Japan and Latin America appeared the most promising areas for expansion, while a safe site to better serve the Middle East continued to beckon, despite political instability and censorship problems that varied from country to country. Unfortunately, costs in Japan remained high enough to engender suspicions that they might be one more form of protectionism, while Brazil posed legal problems about ownership of foreign publications. Both might eventually come through, but in the meantime the obvious solution to serv-

The big guns celebrate the Marseilles edition. In front, left to right, Alain
Lecour, Production Director Jean Favre, Publisher Lee Huebner. In the
rear, Richard Morgan, Walter Wells, François Bondy. (SYGMA)

icing a Latin American market that spread beyond the confines of
Brazil and as far as the Caribbean lay in printing in North America.
From there the large number of scheduled flights would enable
relatively rapid delivery throughout Latin America while adding
one big advantage: replacement from the new printing site of the
limited number of copies printed in Europe and flown to New York
for distribution in the United States, where they often arrived
several days late to subscribers.

Advertising salesmen in New York, Huebner argued, had long
worked with one hand tied behind their backs because the paper
had so little circulation in the area: it simply wasn't a familiar,
everyday presence to potential customers. In contrast, the *Financial
Times'* sales of 5,000 copies a day flown from Frankfurt helped it

The *Herald Tribune* is back in the United States! Walter Thayer holds the first number printed in Miami while Lee Huebner and Alain Lecour look on.

a great deal, and the prospect of increasing its presence at lesser cost was what led it to begin a facsimile printing operation in New Jersey in mid-1985. If the *Herald Tribune* owners agreed, a sale of some 7,500 copies of the *IHT* delivered on time in North America might serve to create its own desirable "presence" among potential advertisers. For gut reasons, the board of directors with its *New York Times* representation might never accept a return to printing the *Herald Tribune* in New York itself, but early in 1985 the board agreed to a printing site in Miami, Florida, which could serve both the northern and southern markets.

Huebner had put a lot of energy into getting the decision made. An early memo on his part led the board to decide to carry out a long-range planning study, and to dispatch to Paris a three-man group representing the three owners. Huebner worked with the three closely, seeing their presence as an opportunity to build support for expansion among board members. *Times* representatives saw Latin American distribution as crucial and U.S. circulation as only marginal, while *Washington Post* members saw the U.S. financial community as a key audience and were less interested in Latin America. The Miami decision was an attractive resulting compromise.

The *Herald Tribune* in its various guises had always operated in a complex environment of technological, economic, and political flux, but in recent years the pace of change seemed to have speeded up, and called for unusually rapid adaptation if the paper was to survive at all in the face of the competition that this engendered. Somehow, the paper had successfully managed to adapt in the past, often at considerable cost to its owners, and often on a rather hit-or-miss basis. In the seventies and eighties it adapted on its own, with a good deal more thought and planning on all levels as to how it should do so. As the paper approached its centennial the process of adaption appeared bound to continue.

CHAPTER 15

The *IHT* Today and Tomorrow

IN JAMES GORDON BENNETT'S DAY American trav-
elers could hardly miss the reading room and business offices
of the *New York Herald,* European Edition, halfway down the
avenue de l'Opéra, where they could go in and register and get
their names in the paper—and in the local paper back home. For
almost fifty years, from 1930 on, when American tourists strolling
on the Champs Elysées near the Arc de Triomphe glanced down
the rue de Berri, they couldn't miss the tall "Herald Tribune" sign
in front of No. 21, particularly at night, when it glowed a deep
red. In the fifties and sixties, anyway, they had probably already
seen "Herald Tribune" emblazoned across the bosoms of pretty
vendors near the American Express offices or on the boulevard
Montparnasse or on the Champs Elysées itself.

But the Golden Girls are long gone, and no one strolls casually
down the avenue Charles de Gaulle in Neuilly; in the daytime it's
a roaring, eight-lane commercial artery leading out of the center of
Paris. At night the sidewalks are virtually deserted. A person really
has to seek out the plain glass-and-steel building housing the paper
now, and few do so except to conduct serious business. And that,
in a very real sense, marks the change in the *Herald Tribune*—
from Bennett's time, when a wealthy cosmopolitan made it the
personal newspaper for wealthy cosmopolitans, through Laurence
Hills' time, when Hills made it the village newspaper for Americans
in Paris, through the forties and fifties when it became a better
paper yet failed to break out of the Paris/American tourist mold,
to the Weiss-MacDonald period of merger with the *Times* and the

beginnings of real internationalization, and to more recent times when globalization on the basis of market research has led to the businesslike creation of a product aimed at specifically defined, internationally minded, affluent, mobile audiences.

Few people think about the fact, but a newspaper is always a business that has to make enough money to cover its costs and continuing investment, unless it is subsidized by an individual, an interest group, or a government. For most newspapers this means that to convey the messages in the news columns, the paper also has to convey advertising messages. To secure the necessary advertising it has to convince advertisers that they will reach the audiences they seek. The *Herald Tribune,* like any newspaper or magazine, has always been aimed at particular audiences—positioned in a market, as current talk has it—even when it was subsidized by Bennett.

Editorial room people generally think of themselves as simply dedicated to putting out the news as best they can and as objectively as they can. If this is well done, the newspaper will sell. Pushed a bit, they will admit that the selection of features and the allocations of space between hard news, features, sports, and so on will also have something to do with the paper's success. The back of the book, as the nonnews pages are called, is certainly important. Editorial policy, reflected in the editorial columns, is perhaps admitted to be the owner's business. But when Mort Rosenblum quoted *Washington Post* editor Ben Bradlee about "being an editor with his hat on"—i.e., ready to walk out at any time—who would maintain a healthy mistrust and distance from advertising, promotion, marketing, and the owners represented on the board, he reflected an editorial ideal that has its limits.

Since World War II—with the possible exception of the time Brown and Whitelaw Reid put pressure on Eric Hawkins—*IHT* publishers have by and large kept their hands off the editorial side. But in aiming the newspaper at specific audiences, and aiming it in such a way that it will attract the advertising that now produces 55 percent of the newspaper's necessary revenue, they must exercise some influence over its content. Essentially, they do this through their choice of editors, who steer the editorial side in a way that complements what the particular publisher tries to do with the newspaper as a whole. So when Weld took over in 1960, facing the awesome competition of the *New York Times,* he replaced the aging Eric Hawkins with Cutler, who brought some much-needed professionalism to the newsroom. (It was perhaps lucky that Weld left after a year and a half. His preference was for a small-town, community-style newspaper—just when the American community in Paris was shrinking drastically.) When the *Washington Post* bought in, MacDonald and Weiss came as a team, developing shared views on the necessary reorientation to what Weiss called a mid-Atlantic viewpoint and away from Parisian parochialism. Eckert's choice for editor, Rosenblum, replaced Weiss after MacDonald had left, and Rosenblum saw to some of the editorial changes Eckert had listed in his last report to the board, when he reviewed the process of modernization he had overseen. And not so long after Huebner became publisher he had his own editorial team, of Foisie from the *Post* and Wells from the *Times.*

Huebner, in the early eighties, faced another one of those fundamental changes in the newspaper's milieu of the sort that have, in the past, necessitated basic alterations in the newspaper if it was to survive at all. The technology that made it possible for Huebner to undertake globalization made it possible for competing newspapers and journals to move in the same direction. In the late sixties Richard Morgan was able to take advantage of Weiss' increased business and financial coverage to virtually create a whole new field of international financial advertising: display ads from banks and financial services and for new stock or bond offerings constituted more than half of the display advertising in the paper by the mid-seventies, compared with a meager 1.5 percent two decades earlier. Few things better illustrated the change in the nature of the paper. But the situation couldn't last: the market was too attractive and the new technologies allowed a host of new competitors to enter the field—*Euromoney,* the *Financial Times'* Frankfurt Edition, the *Institutional Investor's* International Edition, *Fortune's* and *Businessweek's* European editions, the *Economist's* International Edition, and last—but far from least—the *Wall Street Journal,* whose Asian Edition began in 1977, and which finally, after years of fits and starts, began a European Edition in February 1983.

The *Wall Street Journal* made all the services at the *IHT* review their operations; as a primarily business journal but with an enormous news hole and vast resources, the *Wall Street Journal* would compete perhaps more directly with the *Financial Times* than with the more generally news-oriented *Herald Tribune.* But along with all the other international financial publications it would be bound to cut into the *IHT's* advertising, and it did: financial advertising lineage dropped 20 percent over a six-year period—primarily from the United States, where, though advertisers were aware of the *Wall Street Journal,* the other journals, and even the *Financial Times,* with its U.S. sales of 5,000 copies, they had to be reminded of the existence of the *IHT.* Rough times in the international advertising field accounted for part of the loss; market researchers at the *IHT* talk of the "fragility" of the market. But it meant that the paper had to turn elsewhere to make up the losses—which it was more than able to do.

Moreover, the new competitive environment within which the *IHT* had to operate in the mid-1980s was not only one of new international financial journals. Start-up costs for new papers were relatively lower than in the past: the old *Rome Daily American* had finally finished its ninth life, but its last editor, Christopher Winner, began a new paper in Rome, the *International Courier*— with access to the *Washington Post* news service! In Athens the new *Athens Star* drew on the *New York Times* news service. And both could offer local readers a hefty rundown on local news. (To Phil Foisie the conclusion seemed clear; in the future the *IHT* might have to include local metropolitan inserts in large metropolitan centers like Rome.) In other areas—Asia, for example—local English language newspapers were improving, drawing more heavily on American news and feature services.

In the meantime papers the world over were finding that faxing to distant locations was possible at reasonable cost: Asian newspapers faxed to the United States; the *Peking People's Daily* was considering faxing to Europe for Chinese residents there; *Al Ahram* faxed from Cairo to London (and offered to share the faxing facilities in reverse with the *IHT*). The *Financial Times,* which had flown its 5,000 copies to the United States from Frankfurt, began to fax to a printing site in New Jersey, near Philadelphia, in mid-1985, and considered faxing to Asia, where the *Economist* had already begun to print. *USA Today,* which had established its familiar and colorful look all over the United States, began a European facsimile edition in 1986; some feared it might well skim off several thousand tourists a day to whom the *Herald Tribune* look was less familiar and to whom *USA Today's* greater sports and pop culture coverage might appeal. It didn't turn out that way, but others might soon join in the international facsimile game. The *Herald Tribune* had begun it all back in 1974. Now competition was rapidly transforming the game by the mid-eighties. For the *International Herald Tribune* to meet the competition, advertising, circulation, marketing, and editorial strategies would all have to intersect, and it was Huebner's job, as publisher, to bring them all together.

Changes on the editorial side under Foisie and Wells were, indeed, all designed to cope with the new competitive environment both by improving news coverage and presentation, and by making important changes in the back of the book. Only five years after the installation of the first computerized composing system, a new higher-speed system allowed better editing, a later deadline, closing stock reports for the first edition, and a physical reorganization and expansion of the newsroom along with a reshuffling of editorial responsibilities and a substantial increase in newsroom personnel. Most editorial personnel agreed that the editing was improved; more care was given to hiring, and trail periods became routine, assuring a greater degree of professionalism. Almost imperceptible changes in margins and subheads provided more space for news;

the paper was laid out more carefully and more tightly edited. Space for business news doubled, and business statistics were expanded and reorganized. (Before the new computer system was installed, statistics had had to be trimmed at the time of paste-up; sometimes it was done, for example, by pulling the listings of the last letter of the alphabet or those listings that hadn't changed. The advent of the *Wall Street Journal,* one editor cracked at the time, with its vast and accurate tables, would be like turning on the lights in the whorehouse. The new system cured all this.)

Regular financial columnists were anchored on different days to encourage regular buying of the newspaper, and new ones were added; in late 1984 a successful effort to tap a new type of advertising came when the former financial editor, William McBride, now stationed in New York, began an internationally oriented, once-a-month personal investment section. A full-time financial correspondent in London and another in Frankfurt meant that in essence, the paper could claim to have four foreign bureaus, counting its own offices at the *Washington Post* and the *New York Times,* with which communications were greatly improved in the eighties, after a moment of some annoyance when two men left the *Times* to come to the *IHT.* In the mid-eighties, in the light of growing Asian circulation, the need for stories aimed at the Asian audience, and a sense that a greater feel for what was necessary in the Pacific Edition could only come from someone on the spot, Huebner persuaded the board that an editor-correspondent in Asia had become essential.

Continuity and familiarity marked the rest of the newspaper, yet there were differences on almost every page. Over time Huebner had finally been able to resolve the burning 1970s issue of whether the *IHT* should have its own writers. He had added them on gradually, and by the mid-eighties the paper sported bylines from three regular in-house reporters and from full-time correspondents in Frankfurt, London, and Asia, and more frequent contributions from regular staffers, all of whom could supplement the enormous volume of material pouring in from the news services and the *Times* and *Post,* and who began to generate news-breaking stories on their own—on the politicization of UNESCO, the development of the European peace movements, or the European lag in high technology. (AP Dow Jones disappeared from the news services with the advent of the *Wall Street Journal,* Europe—not without some rancor—and Agence France Presse reappeared.)

Rearranging the editorial page seems to have been something of a preoccupation in the eighties. The paper prided itself on continuing the American tradition set by Bennett—and admired by his French contemporaries—of separating more or less objective news reporting from editorial opinion, but Foisie thought that the editorial page needed to be less American in orientation, that the paper needed more European columnists to supplement the *Times* and *Post* stable and the other American columnists like William Pfaff, who wrote directly for the *IHT.* The letters column was reinvigorated (and renamed "Letters to the Editor," for presumably good reasons) with a view to stimulating debate on important issues. Rosenblum and Foisie were both conscious of the patchy quality given to editorials by having them come from the *Post* and the *Times* (and followed by a roundup of editorials from newspapers all over the world), and Foisie ultimately secured an editorial writer for the *IHT* to supplant the retired Harry Baehr—John Fay, who could write regular editorials and give the page a sense of direction. In the meantime, reorganization gave the page room for more columns, making it into something more of what has come to be called an op-ed page.

Sports, too, got more room, though the advertising representatives who always complain to each other that it's too American will have to live with a primarily American orientation: as the sports editor says, there are 200 major international sports and thirty-seven countries that play first-division soccer alone. He can give coverage to major international grand slams—world cup skiing, soccer, tennis, golf, or rugby—and occasionally take note of other sports that he can't cover regularly. But basic American sports coverage for Americans abroad remains what the page is all about.

Most significantly, an effort was made within the regular paper to give to features a more systematic worldwide appeal, keeping both advertisers and the more geographically dispersed audience in mind. It wasn't easy; there were strong disagreements, and a considerable shuffling of personnel. The rather hastily conceived "Weekend" was eventually split into a Friday travel section of worldwide scope, to provide a sort of serendipitous pleasure to corporate travelers who make up so much of the *IHT* audience, and the regular Saturday "Weekend," which presented longer articles in an attempt to delineate trends that result from disparate events merely noted in day-to-day articles and features, to inject more controversy over—for example—the politics of culture, to try to attract more name writers on a more regular basis. (Missing now from "Weekend" is that grand holdover from the 1920s, the late Waverley Root, whose final contribution before his death in 1982 harked back to that earlier era: a series of reminiscences about Henry Miller and Anaïs Nin.)

"Arts and Leisure" pages three days a week now draw on an established group of writers on the stage, the international art market, artists, and pop artists and recordings. One star in the mid-eighties was still there after thirty years: Hebe Dorsey, now known throughout the world of fashion, one of the planners of the Metropolitan Museum of Art's 1982–83 costume exhibit, "La Belle Epoque," which drew heavily on *Herald Tribune* fashion supplements of the earlier era, and the poster for which came from the cover of one of them, displaying elegant ladies and gentlemen in "The Stands at Longchamps." Hebe Dorsey and Thomas Quinn Curtiss (who still contributes occasional articles) are the last of the generation of the fifties, if you exempt Art Buchwald, who writes for a wider audience, but whose columns are still among the most popular features in the paper.

A new "Science and Technology" page one day a week reflected the feeling that the Paris milieu had always brought a particular bias to features in the past: most features were written by pickups off the Paris streets, and most Americans in Paris who could write at all were there in connection with the arts, and particularly with the avant garde. Features therefore needed a fairly drastic correction, and science and technology was a part of it. Katherine Knorr, the features and "Weekend" coordinator struggling with the problem in the mid-eighties, argued that on the news side the paper was unique in being largely one big copydesk that could draw on the two foreign desks and the two national desks of the parent papers; this worked for the news, but not for the back of the book, where the features on the parent papers were designed largely for their particular audiences, which were quite different from that of the *IHT*. The *International Herald Tribune* had to have its own orientation, steer its own course, demand from its contributors what fit into this orientation, rather than—as too often in the past—search around for something, anything, to fill some space. Well-designed features could serve the *IHT* audience better as well as bring in the necessary advertising of the kind that resulted from well-designed special reports—those supplements that the paper published in increasing numbers on specific areas or countries or subjects.

For, in fact, special reports under Katherine Knorr's direction had been one of the keys to coping with advertising competition in the early eighties. For decades the reports were anathema to derisive journalists, who viewed them essentially as puffery designed for promotion and advertising purposes, and their relationship to the regular editorial staff was always a matter of contention. (Buddy Weiss put them under his wife Peggy's direction; Mort Rosenblum thought the issue of their control was a key to his dismissal.) Huebner, Foisie, and Knorr viewed them as an opportunity to broaden and deepen coverage in a way the daily newspaper could never do, and thought that serious writers could be attracted to them to make them lively and readable and that the paper need not be compromised by them. Economic reports on

Euromarkets or broad coverage of the state of the Italian economy and polity vied with sections on travel in Venezuela or Egypt, or Latin American nuclear technology. The result, they believed, justified their several years of effort and expense; first-rate people now write for the special reports, which are like a gift of white space to the editorial department that enables the paper to print high-quality, analytic, thoughtful material it could otherwise never print in its normal daily format—while providing close to 15 percent of advertising lineage during a difficult period.

No other daily paper provides as compact and well-edited a view of what's going on in the world, including an attention to basic and underlying trends. To Americans who groan at the weight of their massive and advertising-filled *New York Times* or *Washington Post,* the usual sixteen-to-twenty tightly packed pages of the *IHT,* with only 30 percent of space devoted to advertising, are an extraordinary and delightful relief; to people whose hometown newspapers sometimes lack sophisticated world coverage, the *IHT* is a treat not to be missed when they're abroad. Following its old tradition, the paper downplays neither criticism nor controversy over American institutions and policies; the editorial page continues to carry contrasting points of view culled from columnists and newspapers all over the world.

The *IHT* is certainly no longer an American in Paris, and some older readers miss the old Parisian flavor, finding that a newspaper that is rooted in no specific geographic milieu has a faintly antiseptic air about it, that it's perhaps a little too dignified and serious. Some of the atmospherics of the computerized newsroom, where older personnel miss the ordered chaos of the old-fashioned newsroom— what made it a newspaper rather than just another office—seem to them to have spilled over into the paper. One editor, who shares the opinion of a longtime staff writer that it's a much better paper now than in the past, also shares her opinion that in some ways it's also less interesting and lacks excitement. He is pleased with an off-lead on American Fourth of July celebrations that tells about an immigrant leading a parade, or having an obituary for Chef

Boyardee of spaghetti fame precede that of some well-known but otherwise undistinguished diplomat. To some in the newsroom there's a sense that too much attention is paid to statistics and to market research, that if only the editors edit the paper for themselves and find it interesting, then the paper will be interesting to others. It's practically what James Gordon Bennett said almost a hundred years ago!

In fact, there is a self-conscious effort throughout the newspaper to link today's carefully planned product to the tradition of Gordon Bennett. The internal newsletters are named the "Owl" and the "Owlet"; the promotion department often brings Bennett's name into its activites; the James Gordon Bennett Cup balloon race continues to flourish, and in 1983, on the 200th anniversary of manned balloon flight, the balloons took off again from the place de la Concorde before a crowd of 500,000 as they had back in 1906.

There is also an effort to create a new aura, to attach to the newspaper the romantic image of the global newspaper that can be found everywhere. It circulates, after all, in 164 countries, three times as many as even existed when it started up again at the end of World War II. Internal newsletters delight in printing pictures of notables reading or carrying the *IHT*: former Saudi Petroleum Minister Sheikh Yamani at an OPEC meeting, a Russian delegate to an international security conference, former French President Giscard d'Estaing. A glossy promotion pamphlet once showed the remarkable number of *IHT* subscriptions by diplomatic missions in countries throughout the world; at the time, in Peking, subscriptions went to missions as diverse as those of Canada, Czechoslovakia, Denmark, Pakistan, Sweden, and Yugoslavia, among many others. Subscription lists include a remarkable number of international notables. The late Princess Grace of Monaco told Eckert's wife that she always read it; J. Paul Getty, who by most accounts was the richest man in the world, always subscribed to it. Prime Minister Lee Kwan Yew of Singapore sends out for it if his regular copy is late; Helmut Schmidt has declared publicly that he considers it "the best daily newspaper in the world." Peter Ustinov, Paulette Goddard, the late Howard Hughes, His Holiness the Pope—the list of subscribers in different parts of the world is endless.

Yet Huebner and his circulation people are realistic: 18 countries account for 85 percent of circulation; 26 other countries account for another 10 percent; 7,000 copies—5 percent—are spread around another 120 countries. They have calculated quite carefully whether there would be any savings in cutting marginal circulation in any of the latter countries, particularly in the light of the benefit of being able to claim global circulation, and the answer is no. On the other hand, the figures mean that efforts at increasing circulation will continue to be made primarily in those markets where substantial increases are most likely. Romanticism plays little role.

What does play a role is the enormously complicated organization built up by François Desmaisons across the years, bequeathed in 1984 to his successor, Alain Lecour, who, after directing facsimile operations in London and Zurich, had managed the Asian offices since the inception of the Hong Kong Edition. Editor Philip Foisie has even said that this is perhaps one newspaper where the circulation department is more important than editorial. Facsimile processes allowed the paper to break out of the web of parochialism that stymied Parsons and Weeks earlier. But each new satellite printing plant still depends on a complex of truck, train, plane, local distributor, and local mail service to get the paper to the reader. Plane service to one point must be coordinated with train, truck, or plane service from there to other points, and from those to yet others, with the key being to get the package of the right number of papers to its final destination as early in the morning as possible. Storms, strikes, accidents, delays, require rerouting; different planes fly to the same place on different days.

In Germany and the United Kingdom the paper has set up its own distribution companies. (In England the company is now housed in the same Georgian building—63 Long Acre, close to the

François Desmaisons (right) confers with Phil Foisie outside the present IHT home on the Avenue Charles de Gaulle in Neuilly. (Linda Bell)

Royal Opera House and Covent Garden—that houses extensive advertising activities in hopes that the building will come to be identified as the "Herald Tribune House.") In the Middle East the paper is able to simply sell several thousand copies to an old reliable ally, Levant Distributors, which manages to get papers in and money out where almost anyone else is liable to fail. Even Levant may not succeed in what seemed like a promising boom area—Nigeria—when economic and political upheaval occur. Reliable distributors like Levant may be the key to success in Latin America, where the *IHT* hopes to be able to sell fifteen to twenty thousand copies a day now that the Miami fax site is in operation.

Discount bulk sales to hotels or airlines serve a dual purpose: distributed free by the purchaser, the papers serve as a useful promotion device; they also enter the OJD audit count, for advertising sales purposes. Hotels in the Far East are used to distributing free copies—the Ritz Taipei takes 100 copies a day—but the practice is not well established in Europe. Airline sales, however, have long been a focus of effort; it doesn't cost too much to get packages to major airports, and despite occasional setbacks, sales to airlines have soared to over 37,000 a day, with orders ranging from 9,500 a day for Lufthansa and 5,700 for Air France to 7 for Air Micronesia and 2 for Cyprus Airways. (If a major airline cuts back sharply, as TWA once did in the early seventies, by 3,500, the effect on total circulation figures is almost as great as the overthrow of the Shah of Iran!)

One of the great advantages of the Miami printing site is that it should ease getting current issues of the *IHT* on planes flying to Europe from the United States, thereby exposing travelers to the paper as they get going. Once they see it, so the reasoning goes, they're bound to look for it in Europe. Then, too, Miami should satisfy some of those Americans who have gotten used to the paper elsewhere in the world and dream of subscribing to it in the United States. Getting the paper to the United States from printing sites in Europe has always been a complicated operation. Scheduling problems prevented a cooperative arrangement in shipping Zurich-printed copies from Frankfurt on board the cargo flight used by the *Financial Times*. Kennedy Airport in New York has always been something of a nightmare for shipments to the United States anyway; American customs have not always helped matters on the days the paper has come on a passenger flight rather than airfreight.

Japan is another market area where distribution problems have restricted circulation. Day-late availability seems to mean that if the *IHT* is to compete there with the improved Asian *Wall Street Journal*, printing in Japan itself is a necessity.

And everywhere mail service is an obstacle. To old hands, there is no question that mail services have deteriorated in almost all countries, slowing both home and office delivery of the supremely important subscription copies. As long as people buy the paper on the newsstands, they may remain only occasional readers; in fact, transforming occasional readers into regulars is a primary goal for the future. Subscriptions are an important means of ensuring everyday reading, and subscription promotion is always a big endeavor. But late delivery is an annoyance to everyone. The *Financial Times* and the *Wall Street Journal,* Europe, have tried to circumvent part of the problem by what's called hand delivery, advertising a list of cities where the service is available; it's expensive, but in the existing competitive milieu they've been willing to sink resources into it, and for the present, at least, to accept losses on the service. The result is that the *IHT,* while paying more attention to costs, has had to follow suit.

It is certainly true that the editorial room may turn out a superb product to little effect if it isn't distributed, and the *Herald Tribune* depends upon one of the most complicated—and constantly changing—circulation systems in the world. But at least one recent distribution move that harks back to the days of Gordon Bennett requires little effort: in May of 1982 a refurbished Simplon Orient Express, made up of luxurious railroad cars from another era salvaged from museums and railroad yards all over Europe, began a nostalgic, high-priced, three-times-a-week service between London and Venice—and as in days of yore, passengers find the train has made the *Herald Tribune* and fresh hot croissants available to them each morning in their roomettes or among the crystal and fine china on the linen table cloths in the dining car.

The Simplon Orient Express didn't add much to those important, official OJD audit figures. But by the end of 1985 circulation stood at a record of over 170,000 copies per day; at one point in the middle of the year over 185,000 copies were being sold. Given Miami printing and continued negotiations for other sites, the magic figure of 200,000 did not seem out of sight in mid-1986.

There is no rest in any of the services of the paper. In the chart-filled advertising department, where trends in particular categories of advertising are carefully plotted, and diversification in types of advertising is constantly sought out to protect against the fragility of international advertising markets, there is a continuing search for skilled and knowledgeable advertising representatives in different parts of the world, skilled enough to be able to persuade potential customers that the high-price medium that is the *International Herald Tribune* will reach enough of those readers who are important to them to make the advertising worthwhile. They draw on glossy, chart-filled brochures prepared by the promotion department designed to discriminate between different audiences and to convince advertisers that their dollars, yen, francs, or pounds will produce more in the *IHT* than in competing media—which may soon include Pan-European television. In the face of the presence of new competitors in the 1980s, so-called "tombstone" ads— ads for new syndicated loan bond issues—dropped sharply (from 22 percent of all ads in 1979 to only 8 percent in 1983), and the financial advertising that had soared in the seventies as the paper itself was transformed dropped from 52 percent to 38 percent of all advertising in the paper. The loss was perhaps temporary, other categories more than made it up, and it could be argued that the resulting, more diversified advertising base was healthier. Increased rates improved advertising revenue anyway, despite the difficulties. While part of the increase came from premiums for advertising carried in both the Atlantic and the Asian areas, a good part came from premiums for the four-color ads that were begun in 1979. The ads' appeal lies in the way they stand out against the black and white background, and their space more than tripled between 1981 and 1985. The complications of that first night—when the preprinted rolls shipped from Montpellier for black and white printing in Paris kept tearing—were multiplied as printing sites multiplied: some sites could only print color on some pages, other sites on other pages, and some sites were limited in the amount they could print. As a result, Gerard Piermé, the man who for most of his thirty years at the paper has laid out the advertising on pages onto which the news stories are then pasted, has had to tailor the color ads to take into account a variety of printing plant conditions, while seeing that papers that go to certain Middle East countries include no liquor ads and papers that go to Malaysia have no ads for cabarets, doing special layouts four days a week when papers for Asia are substantially different, and making adjustments for ads that are for the Atlantic area only, those that are for Asia only, and those that are "full run." Piermé may be replaced by a computer when he retires, but he's skeptical about it, and in the meantime may lay out forty to fifty different pages a day for a sixteen-page paper.

Classified ads, going through their own metamorphosis as the paper changed across the decades, provided a third of advertising revenue in the 1980s. They no longer advertised individual pieces of furniture or economy used cars for sale. Rather they tended to offer international business services, expensive real estate, international secretarial or international executive positions available— or services to adapt your Mercedes or Maserati to American exhaust emission requirements. Ever since James Gordon Bennet had trouble with disguised ads for prostitutes in his New York Edition, classified ads have been touchy. In the old days the list of prohibitions included ads for fortune-telling, gambling, nudist colonies, or marriage offers. When someone once sent in an ad to classified that read, "Intelligent, attractive Austrian-American (27) with sweet girl (6) seeks permanent domestic position in cultured motherless home," the classified manager of the time took a few moments to write back that it couldn't be printed as submitted, but could if it read, "Intelligent Austrian-American, 27, with 6-year-old daughter, seeks permanent domestic position in cultured home." The line was perhaps fine.

Sometimes management itself required education: in 1965, when the terms were not yet so common, André Bing had to confirm to Richard Morgan what an ad meant that read, "Gay American, 25, desires camping situation. Photo of site preferable." Back in the 1920s two enterprising American girls set up what may have been the first escort service in Paris and advertised in the *Herald* of those days. It may have been innocuous, but the rash of escort services that broke out in the 1970s was somewhat less so. Sitting with friends around the bar in the Travelers Club one day, Richard Morgan decided, as a joke, to let a couple of escort service ads in. More followed, Weiss objected, and MacDonald raised the obvious issue of how to distinguish legitimate ones from illegitimate ones; but before any decisions were made he had left, and by the time the board debated the issue the ads were bringing in several hundred thousand dollars a year! Some were so obviously code-worded— "Call Emmanuelle" or "Last Tango in London" or "Exciting Parisian parties and interesting night life!"—that Huebner, who would have liked to take them out entirely, drastically restricted wording, shortened the ads, and put them all on an inside page where they presumably provide a legitimate business service and some embarrassment. There are no ads for Parisian escort services, though: the Paris police put a stop to them, and some of the beautiful young women who came to place the ads are missed by the ad takers.

The continued surge in circulation will mean increased advertising revenue in the future, and in the mid-eighties there was reason to think that the *IHT* would continue to hold its own—and more— against increased competition. But as in the past, the paper would have to readjust strategy, move, perhaps, into more travel advertising, more luxury consumer goods, the personal investment category sparked by the new monthly personal investment section. Circulation in new areas might reinvigorate old categories of advertising or bring in new. The board's permission for limited U.S. circulation from Miami may be a big help. Perhaps as an augury of things to come, in late 1984 the *IHT* published its first twenty-four-page paper containing no special report—i.e., justified by a record volume of advertising—and in 1985 record advertising produced a record profit.

The promotion department people don't just do work for advertising. They also do circulation promotion in the form, for example, of mailings to a listing of "Who's Who in Great Britain Finance," or to a listing of diplomats, or to high-income families in particular areas, as well as to the more usual subscriber lists of other publications. Sometimes it works well; sometimes it can be frustrating, when a mailing of several thousand letters brings in only a couple of subscriptions. "Exchange advertising"—space given to other publications to advertise in the *IHT* in exchange for *IHT* ads in the others—has blossomed. Huebner and his promotion people try to get *IHT* reporters on television panels, get them quoted on Paris radio press roundups, provide speakers for special events. The 1984 election led not only to a special edition of the newspaper, but also to radio and TV commentary and debate by *Herald Tribune* reporters and editors, and a bash at the Hotel Royal Monceau in conjunction with Pan American Airways, the American Club, and other American organizations in Paris. *IHT* ads appear on cable TV, which channels news programs to thousands of hotel rooms in the Paris area. Syndication of some *IHT* material began in 1979, and articles about the *Herald Tribune* that appear in magazines like *Town and Country* are widely redistributed by the *IHT* itself. Special events like the winter olympics in Sarajevo or the Geneva summit conference of 1985 call for delivery of several hundred extra copies. A special products division has published a popular book of front pages from the *Herald Tribune*, 1887–1980, a book of superb Magnum photographs from the immediate post–World War II period, whose publication was accompanied by a traveling exhibit, and a book by Hebe Dorsey on La Belle Epoque.

What also began as promotion is now a money-making enterprise headed by its own director: the conference division. The promotion department and financial writer Carl Gewirtz in conjunction with the Forex Research Organization of London arranged a series of conferences on the management of foreign exchange risks, bringing together financial experts and company managers while effectively promoting the paper in the process. A series of oil and money conferences attracted such speakers as Sheik Yamani and Henry Kissinger. Other conferences—all receiving wide media coverage—introduced the new democratic government of Spain and the Mitterand government of France to international business and vice versa. Still others have been held on trade, investment, or international management in places as diverse as Hungary, Portugal, and Singapore, where an ASEAN conference helped put the *IHT* on the map when President Reagan's trade representative, William Brock, called for an ASEAN/U.S. free trade area in a speech to the assembled ministers and business delegates.

On a somewhat different note, on the tenth anniversary of *Herald Tribune* facsimile printing in the United Kingdom, the first basket of *IHT* roses—named by the Royal National Rose Society—was presented to Princess Margaret by Huebner's five-year-old son, with proceeds from sale of the roses to got to charity; the accompanying ad campaign read, "Thanks for helping us grow."

It was all part of an effort to make the *International Herald Tribune* as visible as possible in the face of a ceaselessly changing environment. The only certainty in that environment has been that strategy in all areas—editorial, circulation, advertising, and marketing and promotion—has had to intersect, and that there was no battle to be definitively won, only a continuing and continuous campaign, in which wealthy and powerful opponents like the *Wall Street Journal* and the *Financial Times* posed an enormous challenge, while lesser opponents could never be simply ignored.

The publisher presides over the whole increasingly complex and far-flung business, checking on world trends and on the competition, keeping a wary eye on the editorial operations, determining allocation of space within the paper, managing finances, supervising production, advertising, distribution, and marketing and promotion, fending off pressures and criticisms from the outside and passing on suggestions to the services, reporting back to and consulting with the board of directors, dealing with the unions, coping with the complexities of the law in different countries and in different situations, and making himself available for innumerable public relations activities.

Lee Huebner supervised a wholesale renewal of the top personnel at the paper. François Desmaisons, for over twenty years director of circulation, moved to Marseilles in 1984 to coordinate Mediterranean area circulation and to represent the *IHT* in dealings with circulation and distribution trade organizations. Alain Lecour—whose father had been with the paper for twenty years—became associate publisher, replacing Desmaisions. Lecour, after his years of establishing new facsimile sites and managing Asian operations, would now have overall managerial responsibility for circulation, while continuing to oversee planning for future facsimile sites. The rotund associate publisher Roland Pinson, the former secretary to André Bing who had installed the first facsimile transmission facilities back in 1974 and negotiated the modernization agreements with the production unions in 1978, retired in 1983; his functions were divided between René Bondy and, eventually, several others. The ascetic-looking Bondy, the financial director who had modernized office procedures and dealt with the legal complexities of modernization and globalization, now became deputy publisher, continuing his responsibilities in the areas of finance and accounting, but also taking over relations with the unions, acting as president of the workers Comité d'Entreprise and as the paper's representative at the Paris Publisher's Association. And the archetypical cosmopolitan Richard Morgan—Chevalier du Tastevin, Traveller's Club, etc.—relinquished his duties as advertising director after twenty years to his deputy, Rolf Kranepuhl, becoming, in the process, associate publisher with the duties of supervising marketing and promotion functions and continuing to maintain high-level sales contacts.

By 1985 Huebner had his own team at virtually all services of the paper—Foisie and Wells in editorial, supervising a reorganized staff and system, Lecour in circulation, Kranepuhl in advertising, Bondy in finance, with Morgan still lending his talents to marketing and promotion—and three new regional managers in London, New York, and Hong Kong, whose appointment seemed to symbolize the worldwide spread of the paper's operations. Huebner could well feel that he had a reinvigorated staff with which to face emerging global competition.

When Bob MacDonald wrote his "Facilities Review" back in 1976, he began by saying that Paris would be about the last place to establish an international newspaper such as the *Herald Tribune*. He could cite labor unrest, the relatively high franc, the excessive regulations concerning foreign workers and the difficulties of getting their working papers, the requirements for registration of officers of foreign corporations, elaborate exchange controls, the complex social measures enacted by successive governments designed to humanize capitalism but often requiring enormous amounts of time and paperwork. It was only shortly before his report that he had had to start contributing financially to the activities of the Comité d'Entreprise as it expanded from its original role of representation of workers' grievances and conduct of good works for needy workers, to the organizing of trips abroad to Egypt or Ceylon, the purchase of condominium space in ski resorts, and the acquiring of mobile homes on the Mediterranean and summer apartments on the Normandy coast. MacDonald had had to begin to participate in the de Gaulle project of profit sharing, and the Comité, with access to the books and the opportunity to bring in its own auditor, paid for by the company, had constantly agitated for accounting procedures that would increase immediate profits in which the workers would share. And MacDonald had sufficiently feared their militancy that he had thought a mere expression of intent to modernize would result in immediate seizure of the plant.

Much of this has changed for Huebner. Despite an abortive strike threat in 1983 when the new Atex editorial computer system was installed, union militancy seems much diminished. Paris now appeared to be an ideal center for the paper: the issue of moving to another location virtually disappeared, along with any sense that the paper was actually hampered by its Parisian locale. For Huebner, Paris retained a status as a cosmopolitan world capital that lent the paper a prestige it would not have elsewhere. In the old Paris *Herald* days editors and publishers joined innumerable local organizations to display their presence. For a while, after the move to Neuilly, it appeared that others were emulating Phil Foisie, who—insisting on the international quality of the paper—avoided too much identification with the Paris milieu and the American community in Paris: the only club he joined was the Swedish Club. By the mid-eighties things changed again: there was more security about the image of the *International Herald Tribune,* and as the paper approached its 100th anniversary Huebner and others became much more actively involved in community organizations and activities.

Huebner's relations with the owners appear different, too. Where MacDonald had looked with suspicion upon Huebner's earlier forays on behalf of the board and told people what they ought to say to him, Huebner, in 1984, had found it useful to work closely with a long-range planning group sent over by the board in response to a memo Huebner had prepared about future facsimile printing sites. It meant having allies on the board when decisions later had to be made. It also meant that when the board accepted his draft long-range plan setting targets for the future and authorizing greater investment of earnings in future expansion, he had a greater sense of autonomy than ever before.

Some staff members still thought it was impossible to run a paper with three sets of owners who had to be satisfied. Sydney Gruson, of the *New York Times*—the last publisher of the abortive *Times* International Edition, who wanted to be a publisher of the merged paper in 1967—was long looked upon as the most skeptical and perhaps most difficult person on the board because he was the only man at the *Times* who read the paper regularly with an eye to what *Times* material had not been used. As he once put it, "There's a squalid rumor that I measure each column [of *Times* material in the *IHT*]. I measure inch by inch!" And he was one of those who earlier opposed having the *IHT* originate much of its own material. Yet he and other *Times* representatives on the board accepted the growth of a staff of full-time writers and the creation of the *IHT's* own bureaus, as well as the opening of the Miami facsimile site with its planned sales in the United States. After much effort and discussion, *Times* editors no longer viewed the *IHT* as just another client or just another paper of which the *Times* was part owner. Huebner also argued that with three owners, coalitions could be

Publisher Lee Huebner meets with his Board of Directors in Paris in 1985. In front, left to right, Arthur O. Sulzberger, William S. Paley, Katharine Graham, Walter N. Thayer. In the rear, Donald Graham, Bernard Kiernan, John R. Harrison, Ben Bradlee, Sydney Gruson, Frank Stanton, Martin Cohen, Edwin Singer, Richard Simmons, David Gorham and Lee Huebner.

built on the basis of differing interests, as in the case of selection of the Miami printing site; a single owner might have been harder to deal with.

As it approaches its 100th anniversary, the *International Herald Tribune's* own past is omnipresent. One of the great copper owls whose glowing eyes glowered down from the parapet of James Gordon Bennett's Stanford White–designed Herald Square building in New York graces a corner of Lee Huebner's office; in 1964 B. J. Cutler rescued it from the basement of a New York University building where it had lain for forty-three years among a pile of Bennett memorabilia donated to the university after his death. The building of which Laurence Hills was so proud still stands on the rue de Berri, and in the elegant California Hotel bar across the street a plaque still informs you that this is Hawkins' corner.

Harry's New York Bar is always open on the rue Daunou and still advertises in the *IHT*. Like the *Trib,* it still rather looks the same; the big bar Harry brought over in the twenties is there, along with all the stained wood, the International Bar Flies device on the mirrors, the picture of Helen Traubel and the "Chicago Friends of the St. Louis Browns." But Sparrow Robertson would be at a loss among the clientele—glossy, high-priced-looking, well-manicured, young French and international business types, very much in the mold of those who constitute a large part of *IHT* readership. The most recent audience survey places most readers in the upper-income brackets, world travelers, with university degrees and substantial investments; two-thirds of readers are between the ages of thirty-five and fifty-five.

The paper they read is unique, different both from normal metropolitan and rural newspapers and from its global competitors, and vastly different from what it has been. The whole operation is strange. The newsroom, after all, is like the international desk or foreign desk of most newspapers, without the city desk where the reporters and most of the excitement are. In that sense it's a less complicated operation than that of most newspapers. But this void contributes to the sense of strangeness that affects veteran newspapermen, some of whom invoke a lack of community feeling in the newsroom, a lack of ties to the organization they work for or to the product they turn out—despite all that recent management has done, all the efforts to invoke a great tradition.

The strangeness—the differences between this newsroom and the traditional ones—may increase. Computer experts at the paper who see their task as defining new options and possibilities from which the owners can choose will argue that computerized communications possiblities these days should lead the paper into radically different directions. The paper should decentralize its editorial room, put area-oriented desks in different parts of the world, where deskmen with a sense of the area could draw more on multiple news sources that exist all over the world, conferring and communicating with the ease that modern methods allow, even tailoring local editions that would contain more locally generated news. The trend toward adding *IHT* reporters and bureaus would be reversed in favor of a truly global newsroom, with the composing room no longer necessarily close by. Computerization would take care of most of the supposed complexities of advertising layout and circulation as the changes took place. The paper, they argue, has a flexibility and freedom to move in such new directions that its competition does not have: both the *Wall Street Journal* and the *Financial Times* are burdened by the necessity of carrying enormous volumes of statistical tables that are primarily of domestic interest.

What this demonstrates is that the debate over the nature of the paper, of what its particular role and niche are to be in the general scheme of things, will never stop. Bennett's target was clear; Hills' less so. Parsons, aiming at a Europe-wide elite of government, politics, and business, who needed to know what Americans thought and what Americans were doing in the new American century, missed badly. Willett Weeks would like to have followed Parsons' lead, seeing an opportunity in the emerging European Economic Community, but Eric Hawkins seemed happy to produce for Americans in Paris as he had in the thirties, and if Weld had had *his* way, he would have preferred to do the same thing, rather than follow the *Times'* example of trying to produce what Weld called an "international prestige product." MacDonald and Weiss quickly saw the need to break out of Paris parochialism, yet there remained a constant pull back toward the Paris milieu.

But the issue that really came to the fore was whether the paper was an American one for scattered Americans, an American paper designed primarily to give non-Americans an American view of the world—or whether technological change was producing a new, worldwide elite with a common consciousness that could be served by an American-owned newspaper whose editors could provide that elite with a broadly conceived view of world events, a view that could itself be qualified as "objective." It is this latter view that Huebner and his people have adopted. Unlike other papers, whose nature is defined largely by a particular geographic locale or by a particular interest group they serve, the *International Herald Tribune* is defined by the common interests of a multinational readership scattered about the globe. As one in-house newsletter put it, "There is a striking homogeneity across nationalities and countries of residence which, together with their cosmopolitan lifestyles, clearly demonstrates the 'internationality' of *Herald Tribune* readers." And for now, at least, Huebner will follow a strategy of keeping the different editions basically the same, with only minor modifications: "Our readers [in Asia] are eager to have the same newspaper they read in Europe or that friends or colleagues or competitors are reading in Europe. They want to feel they are in touch with the same body of information available in all parts of the world."

In contrast to competitors' multinational marketing, as a result of which they tailor their product to each market, the *International Herald Tribune* will emphasize what's common throughout its global market. This, so far, is what has guided Huebner in adapting the newspaper itself to global circulation and in attracting the advertising that makes it all possible. And as if to bear out Huebner's view, 1985 witnessed a new surge in circulation and advertising greater than that in any single year before.

The times don't allow the paper to stand still. If it bested its competitors in the past, from *Galignani's Messenger* before the Great War to the *Chicago Tribune* of the interwar period and—in the biggest battle of all—the *New York Times* International Edition of the sixties, its current owners and managers have had to learn to live with the presence of its international and global competition in contemporary times. The presence of that competition and the present state of the paper reflect what the paper's pages have chronicled in the last decade: a world made more interdependent and more closely linked by the extraordinary communications revolution of our time.

Yet in this same time the paper has reported the rise of new religious and nationalist fundamentalisms reacting—sometimes violently—against that interdependence. One relatively minor result has been frequent interference with the *IHT's* distribution. Fifteen years ago a Middle East more and more integrated into the world economy by the oil trade and the resulting investment in vast projects of modernization seemed an obvious site for a new *IHT* facsimile printing plant; the project is still on hold. All through the 1970s the paper reported on growing awareness of a "global agenda" requiring global action to deal with increasing population, pollution, resource depletion, and environmental degradation, and the continually growing income gap between rich and poor countries—as well as reporting on efforts to cope with the problems. But its pages were also filled with stories on the political and military conflicts that continuously turned attention away from that agenda and interfered with any remedial action: wars in the Middle East, Southeast Asia, Central America, and throughout Africa, as well as the rise of terrorism. It chronicled, too, the rise and fall of detente and the frightening new course that superpower arms competition took in the 1980s, while its editorial page and the enlarged "Letters to the Editor" column provided evidence of lack of global concensus on how to deal with all these issues. The world on which the first global newspaper reported was certainly no simple one.

James Gordon Bennett would not have been surprised. But he would certainly have been surprised at much in the lineal descendant of his Paris Edition of the *New York Herald*. He would chafe at boards, committees, government regulations, unions, market research. One can imagine the purple explosion at what it takes to hire or fire nowadays. He might be hard put to understand the job of financial director in this day and age. But we may imagine that he would be delighted that as his newspaper approached its centennial year it had taken advantage of every technical innovation to improve its coverage and presentation of world news, that it had survived all these years, that out of those modest offices on the avenue Charles de Gaulle comes a paper now circulated and known throughout the world, where its reputation in leading circles is greater than ever.

Don Cook, the former *New York Herald Tribune* foreign correspondent, once growled about the Neuilly-based *IHT,* shortly after it had made its move from the rue de Berri, "That's not a newspaper they're running out there, it's a computer center!" But Art Buchwald was much more to the point about the paper he called the "only newspaper he ever really loved" when he wrote at about the same time "It's alive and well and living in Neuilly!"

Bibliographical Note

OST OF THIS account has been drawn from the extensive collection of memoranda, letters, publisher's reports, and financial and other records to be found in the archives of the *International Herald Tribune,* from a reading of a major part of the press run of the newspaper since its beginnings on October 4, 1887, and from the papers of the Reid family to be found in the Library of Congress. Unfortunately, many of the paper's records for the period before World War II were burned during the war to keep occupants of the building warm; for this period, in addition to the press run, I have had to rely on memoirs and the autobiographies and biographies listed below, some of which are rather inaccurate.

The people who were willing to talk to me and help me out were legion: Geoffrey Parsons, Jr., B. J. Cutler, Murray (Buddy) Weiss, Mort Rosenblum, all of them former editors; their associates Nat Kingsley, Bill Holden, and Harry Baehr (who contributed editorials from New York for almost forty years); current editors Phil Foisie, Walter Wells, Sam Abt, Robert McCabe, and Carl Gewirtz; and Buel Weare, Walter B. Kerr, Whitelaw Reid, Ogden Reid, Jr., Sylvan Barnet, Willett Weeks, Philip Weld, Robert MacDonald, and Robert Eckert, all former directors, publishers, or publisher's representatives. I owe a special debt to present publisher Lee Huebner and to former associate publisher Roland Pinson and his secretary Micheline Personnaz.

Journalists and columnists include, from the pre–World War II period, Eric Sevareid, John Elliott, William Shirer, and the last managing editor of the Paris *Chicago Tribune,* Jules Frantz; from the postwar period, Art Buchwald and his former secretary, Ursula Naccache, Robert Yoakum, Les Midgeley, Herbert Kupferberg, Everett Walker, Don Cook, Nan Robertson, Naomi Barry, Hebe Dorsey, Thomas Quinn Curtiss, Ron Koven, James Goldsborough, Axel Krause, Frank Brackle, and Dave Stevens; other long-term newsroom and special section people Roy McMullen, Sim Kantin, Tom Kennedy, Larry Rampersad, Peggy Sunde Weiss, Barney Kirchoff, Katherine Knorr, the touch-up artist of so many years known as Picasso II, Maurice Van Grasdorf, and the indefatigable and ever-helpful librarian Maggie Shapiro.

In the various business and production services I spoke at length to Richard Morgan, René Bondy, François Desmaisons, Claudie Lucas, Larry Sackett, Stephan Conaway, Hugh Pryce-Jones, Pierre Rousseau, Jim Nolan, Juanita Caspari, Chris Lanoue, Bruce Singer, Danielle Meunier, Gerard Piermé, Robert Palmacci, Marc Gara, Jean Favre, Guy Lebreton, Roland Massuard, and longtime secretary Anik Cretu. From among the owners I must single out at Whitney Communications Walter Thayer and John Prescott, at the *Washington Post* Katharine Graham, Ben Bradlee, and Fred Farris, at the *New York Times* Arthur Ochs Sulzberger and Sydney Gruson. Robert M. White II, former editor of the *New York Herald Tribune,* was most courteous and helpful.

And at innumerable lunches with so many other people on the paper, I learned much from gossip.

I made use of the following books:

Alsop, Susan Mary. *To Marietta from Paris: 1945–1960.* Garden City, N. Y.: Doubleday, 1975.

Attwood, William. *The Man Who Could Grow Hair.* New York: Knopf, 1949.

Beach, Sylvia. *Shakespeare and Company.* New York: Harcourt, Brace, 1956.

Blumenfeld, R. D. *R. D. B.'s Diary*. London: Hennemann, 1930.

Buchwald, Ann (Interrupted by Art Buchwald). *Seems Like Yesterday*. New York: Putnam, 1980.

Buchwald, Art. *Art Buchwald's Paris*. New York: Lion Books, 1956.

Calmer, Ned. *All the Summer Days*. Boston: Little, Brown, 1961.

Crockett, Albert Stevens. *When James Gordon Bennett Was Caliph of Bagdad*. New York and London: Funk and Wagnalls, 1926.

Flanner, Janet. *Paris Was Yesterday: 1925–1939*. New York: Viking, 1972.

Ford, Hugh. *The Left Bank Revisited*. University Park, Penn.: Pennsylvania State University Press, 1972.

——*Published in Paris*. New York: Macmillan, 1975.

Gallico, Paul. *Trial by Terror*. New York: Knopf, 1952.

Hawkins, Eric (with Robert Sturdevant). *Hawkins of the Paris "Herald"*. New York: Simon and Schuster, 1963.

Holt, Edwin P. *The Whitneys: An Informal Portrait*. New York: Weybright and Tally, 1976.

Laney, Al. *Paris "Herald": The Incredible Newspaper*. New York: Appleton-Century, 1947.

Mott, Colonel T. Bently. *Life of Myron T. Herrick*. Garden City, N. Y.: Doubleday Doran, 1929.

Seitz, Don. *The James Gordon Bennetts, Father and Son*. Indianapolis: Bobbs-Merrill, 1928.

Sevareid, Eric. *Not So Wild a Dream*. New York: Doubleday Doran, 1947.

Shirer, William L. *Twentieth-Century Journey*, Vol. 1. New York: Simon and Schuster, 1976.

Steel, Ronald. *Walter Lippmann and the American Century*. Boston: Atlantic Monthly/Little, Brown, 1980.

Stewart, Kenneth. *News Is What We Make It*. Boston: Houghton Mifflin, 1943.

Wickes, George. *Americans in Paris, 1903–1939*. Garden City, N. Y.: Doubleday, 1969.

Wood, Thomas W., Jr. *Influence of the Paris "Herald" on the Lost Generation of Writers.* Ann Arbor, Mich.: University Microfilms, 1967.
Woodward, Stanley. *Paper Tiger.* New York: Atheneum, 1964.

Among a great many articles, three provided supplementary information:
Burnett, Whit and Martha Foley. "Your Home-town Paper: Paris." *American Mercury* (January 1931), Vol. 220.
Dowell, William. "The Graying of the *Herald Tribune.*" *The Paris Metro,* October 13, 1976.
Goldsborough, James. "An American in Paris: The *International Herald Tribune.*" *Columbia Journalism Review* (July 1974), Vol. 13.

Index